'TIS NATURE'S FAULT

'Tis Nature's Fault

Unauthorized Sexuality during the Enlightenment

Edited by
ROBERT PURKS MACCUBBIN

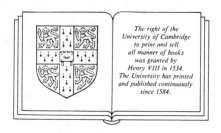

The right of the
University of Cambridge
to print and sell
all manner of books
was granted by
Henry VIII in 1534.
The University has printed
and published continuously
since 1584.

CAMBRIDGE UNIVERSITY PRESS

Cambridge

New York   New Rochelle   Melbourne   Sydney

Published by the Press Syndicate of the University of Cambridge
The Pitt Building, Trumpington Street, Cambridge CB2 1RP
32 East 57th Street, New York, NY 10022, USA

First published 1987

Printed in the United States of America

Library of Congress Cataloging-in-Publication Data

'Tis nature's fault : unauthorized sexuality during the Enlightenment
edited by Robert P. Maccubbin.
p.   cm.
English, with some essays translated from French or Italian.
1. Sex customs – Europe – History – 18th century.   2. Europe – Social
life and customs – 18th century.   3. Europe – Moral conditions.
I. Maccubbin, Robert P.
HQ18.E8T57   1988   87-19715
306.7'094 – dc19

British Library Cataloguing in Publication Data

'Tis nature's Fault : unauthorized sexuality
during the Enlightenment.
1. Sex customs – Europe – History – 18th century
I. Maccubbin, Robert P.
306.7'094   HQ18.E85

ISBN 0-521-34539-1 hard covers
ISBN 0-521-34768-8 paperback

CONTENTS

Introduction

In the last several years, and partly in the wake of Michel Foucault's argument that we need to abandon a categorical approach to human sexuality, a body of scholarship has, with increasing subtlety, investigated sexualities. The present volume addresses sexual phenomena that during the 18th century were for one reason or another outside the legal or sanctified systems of acceptability — most notably unwed heterosexual domesticity, masturbation, prostitution, libertinism, homosexuality, erotic literature (from the metaphorically indirect to the explicitly obscene). To place the unauthorized phenomena into a focusing context, the volume is prefaced by Roy Porter's exposition of *Aristotle's Master-piece*, a sexual primer for married couples that, whether a compilation of vernacular practice or medical wisdom, is an encomium to marriage and procreation. It contains nothing about the behaviors addressed by the other authors in this volume, and its exclusiveness is its importance.

The two essays which follow Porter's reveal tensions within the heterosexual domestic world. J. M. Goulemot finds in the abbé Thiers' *Traité* an earnest attempt to discriminate between orthodox sexual practices and those that were purely superstitious and magical, especially those concerned with overcoming impotence and infertility; and John Gillis, in investigating such phenomena as massive noncompliance with the 1753 Marriage Act, outlines an "historical anthropology of marriage that takes into account class and gender variation, and thereby calls into question the evolutionary perspective that has so dominated our thinking about the history of heterosexuality."

Théodore Tarczylo's analysis of the argument and rhetorical strategies of Diderot's *Suite de l'Entretien* reveals how mechanism and the laws of nature affect Enlightenment thinking and question orthodox bases of judgment about such actions as masturbation and homosexuality, issues further treated in the essays of Michel Delon and Robert Ellrich. Ellrich's essay also establishes the role of sexual discourse in helping to undermine the old order, an issue which is implicit in the essays by Robert Dawson and Armando Marchi on the diffusion of pornography and obscenity in France and Italy, and which is central to David Coward's psychological study of Restif de la Bretonne. Other essays on erotica, by P.-G. Boucé and Peter Sabor, help define the linguistic parameters of erotic discourse in fiction.

Prof. Coward's essay is one of three on libertinism. The other two are James Turner's overview, which shows the "instability and complexity" of the concept, but tries to establish the connections between illicit libertinism and the "religious and moral systems it purports to reject," and J. P. Guicciardi's examination of how the public image of the sexual excesses of Louis XV helped undermine the conception of the kingly role.

The largest single group of essays concerns homosexuality, beginning with Randolph Trumbach's review of the recent historiography, an essay like Turner's in that he establishes a general background for the essays which succeed it. The essays on homosexuality discuss three different cultures — England, France, and Holland. Michel Delon, who focuses his remarks on Voltaire and Diderot, demonstrates how the Enlightenment "hesitated between secularization of traditional thinking and more radical rethinking" about homosexuality; Arend Huussen and Michel Rey, working with court records and police archives, develop insights into both changing attitudes toward homosexuality and the existence of homosexual subcultures. Finally, in a fully developed but explanatory statement that won the James L. Clifford Prize of ASECS for 1986, G. S. Rousseau's attention to the literary record shows us how rich and untapped are the annals of homosexuality. His opening endnote defines his reasons for choosing to use the admittedly anachronistic term "homosexuality," rather than "sodomy," to denote the entire complex of homo-erotic behaviors; and I direct your attention to his definitions because the lexical problem is complex and important.

In editing this volume I thought it desirable to normalize the use of terms referring to same-sex erotic feeling and action; and inasmuch as most of the authors in this volume had already used the term "homosexuality," and because I share G. S. Rousseau's reasons for his lexical choices, the umbrella term "homosexuality" is used throughout this volume except in Randolph Trumbach's review of the extensive recent historiography, an essay whose subject makes it a special case, and in which therefore I gladly accede to his wishes to avoid anachronism by using the term "sodomy." In the past, Michel Rey's choice has been to use "sodomy" as the umbrella term, so the different usage in the essay translated for this volume should be noted. The lexical issue is not trivial, and is complicated by the fact that this volume discusses four different national cultures, and includes essays in French and Italian that have been translated into English. With the permission of the individual authors, an essay originally written in French or Italian will be made available to anyone wishing to consult the original text. Without clarifying the semantic field, as editor I would have felt like the narrator of *A Tale of a Tub:* "What I am going to say is literally true this minute I am writing."

One final and most important point: I want to identify what I regard as the most conspicuous lacuna in this volume—a feminist perspective. All of our eighteen authors are Peter, Martin, or Jack. I would, therefore, like to encourage a feminist review of the present volume, as well as feminist essays on the same or related topics.

ROBERT P. MACCUBBIN

"The Secrets of Generation Display'd":
Aristotle's Master-piece
in Eighteenth-Century England

The histories of sex and sexuality have been focused in recent years by the powerful reconceptualizations of scholars such as Michel Foucault, Edward Shorter, and Lawrence Stone.[1] Yet one enormous obstacle, which keeps this key dimension of life singularly opaque to understanding, remains: our almost total ignorance of the sexual beliefs and behavior of all but the tiniest minority of people in the "world we have lost." Certainly, as Peter Gay has recently reminded us,[2] more intimate secrets survive in the archives than we sometimes credit; yet it is safe to predict that we shall remain forever in the dark about the love lives of otherwise well-known public figures, about John Milton as well as the mute inglorious Miltons.[3] For this reason it is worth exploring the history of sexual advice literature, which promises to throw at least a few dim rays upon the broader contours of sexual values and practices of earlier times.

It goes without saying, of course, that extrapolating from the guidance of advice books to what people actually thought and did is immensely hazardous, for reasons that need little rehearsal here. We know next to nothing about who read such publications, for what reasons, and with what effects. In many cases we know little about the authors or their intentions. These uncertainties apply even to the best-sellers. It is not clear, for example, whether the many-editioned antimasturbation polemic *Onania* was written or read as either a puritanical morality tirade or a catchpenny emission of lewd softporn.[4]

What is clear, however, is that from the late seventeenth century in England, France, Holland, Germany, and, increasingly, North America, self-education sex literature started flooding off the presses. A few works aimed at "the common reader" became wildly successful, running into scores of editions and being energetically pirated, vulgarized, and recycled. In France the best-seller by far was Nicholas Venette's *Tableau de l'amour conjugal*, which first appeared in 1696, went through at least thirty-one editions in the eighteenth century for a chiefly bourgeois readership, and became in the nineteenth century the "Bible of the French peasantry."[5] Venette's work was translated into English, German, Dutch, and, eventually, Spanish. It enjoyed notable popularity in Enlightenment England, though perhaps the title page of a late eighteenth-century edition should not be believed when it boasts of being the "twentieth edition."[6] The most successful primer in English, however, was *Aristotle's Master-piece*.[7] Surviving copies prove that this work, printed either separately or with other pseudo-Aristotelian writings, went through over twenty editions in the eighteenth century and far more in the nineteenth century in both Great Britain and America.[8]

The provenance of *Aristotle's Master-piece* presents problems barely yet tackled by scholars.[9] Fragments of the sexological doctrines of antiquity had begun to be codified in Latin in the late Middle Ages, and Renaissance humanism ushered in the publication of scholarly treatises on sexual topics, most notably Giovanni Sinibaldi's *Geanthropeia* (1642).[10] *Aristotle's Master-piece*, first appearing in English in 1684, drew heavily on these and other sources. It is, of course, not by Aristotle, and its compiler or compilers remain unknown, though the medical popularizer William Salmon may have had some hand in writing it.[11]

Considering its vast circulation and staying power from the end of the seventeenth to the present century, *Aristotle's Master-piece* has received oddly little scholarly attention. Of course, it is readily dismissed because it contains a "great deal of nonsense."[12] Condemning it as a "hoary old debauchee acknowledged by no-one," D'Arcy Power concluded: "The Master-piece at its best is a mere catchpenny production written for the prurient-minded and the less said about it the better."[13] Examining its fortunes in America, Otho Beall, Jr., labeled it a scrapbook of "pre-objective" and "occult" sexual "folklore," a "medical anachronism," which—like P.-G. Boucé's statement that it is a "rich lode of startling beliefs and myths"—pigeonholes it too neatly and disparagingly.[14] Similarly, in a study that focuses on nineteenth-century editions, Janet Blackman sees it as a "patchwork" or an "anachronism"—another label that prejudges too many issues: "It is almost too exact in the imprecision or ineffectiveness of much of its advice, and this stems from lack of thought and explanation rather than cogency or simplicity."[15]

The format, fame, and fortunes of *Aristotle's Master-piece* pose intriguing problems. Was the work primarily a compilation of vernacular sexual and gynecological know-how, or did it codify chiefly professional medical wisdom? What pressures were there on publishers, hack writers, and editors to modify successive editions to meet changing public expectations and medical teachings?[16] What did readers get out of it? Did it confirm their prejudices or open their eyes? Did it teach or titillate? Above all, who actually read it: the married or the unmarried, men or women?[17] Existing studies give us few leads on these questions, and this present article will illuminate them only indirectly.

My approach here will be primarily exegetical. I aim to anatomize *Aristotle's Master-piece* in order to bring out its main arguments and reveal its inner structure and assumptions. The book has been disparaged generally as a slipshod ragbag of myths and old wives' tales randomly sandwiched between two covers. My contention, by contrast, is that it possesses a logical, sequential plan and aim and operates within a consistent intellectual paradigm; I shall explore what these are.

I shall also place the teachings of *Aristotle's Master-piece* in the context of other sexual popularizations of the Enlightenment[18] by making glancing comparisons between its views and those of highly visible treatises, such as Nicholas Venette's *Tableau de l'amour conjugal,* James Graham's *Lecture on Generation* (1783),[19] and Ebenezer Sibly's *Medical Mirror* (1784).[20] I shall also hint more speculatively at what its contents might tell us about popular sexual outlooks in pre-Victorian England.

First is is necessary to clarify the nature of the text itself. Scholars have long recognized that there is no single text of *Aristotle's Master-piece* reprinted verbatim down the ages. Janet Blackman in particular has noted that the text was apparently transformed through time; and she has drawn on editions from the late seventeenth, late eighteenth, mid nineteenth, and early twentieth centuries to highlight shifts in tone and teaching. A lucky-dip sampling of this kind can be dangerous, however, since it fails to trace the true pedigree of the work. Blackman, in addition, seems to have fallen into the error of reading as long-term textual transformations what really were substantially distinct, simultaneously circulating versions of the opus. *Aristotle's Master-piece* should not be seen as a single text that evolved or was adapted over time but as several different books with a single title. By the early eighteenth century, three quite distinct versions had appeared, of which at least two remained in print sporadically through the eighteenth century and beyond; another utterly distinct version appeared in the Victorian period. This publishing story is most simply set out in the appendix.[21]

In outlook and content, what I shall for convenience call Versions 1, 2, and 3 are broadly commensurable; they cover much the same ground, though certain topics are treated only in some versions. For example, Versions 1 and 2 contain chapters that explain the endowment of fetuses with souls, whereas Version 3 has no such chapter. All three versions, however, contain comparable sexual and medical information that is explained in similar, often identical, terms. There is, however, one major and intriguing distinction between the first two versions and the third. The first two are essentially neutral in tone. They convey their information in direct, didactic prose. By contrast, Version 3 (which seems to have gone through the most editions) is altogether lighter and more jaunty, with an ear for innuendo and suggestion redolent of popular bawdy.[22] In this version, sexual arousal and male-female relations are subjects of wit, of raciness, and of sly irony. Thus Version 3 praises chastity: "Virginity untouch'd and taintless, is the boast and pride of the fair sex," while inserting a barb in the tail: "But they generally commend it to put if off, as good as it is care not how soon they are honestly rid of it."[23] Similarly, the newlywed husband, fired to feats of love by the beauty of his bride, is urged to embrace her; if, however, she is plain or ugly, the advice is to do it in the dark (3:47[40]). Moreover, in Version 3 alone, each chapter has a tailpiece of light, mildly suggestive doggerel. Thus, rounding off the chapter on marriage, the husband is advised to go to it:

> Now, my fair bride, new will I storm the mint
> Of love and joy, and rifle all that's in't;

4

> Now shall my infranchis'd hand, on ev'ry side,
> Shall o'er thy naked polish'd ivory slide.
> Freely shall now my longing eyes behold
> Thy bared snow, and thy undrained gold;
> No curtain now tho' of transparent lawn,
> Shall be before thy virgin treasure drawn,
> I will enjoy thee now, my fairest, come,
> And fly with me to love's elysium;
> My rudder with thy bold hand, like a try'd
> And skilful pilot, thou shalt steer and guide,
> My bark in love's dark channel, where it shall
> Dance, as the bounding waves to rise and fall.
> Whilst my tall pinnace in the Cyprian streight
> Rides safe at anchor and unlades the freight . . .
> Perform those rites nature and love requires
> 'Till you have quench'd each others amorous fires.
>
> (3:40–41[31–32])

It may be a sign of the greater sexual frankness of this version that it opens, as does Venette's *Tableau,* with a long, anatomically explicit exposition "of the parts of instruments of generation, both in men and women" (3:11[7]), whereas Versions 1 and 2 begin with an encomium on marriage.

At least, two of the three versions (2 and 3) were reprinted frequently during the eighteenth and into the nineteenth centuries. Once the separate versions had appeared, they underwent little change beyond trivial stylistic updating, some paraphrasing, and the inevitable descent to textual corruption (in an early nineteenth-century printing, Avicenna has become, rather symbolically, Advicene).[24] In other words, it would, pace Blackman, be a mistake to regard the texts as undergoing modification through time either to create or to reflect shifts in public or medical opinion. That did not happen (though it probably did with English translations of Venette's *Tableau de l'amour conjugal*).[25] Indeed, both the longevity and the stability of these texts are truly remarkable. In a commercializing culture dominated by fashion and speedy cultural turnover, why did the common reader desire the facts of life from so venerable, not to say out of date, a book?

The great exception to the general tone of successive editions of *Aristottle's Master-piece* is Version 4, first published at some point in the nineteenth century. Though retaining the original title and reproducing much of the advice about women's diseases contained in Version 2, it is a fundamentally different work. Above all, in this Victorian version the sex has disappeared. Here there is no anatomy of the genitals, no tips for creating the "soft lights and sweet music" atmosphere for lovemaking, no advice on conceiving a boy or a girl—none of the facets of making love and making babies that dominate all earlier versions. Rather, the burden of this version is captured by the chapter heading: "Words of Warning." Addressed primarily to young men, it has become a moral tract to open eyes to the perils of that "foolish infatuation" (4:18) youths may so readily contract for flighty belles or even for "unfortunates," women of the street (4:15). Men need to be on guard against their own weaknesses; they must recognize that "eager pursuit of sensual gratification disqualifies for the exercise of the loftier powers" (4:43) and instead cultivate "self-command" and "abstinence" (4:18, 43). Young ladies, for their part, must learn the folly of flirtatiousness; "La Traviatas" will go down the roads to moral and physical ruin in the end. Marriage is the true goal for the virtuous, with emphasis on its "obligations" and "duties" (4:43) (though as a concession the text adds, "There is nothing debasing in connubial love" [4:43]). Marriage itself must be deferred until the husband has "adequate means of support" (4:36). Thus *prudentia carnis* has given way to prudence over pounds and pence, desire has been unveiled as danger, and sex has been replaced by the higher ideals of "family affection" and sentimental companionship (4:47). This is *Aristotle's Master-piece* for Charles Pooter. In the discussion that follows I shall ignore this degenerate edition and consider the earlier three versions collectively as a whole.

❖

One of the great debts we owe the late Michel Foucault is for his emphatic denial that sexuality is timeless. He contended that our notion of the sexual economy is distinctively modern; we should not foist it on the past.[27] This advice is well taken when approaching *Aristotle's Master-piece*, since one of the reasons it appears such a hodgepodge of obsolete fragments is precisely because few of the topics prominent in modern sexology receive even a mention. Little is said of sexual desire as a source of fear, guilt, or danger (medical, moral, or religious). There is no inkling of perversion or of *psychopathia sexualis*, nothing about homosexuality, masturbation, sadomasochism, prostitution, and nymphomania or about any intimate dialetic of sex with neurosis. Most fundamentally, *Aristotle's Master-piece* conveys no awareness of sexual problems inseparable from the psyche and the problems of the self: sex is not seen as a psychological category; it is not "in the mind" at all.

Neither does *Aristotle's Master-piece* anticipate the therapeutics of modern liberal sexology. There are no inducements to "the joy of sex" that show how to transcend shame, repression, and guilt, no advice on avoiding unwanted pregnancies, no drill of coital positions for maximizing erotic pleasure. Rather, *Aristotle's Master-piece* assumes that sex is nature's way of providing for "the business of generation." Far from being a potpourri of remnants of sexual lore, it is an integrated and coherent work whose unifying theme is the subject of reproduction. This organic scheme is apparent from even a casual glance at the chapter headings (most editions unfortunately lack a table of contents). For example, the 1690 edition (Version 1) opens with a discussion of the optimal age for marriage (i.e., the rite of passage that translates the biological potential for reproduction into social and moral actuality); by the second chapter it is already advising couples how to beget specifically male or female children. Successive chapters explain, among other things, why children resemble their parents. I shall analyze this structural plan in greater detail below, but here stress that the compiler did not see his main task as giving readers instructions in the art of lovemaking itself. That, it is assumed, would be as redundant as teaching your grandmother how to suck eggs (was *anyone* before certain eminent Victorians and the likes of Marie Stopes ever ignorant of the mere mechanics of copulation?). Clearly the editor also did not anticipate James Graham's later anxiety that desire might dwindle unless one celebrated "the rites of Venus in a variety of ways."[28] Rather, instruction was not just in "the bare performing of that act . . . but the performing it so as to make conducive unto the work of generation. And since this act is the foundation of generation, and without which it cannot be, some care ought to be taken and consequently some advice given, how to perform it well" (3:39[31]).

Thus *Aristotle's Master-piece* takes it as axiomatic that sex forms part of the larger plan of the preservation and multiplication of the species.[29] This notion is expressed on a number of different levels. In part it is simply assumed that couples do indeed want children:

> Though there are some that desire not to have childbirth and yet are very fond of nocturnal embrace to whom these directions will be no way acceptable, . . . yet I doubt not but the generality of both sexes, wherein a married state, have such a desire to produce the fair image of themselves, that nothing can be more welcome to them than those directions, that they make their mutual embraces most effectual to that end. (3:39[30]).

Indeed, the compiler states that anticipation of motherhood is the chief pleasure certain women take in the marriage bed (3:45[35]). But procreation is also explained as both the telos of nature and the command of God ("go forth and multiply").[30] As Version 1 states, only the most hardened lechers could pretend to be ignorant "to what end they were created Male and Female, which was to beget children and propagate their kind" (1:51); and all versions set the reproductive history of mankind against a panorama of "the plastic power of Nature" (3:9[5]), viewed as *natura naturans*, a great creating Mother in the "dark recesses" of whose "womb" the labors of fresh creations are constantly coming to fruition (3:9[5]).[31] Furthermore, if nature is the eternal mother who instills mankind with the instinct of generation, God is the Father who commanded Adam and Eve (and through them, all successive generations) to people the Earth. God is also the Holy Ghost, the fecundating agent in the divine *fiat*. Thus, as both Father and Holy Spirit, God made the cosmos fruitful:

> It plainly appears in Holy Writ, that this glorious Universe . . . everywhere adorned with wonderful objects, proclaiming the Wisdom and Omnipotence of the Great Work-Master who in six Days Erected all Things for his pleasure, was at first drawn out of Nothing, or at most a Formless Chaos of Confusion; no Fruits nor Pleasure, no creature that hath breath, had being in the place this lower World possesses, till GOD out of the Abundance of his Goodness, sent forth his Holy Spirit, who Dove-like, with mighty out spread-Wings, sat brooding on the Vast Abyss, and made it pregnant . . . all Creatures soon had being, and every Plant, Tree, Herb, or Flower . . . sprung from the Verdant Earth . . .; every thing of life having Seed in it self, that no second Creation was needed. (1:[i]).

Since then every human coupling has been a sacramental love feast that reiterates the Creation: "The natural inclination and propensity of both sexes to each other, with the plastic power of Nature, is only the energy of the first blessing, which to this day upholds the species of mankind in the world." (3:9[5]).

Thus the subject of *Aristotle's Master-piece* is reproduction. That both men and women will desire to copulate, that copulation can be accomplished without biological and psychological impediments, that desire will not prove delusive or destructive, that there is a love above brute lust—these are taken for granted and require no rhetoric, special pleading, or elaboration. There seems nothing problematic about mutual sexual attraction. No chapter is felt necessary to deal with loss of libido; no mention has to be made of homosexual desires or practices, bestiality or buggery, erotic mania, or even that great bugbear of the age, masturbation.[32]

It is not assumed, of course, that sex is all plain sailing. It is noted that a woman becomes barren earlier in life than a man, but this is readily explained within the framework of humoural medicine: being cooler and moister in constitution, women are less vigorous than men. Instructions, indeed, are given to ensure that copulation be most enjoyable and certain. Relax, the reader is told, cast care aside, indulge in fine wines and delicacies:

> When a married couple, from a desire of having children, are about to make use of those means that nature ordained to that purpose, it would be very proper to cherish the body with generous restoratives, that so it may be brisk and vigorous; and if their imaginations were charmed with sweet and melodious airs, and care and thought of business drowned in a glass of racy wine, that their spirits may be raised to the highest pitch of ardour and joy, it would not be amiss; for any thing of sadness, trouble, and sorrow, are enemies to the delights of Venus. And if, at any such times of coition, there should be conception, it would not have a malevolent effect upon the child. (2:76–77[43])[33]

Nevertheless, the prime concern of *Aristotle's Master-piece*—more so than in the writings, for example, of Venette or Graham—lies not in overcoming anticipated snags in copulation but in tackling hindrances to conception and overcoming the spectre of sterility.

The best solution to this problem was marriage. Within marriage, sex was not merely moral and civilized, not merely "happy," "pleasant," and "delightful," but also more likely to prove fertile.[34] Promiscuity was attacked as brutish and barren. Marriage, however, was not viewed merely as a means of taming the flesh, as was depicted in Daniel Defoe's *Conjugal Lewdness*; nor was it seen as an instrument of proto-Malthusian "moral restraint" to control runaway population growth by deferred gratification.[36] Rather, marriage, it was emphasized, had been instituted in paradise as the divine instrument for peopling the world (1:1). The pronatalist *Aristotle's Master-piece* was unambiguously in favor of early marriage and against all obstacles to matrimony. In particular, it urged that women marry while in their teens, as soon as their bodies had ripened. The ages of eighteen to twenty were recommended—markedly below the typical age of bonding in late Stuart and early Hanoverian England, when social retrenchment and economic anxieties induced late nuptuality as the norm.[36] Parents were urged under no circumstances to obstruct the marriage of their children, especially their daughters, for reasons of family policy, matchmaking, or the quest for "a large dowry" (1:62). For one thing, the work warned, characteristic diseases of pubescent girls such as the green sickness were caused by enforced sexual abstinence (1:3).[37] Even worse might follow: prevent young people from copulating lawfully within marriage, and they would merely do so promiscuously. The evils following that would be not merely sin, vice, disease, and social confusion but also frustration of what nature intended, because casual copulation or prostitution rarely resulted in pregnancy (1:58). Mirroring other pronatalist sex educators such as Venette and Graham, the message of *Aristotle's Master-piece* was that married unions would prove fertile, but irregular fornication would breed only sterility and disease. Pronuptualist as well as pronatalist, *Aristotle's Master-piece* thus contributed to the climate of opinion that repudiated "libertinism" and promoted marriage as more than a prudent economic contract. Marriage was companionable and sexually fulfilling, as well as healthy, both for the couple concerned and also (in a mercantilist way) for the body politic. Although "matrimony, in the present age, is looked upon as a most insupportable yoke—wives and husbands are accounted the greatest clogs and burdens to those who give up the reins to their unbridled appetites" (3:27[20]), in reality marriage was both blessed and enviable, "of all conditions the happiest" (1:55).

Within marriage, *Aristotle's Master-piece*'s advice was that regular, though not excessive, sex was most favorable to generation: "They that would be commended for their Wedlock Actions, and be happy in the fruit of their Labour, must observe to copulate at distance of time, not too often, nor yet too seldom, for both these hurt Fruitfulness alike" (1:10). The text clearly assumes no need to recommend a specific frequency or timetable of the right hours of the day or seasons of the year for sex, in the manner of Venette's *Tableau de l'amour conjugal*. It does, however, ban intercourse during menstruation (1:10), which (reflecting both medical and popular opinion) is seen as both filthy and liable to engender defective or monstrous children, such as infants with purple birthmarks.[38] Abstinence is also advised during most of pregnancy, lest miscarriage be induced, but in general, the work avoids "policing" sex with any rigid scheme of medical or moral rules.

Most of the advice on sexual intercourse follows a different tack, its chief concern being to aid conception. In particular, *Aristotle's Master-piece* stresses that the best chances of conception will follow when the wife as well as the husband is aroused:

> It is . . . necessary, that in their mutual embraces they meet each other with
> equal ardour; for if the spirit flag on either part, they will fall short of what

nature requires, and the woman must either miss of conception or else the children prove weak in their bodies, or defective in their understanding and therefore I do advise them, before they begin their conjugal embraces, to invigorate their mutual desires, and make their flames burn with a fierce ardour.   (2:47[43])

Arousing female desire is, however, no great problem, since the compiler views women as no less libidinous than men. In this context, the author debates at length the Hippocratic belief that the mingling of both male and female seeds, which requires mutual orgasm, is needed for conception, but rejects it as physiologically unsound; there being no evidence that women ejaculate seed (1:6).[39]

On top of this general advice for promoting conception, were offered further hints on producing a boy or a girl (assuming a preference for boys). Here *Aristotle's Master-piece* retails the popular belief (repudiated by Venette from his lofty vantage point as a learned physician battling superstition) that males can be produced if the woman lies on her right-hand side in intercourse (because boys are engendered in the right side of the womb). Copulating when the moon is on the wane will, symbolically, produce girls (1:8; 3:41[32]; 2:[8]).

The remainder of the book spells out the biological consequences of copulation. How is one to know if the woman has conceived (3:37–43[29–33])? A choice of pregnancy tests, mainly involving the inspection of urine (largely dismissed by Venette), is suggested:

If urine be put in a glass three days, and the woman have conceived certain live things will appear to stir in it. If a bright Needle be put in a whole night and she have conceived, divers little red Specks will be thereon, but if not it will be blackish or rusty. Nor are these imaginations, but the proved assertions of the Learned in Physick and skilful in Midwifery, who have made it their study to search into the depth of Nature's Secrets.   (1:114; 3:55[44])

Once pregnancy itself is established, how is one to determine the fetus' sex? Once again, a range of signs is listed. Boys give less painful pregnancies than girls; similarly, it is a sure sign of a boy if the right side of the womb is agitated (3:44[34]).[40]

Subsequent chapters advise for pregnancy management (3:37–50; 1:50). Tight lacing is to be avoided, and charms and medicaments are prescribed to prevent or ease the swelling of breasts caused by the plethora of blood that pregnancy produces (3:[50]). A rudimentary physiological sketch of the quickening and maturing of the fetus in the womb follows. Unlike the works of Venette or Sibly, which contain elaborate embryologies, *Aristotle's Master-piece* is little concerned with anatomical niceties; instead it addresses problems that would most worry pregnant women (1:16, 34; 3:48[38]).[41] One section answers whether the fetus derives all its nourishment through the umbilical cord or takes in some through the mouth (the latter view is, wrongly, accepted); another explains what stage of development the fetus has reached in each successive month of pregnancy (1:9).

The latter half of *Aristotle's Master-piece* looks forward to childbirth itself (a theme handled more copiously in the other pseudo-Aristotelian works, the *Compleat Midwife* and the *Last Legacy*, which were often printed with *Aristotle's Master-piece* (1:94ff.)[42] I shall not here analyze the account of midwifery techniques, though, in the light of recent scholarly controversy about the rise of male midwives, it is worth noting that from the earliest editions of *Aristotle's Master-piece* it is taken for granted that although normal births will be attended by women, men will deal with difficult confinements.[43] Nor shall I explore the group of chapters entitled, "A Private Looking Glass for the Female Sex," tagged onto later editions and announcing that it will treat "of several maladies incident to the womb, with proper remedies for the cure of each" (2:[12]). The presence of this section in most late Georgian editions probably reflects an increasing awareness of how extensively ill-health in women was caused by repeated or difficult lyings-in (in another perspective, its prominence could be said to mark a further stage in the medicalization of women).[44]

It is a measure of how far *Aristotle's Master-piece* is about "the business of generation" that almost all the problems confronted in the text relate not to sexual intercourse itself but to child-bearing. The problem treated in greatest depth is barrenness (indeed, it is so prominent that it actually heads the contents list on the title page of the 1690 edition).[45] The text assumes that failure to conceive will be experienced on all sides as calamitous. It lays responsibility on the woman (the idea is not even entertained that a potent man may nevertheless be sterile),[46] for women by their nature are less vigorous than men. Defects in the female constitution are examined—she may, in humoural terms, be too dry, too moist, too cold, or too hot—and these excesses or deficiencies, it is suggested, can be rectified by appropriate medicaments and restoratives, recipes for which are detailed (1:7). Changes in everyday living may also help, and above all luxurious habits are to be avoided: "City dames that live high and do nothing, seldom have children" (3:45[36]). Relaxation, contentment, and satisfaction are recommended as conducive to fertility (3:45[36]). The tone of this advice is not of the victim-blaming kind (it is not assumed that barrenness is a divine punishment for vice or sin). Rather, it appears a constructive attempt to provide a measure of reassurance capable of being translated into practical action, thus helping partners to restore some sense of control over their reproductive destiny.

Aristotle's Master-piece tackles head-on the most terrifying outcomes of reproduction. What if pregnancy did not result in a normal live baby but was either false or issued in an abortive, hideous lump of dead flesh (1:53, 118ff.)? The text offered a physiological rationalization of these "moles" by explaining that they were generally caused by weakness in either the male seed or a womb that lacked due heat or spirits to generate a normal child. Intercourse during menstruation was another cause of such "moles" (1:44–45). Restoratives and tonics were recommended to prevent recurrences.

This raised the problem of the status of such abortions in nature and under God. Were they truly human? If so, did they have souls? And, in that case, what was the natural history of the soul? How and when did the infusion of the soul into the fetus take place (1:30; 2:26[15])? Such problems were agonizing for individual parents (was this fruit of one's womb immortal?) but no less so for the community at large (who was to be baptized and who buried in holy ground?). Not surprisingly, therefore, most versions of *Aristotle's Master-piece* include a chapter on the soul, which explains in orthodox theological terms that souls are not engendered by the copulation of male and female but are superadded by God to fetuses during their development in the womb. For ensoulment, two criteria must be satisfied. First, the fetus must be independent and live, with a human form. This excludes shapeless accumulations of flesh such as "moles." Second, the fetus must be the fruit of regular intercourse between a man and a woman. This stipulation addresses the problem of live-born "monsters," which is examined in most versions of *Aristotle's Master-piece.*

Producing a severely malformed child was not just a ghastly trauma for the parents but was also regarded as an ominous social event, a portent, a punishment.[47] Most editions of *Aristotle's Master-piece* carry horrifying illustrations of grotesque monsters (all the more conspicuous since they are often the only illustrations in the whole book). These include what later ages were to call Siamese twins, but chiefly depict black, hairy, or simian infants. In offering explanations for these, *Aristotle's Master-piece* lapses into a misogyny uncharacteristic of the text as a whole. It attributes the mother with responsibility, seeing malformations as the consequence of one of four possibilities. Perhaps the mother has a grave internal disorder, or had copulated with an animal, the latter of which would result in a hybrid man-beast (this offspring, being subhuman, would have no soul) (1:52).[48] Perhaps the woman has lain with some demon (1:52). This view—scotched as a biologically absurd superstition by Venette— continues to appear in editions of *Aristotle's Master-piece* until well into the nineteenth century and may indicate through its clear acceptance of incubism the lingering of lurid popular witch beliefs.[49] The last explanation offered is that the monster is a product of the mother's imagination (1:46; 2:18).

The belief in a woman's power to imprint upon her baby whatever was in her imagination at the moment of conception or during pregnancy was widely accepted within both regular medicine and popular culture (1:43).[50] It was challenged by the science of the Enlightenment and, indeed, was rejected by Venette and various eighteenth-century medical figures,[51] but it was endorsed by *Aristotle's Master-piece* throughout its publishing career. Its implications were extraordinarily equivocal. It could serve as a comforting rationalization of what was otherwise terrifying and inexplicable (2:[11]): why was a child born with red stains on its skin or with a harelip? Because at a crucial juncture its mother had eaten a strawberry or had been crossed by a hare (1:20). Yet it also endorsed what was clearly perceived to be the dangerous power of women. The future of the race seemed to depend on what chanced to be racing through the mind of the weaker vessel, whose rationality was doubted at the best of times (a theme, of course, exploited in Laurence Sterne's *Tristram Shandy*).

Moreover, though the chapter on imagination blamed women for producing deformities, it also—bizarrely—instructed them in committing adultery undetected (1:19). If, in the hot embraces of her lover, a woman called to mind her husband, then the resulting issue would indeed resemble him. Thus, the text fanned the flames of distrust against women while also spelling out to them the art of foolproof infidelity.

This instance runs against the grain of the book, which is not generally misogynistic or, to use Alex Comfort's terms, "anxiety-making," and which aims to promote better understanding and reconciliation between spouses. Male suspicions against women are allayed at length in two particular chapters. One deals with the dilemma created by the cultural fetish of virginity. If on your wedding night your wife does not bleed on first penetration, does this prove that she was no virgin? Not at all, *Aristotle's Master-piece* answers reassuringly (1:87; 2:84). There are many natural ways for the hymen to be ruptured before the first encounter with a man (Version 3 mischievously suggests that the lady, fired by erotic arousal, possibly had been exploring herself rather too energetically with her own fingers (3:34–35[26]). In any case, not all virgins bleed when the hymen is ruptured. Hence the brisk, no-nonsense advice:

> When a man is married, and finds the tokens of his wife's virginity upon the first copulation, he has all the reason in the world to believe her such, and to rest satisfied that he has married a virgin; but if on the contrary, he finds them not, then he has no reason to think her divirginated, if he finds her otherwise sober and modest.   (3:36[28])

If, however, your wife bears a child just seven months after marriage, does this mean she was unfaithful to you in advance? By no means necessarily. Medical and legal testimony are drawn on to show that live births are occasionally brought forth many weeks prematurely. Once again, the wife deserves the benefit of the doubt (1:65).

❋

I have been locating the concerns and interpreting the strategy of *Aristotle's Master-piece*, suggesting that these are fundamentally different from the sexual preoccupations of the last two centuries. Modern discourse has commonly associated sex with danger (in prostitution, perversions, or overpopulation), recreation, or the psyche; *Aristotle's Master-piece*, by contrast, sets sex in a context that is fundamentally natural and functional. It is neither tainted by sin nor warped by the phantoms of the conscious or unconscious psyche. Physically embedded in the biology of reproduction within an authentically Aristotelian teleology, it is portrayed as nature's way of ensuring generation and safeguarding the life of the species within the wider rhythms of the cosmos.[52]

How typical of its times was this outlook? No firm answers are yet possible, but other contemporary works of sexual instruction also privileged sex-as-generation in a comparable fashion. There are, of course, major differences between *Aristotle's Master-piece* and the writings, for instance, of Nicholas Venette, James Graham, and Ebenezer Sibly (not to mention Diderot or the Marquis de Sade). Both physicians, Venette and Sibly produced texts that claimed to establish new discoveries in physiology and in embryology. Venette made a luxuriant parade of book learning, citing scores of medical and theological authorities and indulging in subtle plays of learned wit and irony. Yet, for all their differences, these texts share with *Aristotle's Master-piece* the common assumption that "sensual felicity" is not a taboo but a natural function that is both pleasurable and health-giving when pursued with "reciprocal love" within the social institution of marriage and directed toward the biological end of reproduction.

But did *Aristotle's Master-piece*'s pronatalism square with the outlooks of its readers? The triumph of modern historical demography has been to demonstrate how extensively and successfully families limited and regulated their progeny in time past.[53] Fearing the fate of the nursery rhyme old woman who lived in a shoe and worried about producing too many children too closely crowded together, would couples really have taken to heart the pronatalist message of *Aristotle's Master-piece*? It is perhaps most likely that the readership of *Aristotle's Master-piece* fell principally amongst those who did not have either any or enough children or amongst those who experienced difficulties in producing them (particularly male heirs). Though we have scant concrete evidence about who actually read the work in the eighteenth century, it may be illuminating that the 1690 edition advertised itself as being "very necessary for all midwives, nurses and young married women." Probably both newlyweds and those about to marry as well as those experiencing sterility problems purchased it and turned to it for reassurance and guidance. Its steady sales, spanning more than two centuries, suggest that it was at least somewhat successful in meeting readers' wants; for want of competition, however, that may have been *faute de mieux*.

The social profile of the readership of *Aristotle's Master-piece* is largely guesswork, though its steady sale suggests a broad social mix. The text is not as self-preeningly erudite as Venette's; it does not go out of its way to talk down chapbook-style to the barely literate, nor was it ever issued in abbreviated, simplified, diluted form. Though mostly in plain speech ("yard" is the standard term for penis),[54] the text is also sprinkled with Latin phrases and medical terminology and contains some quite technical anatomical discussion. Readers are assumed to be able to take references to "the Galenists" or to Avicenna in their stride. Arguably, however, this display of hard learning was designed to attract more readers by conjuring an aura of expert authority. The same explains the lofty social settings it depicted. The reader was assumed to be of such social standing as to be able to relocate her residence during pregnancy (3:45[123]), to have access to an elaborate *materia medica*, to be able to order pheasant, quinces, and pomegranates as aphrodisiacs, and to sip muscatel and Malaga to make the night right for love (2:44[24]). Readers were apparently expected to hire wetnurses and to have parents who might act as marriage brokers (2:44[24]). Presumably only a tiny proportion of readers were actually able to do any of these. These unrealistic assumptions perhaps pandered to reader fantasy and snobbery and were thus good advertising strategy. Popular publications such as children's books were commonly aimed at higher social groups than their actual readers comprised; such is the stuff of flattery and hegemony (2:26[24]).[55] This may, however, merely reveal that editors were out of touch with the real nature and quality of their customers (just as Marie Stopes believed that her women readers could insert their contraceptive pessaries while dressing for dinner). Certainly, the glacial changelessness of the text over the course of two centuries suggests that little care was taken to adjust the text to changing needs. It is possible that the continued free circulation of what in the eyes of the Dr. Bowdlers and Mrs. Grundys must have seemed a dubious, if not a dirty, book was facilitated precisely because of its venerability.

How far did readers absorb a "hidden agenda" along with the facts of life? I shall address, in conclusion, three questions on the aspects of the ideological load of *Aristotle's Master-piece*. First, did the text aim to induce the common reader to abandon traditional beliefs about the mechanisms and morality of sex and to defer instead to the "opinions of the learned" (2:44[26])? How far, in other words, was a new sexual discipline being instilled? In many respects, *Aristotle's Master-piece* is not a text that tries to create a mystique of science or to mystify expertise; on the contrary, it proclaims a democratic epistemology that promises explicitly to unfold the "secrets of generation" (1:i),[56] and asserts in particular that sexual information should not be withheld from women (2:[iii]). Admittedly, it passes itself off as the teachings of the incomparable Artistotle, praises his wisdom to the skies, and decries "vulgar errors."[57] Yet, it also cheerfully admits that the ancients were far from infallible oracles; indeed, it asserts that most of their anatomical teachings were wrong![58] When it cites the opinions of the "learned" as authorities, it is generally to *confirm* popular lore and to reassure rather than to penalize. Certainly, the text instructs the sick reader to summon professional medical advice, yet it assumes that self-dosing is generally the norm and tables recipes for self-physicking readers (2:89[50]). *Aristotle's Master-piece* is better seen as part of the commercialization of popular sexual beliefs into print culture than as an arm of hegemonic medical policing.[59]

Second, how instrumental was *Aristotle's Master-piece* in reinforcing gender roles?[60] It is a complicated issue that warrants a more nuanced answer than space permits. Undoubtedly, the text was operating within a holistic medical system derived from the Greeks, which viewed males as comprehensively stronger and healthier than women (being in humoural terms both hotter and drier). Women were more disease-prone, partly because they were instrinsically weaker and partly because they suffered the diseases of child-bed. The text discusses notably the anatomy and diseases of *women*. The assumption is pervasive that maleness is normal, natural, and healthy, hardly requiring sustained attention.

Yet, *Aristotle's Master-piece* does not celebrate crudely "macho" qualities.[61] There is no hint of a "double standard," and the book is generally free of the gross misogyny that disfigures so many Renaissance texts on women and marriage.[62] Women are not portrayed as nymphomaniacs or hags. Nor does the text project either that ideal of women as sexless, passionless, delicate, and liable to hysteria and neurasthenia if physically or mentally exerted, which became so dominant in the Victorian age or, indeed, the Victorian cult of motherhood.[63] Men and women were indeed seen as different, and these distinctions embodied prejudices (e.g., the assumption that a male fetus gives a mother-to-be an easier pregnancy than a female fetus [1:13]). A key aspect of this view of the simultaneous difference and complementarity of the genders is the belief that in reproduction men supply the active component, women the passive (1:15). Yet the text also stresses the power of women: children take after their mothers more than their fathers.

Overall, the similarities between the sexes rather than the polarities are emphasized.[64] Women enjoy parity in sexual desire, and female desire is not viewed as grotesque or psychopathological but is portrayed sympathetically as contributing to the well-being of both woman and child.[65] Moreover, there is a physical guarantee for this parity in esteem, since (as *Aristotle's Master-piece* insists) men and women are actually anatomically similar; there is no "vast difference between the Members of the two sexes" (1:93), because the "use and action of the clitoris in women is like that of the penis or yard in men, that is, erection" (3:23[18]). Admittedly, female genitalia are inverted from men's, but they amount to the same in the end:

> For those that have the strictest searchers been
> Find women are but men turn'd outside in;
> And men, if they but cast their eyes about,
> May find they're women with their inside out.

Or:

> Thus the woman's secrets I have survey'd
> And let them see how curiously they're made
> And that, tho' they of different sexes be,
> Yet in whole they are the same as we.   (3:22[17–18])

Finally, what overall sexual values did *Aristotle's Master-piece* instill? Above all, it is pronuptualist and pronatalist. Does this propaganda for "sweet conjugal love" and child-bearing represent an attempt to sell these institutions to reluctant young people, especially women? This seems unlikely; most of our evidence from common life indicates that young people were generally eager to marry and set up households (even if that eagerness largely registered the desire to escape the tutelege of parents and—in the case of women—to avoid the fate of spinsterhood). It may, however, resonate with the anxiety expressed by a great number of social commentators at the close of the seventeenth century that the nation was being weakened by underpopulation.

If we assume that *Aristotle's Master-piece* was read by people for whom marital union was both destiny and choice, then for that readership it must have appeared positive and reassuring. Sex was not stained with stigmas of sin, decadence, libertinism, enslavement to passion, or psychological disturbance.[66] Neither did it need to be sublimated, suppressed, or sentimentalized. Rather, it was viewed as an agency of nature.[67] The text's trust in nature perhaps interweaves into one fabric the organic philosophy of Aristotle, the optimistic naturalism of the early Enlightenment, and the earthy realism of popular culture.[68] *Aristotle's Master-piece* is generally relaxed about what Christian churches had made an inflammatory subject. This might help to explain its enduring success.

Roy Porter
Wellcome Institute for the History of Medicine

APPENDIX

Aristotle's Master-piece: Generations of Editions

Version 1	*Version 2*	*Version 3*	*Version 4*
1690: London	1710: London and subsequent	early 18th-c.: London, 12th edn.	
		(Entirely new format in table of contents; division of materials into three parts; divisions of chapters into sections, etc. Remains unchanged at least until the 15th edn. of 1723).	
		1749: London, 23d edn. (Aristotle's Masterpiece remains identical to the format of the 12th, 13th, and 15th edns. New material added: *Aristotle's Compleat Midwife; Aristotle's Book of Problems*; and *Aristotle's Last Legacy*. This publication remains constant up to latest edns. so far found, which appear to be dated early 19th c.)	
	First part almost identical to chaps. 1-15 of the London edn. of 1690. In remainder of the edn., order of contents unique.		Victorian edns. (dates unclear)

NOTES

1. Foucault, *The History of Sexuality*, vol. 1: *An Introduction* (N.Y.: Pantheon Books, 1978); Shorter, *The Making of the Modern Family* (London: Collins, 1976); Stone, *The Family, Sex and Marriage in England, 1500–1800* (London: Weidenfeld and Nicolson, 1977).

2. *The Bourgeoisie: 1. The Education of the Senses* (N.Y.: Oxford Univ., 1984); this work contains an important bibliographical essay.

3. For general background, see Iwan Bloch, *A History of English Sexual Morals* (London: Corgi, 1965); Morton M. Hunt, *The Natural History of Love* (London: Hutchinson, 1960); Nina Consuelo Epton, *Love and the English* (London: Cassel, 1960); G. Rattray Taylor, *Sex in History* (London: Thames and Hudson, 1953); and Denis de Rougemont, *Love and the Western World* (Princeton: Princeton Univ., 1983). For Milton, see Edward Le Comte, *Milton and Sex* (London: Macmillan, 1978).

4. On the erotic and the medical, see Roger Thompson, *Unfit for Modest Ears* (London: Macmillan, 1980), and Peter Wagner, "The Pornographer in the Courtroom: Trial Reports about Cases of Sexual Crimes and Delinquencies as a Genre of Eighteenth-Century Erotica," in *Sexuality in Eighteenth-Century Britain*, ed. Paul-Gabriel Boucé (Manchester: Manchester Univ., 1982), pp. 120–40.

5. For Venette, see Jean Torlais, *Médecine du passé en Aunis et Saintonge* (La Rochelle: Impr. de l'Ouest, 1931), pp. 51–72, and André Pecker, "Nicholas Venette (1633–1698): Est-il le fils de Guy Patin?" *Bulletin des Sciences Médicales* 16 (1983): 167–74.

6. Roy Porter, "Spreading Carnal Knowledge or Selling Dirt Cheap? Nicholas Venette's *Tableau de l'Amour Conjugal* in Eighteenth-Century England," *Journal of European Studies* 14 (1984): 233–55.

7. The work is, of course, not by Aristotle. For Aristotle's own sexual views, see Johannes Morsink, *Aristotle on the Generation of Animals* (Washington, D.C.: Univ. Press of America, 1982).

8. I do not claim to have seen all surviving editions published in eighteenth-century England. A proper bibliographical study would be highly desirable.

9. For the development of comparable sexual texts from antiquity, see G. E. R. Lloyd, *Science, Folklore and Ideology* (Cambridge: Cambridge Univ., 1983); M. Anthony Hewson, *Giles of Rome and the Medieval Theory of Generation* (London: Athlone Press, 1975); H. R. Lemay, "Human Sexuality in Twelfth- through Fifteenth-Century Scientific Writings," in *Sexual Practices and the Medieval Church*, ed. Vern L. Bullough and James Brundage (Buffalo, N.Y.: Prometheus Books, 1982), pp. 187–202; Brian Lawn, *The Prose Salernitan Questions* (London: Open University Books for the British Academy, 1979); and Beryl Rowland, *Medieval Woman's Guide to Health* (London: Croom Helm, 1981).

10. Alex Comfort, *The Anxiety Makers* (London: Nelson, 1967), p. 20.

11. Janet Blackman, "Popular Theories of Generation: The Evolution of Aristotle's Works; the Study of an Anachronism," in *Health Care and Popular Medicine in Nineteenth-Century England*, ed. John Woodward and David Richards (London: Croom Helm, 1977), pp. 56–88. See also Vern Bullough, "An Early American Sex Manual; or, Aristotle Who?" *Early American Literature* 7 (1973): 236–46; Angus McLaren, "The Pleasures of Procreation," in *William Hunter and the Eighteenth-Century Medical World*, ed. W. F. Bynum and Roy Porter (Cambridge: Cambridge Univ., 1985).

12. Comfort, *Anxiety Makers*, p. 20; see also G. L. Simons, *Sex and Superstition* (London: Abelard-Schuman, 1973).

13. "Aristotle's Master-piece," in *The Foundations of Medical History* (Baltimore: Williams and Wilkins, 1931), pp. 147, 168.

14. Otho J. Beall, "*Aristotle's Master-piece* in America: A Landmark in the Folklore of Medicine," *William and Mary Quarterly*, 3d ser., 20 (1963): 207–22, quote on p. 220; Boucé, "Some Sexual Beliefs and Myths in Eighteenth-Century Britain," in *Sexuality in Britain*, ed. Boucé, pp. 28–46, quote on p. 36. Boucé suggests that the "myths" contained in *Aristotle's Master-piece* are redolent of the "pre-logical mentalité" (p. 30).

15. "Popular Theories," p. 83. It is, she suggests, a "substitute for thought" (p. 84).

16. For general discussion of the problems of establishing the publishing history of such works as this, see *Books and Their Readers in Eighteenth-Century England*, ed. Isabel Rivers (Leicester: Leicester Univ., 1982); David Foxon, *Libertine Literature in England, 1660–1745* (London: Shenval Press, 1965); and John Feather, "The Commerce of Letters: The Study of the Eighteenth-Century Book Trade," *Eighteenth-Century Studies* 17 (1984): 405–24.

17. Amongst those was Francis Place, who read it while still a schoolboy: "I had read a book at that time openly sold, on every stall, called Aristotles Master-Piece, it was a thick 18 mo, with a number of badly drawn cuts in it explanatory of the mystery of generation. This I contrived to borrow and compared parts of it with the accounts of the Miraculous Conception in Mathew and Luke" (*The Autobiography of Francis Place*, ed. M. Thale [London: Cambridge Univ., 1972], p. 45).

18. For broad background to Enlightenment ideas on sexuality, see Jean Hagstrum, *Sex and Sensibility* (Chicago: Univ. of Chicago, 1980), and Paul Hoffmann, *La Femme dans la pensée des lumières* (Paris: Editions Ophrys, 1977).

19. Roy Porter, "The Sexual Politics of James Graham," *British Journal for Eighteenth-Century Studies* 5 (1982): 199–206; see also Graham, *Lecture on the Generation, Increase and Improvement of the Human Species* (London, 1783).

20. Ebenezer Sibly, *The Medical Mirror; or, Treatise on the Impregnation of the Human Female* (London, 1784); A. G. Debus, "Scientific Truth and the Occult Tradition: The Medical World of Ebenezer Sibly, 1751–1799," *Medical History* 27 (1982): 259–78.

21. It should be stressed that this table must be provisional. Most editions of *Aristotle's Master-piece* lack both a date of publication and a publisher. Some give an edition number, but it is dubious whether these may be relied on. I have consulted the following editions:

Version 1: *Aristotle's Master-piece or, the Secrets of Generation Displayed in all the Parts Thereof* . . . (London: J. How, 1690; 1694);

Version 2: *Aristotle's Master-piece*, (London, 1710); *Aristotle's Master-piece Compleated* (Glasgow, 1782); *The Works of Aristotle, the Famous Philosopher* (London: Archibald Wisleton, [c. 1810]); ibid. (undated but probably early Victorian, published by Thomas Richardson in Derby);

Version 3: *Aristotle's Master-piece*, 12th edn. (London: The Booksellers, early 18th-c.); ibid., 13th edn. (London: The Booksellers, early 18th-c.); ibid., 15th edn. (London: The Booksellers, 1723); ibid., 23d edn. (London: The Booksellers, 1749); *Aristotle's Works Compleated* (London: The Booksellers, 1753); 28th edn. (London: The Booksellers, 1764); ibid., 31st edn. (London: The Booksellers, 1776); *The Works of Aristotle* (London: The Booksellers, 1790); ibid. (1791); ibid. (1793); ibid. (1796).

22. Compare Margaret Spufford's comment on sex in contemporary chapbooks: "The whole tenor of the merry books conveys that seventeenth-century women enjoyed their own sexuality and were expected to enjoy it" (*Small Books and Pleasant Histories: Popular Fiction and its Readership in Seventeenth-Century England* [London: Methuen, 1981], p. 63); Victor E. Neuburg, *Popular Literature: A History and Guide* (Harmondsworth: Penguin, 1977).

23. Version 3 is hereafter cited in text from *Aristotle's Master-piece*, 12th edn., (London: The Booksellers [early 18th-c.]). Figures in brackets give the page numbers of *The Works of Aristotle in Four Parts* (London: The Booksellers, 1796); 3:32[25].

24. Version 2 is hereafter cited in text from *Aristotle's Master-piece* (London, 1710). Figures in brackets give the page numbers of *The Works of Aristotle, the Famous Philosopher* (London: Archibald Wisleton, c. 1810); 2:9[8].

25. Porter, "Spreading Carnal Knowledge."

26. This 4th version is hereafter cited in text from *The Works of the Famous Philosopher Aristotle* (London: The Booksellers, n.d.); clearly Victorian, it claims to be the "original edition unabridged" (4:13). An undated but late Victorian edition of this version carries an "Advertisement" that reassures the reader that "The odium in which the book has been held by the moral and the virtuous, does not apply to the present edition. That which was good and useful has been retained, and that only; the omission being supplied by new matter of an interesting and valuable character. . . . To supply a good and moral edition of a work hitherto accounted the reverse of either, is he (the publisher) believes, both important and useful."

27. *History of Sexuality*, Vol. 1: *Introduction*. For helpful warnings about the pitfalls of back-projecting modern sexology, see Jeffrey Weeks, *Sex, Politics and Society* (London:

Longman, 1981); Michael Ignatieff, "Homo Sexualis," *London Review of Books*, 4–17 Mar. 1982, pp. 8–9; Stephen Heath, *The Sexual Fix* (London: Macmillan, 1982); and Paul Robinson, *The Modernization of Sex* (N.Y.: Harper and Row, 1976).

28. *Lecture on Generation*, p. 42.

29. Venette and Graham would have agreed. See Porter, "Spreading Carnal Knowledge," and "Sexual Politics of Graham."

30. Version 1 is hereafter cited in text from *Aristotle's Master-Piece; or, The Secrets of Generation Display'd in all the Parts Thereof* (London: J. How, 1690). Here see the introduction: God, having created man, "added Allurements, and desire of mutual Embracing, so that they might in Procreation be sweetly affected and delighted by wonderous ways: For unless this was natural to all kinds of Creatures, they would be regardless of Posterity, and Procreation would cease; whereby Mankind would quickly be lost, and the Affairs of Mortals of no Continuance." See also *Aristotle's Master-piece* (2:9[5]).

31. For the natural philosophy of organic growth (surviving, despite the mechanical philosophy of the Scientific Revolution), see Carolyn Merchant, *The Death of Nature* (San Francisco: Harper and Row, 1980), and Desirée Hirst, *Hidden Riches* (London: Eyre and Spottiswoode, 1964).

32. For discussions of homosexuality, see Paul-Gabriel Boucé, "Aspects of Sexual Tolerance and Intolerance in Eighteenth-Century England," *British Journal for Eighteenth-Century Studies* 3 (1980): 173–89, and "Some Sexual Beliefs and Myths in Eighteenth-Century Britain," in *Sexuality in Britain*, ed. Boucé, pp. 28–46; see also Alan Bray, *Homosexuality in Renaissance England* (London: Gaymen's Press, 1982). For erotic mania, see G. S. Rousseau, "Nymphomania, Bienville, and the Rise of Erotic Sensibility," in *Sexuality in Britain*, ed. Boucé, pp. 95–119. It is remarkable that no edition of *Aristotle's Master-piece* seems to have jumped on the bandwagon of fear of masturbation, for which see R. H. MacDonald, "The Frightful Consequences of Onanism," *Journal of the History of Ideas* 28 (1967): 423–41.

33. The contrary belief, that Venus and Bacchus did not mix, became common in the works of such Enlightenment figures as James Graham and Erasmus Darwin. See Porter, "Sexual Politics of Graham."

34. For broader contexts on perceptions about the relations between sex and the family, see Jean-Louis Flandrin, "Amour et mariage," *Dix-huitieme siècle* 12 (1980): 163–76; Philippe Ariès, "L'Amour dans le mariage," *Communications sexualités Occidentales* 35 (1980): 116–22; and J.-L. Flandrin, *Le Sexe et l'Occident* (Paris: Editions du Seuil, 1981).

35. On *Aristotle's Master-piece* and 19th-c. Malthusianism, see Angus McLaren, *Birth Control in Nineteenth-Century England* (London: Croom Helm, 1978), pp. 28–29, 78–79, 84–85, 222–23, 238–39.

36. See E. A. Wrigley and R. S. Schofield, *The Population History of England, 1541–1871* (London: Edward Arnold, 1981).

37. Medical means such as purges were also suggested (1:71ff). See also *Aristotle's Master-piece* (3:30[22]), and I. Loudon, "Chlorosis, Anaemia and Anorexia Nervosa," *British Medical Journal* 271 (1980): 1–19, and "The Diseases called Chlorosis," *Psychological Medicine* 14 (1984): 27–36.

38. See Patricia Crawford, "Attitudes to Menstruation in Seventeenth-Century England," *Past and Present* 91 (1981): 47–73. For menstruation as polluting, see Edward Shorter, *A History of Women's Bodies* (Harmondsworth: Allen Lane, 1983).

39. See McLaren, "Pleasures of Procreation."

40. For the body symbols of left and right, etc., see Brian Turner, *The Body and Society* (Oxford: Basil Blackwell, 1984).

41. For backgrounds to contemporary embryology, see Joseph Needham, *A History of Embryology* (Cambridge: Cambridge Univ., 1934); Elizabeth Gasking, *Investigations into Generation, 1651–1828* (London: Hutchinson, 1967); F. J. Cole, *Early Theories of Sexual Generation* (Oxford: Clarendon Press, 1930); and Shirley Roe, *Matter, Life and Generation* (Cambridge: Cambridge Univ., 1981).

42. See Pierre Darmon, *Le Mythe de la procréation a l'age baroque* (Paris: J. J. Pauvert, 1977).

43. Audrey Eccles, *Obstetrics and Gynaecology in Tudor and Stuart England* (London: Croom Helm, 1982); Jean Donnison, *Midwives and Medical Men* (London: Hienemann, 1977); Adrian Wilson, "William Hunter and the Varieties of Man-Midwifery," in *William*

Hunter, ed. Bynum and Porter.

44. Shorter, *History of Women's Bodies,* and Babara Ehrenreich and Dierdre English, *Complaints and Disorders* (London: Feminist Press, 1973).

45. See also Germaine Greer, "The Curse of Sterility," in *Sex and Destiny* (London: Secker and Warburg, 1984).

46. Some brief advice, however, is given on how to restore "flaggy yards" (1:7).

47. Kathleen Park and Lorraine Daston, "Unnatural Conceptions: The Study of Monsters in Sixteenth-Century France and England," *Past and Present* 92 (1981): 20–54; C. J. S. Thompson, *The Mystery and Lore of Monsters* (London: William and Norgate, 1930); Leslie Fiedler, *Freaks* (N.Y.: Simon and Shuster, 1978). See also the discussion in John Sergeant, *Solid Philosophy* (London, 1697).

48. For men-beasts, see Keith Thomas, *Man and the Natural World* (Harmondsworth: Allen Lane and Penguin, 1983).

49. For the wider perspective on witchcraft, see Keith Thomas, *Religion and the Decline of Magic* (London: Weidenfield and Nicolson, 1971).

50. Compare this report in the *Gentleman's Magazine:*
The wife of one Rich. Haynes of Chelsea, aged 35 and mother of 16 fine children, was deliver'd of a monster, with nose and eyes like a lyon no palate to the mouth, hair on the shoulders, claws like a lion instead of fingers, no breastbone, something surprising out of the navel as big as an egg, and one foot longer than the other.—She had been to see the lions in the Tower, where she was much terrify'd with the old lion's noise. (16[1746]: 270)

51. See, e.g., Jean Blondel, *The Strength of Imagination in Pregnant Women Examin'd* (London: J. Peele, 1727).

52. For different approaches to the flesh and the body, see Frank Bottomley, *Attitudes to the Body in Western Christendom* (London: Lepus Books, 1979), and Thomas R. Frosch, *The Awakening of Albion: The Renovation of the Body in the Poetry of William Blake* (Ithaca: Cornell Univ., 1975).

53. Wrigley and Schofield, *Population History.*

54. Contrast the flowery language of John Armstrong's *The Economy of Love* (London, 1736):

> Recline your Cheek, with eager Kisses press
> Her balmy Lips, and drinking from her Eyes
> Resistless Love, the tender Flame confess,
> Ineffable but by the murmuring Voice
> Of genuine Joy; then hug and kiss again
> Stretch'd on the flow'ry turf, while joyful glows
> Thy manly Pride, and throbbing with Desire
> Pants earnest, felt thro' all the obstacles
> That intervene: but Love, whose fervid Course
> Mountains nor Seas oppose, can soon remove
> Barriers so slight . . . (lines 181–91)

55. Compare James Secord, "Newton in the Nursery: Tom Telescope and the Philosophy of Tops and Balls, 1761–1812," *History of Science* (1985); forthcoming.

56. For the dynamic interaction of popular and polite culture, the "great" and "little" traditions, see Peter Burke, *Popular Culture in Early Modern Europe* (London: Temple Smith, 1978).

57. *Aristotle's Master-piece* plays elaborate games over "Aristotle" as the author of the work. Cf. "To The Reader," *Aristotle's Master-piece* (2:3).

58. For mixed feelings about the ancients see Richard Foster Jones, *Ancients and Moderns* (St. Louis: Washington Univ., 1962), and Barbara J. Shapiro, *Probability and Certainty in Seventeenth-Century England* (Princeton: Princeton Univ., 1983). See also *Aristotle's Master-piece* (2:25–26[14]).

59. Here I endorse the views of Peter Burke as expressed in "Popular Culture between History and Ethnology," *Ethnologi Europaea* 14 (1984): 5–13.

60. See L. J. Jordanova, "Natural Facts: A Historical Perspective on Science and Sexuality," in *Nature, Culture and Gender,* ed. Caroline MacCormack and Marilyn Strathern (Cambridge: Cambridge Univ., 1980), pp. 42–69.

61. For the history of "macho man" and "viriculture," see Brian Easlea, *Science and Sexual Oppression* (London: Weidenfeld and Nicolson, 1981).

62. Although there is mention of Lamia in *Aristotle's Master-piece* (1:59–60), for misogyny, see K. L. M. Rogers, *The Troublesome Helpmate* (Seattle: Washington Univ., 1966).

63. Nancy F. Cott, "Passionlessness: An Interpretation of Victorian Sexual Ideology, 1790–1850," *Signs* 4 (1978): 219–36; Sara Delamont and Lorna Duffin, eds., *The Nineteenth-Century Woman: Her Cultural and Physical World* (London: Croom Helm, 1978); G. J. Barker-Benfield, *The Horrors of the Half-Known Life* (N.Y.: Harper and Row, 1976).

64. For the perception of female sexuality in the 18th c. see Patricia Meyer Spacks, "Ev'ry Woman is at Heart a Rake," *Eighteenth-Century Studies* 8 (1974–75): 27–46; Roy Porter, "Mixed Feelings: The Enlightenment and Sexuality in Eighteenth-Century Britain," in *Sexuality in Britain,* ed. Boucé, pp. 1–27.

65. *Aristotle's Master-piece* explains that deformed children are the product of weak desire (1:22), and argues that "the greater the woman's desire is, the more likely she is to conceive" (3: 47[37]). The text adds that women approach the marriage bed with "equal vigour" to the man.

66. See Hagstrum, *Sex and Sensibility.*

67. For the complexities of the ideological uses of the concept of nature, see also S. Shapin, "The Social Uses of Science," in *The Ferment of Knowledge,* ed. G. S. Rousseau and Roy Porter (Cambridge: Cambridge Univ., 1980), pp. 93–142.

68. For growing confidence in "nature" see B. Willey, *The Seventeenth-Century Background* (London: Chatto and Windus, 1946), and *The Eighteenth-Century Background* (London: Chatto and Windus, 1946); A. O. Lovejoy, *The Great Chain of Being* (Cambridge: Harvard Univ., 1936), chaps. 7–8.

Sexual Imagination as Revealed in the
Traité des superstitions
of Abbé Jean-Baptiste Thiers

We are all familiar with the difficulties involved in describing the amorous practices of the classical age. We know that contemporary authors, *les moralistes* themselves, spoke of love a great deal, but they did so in terms so general that they never seem to refer to the experiences of an individual or a phenomenon of their society. So we are left to investigate demographic statistics, birth registers, and confessors' handbooks; but the search for information about actual amorous practices continues to prove futile; nothing shows through beyond the fleshless abstraction of figures. For those who remain undaunted, there is the novel, which had already become numerically significant by the seventeenth century and which dominated the eighteenth. Love often provided its subject matter. Some would say that it was the preferred subject matter, if not the only one.[1] The novel was even to come under attack for this reason, on the grounds that it corrupted young men and sullied young women. When Dr. Bienville comes to seek the causes of nymphomania when relating the case history of one of his patients, it does not take him long to point to the harmful influence of servants and the pernicious effects of Marivaux's novels.[2] Ah, who would ever have imagined—and dared say—that it was so! Similarly, when J.-L. Flandrin, in his remarkable *Amours paysannes,* leaves the barren shores of sociological and statistical sources and seeks evidence of actual experience, it is to Restif's fiction that he turns.[3]

Of course, as literary historians, we know that the events related in fiction are not proper matter for sociological studies.[4] First and foremost, a novel yields information about novels: literary devices and their effects on the reader. To use fiction as a source from which to determine social and historical reality is risky and often misleading. Eighteenth-century novels may well deal with love, but can we actually discover in reading them what the experience (or experiences) of love under the *ancien régime* were? The limitations inherent in first-person narratives (which would mean the narratives of the eighteenth-century elite), do not help matters. Aside from those who hold to the most short-sighted view of sociology, who would maintain that the novels of Sade reflect the sexual practices of a corrupt aristocracy that felt threatened in its existence? To argue thus is to accept as true, without the slightest proof, revolutionary diatribe about the decadence and perversity of the nobility. We would do well to abandon denunciations of this kind to those who would wage such dubious wars and to approach the "amorous" novel with somewhat more scientific rigor.

The pornographic novel represents amorous fiction taken to its extreme, and it was very popular in the eighteenth century; but it does not allow any more so than other types of novel a strictly sociological reading. The adventures of Dom Bougre, in *Le Portier des Chartreux,* do not reflect the morals of the clergy by some one-to-one correspondence.[5] The recurrence of certain themes may provide some indication of social practices, but it does not allow us to determine standard behavior. The frequent presence of lewd monks—from Père Girard to Dom Saturnin, by way of the wan bishop of the *Cent-Vingt Journées de Sodome*[6]—is not sufficient for us to draw conclusions about the sexual life of the eighteenth century clergy, just as Sade's novels do not reflect the sexual habits of the aristocracy on the eve of the French Revolution. To carry this even further, it would be a mistake to maintain that given works provide an indication of the sexual activities of their authors, even in those instances in which the painstaking research of biographers enables them to establish links between actual and written experience. At best, one can argue that literature yields, beyond the evidence it gives about itself, evidence about the imagination of writers and their readers, which is far from insignificant.[7] This statement probably applies most fully to erotic (or even pornographic) fiction, where literature is carried to excess both in its function as an effect-producing machine (the effects here being physiological) and in its relation to the imagination of a given period and society. I am convinced that we would be justified in analyzing amorous literature as imagination in concrete form, that is, as a recasting of reality (in an effort to go beyond it, to repress and to conceal) and as an opportunity to shock one's readers, to speak the socially unspeakable and break with accepted practice.

I do not, however, propose to undertake this particular reading of the eighteenth-century amorous, erotic, libertine or blatantly pornographic novel with its view toward reconstructing a fragment of the amorous imagination. I rather propose to examine—through an approach related to ethnohistorical study, as I shall demonstrate—the *Traité des superstitions* of the Abbé Thiers,[8] and more precisely still, those superstitions concerning marriage that take up the eight chapters of book ten.

Just as in the case of sociological studies grounded in literature, the error to be avoided lies in taking Thiers' work as a documented study of eighteenth-century French society. It is nothing of the sort. It is a work of compilation and erudition that contains little direct observation. In many respects, the *Traité des superstitions* is somewhat like a teacher's copy with the right answers; it is supposed to allow its reader to distinguish those practices that are purely superstitious from those that are orthodox. The system of classification by sacrament that Thiers adopts provides both an indication of the pedagogic and didactic character of the work and insight into the reading audience for which it was intended. The work offers, then, not an x-ray of seventeenth- and eighteenth-century French society, but an a-historical picture of the superstitious practices of the Christian West. It is true that in the area of those practices related specifically to marriage we learn of attitudes, patterns of behavior, and certain objects and events that are given unusual importance (most all of these phenomena being difficult to date); but we are essentially given the mind that is behind these practices. How could one fail to see the essential presence of sexual fantasizing beneath the importance attached to the tying and untying of the *aiguillette*?[9] And such sexual fantasizing is unquestionably an integral part of the established social norm; it defines itself in terms of standard behavior, even when rejecting it. Obviously, the superstitions related to the sacrament of marriage do not include all practices and do not cover the whole of sexual imagination, but they reveal the greater part of their society's secrets, far more so than would have been the case in a dechristianized world.

Let us recall who Thiers was and what the *Traité des superstitions* represents. J.-B. Thiers (1636-1703) came from a modest, provincial background. After a brilliant career as a student, first in Chartres and then in Paris, he became a professor in Chartres and Paris and a parish priest in Champrond-en-Gâtine and Vibraye. He was extremely active in the religious and scholarly debates of his time, siding against the Franciscans in Reims, against the Great Archdeacon in Chartres, against Denis de Sainte-Marthe (the leader of the religious order of Saint-Maur, in defense of l'abbé de Rancé), against the famous Père Mabillon in the debate over a miraculous tear preserved in Vendôme, against Jacques Boileau, the poet's brother, and on and on. His most famous work is the *Traité des superstitions qui regardent les sacrements selon l'Ecriture sainte, les décrets des Conciles et les sentiments des Saints Pères et des théologiens* [*Treatise on the Superstitions concerning the Sacraments according to the Holy Writ, the Decrees of the Church Councils and the Opinions of the Holy Fathers and Theologians*]. It appeared in its original (purely theoretical) version in 1679 and in a version considerably enlarged with examples in 1703-04. Extremely popular, the book was published several times during the eighteenth century. It was plagiarized in Diderot and D'Alembert's *Encyclopédie* and parodied in Abbé Bordelon's *L'Histoire des imaginations extravagantes de M. Oufle* (1710), which was reprinted in 1753 and which reappeared in digest version in 1789 in the lawyer Garnier's *Collection des voyages imaginaires*. There is hardly a text written by the *philosophes* that does not draw upon it when it comes to denouncing the fanaticism of the Catholic rural world. More recently, it has been a source of information in the research of ethno-historians and folklorists like Van Gennep—all of which should give some idea of its importance.[10]

It is likely to be some time before consensus is reached as to the credence to be given the accounts of rural folk cultures that constitute Thiers' portrait of the French countryside. The research that has been done over the last few decades on the French peasantry of the Enlightenment has taught us to proceed with caution. In effect, Thiers' frame of reference posits that superstitions have no history and that nothing separates those of the early Christian era from those that existed as he wrote. He allows as well that superstitions can resurface and that there are those that exist underground. The fact that tenets do not vary from one group to another—which for Bossuet was proof of the superiority of Catholicism over Protestantism—is for Thiers true, quite simply, for superstitions too. Insofar as one takes the *Traité des superstitions* as a manual allowing the Church's shepherds to distinguish orthodox practices from those that lead their flock astray, it is meaningless to make distinctions between superstitions that were learned of in books and those that were discovered in the field by Thiers himself or one of his numerous correspondents. It should be noted, however, that the proportion of first-hand accounts is far greater for superstitions dealing with the sacrament of marriage than for others. As to whether this was because Thiers himself was more interested in these superstitions or because their presence among the religious practices of the rural world of the classical age was more real, it would be hard to say. The point, in all events, is worth making.

In the four volumes of the *Traité des superstitions,* one volume, divided into four books, is given to a general (or theoretical) discussion of superstitions: What are they? Why should they be condemned? The remaining three volumes are devoted to specific superstitious practices as they are related to given sacraments. The greater number of practices dealing with "amorous" relations are found in book ten of the fourth volume: "Of those superstitions concerning marriage." This tenth book, which is at the end of Thiers' work, is divided into eight chapters. Three of them—chapters six, seven and eight, which deal with conjugal duty and the tying and untying of the *aiguillette*—are of special interest to our concerns here.

Still, we would do well to be clear about what is involved and to define what we intend to do. Thiers is not one to present the peasants of the classical age in their nightshirts. In fact, although peasant customs dominate the *Traité des superstitions,* Thiers observes that superstitions are no longer a strictly rural phenomenon. He notes that they "have gained access to the world of the nobility, are common among the middle classes, and are popular with commoners; every kingdom, every province, every diocese has its own" (p. 45). Thiers does not invite us into the inner love sanctums of the rich and the poor. He reveals nothing specific about the sexual practices of his time. It thus behooves us to distinguish actual superstitious practices from the imaginative processes that have generated them and that constitute their *raison d'être.* To be sure, there existed remedies for untying the *aiguillette* (to overcome the impotence caused by an enchantment or magic spell) and these remedies represent, in effect, superstitious practices. But how are love and sex conceived in the mind so as to foster belief in the tying and untying of the *aiguillette*? That is what is essential here: the underside of superstitious behavior. Still, we should not overlook the fact that through their gestures and symbolism these practices reveal, in their own way, another dimension of the contemporary mind.

The practices that deal with love do not constitute a particular kind apart from the rest. They clearly show the characteristics of superstitions in general (as Thiers defines them) and even the folk cultures from which they are drawn: a world in which every object functions on both the natural and supernatural levels and in which future events can be known before they occur (p. 24). Nothing especially new here, still some of the givens are worth noting.

First of all, Thiers maintains that there exists a standard behavior for love: marriage, which he valorizes by virtue of its longevity. "Marriage is hardly less ancient than the world itself," Thiers claims, and the proof of it lies in its creation by God in earthly paradise (p. 234). Reading Thiers' work one might well infer that all sex life was limited to marriage and that superstitious practices—anything from those associated with betrothal to those associated with charivari—revolved exclusively around matrimony. But then, is this not a handbook dealing with superstitions as they relate to the sacraments? If Thiers happens to recall the Angevine custom whereby "a young man who was in love with a young woman and who was loved by her would drink with her under promise of marriage, whereafter they would make love as if they were actually married" (p. 251), he deals with it less as another kind of love relationship than as a deviation from the institution of marriage. This explains, moreover, the absence of references to masturbation or even acts that run counter to the ideal of marital fidelity, for the context is the sacrament of marriage, and it is in this context alone that he examines sexuality. Even when Thiers deals with homosexuality, it is in relation to the marriage tie. What he condemns is not so much homosexuality itself as the participants' deviant request for the sacrament of wedlock (pp. 257-58). Those who would hope to find a panorama of the rural and urban sexual practices of the classical age should not look for it in the *Traité des superstitions*.

The superstitious practices associated with marriage expressed foremost a desire to know what lay ahead, for individuals perceived their future as a threatening, or at least unsettling, unknown. Matrimony and baptism came to incorporate a wish to negate time, to merge present and future. Through recourse to the elements (water and fire), the animal world, or the chance happenings of daily life (pp. 236-38), individuals sought to determine the kind of person—young girl, adult woman, young man, widower—they would marry. The marriage sacrament thus engendered the sin of curiosity, for the stakes were high: one's aspirations, one's lineage, one's very future happiness (or misery). When carried away by passion, some sought to change the attitudes or even violate the bodies of those they loved. The sin was then one of brutality. It was commonplace to resort to philters of various sorts, made from bones, holy Spanish flies, infusions, and any and every other natural or artificial product that the rural world could offer (pp. 239-41). People would wear bands made of "leaves or roots, herbs, metal, reptiles, or the intestines or the limbs of birds and animals" (p. 240); or they would hide them in intimate places: in the beds and mattresses of those they desired. Others used figurines to cast spells or simulate the sex acts they sought.

Sometimes they open the chests of these figurines and set their hearts on fire or squeeze them so tightly that they liquefy. And they do so with the hope that the heart of the person they desire will burn, melt, and be softened so that he or she in turn will be compelled to love them.   (p. 240)

Others still made magic rings or mixed their urine with love potions, or even carried on their person some part of their beloved's clothing or body: ribbons, fingernails, hair or pieces of a shoe. To reach their ends, some went so far as to use church ritual and the accessories of religious services: fasting, holy oil and water, religious relics and pieces of priestly garments. Even the eucharistic host was exploited. Some stained it with blood, others pronounced vile words over it; others still had masses said on a "piece of the membrane that covers babies at their birth" (p. 243). So did superstition give way to sacrilege.

Just as the superstititons that take the Eucharist as sacrifice (or that are based on the moment at which one receives the Eucharist) structure time according to a particular logic, the superstitions associated with betrothal and marriage established a division of time wholly unrelated to church ritual or simple secular chronology. It was no longer so much a matter of learning what the future held as of determining it by selecting days guaranteed to bring prosperity and happiness. Engagements and weddings fell under the influence of a rigid chronological determinism. Certain dates were rejected, others came to be preferred. "All these acts of madness are simply vestiges of paganism," Thiers claimed (p. 248). All the more so if one were to add the custom popular in certain areas of getting married at nightfall.

With the aim of assuring a happy future, superstitions added their own ritual to religious ceremonies that were already highly ritualized. Couples who were to be wed were advised to come to church in an inebriated state and to have obscene songs sung for them as their engagement was being blessed. They were advised not to attend the publishing of the banns and to make various ritualized gestures aimed at warding off evil spirits. For the wedding ceremony, everyday clothes were recommended, Sunday clothes being reserved for a visit to the church a few days later so that "the marriage might be happier and the newlyweds might more fully love each other" (p. 249). During the ceremony, the couple would give each other presents, don various objects so as to avoid misfortune, and the groom— to avoid impotence—would urinate through the ring which was to be blessed and presented to his bride. Rings had their place in an entire series of superstitious practices: the man would slip it up just to the first knuckle of his fiancée's finger; one would increase the number of rings; or one would let the ring drop, but "on purpose" (p. 252). Thiers also speaks of buffets and blows, and at greater length of the charivari. He is inexhuastible when it comes to describing the noisy goings on that are a part of or accompany the wedding, such as the *pâté de la mariée*: awakening the newlyweds with singing and shouting on the day following the marriage ceremony (p. 255). All of these practices are difficult to categorize. The fact that a number of them are common to several of the sacraments renders attempts at categorization futile, lest we rewrite the whole of book ten of the *Traité des superstitions* with a different approach to classification. We would be better served by avoiding this tautological detour and analyzing the implicit assumptions of these superstitious practices and the significance of their symbolism and their distinctive characteristics.

What defined marital happiness in this archaic world? Even more than financial security and mutual understanding, it was fecundity, whose importance is apparent in the very symbolic forms that shaped superstitious practices. If a sow grunted in the pigsty as the suitor appeared "at midnight on the eve of Saint Andrew," this meant that he would marry a widow, whereas the grunting of the piglets foretold a marriage with an untested young girl (pp. 236-37). A curious way, indeed, to designate the proven capacity to reproduce! The whole of Thiers' study is a demonstration of the importance attached to the fruitful completion of the sex act. Desire and orgasmic pleasure are expressed as well within the context of superstitious ritual, but in their own way. First of all, by the very choice of words. The prudish language of love ("se faire aimer": to be loved by) is followed, most unexpectedly, by the brutish description of love-making: not only "aimer éperdument" and "aimer à la folie" (to love madly), but above all "jouir d'elle plus aisément" (to take pleasure of her more fully) (pp. 242 and 240). More often than not, the symbolism of superstitious practice is rooted in eroticism. It is easy enough to grasp the meaning of touching someone's foot or hand or having in one's possession a piece of clothing of the person desired, and no more difficult to decipher the significance of urine and secretions and the choice of one's bed as a place on which to cast magic spells. At times, the symbolism is little more than a simulation of the act: pissing through the bride's ring or slipping the ring up to the first knuckle. Is not one of the remedies proposed for unknotting the *aiguillette* "pissing through the keyhole of a church" (p. 268)? One could hardly be more explicit! Baptismal candles, blows administered to specific parts of the body, the shooting of firearms that was common practice during the charivari, the knotted cord of the *aiguillette*: all of these are just so many obvious sexual references.

Contrasts between the symbolic forms of sexual imagining are undoubtedly most apparent within the range of superstitious practices associated with the tying and untying of the *aiguillette*. Two types of remedy are offered to those whom the devil has struck with impotence. One is direct:

> Place the newly weds naked on cobblestones or the ground; have the bridegroom kiss the big toe of the bride's left foot and the bride kiss the big toe of the groom's left foot; have each of them make the sign of the cross with their heels.   (p. 266)

The other, while it assumes more symbolic distance, is no less transparent:

> Pierce a barrel of wine that is as yet untapped and direct the very first wine coming out through the ring that was given to the bride on her wedding day.   (pp. 267-68)

One notices, moreover, that whereas superstitions dealing with conjugal duty and designed to reduce its frequency are very few, sexual impotence holds an important place. The anxiety generated by the fear of not being able to reach orgasm and/or procreate finds an outlet in superstitious practice. Thiers, who categorically denies the influence of the devil's power in non-sexual areas, acknowledges that the devil is at work in the case of impotence:

> Those free-thinkers and libertines for whom everything is a matter of nature and who judge things through reason alone refuse to be convinced that newly weds can have the *aiguillette* knotted and be kept from performing their marital duty by the devil's trickery. (p. 261)

He expresses thereby one of the principal fascinations that haunted the rural world of the classical age, a fascination that was fostered by the high rate of infant mortality, the obsession with virility in the Christian West, and the anxious concern that demographic decline created among commoners and *philosophes* alike.[11] Thiers does not consider those devil-inspired practices that would knot the *aiguillette* to be superstitions: "This evil spell is not imagined, it is real," he says (p. 260). He maintains, however, that the means used for unknotting the *aiguillette* are mere superstition when not sanctioned by the Church. The difference in attitude toward the tying and untying of the *aiguillette* is not trivial. It reveals the very working of the sexual imagination. Positive and negative practices are numerically equal within the system of popular beliefs, but the different manner in which one deals with the causes of evil and the remedies proposed to counter them stands as proof that the contemporary sexual imagination was dominated by a fear of deprivation. And it is indeed the fear of castration that one finds running throughout men's dreams in the classical age.

In fact, closer analysis reveals that all of the sexual imagery in the *Traité des superstitions* draws upon similarly contradictory values. From beneath the recurrent libidinous pleasures there appear a host of fears and anxieties, expressed as a rule in symbolic terms. The chance encounter with a virgin or a dishevelled or pregnant woman was felt to be ominous, whereas meeting a courtesan or a toad was supposed to be a sign of future happiness. The interpretation given to symbolic events or chance meetings thus did not always reaffirm the value of sexual pleasure; the symbols themselves seemed at times to contradict it. One finds the same contradiction in the "innocent possessing" of one's beloved that individuals fantasized, thereby exalting sexual enjoyment, with the aid of philters and magic spells they created from skeletons and excrement. In a similar perspective, one might note that symbols of violence—weapons, blows, blood—permeate the imagery of lovers' bliss.

The above should give some idea of the complex nature of sexual imagination, even, as in this instance, when it is presented under the aegis of accepted social behavior and within the framework of the normative and pedagogic discourse of the militant Church.

Translated by
Odile Wagner & Arthur Greenspan

Jean-Marie Goulemot
Université de Tours

NOTES

1. This is one of the themes of 18th-century criticism of the novel. See especially the attacks by Abbé Jaquin (*Entretiens sur les romans* [Paris, 1755]) and Marmontel (*Essai sur les romans considérés du côté moral* [Paris, 1787]). The "Entretiens sur les romans," which opens Rousseau's *La Nouvelle Heloïse* (Paris, 1761) is especially important on this subject.

2. *De la Nymphomanie ou fureur utérine* (Amsterdam, 1771; rep. Paris: Sycomore, 1981).

3. Collection "Archives" (Paris: Gallimard-Julliard, 1975).

4. On this issue see J.-M. Goulemot's "Introduction" to Jamerey Duval's *Mémoires, enfance et éducation d'un paysan au XVIIIe siècle* (Paris: Sycomore, 1981).

5. Attributed to Gervaise de la Touche, *Le Portier* (Amsterdam, 1745) was a famous and much reprinted erotic novel.

6. Father Girard is the pseudonymous hero of the Marquis d'Argens' novel, *Thérèse philosophe* (Amsterdam, 1748). Dom Saturnin appears in *Le Portier*.

7. I have tried to explore the operations of the sexual imagination in Laclos' *Les Liaisons dangéreuses* in "Le Lecteur voyeur et la mise en scène de l'imaginaire viril . . . ," in *Laclos et le libertinage* (Paris: Presses universitaires de France, 1983).

8. The text cited will be the edition of extracts from the *Traité*, edited with "Introduction" and notes by J.-M. Goulemot (Paris: Sycomore, 1984).

9. The *aiguillette* was a cord or ribbon which a supernatural power could knot. When knotted, it was an image of impotence or infertility.

10. For biographical matter and further detail on other points in this paragraph, see Goulemot's "Introduction" to the *Traité*.

11. See in Montesquieu's *Lettres persanes* the letters concerning the demography of the Roman Empire, and see the discussion by Diderot in the *Supplément au voyage de Bougainville*.

Married but not Churched: Plebeian Sexual Relations and Marital Nonconformity in Eighteenth-Century Britain

The study of the history of sexuality is dominated currently by a powerful teleology first bestowed by the Victorians and subsequently reinforced by those who would see the past as a singular, unilinear progression from tradition to modernity. All that does not fit neatly into this concept of change is defined as either deviant or anachronistic, in any case of lesser interest because it does not lead to the prescribed future. In this sexual telos the eighteenth century has come to occupy a special place, for it is seen as a turning point, the moment when, to use Lawrence Stone's term, a new "affective individualism" finally pushed aside the ancient obligations to kin and community, permitting men and women for the first time to construct relationships on the basis of personal likes and dislikes. The eighteenth century is perceived as the moment when traditonal arranged marriage gave way to the modern love match, when sexuality was finally domesticated, and when the nuclear family based on companionate marriage became the central focus of social and emotional life.[1]

This conception of the past does not give sufficient recognition to regional and class variations, to the dialectical, as opposed to the evolutionary, features of change. What is more, it attributes too much to the eighteenth century itself. The notion that personal relations in earlier centuries were uniformly cold and calculating has been challenged by numerous recent studies. Relations between seventeenth-century parents and children have been shown to have been quite affectionate and understanding.[2] Nor was love absent from Early Modern courtship and marriage. Apart from among the very rich and powerful, arranged marriage in the strict sense seems to have been the exception. Parents took an interest in their children's choice of mates and were obstructive at times where vital religious or economic interests were at stake, but they possessed few of the dictatorial powers imagined by those historians who have portrayed the sixteenth and seventeenth centuries as uniformly repressive and the eighteenth century as uniquely liberating. Keith Wrightson has recently summarized the evidence on this point: "There is little evidence of cold-bloodedly 'arranged' matches outside the very highest ranks of society. The likelihood of parents initiating or proposing a match was not uniform even at the highest social levels, while even when they did so, children usually seem to have enjoyed a right of refusal."[3]

On the issue of the capacity for affection, new evidence also contradicts a simple evolutionary conception that assigns to the eighteenth century the dubious honor of having invented romantic love. The content of folk ballads, the symbolism of rural courtship, and the idioms of ordinary speech all provide abundant evidence of irrepressible affections in earlier centuries. Recent studies of popular mentality, which provide additional evidence of deep and often disturbing emotions, also should alert historians to the fallacy of assuming a progressive development of the capacity for affection. The Reverend Richard Napier's notes on the lovesick in his early seventeenth-century Buckinghamshire parish reveal a previously undetected depth of unrequited feeling.[4] Passion was not something waiting to be invented by the novelists of the next century. It was already a powerful, if sometimes frustrated, force in the life of every stratum of British society.

It would seem that the eighteenth century's claim to uniqueness must now be discounted. I do not, however, wish to disappoint those who regard it as having its own special characteristics, though I remain critical of historians who would force its changes into a single, unilinear perspective. There can be no doubt that the already strong thrust of "affective individualism" gained additional impetus, especially among the propertied and educated classes. At that level there was general acceptance of the norm of monogamous companionate marriage and an intensification of commitment to the nuclear family. Whether these things meant the same thing to men as they did for women is open to question, but even if Lawrence Stone's description is not entirely correct, it is nevertheless evident that Great Britain's propertied classes had reached a conscensus on what was to be regarded as public sexual morality, even if private lives sometimes violated the prescribed norms. Overt libertine behavior now met with censure; concubinage and bastardy equally were stigmatized. Between the passage of Lord Hardwicke's Marriage Act in 1753 and the harsh bastardy clauses of the New Poor Law in 1834, the established church and the state threw their full weight behind monogamous marriage and the nuclear family, denying legitimacy to all other arrangements.[5]

The triumph of new conceptions of family and sexual life among the upper classes seems clear. What is less certain is the success of the elite in imposing their values on other elements of British society. Lesser folk seem not to have been driven by the same sexual telos. Their notion of moral development diverged from that of the elite, and their sexual practices ran counter to the prescriptions of church and state. Groups just below the master artisan and independent smallholder class were developing modes of marriage and family life suited to the unprecedented social and economic conditions of early industrialization. At first unobtrusively and then with increasing distinctiveness, they constructed plebeian morality that directly challenged the prescriptions of affective individualism, contrasting the newly enshrined virtues of monogamous marriage and the nuclear family with a very different set of moral imperatives that emphasized the value of love and commitment both in an out of marriage and recognized the necessity of parenting and family arrangements beyond the nuclear family.

The realities of eighteenth-century plebeian culture present a no less powerful challenge to the sexual telos that dominates so much of current historical writing. In the pages that follow, I cannot do full justice to the rich and complex dialectical relationship between plebeian and elite values and practices. Instead, I wish merely to suggest the outlines of an historical anthropology of marriage that takes into account class and gender variation and thereby calls into question the evolutionary perspective that has so dominated our thinking about the history of heterosexuality.

Marriage discipline was of great concern to the elite throughout the eighteenth century. In 1753 they had successfully abolished clandestine marriage and deprived betrothal of its legal standing only to find that by the 1790s sexual license was once again threatening both parental and parish control. Concern intensified during the Napoleonic Wars to the point that the Reverend W. Sharp, parson of a sprawling Derbyshire parish, was convinced in 1813 that:

> the lord of misrule has erected his most despotic throne: that in that place are found all the practical blessings of perfect equality; that subordination is totally unknown, that scarcely anyone possesses influence to control even over those whom 'the laws of God, the laws of their country, and of reason' had placed under their jurisdiction; that everyone does just 'that which is right in his own eyes,' and nothing else; that, in short, liberty has degenerated into perfect licentiousness, and general independence into universal impudence.[6]

In the backwater Lancashire weaving village of Culcheth, where the rate of illegitimacy had mounted steadily from the 1780s until reaching well over 30 percent in the 1820s, the clergyman there railed against what he called the influences of "domestic republicanism."[7] In 1840 the editors of the *Christian Lady's Magazine* were convinced that the apocalypse had arrived with the advent of Owenite socialism:

> The main plan . . . is, first to wholly abolish marriage . . . second, to take every child from its mother at the time of its birth . . . and to commit the infants to persons appointed for that charge, who shall nourish them like a promiscuous litter of pigs. . . . Thirdly, to do away with that sacred and endearing thing—home. . . . There is to be no separate dwelling, no husband, no wife, no parent, no child, no brother, no sister, no neighbour, no friend, no pastor, NO GOD.[8]

The rhetoric was hyperbolic, but the reality pervasive. It was said that in the metropolis that "the prodigious number among the lower classes . . . cohabit without marriage."[9] Even in out-of-the-way places such as quiet Ash-next-Sandwich in Kent, at least 15 percent of couples living there in the period 1750–1834 were not to be found in marriage registers.[10] The known proportion "living tally" in certain Lancashire and Welsh areas was even higher.[11]

Demographers puzzled by declining marriage and baptism rates in the late eighteenth and early nineteenth centuries have usually attributed this to faulty registration, but the truth is that there was massive noncompliance everywhere with Lord Hardwicke's 1753 Marriage Act, which mandated that valid marriages be celebrated at established churches. Only Quakers and Jews were exempted, a condition that has led some historians to argue that resistance to the marriage law must have been a reflection of religious dissent.[12] But the major dissenting bodies never advocated civil disobedience, even as they pushed for reform. A more obvious source of resistance was secular libertarianism; but while it was common in the 1790s for the marriage law's upholders to blame the works of the "infamous Tom Paine, which have eradicated the principles of religion from the minds of the lower orders of the people," organized free thought was more a manifestation of than a cause of popular noncon-formity.[13] The true epicenter of this sexual earthquake was among a plebeian population whose notions of marriage and family were at odds with those expressed in the marriage law. The tremors registering on the Christian Richter scale ran along a fault that had opened between the increasingly narrow definition of marriage and family insisted on by the propertied elite and broader conceptions of heterosexuality as these were being lived at lower social levels. The religious and political expressions of resistance followed, rather than defined, this fissure, gradually gathering strength throughout the late eighteenth century and culminating in the socialist and feminist movements of the 1830s and 1840s.

Because the most articulate expressions of sexual radicalism lagged so much behind the actual behavior, many historians have concluded that sexual nonconformity was principally the product of the rapid urbaniza-tion and factory industrialization that took place in the nineteenth cen-tury. In reality, this was a rural and small-town sexual revolution. More specifically it was the product of social and economic changes associated with what we have come to call protoindustrialization, the prolonged, crucial transition to the urban-industrial world that had its roots deep in the British past but was accelerating rapidly in the late eighteenth cen-tury.[14]

Defiance of the marriage law had a long and honorable standing in Great Britain. The church had not claimed a role in the marriage process until the twelfth century and had never wholly displaced the popular practice of self-marriage and self-divorce. Betrothal in verbis de praesenti continued to be a valid marriage until the Marriage Act of 1753. Further-more, clandestine marriage flourished throughout the first half of the eighteenth century, and when Lord Hardwicke's act put an end to it, many of those who had previously carried on the marriage trade in places like the London Fleet scurried across the Scottish border, where the practice of hasty, private marriages lasted until 1857. Even after it ceased to constitute a legal marriage, the legitimating function of betrothal was widely honored. Sexually active couples exchanged rings and vows to publicize their relations, thus insuring both their own sexual honor and the social legitimacy of their children in situations where a regular marriage was for any reason postponed or prevented.[15]

In effect, there had long existed a dual system of irregular, or "little," and formal, or "big," marriages, in which betrothal and clandestine marriage served as alternatives for men and women with affection for and commitment to one another who could not establish the separate household that normally signaled a big church wedding. The Hardwicke Act removed legal recognition of these "little" marriages. It imposed the narrower definition of marriage and family that, as Lawrence Stone and Randolph Trumbach have demonstrated, had become the standard for the educated elite by the mid eighteenth century.[16] Henceforth only one form of heterosexual union would be sanctioned, a situation that George Haldane warned "will force the poor to make the best shift they can without marriage."[17] Sir William Blackstone called Hardwicke's legislation "an innovation on our antient laws and constitution," and argued that "restraints upon marriages especially among the lower class, are evidently detrimental to the public, by hindering the increase of the people; and to religion and morality, by encouraging licentiousness and debauchery among the single of both sexes."[18] Nevertheless, the law withstood all efforts at reform until 1836, when civil marriage and the dissenters' right to marry in their own chapels were finally established.

The critics were correct. There was massive resentment of the church's monopoly, and not just among dissenters. Hostility to marriage fees was a potent source of anticlericalism well into the nineteenth century. In many places people refused to pay. When he visited South Wales in the 1760s, Lewis Morris found that "the late Act of Parlment is looked upon only as a Cruel and wicked restraint upon the liberties of the Mine Country." He also discovered that many people there were no longer bringing their weddings to the church, but marrying in their own way:

> Some Couples (especially among the miners) either having no friends, or seeing this kind of public marriage too troublesome and Impracticable, procure a man to wed them privately which will not cost above two or 3 mugs of ale. Sometimes a half a dozen Couples will agree to a merry meeting, and are thus wedded and bedded together. This they call *Priodas vach* (i.e. the Little wedding) and is frequently made use of among miners and others to make sure of a woman. . . . The little wedding doth not bind them so Effectually, but that after a months trial they may part by Consent, when the Miner leaves his Mistress, and removes to a Minework in some distant Country, and the Girl is not worse look'd upon among the miners than if she had been an unspotted virgin, so Prevalent & Arbitrary is Custom.[19]

About the same time John Evans observed that "in the little weddings persons cohabit together; and, if after trial they have reason to be satisfied with each other, the friends are invited to witness the intentions of the parties; they are considered as man and wife. If the parties, prior to this, are dissatisfied the woman is dismissed; and such repudiation is not considered a hindrance to future marriage."[20] Similar practices were noted among the mining populations of Yorkshire, who were said to have "exchanged" spouses. An agreement to part and remarry would be made and witnessed in a public house; there would be a feast and the men would make token gifts to their new brides, "whom they now maintain together with the 'childers' of the former union."[21] In the Midlands, miners were also known to have engaged in "swappin' " or "sellin' " of wives, and "those engaging in the transactions never seem to doubt about their right to do so."[22] As Samuel Pyeatt Menefee has demonstrated, the incidence of "wife sale," the most visible of these popular divorce rites, rose and then fell in roughly the same period, 1750–1840.[23]

Sailors formed another group that developed its own rules of common-law marriage and divorce. In the early eighteenth century sailors would have resorted to the clandestine facilities of places like The Fleet; now they made their own marriages without benefit of any clergy. John Carmichael, already married to one woman, wrote out a special contract in taking Sarah Stubbins as his common-law wife. They were said to have made their vows according to what John called the "customs of Devon."[24] In the nineteenth century, Southampton women were still following the practice of working out special arrangements with mariners, drawing their half-pay and looking after them when they were in port. This was "looked upon as nearly as good as marriage among that class." When asked if she were a prostitute, Harriet Hicks replied, "No, only to one man." Magistrate: "You mean that you are not a prostitute, other than as living with one man without marriage?" Harriet: "Yes, that's what I mean."[25]

Common-law arrangements appealed especially to the itinerant worker, but similar rites were also common among the more settled plebeian communities that supplied Great Britain's vast trade empire. Our most complete description of common-law practice comes from the Ceiriog Valley of North Wales, where there had developed what locals called "besom weddings":

> A besom wedding was a wedding after this manner: A birch besom was placed aslant in the open doorway of a house, with the head of the besom on the doorstone, and the top of the handle on the doorpost. Then the young man jumped over it first into the house, and afterward the young woman in the same way. The jumping was not recognized a marriage if either of the two touched the besom in jumping or, by accident removed it from its place. I should think this form of marriage was very common in this part of the country at one time.[26]

Those who had gone through the besom ceremony were considered "married but not churched"; if they decided to separate, they would call together a group of witnesses and, by jumping backwards, divorce themselves: "By jumping backwards over the besom the marriage was broken. The wife had the right to jump back, too. But this step had to be taken by either within the first year. Both of them, afterward, were free to marry again. If there was a child the father was responsible for its upkeep."[27]

Lest this be thought of as a mere survival of ancient custom among

Welsh peasants, it should be noted that Ceirog people were no longer engaged in subsistence agriculture. Men quarried and women prepared wool for developed markets. "Little weddings" seem to have flourished in places where industry was introduced into the countryside and changed the pattern of household formation. They are also evident in situations where the workforce was particularly mobile, as in the case of miners, sailors, or construction workers. At Woodhead, Cheshire, where a thousand navvies were camped in 1845, it was reported that "the couple jumped over a broomstick in the presence of a roomful of men assembled to drink on the occasion, and were put to bed at once, in the same room."[28]

❉

These "little weddings" served many of the functions that the now illegal betrothal and clandestine marriage previously had done. They legitimated those couples and their offspring who could not or would not form their own separate households and nuclear families as mandated by law. As the law became stricter, the resort to common-law rites became more frequent. Among the protoindustrial population the need for flexibility was greater than it had ever been among the traditional peasant or artisan classes. Not only among itinerants—miners, sailors, construction workers—but also more settled communities was there a need for a marriage discipline that would legitimate sexual relations outside the nuclear family and household. Plebeian couples were extending the well-established artisan and peasant tradition of the love match, but without the same access to property and household were broadening the definition of affection to include relationships that were of necessity nonconjugal and even temporary.

Because of the opportunities offered by the protoindustrial household mode of production, the children of weavers, smiths, and potters were induced to stay at home longer. Girls no longer needed to go into service; boys also could earn their keep at home. Consequently, the shape of the family and household altered in an opposite direction from the propertied elite during the same period.[29] Households extended to make room for additional workers, becoming multigenerational because parents were now reluctant to part with the labor of their children and grandchildren. There was less incentive to set up a separate household: in the weaving village of Culcheth young women preferred to stay home with their own families, postponing, and sometimes rejecting, conjugality, even after bearing one or more children.[30] In the nail-making area of Cradley Heath something of a compromise was worked out by which marriage took place but the young people "continue to work, living in the home of their respective parents. . . . This tendency has been sufficiently strong to overcome the usual practice of making a home first."[31] In the Ceiriog as well, couples who could not or would not establish their own nuclear households used the besom ceremony to legitimate both their status and that of their children. The local parson accommodated them by distinguishing the offspring of besom marriages from the children of no known father. Motherhood took on a new meaning, becoming a collective rather than an individual responsibility. The children of a besom wedding took the maternal name and became indistinguishable from the legitimate children of the mother's family. They became "grandmother's children" who often regarded their natural mothers as sister or aunt.[32]

While this ran directly counter to the law and to the upper-class insistence on monogamy and conjugal love, the advantages for plebeians of both sexes was obvious. Sam Bamford was enormously relieved when he found out that the girl he had made pregnant demanded only maintenance and not marriage.[33] Women were able to use existing bastardy laws to enforce male obligations, a strategy preferred by those families that wanted to retain their daughters. In the agrarian south and east, where women's labor had been vastly depreciated by the advance of agricultural capitalism, forced marriage—the so-called "knobstick weddings"—were common. But in the protoindustrial north and west, where the earnings of both women and children were at a premium, flexible common-law arrangements were preferred.[34] Many women found it an advantage to remain single even when they lived with a man. Under the marriage law, a woman's children and earnings were the property of her husband; she was also subject to his authority and his violence. By remaining legally single a woman retained her property, her children, and her rights of settlement. It was probably these advantages that Mary Vinson, a self-employed London sweep, was thinking of when she placed this notice in a London newspaper in 1787: "Many in the same Business have reported I am married again, which is totally false and without Foundation, it being calculated to mislead my Customers."[35]

❊

We can now begin to understand the panic of those Christian ladies and why, as Lady Shelley put it, "every *man* felt the necessity for putting his house in order."[36] From the 1790s, propertied classes listened with growing anxiety to the voices of those such as Tom Paine, who, himself illegally divorced before leaving England, praised the Native Americans for having "no other ceremony than mutual affection."[37] Paine's fellow freethinkers believed that everyone should have the right to marry and to divorce. Thomas Spence, for one, explicitly recognized the personal as the political. For him, sexual and political revolutions were one and the same: "This subject is so feelingly understood in this country, that it is supposed the Chains of Hymen would be among the first that would be broken . . . in case of a Revolution, and the family business of life turned over to Cupid, who though he may be a little whimsical, is not so stern a jailor-like Deity."[38]

Early feminists also agreed that marriage law needed reforming but were not so sure they wanted everything turned over to Cupid. It was Mary Wollstonecraft who warned that "love from its very nature must be transitory."[39] Feminists remained suspicious of any project that ignored the social consequences of heterosexuality. Here they parted with those male radicals who sometimes argued a libertarianism that bordered on libertinism.

Throughout the eighteenth century, single, widowed, and unhappily married women had been attracted to movements that offered an alternative to conventional marriage and the family. Often the alternative was some form of religious asceticism, as exemplified by Ann Lee, the founder of the Shakers, who was reacting to her unhappy experience of marriage and motherhood. Later, many women of similar plebeian origins were attracted to the asceticism of the Southcottian movement, abandoning their marriages to become, like the holy Joanna herself, brides of Christ.[40] By the 1820s and 1830s, however, many of these same women were turning to a more secular vision of redemption. They were flocking to Owenite socialism, which offered an alternative to monogamous marriage and the nuclear family without discounting sexuality. Because socialism took into account the social consequences that earlier radical and religious movements had ignored, it was the first to attract a mass following among both working men and women.

To Robert Owen and his followers legal marriage was an "artificial union of the sexes, as devised by the priesthood, requiring single-family arrangements and generating single-family interests."[41] They were convinced that the nuclear family reproduced class, age, and gender divisions. Affective individualism was no better than possessive individualism: 'It is *my* house, *my* wife, *my* estate, *my* children, or *my* husband. . . . No arrangement could be better calculated to produce division and disunion in society."[42]

Beginning with his American New Harmony experiment in the 1820s, Owen began to devise ways to replace affective individualism. The plans for what he called the "enlargement of the home" included collective housekeeping and childrearing. Parenthood was to be socialized and marriage constructed so that as Robert Cooper wrote, "our females are not considered by the males . . . as their inferiors . . . mere creatures made for their sexual pleasure and indulgence; but . . . as their equals, confidential companions."[43] The Owenite marriage rite not only explicitly recognized the equality of women, but also involved the community in such a way that the collective took responsibility for any children that might result from the union. It was Owenite women who were most insistent on this provision, for, as one put it in "Syrtis," "love with men rarely exists as a sentiment, and with women, as seldom sinks to a passion."[44]

The principles of socialist marriage and family were consistent with plebeian practice, and the actual ceremonies were virtually a direct copy of existing popular rites. Owenite couples were required to make their intentions known to the community three months before they took final vows, which were attended with much secular festivity. Divorce could not take place until the marriage had endured at least twelve months. It, too, required public notice to the community and a waiting period before it was finalized. Care was taken that no party to the marriage, especially children, be harmed by its dissolution.[45]

❧

I am not arguing that Owenite marrige was a mere reflection of plebeian practice. There were many elements of popular practice, such as divorce by "wife sale," which the early socialists abhorred.[46] But there is no question that the socialist critique of affective individualism and the nuclear family was based on experience. All Owenite leaders may not have been of the plebeian world, but the vast majority of their followers were. Both early feminism and socialism drew strength and inspiration from those men and women whose lives had been transformed by the protoindustrial phase of British social and economic development.

By the 1840s that phase was ending and the social conditions it had produced were disappearing. Illegitimacy rates in places like Culcheth and the Ceiriog were dropping sharply, the besom wedding and "wife sale" were in eclipse, and London City Missionaries were reporting success in persuading common-law couples to marry.[47] In the next half century, the British working classes would return to church, chapel, and register office in massive numbers. By 1900 sexual nonconformity was a mere memory, and, for most, a distasteful one at that.[48]

The new conformity was in part the product of the liberalization of the marriage laws begun in 1837, but more important were changes in the mode of production, which created a sharp distinction between men's and women's work. Factory replaced cottage industry and with it the kind of family economy that had sustained the alternative forms of marriage and family. Factory industrialization meant the separation of work from home and the eventual segregation of sex roles into male breadwinner and female housekeeper. Children once again became a burden when the family ceased to be a unit of production. Parents encouraged daughters to wed and sons to establish their own households. Investigators found that by 1900 London women felt compelled "to be legally married to the man they live with," except when a previous marriage had broken down and the couple, being unable to afford legal divorce, were forced to live together outside the law.[49] The "domestic republicanism" that had found its expression in free thought and in socialism had dissipated similarly. From the 1840s both the socialists and the feminists retreated from their earlier advocacy of sexual nonconformity. In time they became staunch defenders of monogamous marriage and the nuclear family, reflecting the attitudes of their social base.[50]

Some historians would have us believe that sexual nonconformity is the product of industrialization and urbanization, but the evidence presented here suggests that the history of heterosexuality is a good deal more complex. It was neither uniform nor unilinear; instead it proceeded in a series of dialectical phases, each with its own unique shape and consequences. The new forms of sexuality associated with the plebeian classes of the late eighteenth and early nineteenth centuries deserve to be understood on their own terms and not as examples of deviance or as anachronisms destined to be pushed aside by the march of sexual progress. They were the product of the conjuncture of certain unique social and economic conditions associated with the early phases of industrialization. These conditions would change by the 1840s and 1850s, as would working-class attitudes toward marriage, family, and sexuality. Yet this episode in the complex history of sexual relations was not without its lasting consequences, not only for working men and women but also for class relations in Great Britain. Plebeian sexual nonconformity provoked the powerful reaction we have come to know as Victorianism. To the victors went the privilege of designating their own norms as liberating and progressive. Only now are we beginning to understand what occurred from another perspective, thus recapturing the complex, contradictory nature of eighteenth-century sexuality.

John R. Gillis
Rutgers University

NOTES

This paper was originally presented in an earlier form at the 1984 Boston meeting of the American Society for 18th-Century Studies. I wish to thank Randolph Trumbach for arranging the panel. I do not pretend to document all the arguments made here. For further evidence on popular heterosexuality, see my *For Better, For Worse: British Marriages, 1600—Present,* Oxford University Press, forthcoming.

1. Lawrence Stone, *The Family, Sex and Marriage in England, 1500–1800* (N.Y.: Harper & Row, 1977), chaps. 6–7; Edward Shorter, *Making of the Modern Family* (N.Y.: Basic, 1975), chaps. 3–4; Philippe Ariès, *Centuries of Childhood: A Social History of Family Life* (N.Y.: Vintage, 1965); part 3, Jean-Louis Flandrin, *Families in Former Times* (Cambridge: Cambridge Univ., 1979), chaps. 3–4; M. Mitterauer and R. Seider, *The European Family: Patriarchy to Partnership from the Middle Ages to the Present* (Oxford: Blackwell, 1982).

2. Linda A. Pollack, *Forgotten Children: Parent-Child Relations from 1599–1900* (Cambridge: Cambridge Univ., 1983).

3. *English Society, 1580–1680* (New Brunswick: Rutgers Univ., 1982), pp. 78–79. See also Alan Macfarlane, *The Family Life of Ralph Josselin* (N.Y.: Norton, 1970), p. 95, and Ralph A. Houlbrooke, *The English Family, 1450–1700* (London and N.Y.: 1984), chap. 4.

4. Michael MacDonald, *Mystical Bedlam: Madness, Anxiety, and Healing in Sixteenth-Century England* (Cambridge: Cambridge Univ., 1981), pp. 88–105.

5. John R. Gillis, "Conjugal Settlements: Resort to Clandestine and Common-Law Marriage in England and Wales, 1650–1850," *Disputes and Settlements: Law and Human Relations in the West,* ed. John Bossy (Cambridge: Cambridge Univ., 1983), pp. 262–73.

6. M. R. Austin, "The Church of England in the County of Derbyshire, 1772–1832," unpub. Ph.D. diss. (Univ. of London, 1969), p. 146.

7. G. N. Gandy, "Illegitimacy in a Handloom Weaving Community: Fertility Patterns in Culcheth, Lancashire, 1781–1860," unpub. Ph.D. diss. (Oxford Univ., 1978), p. 776.

8. Barbara Taylor, *Eve and the New Jerusalem: Socialism and Feminism in the Nineteenth Century* (N.Y.: Pantheon, 1983), p. 119.

9. Edward Thompson, *The Making of the English Working Class* (N.Y.: Vintage, 1966), p. 56; D. J. Steel, *National Index of Parish Registers* (London, 1968), 1:62–63.

10. Anthea Newman, "An Evaluation of Bastardy Recordings in an East Kent Parish," *Bastardy and its Comparative History,* ed. Peter Laslett, Karla Oosterveen, and Richard M. Smith (Cambridge: Harvard Univ., 1980), p. 151.

11. William Rhys Jones, "A Besom Wedding in the Ceiriog Valley," *Folk-Lore* 34 (1928): 153–54.

12. Gillis, "Conjugal Settlements," pp. 272ff.

13. Entry in a 1798 Derbyshire parish register, cited by M. R. Austin, "Religion and Society in Derbyshire during the Industrial Revolution," *The Derbyshire Archeological Journal* 93 (1973): 85–86.

14. On the question of protoindustrialization, see Hans Medick, "The Proto-Industrial

Family Economy: The Structural Function of Household and Family during the Transition from Peasant Society to Industrial Capitalism," *Social History* 3 (1976): 291–315. See also articles in *Proletarianization and Family History*, ed. David Levine, (N.Y.: Academic Press, 1984).

15. Gillis, "Conjugal Settlements," p. 271.

16. Stone, *Family, Sex and Marriage*, chap. 8; Trumbach, *The Rise of the Egalitarian Family: Aristocratic Kinship and Domestic Relations in Eighteenth-Century England* (N.Y.: Academic Press, 1978).

17. William Cobbett, *The Parliamentary History of England* (London, 1813), 15:41.

18. *Blackstone's Commentaries* (Philadelphia, 1803; rep. South Hackensack, N.J.: Rotham, 1969), 1:428.

19. Dafydd Ifans, "Lewis Morris ac Afrerion Priodi yng Ngheredigion," *Ceredigion* 8, no. 2 (1972): 251.

20. See also Leonard T. Davies and A. Edwards, *Welsh Life in the Eighteenth Century* (London, 1939), p. 231.

21. *Notes and Queries*, 10th ser., 9 (14 Mar. 1908), p. 201.

22. Ibid., (23 May 1908), p. 416.

23. *Wives for Sale* (N.Y.: St. Martins Press, 1981).

24. *Notes and Queries*, 11th ser., 1 (18 June 1910), p. 485: J. S. Burn, *The Fleet Registers* (London, 1833), p. 100.

25. Judith Walkowitz, *Prostitution and Victorian Society: Women, Class, and the State* (Cambridge: Cambridge Univ., 1980), pp. 203–05.

26. Jones, "Besom Wedding," pp. 153–54.

27. Ibid., p. 155.

28. Terry Coleman, *The Railway Navvies* (London: Hutchinson, 1965), p. 22. An extended discussion of common-law marriage and divorce is provided by John Gillis, *For Better, For Worse: British Marriages, 1600–Present* (Oxford: Oxford Univ., forthcoming), chap. 7.

29. David Levine, *Family Formation in an Age of Nascent Capitalism* (N.Y.: Academic Press, 1977), pp. 40–45.

30. Gandy, "Fertility Patterns," pp. 167–69.

31. E. Orme, "Conditions of Work in the Nail, Chain, and Bolt Making Industries of the Black Country," Royal Commission of Labour, *Parliamentary Papers* (1892), 16:573.

32. Gandy, "Fertility Patterns," pp. 186–200; Jones, "Besom Wedding," pp. 149–60.

33. *Passages in the Life of a Radical and Early Days* (London: Unwin, 1904), p. 192.

34. This is explored at length in Gillis, *For Better, For Worse*, chap. 7.

35. Ivy Pinchbeck, *Women Workers and the Industrial Revolution, 1750–1850* (London, 1930), p. 285.

36. Italics mine; Taylor, *New Jerusalem*, p. 12.

37. J. Wilson and W. Ricketson, *Thomas Paine* (Boston: Twayne, 1978), p. 28; also, Eric Foner, *Tom Paine and Revolutionary America* (N.Y.: Oxford Univ., 1976), pp. 3, 16.

38. Thompson, *English Working Class*, p. 163.

39. *A Vindication of the Rights of Women* (London, 1792; rep. Harmondsworth: Penguin, 1982), p. 113.

40. J. F. C. Harrison, *The Second Coming: Popular Millenarianism, 1780–1850* (New Brunswick: Rutgers Univ., 1979), pp. 25–29, 86–109.

41. Taylor, *New Jerusalem*, p. 39.

42. Ibid., pp. 39–40.

43. Taylor, *New Jerusalem*, p. 53.

44. Taylor, *New Jerusalem*, p. 214.

45. *Crisis*, 18 May 1833; c.f. Robert Owen, *Lectures on the Marriages of the Priesthood of the Old Immoral World*, 4th edn. (Leeds, 1840), pp. 88–89.

46. The Owenites explicitly rejected wife sale, but were understanding of the reasons why ordinary people took divorce into their own hands.

47. Jones, "Besom Wedding," p. 156; Gandy, "Fertility Patterns," pp. 412–14; Taylor, *New Jerusalem*, p. 205.

48. Gillis, "Conjugal Settlements," pp. 284–86; *For Better, For Worse*, chap. 8.

49. Evidence from Mr. A. Blott, Evidence to the Divorce Commission, *Parliamentary Papers* (1912–1913), 18:201.

50. Taylor, *New Jerusalem*, chap. 9.

Moral Values in "La Suite de l'Entretien"

In the *Encyclopédie* (1765), the anonymous author of the article, "Manstupration" ["Masturbation"] states: "Masturbation that is not habitual, not prompted by impulsive and passionate desires, and is, all things considered, motivated only by need is not in any way harmful and, therefore, in no way wrong (10:51, col. 2). This bold assertion appears again in Denis Diderot's *La Suite de l'Entretien* [*Continuation of the Discussion*] (1769) in a delightfully impudent manner: "Nature tolerates nothing useless, how then am I to blame for assisting her when called to do so by unmistakable promptings? Rather than resisting nature, should we not lend a helping hand when the need arises?"[1]

More attentive perhaps to the similarity of theme than to the differences in style, J. Assézat and Maurice Tourneux included the article in their edition of Diderot's *Oeuvres Complètes* (16:97), at the cost, however, of a small but vital alteration.[2] When annotating the same passage of *La Suite*, Jean Varloot wrote: "Diderot had placed in the *Encyclopédie* the article "Manstupration" in which the same ideas are expressed."[3] Varloot mistook the article's cogent manner of expression as Diderot's ("la phrase diderotienne"), whereas the article's substance is actually a faithful resumé of Samuel Tissot's treatise, *L'Onanisme, ou dissertation physique sur les maladies produites par la manstupration* [*Onanism, or scientific dissertation on illnesses caused by masturbation*] (Lausanne, 1760)[4]. Meanwhile, Jean Mayer pointed out the false assertion of Assézat-Tourneaux but mistakenly attributed the article in question to Hugues Maret, secretary of the Académie de Dijon. Worse yet, he contrasted the academician's "morality lesson . . . designed to shock and to reform the libertine," with Diderot's admirable audacity.[5] It was finally up to John Lough to identify the true author of the article, uncontestably Ménuret de Chambaud.[6]

Such meanderings reinforce Jacques Proust's remark that the assigning or not assigning to Diderot any *Encyclopédie* article always reveals an ideological bias.[7] Let us add: the very reading of the article reveals such bias.

To begin with, Ménuret demonstrates a certain free-thinking point of view. His definition of masturbation, in fact, is distinguished by a realistic attitude unequalled in any of the anti-onanistic literature of the eighteenth century. Even more remarkably, not satisfied merely with advocating therapeutic masturbation, he invokes the authority of Galen:

> the ancients, who were insufficiently stern and scrupulous as judges, thought that when kept in bounds masturbation did not violate the laws of continence. Galen, moreover, did not hesitate to affirm that the infamous cynic (Diogenes), who had the effrontery to resort to that shameful practice in the presence of the Athenians, was very chaste . . . because . . . he practiced it only to avoid the ill effects of retaining the semen.   (pp. 51-52)

Such persistence keeps us from dismissing our preliminary citation as merely accidental.

The reader will have observed, in passing, the device of submerging a provocative opinion beneath a torrent of damning epithets. Must one attribute to this same duplicity Ménuret's own judgment of Tissot's treatise as excellent and therefore a source for "a great deal" for his article (10:51, col. 2)? As a matter of fact, of the three pages devoted to masturbation (which is far from negligible) scarcely a half-page is actually derived from Ménuret; yet having accumulated observations borrowed from Tissot, he insists at length on "the frightful picture of all the ills caused by masturbation." Did prudence demand such extravagance? Did it push Ménuret to accommodate public opinion to the point of adding his own observations, such as: "I was pained to see several of my classmates, carried away by this criminal passion, visibly waste away, become thin, weak, languid, and later succumb to incurable consumption" (10:53, col. 2)? Such excessive precaution seems to represent either divided conviction or a machiavellian circumspection which borders on perversity. One must choose. The article "Mariage" ["Marriage"] will help us. Signed with Ménuret's symbol, this article uses a refined circumspection which nevertheless lends its eloquence to the healing powers of the dildo.[8] The first hypothesis still remains. Must we then accuse the author of being inconsistent? To do so would seriously underrate his scientific merit.[9] It would above all mean judging according to wholly anachronistic criteria: among Diderot, Ménuret, and (even) Tissot, agreement is broader than is usually suspected and is even more profound, since it rests on the basic principle that the physician and the theologian share competence in this area, with supremacy in questions of morality given to the former.[10]

Diderot unreservedly subscribes to this principle. His keen interest in medicine—his numerous relationships with doctors, notably Bordeu, and his well known interest in visiting the sick—and after 1765 the editing of the *Eléments de physiologie* raised him above the level of mere amateur, and laid the ground for his burst of creativity in the summer of 1769. This scientific curiosity and scientific study of sexuality in the *Eléments* illuminates *La Suite*, which may be read as a continuation of the *Eléments* in that it postulates—from the very beginning of the dialogue—the moral authority of the doctor: "Doctor . . . you will answer . . . a question . . . which I wouldn't dare ask anyone but you" (p. 372). The axiomatic force of this beginning and the presence of Bordeu, as guarantor of sound knowledge, relieve *La Suite* of any need for pedantic argumentation—which would have slowed its lively pace.

The dialogue between Mademoiselle de l'Espinasse, its initial instigator, and Bordeu demolishes the role of the priest with respect to women, symbolically at least. It would be too much, however, to demand equal audacity from all three authors considering the very real risks of treating so controversial a subject entailing, as it does, grave and multiple personal involvements. Nor should one expect the same tone or the same argument from three texts so different in nature and purpose. Tissot claims to discuss, *ex professo*, "the illnesses caused by masturbation." *L'Onanisme* is, as we would say today, a monograph on sexual pathology, with all the term implies in the way of narrow specialization and prophylactic intent; it has all the didactic dryness of an academic treatise. In the cross-referenced articles on marriage, masturbation, and wet dreams, Ménuret undertakes to popularize science. An active collaborator on the *Encyclopédie* and close to Bordeu, he presents his thesis in a militant way. With the unusual freedom that a quasi-confidential diffusion guarantees and the candor the dialogue form permits, Diderot, by contrast, writes with undisguised glee, as an artist virtuoso as well as a philosopher, adding to *Le Rêve de D'Alembert* "five or six pages capable of making his mistress' hair stand on end."[11] In comparison with such formal and rhetorical diversity, the underlying harmony becomes all the more significant.

All three writers espouse the same mechanistic image of the body, a reductionist concept whose serious inadequacies cannot be ignored. But the real, and much debated, nature of life itself is of little consequence here. The point in question boils down to this: is ejaculation necessary or not? If it is, then in what measure, by what methods?[12] Observing that all sexual activity obeys the cycle of secretion-elimination renders the details unimportant.[13] In one of the rare technical arguments granted him, Bordeu is allowed to say: "bleeding is a frequent form of treatment, so what matters the nature or color of the superabundant 'humour' " (p. 377). All three authors, moreover, agree in judging total chastity to be detrimental, even fatal, to good health.[14] Variations on this hoary theme abound in Diderot's works, now serious, now playful, according to the context. Indignation against chastity bursts out in *La Suite*: "there's nothing as childish, as absurd, as idiotic, as harmful, as contemptible; nothing is worse except absolute evil itself" (p. 375). And how does Mademoiselle de l'Espinasse react to Bordeu's diatribe against chastity— "Advantage?" "Pleasure?" "None at all!" ? She can only cede, "One could grant that." react? How, indeed, could she resist, "she who is not a prude," that which from Buffon to Rousseau was the unanimous voice of the Enlightenment?[15]

The notion of total chastity rejected, Ménuret writes that "the only natural way to get rid of excess semen is that ordained by nature herself, through intercourse with a woman" (10:51, col. 2). Would this not mean yielding to the Church, which sanctifies the union of the sexes through the sacrament of marriage, even lending it the sanction of science? Such a conclusion, which is not infrequent, results from the fact that our conscience, and perhaps the very teachings of the Church, are not always clear as to the true meaning of Christian marriage, to the point of its being confused with a mere desire to increase population. For the Christian, marriage is not an end unto itself. Marriage represents, rather a toleration, a benevolent outlet granted those who "burn." "Marital purity" (a term significant in itself) is not just a means to procreation, which is not essential. The procreative intent, quite to the contrary, is supposed to foster marital purity and carnal activity to spur spiritual elevation. Thus marital virtue is not radically opposed to absolute continence: it is a relative form of chastity whose practice, hedged about by a detailed set of rules, is designed to prepare the soul for its ultimate victory over the body. It would be impossible to reject one without rejecting the other. To return to Ménuret's "natural way," he goes on to say, "nature has consecrated it so as to reinforce it through the most delectable pleasures." This amounts to inverting the relationship of pleasure to procreation, of the body to the soul perhaps. Is it not a matter of elevating something vile to the level of something indispensably auxiliary, of actually "consecrating" it, of expecting from it a kind of happiness approaching bliss? Bordeu choked with rage at the very mention of chastity, that "lily of virtue" according to Saint Francis of Sales. When he mentions the carnal act (an abomination according to the Church), the doctor takes up the poet's lyre to sing of "the greatest happiness imaginable, the joy, of blending my senses with the senses, my ardor with the ardor, my soul with the soul of the one my heart would chase, reproducing myself in her and with her" (p. 337). Obviously, the inversion of values here is blasphemous. For whatever Bordeu may say, more than trading Hippocrates for Horace he is parodying the language of the Church, stigmatizing chastity in the style of a preacher denouncing sin.

It is with the same sense of horror that he leads us, step by step, from its "childishness" to the very abyss of its "absolute evil." He is doubtless a poet when he exalts carnal pleasure, but his poetry is stolen from the mystic. It has the lyrical effusiveness of someone who, in a fervent embrace, becomes ecstatic, or someone who, in self-transcending union expires in the arms of his beloved to be reborn in the eternity of the species. All malice aside, this leaning toward poetry had already inspired Diderot to write the article "Jouissance" ["Orgasmic Pleasure"]. It even appears not infrequently in medical treatises, where, as a choice morsel of bravura, it seems to carry on the tradition of literary eroticism. Neither Ménuret[16] nor even the prudent, "cold" Tissot fail to conform.[17] It is a denial of the conjugal morality of the Catholic Church.

What if copulation, deemed necessary, proves to be impracticable? Wet dreams and masturbation will substitute. We saw that Tissot considers the former "a benevolent spasm" (see note 14), and Ménuret, agrees.[18] The theologian tolerates it, within strict limits. It is not even mentioned in *La Suite*. A subsidiary matter? Bordeu takes the time to underscore the ill effects of reabsorbing semen into the body's other "humors."[19] Masturbation causes far more delicate problems. Bordeu compares it with bleeding; a nocturnal emission, being spontaneous, would thus be a form of hemorrhage. Actually, the real Bordeu, in the celebrated article "Crise" ["Crisis"], speaking of the interventionist school of contemporary medicine, observed:

Nature, they say, left to herself, causes hemorrhages . . . as a consequence, it is essential that we produce artificial bleeding to supplement natural bleeding; but we are not always alert to the fact that nature follows particular laws in its system of "drainage," that nature chooses precise times to act. How have we come to believe that we can change at will the place, the time, and the order of our artificial evacuations? (*Encyclopédie*, 4:481, col. 2).

Suggesting that nature not be challenged, Bordeu, in *La Suite*, seems faithful to his real-life model. Like him, he "condemns any excess," which does not necessarily prohibit all therapeutic devices. The issue is rather that of avoiding untimely interventions, of being the servant of nature, of "lending a helping hand." Ménuret, as Bordeu's disciple, recommends it.[20] It is a matter of understanding thoroughly the laws of nature and of not giving in to the theoretical chimeras, "to disorders of the imagination," as the dogmatic doctors are wont to do ("Crise"). Acting as his own practicioner, the masturbator, before "lending nature a helping hand," is invited, in *La Suite*, to listen only to the "most obvious indications." Alas, too often he behaves like his dogmatic colleagues: "it is rare," Ménuret observes, "for one not to fall into excess. Passion gets the upper hand: the more one indulges in it, the more one gets carried away, and as one gives in to it, one manages only to excite the desire" (10:52, col. 1). There is no contradiction, then, in recommending therapeutic masturbation (or the similar use of the dildo) while severely condemning its abuse. This justifies the disproportion among favorable and unfavorable arguments in "Manstupration" and explains the exclusive use of negative arguments for the former. Ménuret's considerable borrowings from Tissot have no other excuse. Both retention and ejaculation, if immoderate, are the two antithetical but complementary aspects of excess. The same general principle applies equally to wet dreams or to copulation. Ménuret, following Tissot, carefully distinguishes between the harms of retention and those self-indulgences which are "provoked less by need than by the perverted tendencies of the sexual organs or of the mind" ("Pollution nocturne," 10:923, col. 1). One finds a good example of the same language in "Mariage."

People have praised Diderot's boldness here but, as it seems to me, without really understanding him. First of all, because he shares the honor with the physiologists whose concepts he adopts. Next, because he himself sets limits to its actual application through the reactions of Mademoiselle de l'Espinasse (pp. 376-78). It is a question of a mortal sin, and one expects her indignation: "What on earth are you saying, Doctor!" In a long speech (the longest one in *La Suite*) which shows the onanist not at all eager to choose between venereal disease (or dishonor) and the disastrous results of continence, Bordeu finally succeeds in reassuring Mademoiselle de l'Espinasse. Yet he fails to win her full agreement: "that's certainly a doctrine you wouldn't want to preach to children." But when he appeals to her maternal instinct ("will you allow me a hypothetical case? You have a daughter. . . ."), she accepts the doctor's arguments: "To tell you the truth, I believe . . . but this situation never arises. . . ." This final reticence, so delicately noted, seems to mark a point beyond which it is impossible to go, such as one reaches in all moral systems. Thus, the theologians persisted in describing in detail all circumstances in which emissions were voluntary without ever succeeding in reaching general agreement, leaving the confused faithful no alternative except that of a deterring confession. The same moral dilemma applied to therapeutic masturbation: even though the doctors recognized the need for it, where is the definitive criterion for distinguishing clearly the roles of the organs and the imagination? We can make some allowance for those who oppose Diderot to Tissot in this matter. They are none the less in error. Bordeu minimizes the dangers of masturbation, *without denying them*; Tissot exaggerates them. Though he may seem never to advocate the practice directly, he does so in his own way, through case histories.[21]

Bordeu prepares later to defend homosexuality (p. 379). Mademoiselle de l'Espinasse covers her eyes. The moment of real audacity has come! Law itself is outraged, law which punishes sodomy with death. Bordeu appeals to "common sense," but in vain: "such problems are too lofty for me." But have the principles of physiology invoked up to now prepared Mademoiselle de l'Espinasse for such a conclusion? In fact, Bordeu betrays them.

Nocturnal emission and therapeutic masturbation, both sterile phenomena, are less in conflict with each other than with the reproductive instinct: rather, they confirm its imperious necessity. Deprived of its ultimate purpose, the motor is temporarily idling. Yet the pleasure provided by ejaculation remains the same, is just as legitimate as in copulation. Better still, "it often compensates for reality, with interest added" ("Pollution nocturne," 10:923, col. 1).

Not a single doctor comes forward, however—and one can understand such providence—to praise the pleasure of therapeutic masturbation, whereas unhealthy emissions and merely playful masturbation—products of the imagination—are said to provoke and foster malfunctions of the machine, diverting it from its natural purposes. There is no real pleasure in such emissions; they are "sacrifices" to a "false Venus" ("Pollution nocturne, 10:924, col. 1). Worse yet "the semen burns and erodes all the tissues through which it flows." (10:923, col. 1). No image is frightful enough to depict the sufferings of a masturbator once in the grip of his fantasies. As for homosexuality, even more clearly in conflict with the procreative instinct, it borders on insanity.

"It [masturbation—a word Diderot *never* uses] is a need, and even should you not be impelled by the need, it is still an agreeable thing" (p. 376): now we come, in a long dissertation in favor of therapeutic masturbation, to a new option, surreptitiously introduced, the notion of pleasure for its own sake. Scarcely do we glimpse it before it disappears under a mass of physiological arguments which contradict it and which alone succeed in convincing Mademoiselle de l'Espinasse. But, one may object, has not an "aesthetic order" been exposed from the very start? And does not Mademoiselle de l'Espinasse scrupulously renounce the very "cursed syllogisms" she had up to that point accepted? Perhaps, and at the forefront of this "aesthetic order" comes "the pleasant and useful act," namely copulation—or, as we might say, the pleasure in procreation. In second place comes the "useful," that is, therapeutic masturbation, which, according to Bordeu (p. 376), is "not as sterile" as chastity. The merely "pleasant" comes third. Does this refer to homosexuality only? No, but to "two acts, equally tied to lust which can provide *only* pleasure, without utility" (p. 379). Is masturbation then useful or pleasurable? Does it belong to the second or the third category?

It is noteworthy that this particular ambiguity arises in the case of masturbation, a limiting case. In fact, Bordeu does not rigorously differentiate between the two sides of this key question. And what if Diderot, taking advantage of this inherent equivocation, were actually declaring his independence in respect to a physiological ethic he found too timid? And what if he were giving so much attention to masturbation precisely because it belongs to those frontiers where rigid systems with all their certainties come unravelled, frontiers where the human spirit ventures toward a new world (our own, perhaps)? Might not masturbation be, on the scale of moral values, what the zoophyte is on the scale of living things?

Mademoiselle de l'Espinasse must still be convinced. So, Bordeu is not afraid to imperil all morality and first of all the very principles he has successively made use of: "Whatever is, can be neither contrary to nature nor outside of nature. I would not even except chastity and voluntary continence, which would be major crimes against nature, if indeed it were possible to sin against nature" (p. 380). A final audacity, and not the least of them. Is homosexuality thereby justified? Turning from these inflammatory statements, let us listen to him: "Where do these abominable tastes come from?—Wherever you look, from lack of organization in the young, and from mental depravity in the old" (p. 385). After the intellectual intemperances of the philosopher, we are given the stark realism of the physician. Does this amount to a recantation?

Are we to conclude from what follows that he is preaching bestiality? We have arrived in the realm of pure fantasy, and Mademoiselle de l'Espinasse gracefully participates: "Already I seem to see five or six huge, insolent satyrs pursuing the carriages of our duchesses, and that delights me" (p. 383). Even her scruples now ring false: "I've had enough, enough, be quiet now! (p. 384).

Which of these three incompatible systems inspires Diderot's allegiance? Is it the physiological ethic, hedonism, or amoral ambiguity? A perplexing question, and even insoluble if what has just been said about homosexuality and bestiality gives no hint what practical difficulties they present and therefore what merit they might possess. Furthermore, is not Bordeu manipulating and being amused by these contradictions? We may be revealing our own mind-set in asking which particular ethic is the one that would be all permissive, whereas we should ask what sort of morality, for Diderot, is utterly worthless? Against what do his incompatible systems conspire, and who is imposing their coexistence?

Moral theology and the laws derived from it are clearly the real subject of *La Suite*. Bordeu informs us: "I am just as unhappy with civil laws as I am with religious ones" (p. 372).

Before investigating Diderot's restructuring of values, we should glance at the spirit of *La Suite*, which is the same as that of Grandval's conversations, whose echoes embellish the *Lettres à Sophie Volland*. It is a play of contrasts between the most noble meditations and the most commonplace, even nonsensical, of trivialities, between the reasonableness of the real and the "follies" of reason—a parlor game in which a "despicable ass" interferes with learned discussions of the Mohammedan religion (30 October 1759), where the paradox of the philosopher ("feeling and life are eternal," for example) earns him an offering of "lovely pears that were actually living," or "grapes that were thinking" (15 October). This paradox appears again in *Le Rêve*, in almost identical terms (p. 313). This game inspires the first speeches of *La Suite*: "This Malaga is excellent. . . . And your question?—What do you think of the mixing of species?—Heavens, that too is a fine question . . . ," a proposition well worth pondering, "once the servants are out of the room."

"What will surprise you," Diderot nonetheless wrote to Sophie, "is that there is not a word about religion . . ." (2:224). How is one to interpret that? The fantasy regarding the satyrs ends with Mademoiselle de l'Espinasse's bantering sarcasm: "And the problem of their baptism?—That would cause quite an uproar at the Sorbonne" (p. 384). As for the parody of the language of the Church, is it discreet? Merely provocation. Diderot does not use ecclesiastical terminology, except "absolute chastity." "Solitary activity," for instance, is not a theological term. "Not a single dishonest word," he adds justifiably in the same letter to Sophie. The linear order of sexual practices mentioned in *La Suite* rigorously corresponds to the traditional and unchanging order of moral judgments in theological treatises. Diderot omitted incest, fornication, rape, etc., etc.; he retains only the key concepts in their basic meaning. He reduces the *theological order* to its essential schema as follows:[22]

> +chastity, copulation/therapeutic masturbation,
> hedonistic masturbation, homosexuality, bestiality-.

A metaphysical order in which, because of the eminent superiority of spirit over matter, the struggle for salvation between extreme virtue and total depravity is engaged. The schema is thus read (from beginning to end) as a progressive wasting away of being, a basic tension onto which has been grafted the secondary contrast (indicated here by the virgule) between acts conforming to nature and acts contrary to nature.[23]

A critical reading of Diderot—which in effect amounts to a rewriting—begins by devaluing the virtue of chastity, which results after shifting the secondary contrast in an inversion of values. When sexual practices are thus revised and arranged hierarchically according to the "aesthetic order," the theological order would become:

> -chastity/++ copulation, therapeutic masturbation,
> hedonistic masturbation, homosexuality, bestiality+.

This *apparent axiological order*, generally held to be the real moral stance of Diderot (the audacity!), assumes in fact a single syntactical rule (a homogenity of principles) and a uniformly negative reaction on the part of Mademoiselle de l'Espinasse. It implies a universal apology for sexual practices. All this is lacking in *La Suite*. In order to demolish the tenets of moral theology, Bordeu required no less than three logical systems: 1) physiology, 2) hedonism, 3) amorality. The first of these doubtless permits shifting the contrast between acts contrary to nature and acts conforming to nature; yet far from abolishing it, it introduces a second schema embodying the principle of "double excess":

> ⁻chastity/copulation, ⁺therapeutic masturbation/hedonistic masturbation, homosexuality, bestiality⁻.

The second system aims at pushing back even farther the boundary of the natural; but since it is incompatible with the preceding one, it fails to justify homosexuality. If it seems to be successful in the case of "playful" masturbation, it does so only at the price of extending the confusion:

> ⁻chastity/⁺copulation, therapeutic and hedonistic masturbation/homosexuality, bestiality⁻.

The critique ends with the third system; the theological order is effectively domolished but, along with it, everything written on the subject. In tandem, the three systems enable one to discredit the whole corpus of moral theology with respect to sexuality, their power to criticize outweighting their actual intrinsic value. Beneath the appearance of a logical continuity which presses us either "to deny everything or to accept everything" (p. 381)—a trap into which Mademoiselle de l'Espinasse seems to fall (and along with her more than one reader)—the real linear order of *La Suite* is made up of three heterogenous segments placed end to end whose *textual order* can be shown in steps as follows:

chastity/copulation, therapeutic masturbation	(System 1) physiology
hedonistic masturbation, homosexuality	(2) hedonism
homosexuality, bestiality	(3) amorality

The two ruptures thus clearly revealed are more or less skillfully sutured so as not to be immediately perceptible. We could inventory the methods Diderot used to "mend" his text to give it the appearance of having an axiological order. First of all, he juggles the syntactical rules: sometimes masturbation is "written" according to the first system, sometimes according to the second. More precisely, in effecting their fusion the "aesthetic order" conceals their incompatibility. Having amusingly introduced it like one of those paradoxes, one of the "follies" in the manner of Grandval, he succeeds in preserving the logical continuity of his argument. Such is its essential function. The same maneuver is used in respect to homosexuality; but in this case the systems follow one another without blending (2, then 3), without even a ligature, since a definite break separates them. In effect, unable to convince and having given up trying to deal with Mademoiselle de l'Espinasse as if she were "a man" ("you are taking back your coif and your petticoats"), the doctor-philosopher is metamorphosed into a frivolous gossip-columnist, abandoning for a moment his serious subject for the scandals of the court (p. 380). A second device reinforces the preceding one: Diderot does not rigorously apply the syntactical rules. Erasing from system 1, for instance, whatever won't fit with system 2, he keeps only that which argues for sexual appeasement. Immoderate secretion is not mentioned in connection with coitus, and only barely and abstractly in the case of masturbation. On the other hand, he insists at length on the dangers of continence, backing his argument with physiological details, and even resorting to a fictional example. Furthermore, if he totally leaves out wet dreams, it is because it could have weakened his apology for masturbation. Finally, he never deals with the potentially dangerous role of imagination. Looking back at the *Eléments de Physiologie* (where, for example, the problem of imagination takes up the whole of Chapter 4 in Part III), we can see that these omissions are not due to chance. But that is hardly necessary. In *Le Rêve*, Bordeu himself discusses all these matters together. The disorders prompted by imagination are there analyzed by means of a striking image: the tyranny of the "center" on our organs.[24] Reciprocally, the autonomy of the organs (Bordeu speaks of "vapors") leads to "a kind of anarchy": the two faces of excess are plainly displayed. Also present is the respect due the rhythms of nature, an idea dear to *la médecine expectante* (the wait-and-see school of medicine).[25] Wet dreams are not neglected but rather linked with the imagination.[26] From *Le Rêve* to *La Suite*, Bordeu seems to have come down with amnesia, an amnesia as selective as it is sudden (p. 370). He takes leave of Mademoiselle de l'Espinasse and D'Alembert at 11:30 . . . to return "around two."

Let us now examine the negative reactions of Mademoiselle de l'Espinasse. When are they expressed? At each of the two sutures. And the less successful the suture the more intense is her response. To the first and best concealed, the resistance is moderate and short lived. The second elicits the only pejorative terms she uses in the dialogue; "monstrous," "a slough of depravity," "abominable." Then comes a break, the third argument, and the final abandonment of the "question of morality": "let's leave that vexing problem aside" (p. 381). The art of dissimulation here reaches its consummation. The logical breaks, highlighted and amplified by Mademoiselle de l'Espinasse, are thus blamed on her scruples. The real weakness of Diderot—his inability to propose a single, coherent, and positive alternative to theological morality—passes for the dialectical acumen of Bordeu. Diderot's inconsistencies are growing frenzied. Mademoiselle de l'Espinasse's eventual rescue, Bordeu's definitive failure to convince her, will be passed off as a victory of logical rigor over a woman's modesty aroused by a moment of recklessness (p. 373): "no, no, please do go on." We can see what an essential role is played by Mademoiselle de l'Espinasse: her mounting resistance calls for intensified energy, all the while masking the contradictions. She is the one who launches the dialogue, she again who allows the assault to reach its goal. "Not a prude?" Neither is she an innocent goose: "a friend of ours who wanted to find husbands for us . . . gave a sylph to the youngest, an angel of annunciation to the eldest, and a disciple of Diogenes to me; he knew the three of us very well" (pp. 373-74). She is neither a Présidente de Tourvel, besieged by a Bordeu-Valmont, nor a Justine, attacked by a Bordeu-Sade, but more like Socrates! The same apparent weakness: now false naiveté, now feigned indignation: the same Socratic method which puts the bold questioner on the defensive, forcing him progressively to refine (in this case, to firm up) his reasoning. Far from being passive, Mademoiselle de l'Espinasse constantly maintains the initiative. *La Suite* is a *Little Hippias* in the taste of the century. But the lightness of the dialogue (along with the "bourgeois" décor, the choice of vocabulary, the spirit of Grandval) is not merely and extrinsic ornament, an affectation like Fontenelle's roses; it is a formidable philosophical instrument! The artist comes to the rescue of the philosopher: from a hodgepodge of ideas he fashions a corrosive whole.

One must "leap over the mire." Mademoiselle de l'Espinasse's scruples are designed to lead us finally to the physical sciences, experiments with growth, gradations within kingdoms. From one species to another we are now back to the scientific universe of the *Entretien*; and *La Suite* is going to become, formally, what it claimed to be, justifying its title, at last. "That's where we left off," Bordeu asserts. "Cause," "effect": there, in passing, the detour through the question of morality is justified. But since that's what you want . . ." (p. 381), we won't mention "it" again. The "it" has never been named. Superlative silence! Bestiality is only more intensely present, only more insolently justified. "It's like asking me to begin with the end": a treacherous regret, just when you're getting ready to finish your critical journey! The renouncement is but a pretence since physical science, under the guise of objective observations, eventually (in the discussion of bestiality) carries the moral issue into its proper sphere, that of metaphysics. Thanks to Mademoiselle de l'Espinasse, once again.

But why bestiality, a practice from another era which seems no longer to be a real problem to anyone? What matters here is less its actuality than the reality of an essential concept. Negative pole of the theological order, antithesis of total chastity, bestiality provides that tension which is at the very heart of moral theology. It is equally necessary to Diderot's thesis, as we shall see.

We should recall, first of all, that however rational, theological language does not altogether exclude the emotions. Nothing is really alien to the drama of salvation, not even language. The theologian (even more, the preacher) gladly uses the most frightful, even loathsome, images to lend emotional power to his definitions of sin. Bestiality, *gravissimum inter omnes*, even more than masturbation and homosexuality, inspires fear and disgust. As the ultimate transgression of the sacred order of nature, it calls down the purifying fire on sinner and victim alike. To the metaphysical distress of defilement is added the disgust aroused by imagining the act itself.

Diderot severs these two aspects. He strips bestiality of every repulsive detail. The act itself is none the less suggested, on three occasions . . . and by Mademoiselle de l'Espinasse. As the outcome of her fantasy of the satyrs, first of all; next, by a surprising invitation: "Quick, quick, doctor! Get to work and conjure us up a few satyrs!" That's enough to surprise even the "cynical" Bordeu: "and you'd have no objection to it?" Finally, "stop now, for I see one coming for me; your satyrs are dissolute to the point of frenzy. . . . No honest woman will be safe; they'll go on multiplying forever; eventually, we'll have to slaughter them, or become their slaves." Precious Mademoiselle de l'Espinasse. In this sordid travesty of Utopia, bestiality is dressed up in the prestigious words and tales of the poetic imagination by whose fruits, here borrowed from classical mythology, the whole thing even takes on the dignity of the fable. And to top it all, it pretends to be a highly moral production: "we shall no longer degrade our brothers by subjecting them to tasks unworthy of them and of us. . . . We shall no longer reduce the people in our colonies to beasts of burden" (p. 383). Thus purged, the concept of bestiality is presented to the intellect alone, a mere excursion outside the boundaries, a metaphysical matter.

Repugnance is not, for all that, missing from La Suite. Diderot finds other uses for it: among animals (p. 382). The breeding of hybrids is described in realistic detail (in the name of scientific objectivity?): "copulation," "a rabbit acting as rooster to some twenty hens." The resulting offspring are inevitably repulsive: "chickens covered with hair." Physically deformed, these creatures are further insulted, accused of transgressing both moral norms and the law: "vile rabbit," "vile chickens."[27] Deprived of reason and amoral by nature, they are nevertheless enrolled in the conflict, guilty of beastiality! This perverse use of disgust and censure aims to whitewash human bestiality. The very idea of animal bestiality shows up the absurdity of moral theology and the childishness of its attempts to impose its arbitrary norms on nature, and gives concrete form to Bordeu's final argument: "Whatever is, can be neither contrary to nature nor outside of nature." "Nothing in nature is perfect," Bordeu was saying in Le Rêve (p. 311): so bestiality, however gross, redefined in this way, undermines the structure of moral theology in the same way that physiological monsters spoil those of scientific theory. No form is completely stable, no concept is so eternally fixed in nature that one has only to discover it there. Knowledge is a continuing process, not a definitive revelation. La Suite applies this lesson in relativity to ethics. The task is indeed philosophical since it deals with the rational and metaphysical foundation of Catholic doctrine, but the depreciation of absolute chastity alone was not enough to accomplish its aim. Pointing out its dangers to the body, after all, does not prove that it is noxious for the spirit. On the contrary, it only restates what Christianity, in its highest form, has always required. If one is wholly to abolish this requirement one must, therefore, totally deny the rationality behind the concept of bestiality. Its negative pole once amputated, the whole structure of moral theology collapses.

Bestiality and chastity, the opposite poles of vice and virtue, fuse, at this point, into nothing less. Were not the first words Bordeu used to describe the latter "childishness," "ridiculous," "absurd"? In nature's view, theological extremes amount to the same thing. They get the same treatment in La

Suite. Each negative is paired with a positive—⁻chastity/⁺copulation or ⁻animal bestiality/⁺human bestiality—and is entitled to the same stylistic inversion. If the language of sin is used in respect to chastity and animal bestiality, the lyricism of virtue is reserved for coitus and for the fantasy involving the satyrs. In the case of the negative poles, we're back in a universe destined to evil: "there is nothing more," "because circumstances deprive me," "they have seen," "they were shown." In the case of the positive poles we are in a future on its way to the reign of liberty, benevolence, and pleasure: "my heart itself will choose," "I shall forbid myself," "We shall gain from it," "we will no longer debase." For her to appreciate to the full this systematic demolition, this "sweetheart" certainly needed a good head for theology.

In form a philosophical dialogue, *La Suite* is first and foremost a theoretical treatise, especially in that sexual acts in all their concrete reality are here treated as moral concepts or values. *La Suite* is, moreover, a polemical work; it aims less to propose a positive morality than to prove the absurdity of theological ethics in this domain. With just what other kinds of morality might it be concerned? There are three! Bordeu alerts us: "whatever opinion you may have of my ideas, you will not, I hope, draw any unfavorable conclusions as to my own moral integrity (p. 373). The same thought is expressed in the case of homosexuality (p. 379). "A piece of casuistry," it is generally remarked. The philosophical literature of the eighteenth century, by accustoming us to ruse, risks making its readers overwary. Let us take Bordeu's statement as it stands. The confusion of the thought with the man is built into the very structure of both intra- and anti-theological polemics. By rejecting such and such a point of doctrine, the heretic errs; since he is an inexact thinker, his moral behavior must also be faulty. The atheist rejects the doctrine as a whole, utterly rejecting the principle of the soul's transcendence of the body; he thus rejects the moral order of theology with all its various values in one fell swoop (as Diderot does here). He will be accused of the worst depravities. If the heretic is immoral, the atheist then is amoral. The error of the former is that of "spiritual fornication"; "spiritual bestiality" is the madness of the latter. Bordeu inverts the process: chastity = bestiality. A philosophical prank. He is not asking us to couple with animals! In *La Suite*, moreover, the place and prominence given to such and such a practice is always a function of its theoretical importance, its demonstrative or polemical value, not of its sociological reality, even less of the author's personal tastes. It is not surprising then to find some six pages are devoted to masturbation and bestiality, whereas the other practices are given only a few lines each. Furthermore, masturbation and homosexuality are dealt with in the present tense and in the "neutral" style of deductive reasoning.

As for the postive morality of Diderot, it is neatly summarized in a statement like this one in the *Eléments*: "nature decrees the use of semen; wisdom controls it" (p. 178). Such concession is a measure of the distance between the philosopher engaged in polemics and the physiologists trying to be true to scientific method. Having noted that "a surplus of spermatic fluid produces cancer and consumption," Diderot at first concluded, "the remedy is simple"; but in revising his text, he was to discard the dangerous solution. We have already discovered the same morality in *Le Rêve*, and it has left some traces in *La Suite*—for example, the final retraction regarding homosexuality. Let us add that the weight actually given the latter is indeed slight. Homosexuality, justified in the name of pleasure, is not for all that considered to be an autonomous activity, but rather to be an extension of masturbation, a kind of mutual masturbation. It could hardly be otherwise for one who persists in opposing procreative to sterile acts. It lacks weight in the logical structure also: it is only the consequence of a consequence, a product of "common sense." Unable to cope with the concept of sin, the argument is much too frail to support the eventual apology: it is paradoxical. As for bestiality as a practice: utter nothingness. Though he recommends neither the one nor the other, Diderot nonetheless modifies their axiological value. Homosexuality and bestiality do not upset a supposed sacred order: they do not sully nature. But even if the monster is not destined to inspire horror, even if it is an integral part of nature, it remains nonetheless a monster. The behavior of the homosexual as well as that of the zoophile stem from a "poverty of organization" or a "depravity of the mind"; erratic as they are, they belong in the domain of mental therapy—not to the executioner. Victims of the imagination, of the tyranny of the "center" over the organs, the homosexual and the zoophile are sick, in the same way as the frenetic masturbator, or the witches of former times, or the fanatic or ecstatic.

Here we are back to our point of departure: the positive morality of Diderot in *La Suite* is the same as that of Ménuret and Tissot, or nearly so. Nearly so, insofar as the sharing of basic principles does not exclude nuances of feeling. Everything about Diderot indicates a keen sensuality, often truculently expressed both in his correspondence and in his literary works. It is hard to imagine him joining, for example the anti-onanist crusade which was raging in the second half of the century. Yet, in the *Mémoires*, written for the benefit of Catherine the Great, Diderot, in the role of "counselor," makes his modest contribution. In the public schools, "above all have diligent supervisors in the lavatories because that is where the students are corrupted"[28] in elementary schools. "I have heard there were young children already familiar with the vice. . . . What is the source of it? From the servants, no doubt: one must keep an eye on such people" (p. 223). On the other hand, Diderot, at his most spontaneous, seems rather fond of such crude expressions as "to jerk off" or "to shoot," both of which appear in the first version of the *Eléments* (variants of the Leningrad manuscript, p. 135). The sensibilities of the man and writer must not prejudice our estimate of the thinker: pleasure remains linked to procreation, and therapeutic masturbation remains the extreme limit of the permissible. If there is an element of casuistry in *La Suite*, it is precisely in regard to himself: "I would not take my hat off to any man in the street suspected of practicing what I teach; it would be enough to hear him called a wretch" (p. 378). Limited as it is, the audacity of Diderot's positive morality is not without practical applications: he rebels against the celibacy of the priests; he pleads for the depenalization of homosexualtiy and bestiality.

It is remarkable how this morality stops at the point where Mademoiselle de l'Espinasse's objections begin. Her dialogue with Bordeu merges with one between Sophie Volland and Diderot. One might imagine a dialogue of Diderot with himself. In *Le Rêve*, Mademoiselle de l'Espinasse observes that "there is no difference at all between a doctor who is awake and a philosopher who dreams" (p. 293). We must retreat, but we'll hold the protagonists of *La Suite* where they are. If in her role as a woman Mademoiselle de l'Espinasse borrows much from Sophie Volland, on the plane of ideas, she assumes the role of Diderot the physiologist, the doctor who is awake. As an alter ego for Diderot, Bordeu acts in turn now the doctor awake, now the philosopher who dreams.

If the positive morality thus defined relieves our doubts as to Bordeu's morals, it does not erase the *textual order*. Confronted with the coherence of the theological moral system, Diderot's critical boldness does not succeed in hiding his inability to propose a positive and integrated alternative. The vacillation persists between a morality based on physiological criteria and one based on pleasure. Absurd as the theologian's system of morality may be, it succeeded at least in assigning a precise value to each sexual practice. Physiology excludes as erratic any practice that is "sterile," while pleasure *per se* is outside the purview of physical science and assumes a radical break between eroticism and biology. But one thing remains certain: one must not be fooled by words. The emptiness of all metaphysical moralities demands the banishment of the very word "virtue": "it must be changed to 'benevolence' and its opposite to 'malevolence', " states Bordeu in *Le Rêve* (p. 364). A materialistic morality, we are assured. Is that not answering for Diderot himself? As in other texts, Diderot hesitates to surrender human liberty to the simplistic outlines of a stammering science. Therein lies—if we dare to use the word—his virtue.

Is Bordeu cynical? We should more gladly say: touching. The Bordeu of *La Suite* is in reality Diderot dreaming of a science that would appropriate to itself that whole area left vacant by the bankruptcy of theology.[29] It is the hope of a science in a state of gestation. A form of impatience.

Translated by
James Coke & Michael Murray

Théodore Tarczylo
Paris

NOTES

1. In the *Oeuvres philosophiques,* ed. Paul Vernière (Paris: Garnier, 1964), p. 377. Except where otherwise indicated, refs. are to this edn.
2. *Oeuvres complètes*, 20 vols. (Paris: Garnier, 1876), 16:97. After having defined the

nature of semen, the *Encyclopédie* art. added, "as we proved in a thesis on procreation, defended at the schools of Medicine at Montpellier" (10:51, col. 2). For "we" which suggests a medical doctor, J. Assézat and Maurice Tourneux substituted "one," without which the attribution to Diderot would have been impossible.

3. See his edn. of the three dialogues of 1769 (Paris: éditions Sociales, 1962), p. 96, n. 1. See also p. CXV, n. 3 and p. 97, n. 2).

4. Ed. Théodore Tarczylo (Paris: Sycomore, 1980 & 1981). On Tissot and more general developments on the conceptions of sexuality in the 18th c., see my *Sexe et Liberté au siècle des Lumières* (Paris: Presses de la Renaissance, 1983).

5. *Diderot, homme de science* (Rennes: Impr. Bretonne, 1959), p. 343.

6. *Essays on the "Encyclopedia" of Diderot and d'Alembert* (N.Y.: Oxford Univ., 1968), p. 482.

7. *Lectures de Diderot* (Paris: Armand Colin, 1974), p. 7.

8. "There are numerous occasions when coitus, as legitimized by marriage, is not possible; and religion does not allow one, in such cases, to imitate the fortunate temerity of Rolfink, who, seeing no other possibility for curing a dangerously sick young woman except that of using seminal secretion, and since there was no husband, resorted to an artificial method and cured her completely. . . . I leave it to the theologians to decide whether, in such a case, a *pollution* in no way provoked by lust but rather by a pressing need, is a crime, or whether there are circumstances in which one must avoid the worst of two evils" ("Marriage," 10:116, col. 2).

9. See Jacques Roger, "Méthodes et modèles dans la pré-histoire du vitalisme français," *Actes du XIIe congres international d'histoire des sciences* (Paris: A. Blanchard, 1971): 38, 101-08.

10. Ménuret considers his subject "only in his capacity as a doctor," leaving to the theologians the trouble of making known the enormity of what they determine to be a sin (10:51, col. 2). In this respect he is only returning to the words of Tissot (see my *Sexe et Liberté*, pp. 114-15). The technical freedom of the doctor to explore any corporal function is taken up in order to arouse suspicion about the competence of ecclesiastics, and it is a dangerous premise soon used to discredit the values of the Church, in order—finally—to set up a layman as judge of the ways of salvation. Ménuret wants observation to be the sole instrument of the moralist (*Encyclopédie* art. "Observateur"); and Tissot calls for a medical art of the mind (*Discours préliminaire* to his trans. of Haller's *Dissertation sur les parties irritables et sensibles des animaux* [Lausanne: Bousquet, 1755], pp. xxxi-xxxii.

11. *Lettres à Sophie Volland*, 2 vols. ed. André Babelon (Paris: N.R.F. Gallimard, 1938), 2:224.

12. Thus, in the *Eléments*, the throw-backs to a strictly mechanistic explanation are elucidated the very moment sexuality is a concern. See, e.g., the morphology of eunuchs: "The matter destined to form semen continues to flow toward the area of its secretion; but no longer finding the organs reserved for this function, it turns toward adjacent parts— beyond the stout thighs, plump knees, and wide pelvic bones that everyone attributes to eunuchs. Where is the seminal matter in eunuchs? Where it was in whole males before its separation from the glands" (*Eléments* ed. Jean Meyer [Paris: M. Didier, 1964], pp. 178-79).

13. Ménuret, in the article "Marriage": "In the natural order, every secretion seems to require and to signal the excretion of a distinct humour: thus the release of semen becomes, according to those same laws, a need" (10:116, col. 1).

14. Bordeu evokes "the disastrous consequences of rigorous continence" (p. 376); for Ménuret it is "a state against nature, often the cause of illness" ("Marriage," 10:116, col. 1); and for Tissot "release [nocturnal emmision] is not an illness; rather it is a benign spasm that expels a humour which, if too abundant and unreleased, could be harmful; and although some doctors . . . have denied it, it is nonetheless true that this fluid may, by its abundance, produce such various maladies as priapism or inflammation of the uterus" (*Discours préliminaire*, p. 195). Here is a *de facto* rejection of the Catholic ideal of absolute chastity.

15. The *Encyclopédie* demands more discretion. Ménuret, with the help of historical references, insinuates that this condition might not be the best ("Marriage," 10:117, col. 1). Diderot himself, in the articles, "Christianisme" and "Célibat," attempts a diplomatic balance of arguments *pro* and *contra*. Tissot, though both Swiss and Protestant, does not risk so perilous a terrain. Would it really be charitable to quibble with him, by asking him for a *de jure* denunciation? An explicit warning against excesses of continence, supported by six case histories of illness due to abstinence (against a hundred relating to debauchery), invite us to

value highly Voltaire's good sense, even if we might want to tone down the way he expresses it: "there is no stronger argument against the rash vows of chastity" (*Questions sur l' "Encyclopédie,"* in *Oeuvres complètes,* 52 vols. (Paris: Garnier, 1879), 20:135.

16. He evokes the "keen and permissible pleasures which are amplified and terminated by reciprocal orgasm perpetuated and made precious by the formation of a child" ("Marriage," 10:116, col. 1).

17. See *Sexe et Liberté,* p. 118. The epithet is Gibbon's (*Le Journal de Gibbon à Lausanne,* ed. G. Bonnard [Lausanne: F. Rouge, 1945], p. 60).

18. Cf. "Manstupration" (10:51, col. 2). The same idea may be found in the article "Pollution nocturne" (10:923, col. 1).

19. "and if it is drawn from its reservoirs, distributed throughout the machine only to be evacuated by a longer, more painful, and more dangerous route, will it be any the less lost?" (p. 377).

20. "if I give a few remedies, I aim less to appease than better to carry on the battle, hoping thereby to remove those obstacles that hinder nature in defeating the enemy. . . . I hasten to assist and to facilitate the flight and expulsion of the defeated enemy; even so, always loyal to nature's cause, I encourage when need be, or else I moderate nature's efforts, should I see them growing too impetuous to be lasting" (*Nouveau traité du pouls* [*New Treatise on the Pulse*] [Amsterdam & Paris: Vincent, 1768], pp. XXVII-XXIX).

21. "I saw . . . a widow . . . who for a long time had frequent orgasms during intercourse. . . . [She] succumbed from time to time to such violent attacks of hysteria that she lost her senses; no remedies availed to alleviate these attacks; one could stop them only by means of vigorous massaging of her genitals which at first produced a convulsive trembling followed by an abundant secretion; upon which she would instantly regain her senses" (*Discours préliminaire,* pp. 196-97).

22. The bastardized terminology used herein (since one must give a name to it) is the outcome of a compromise between the need to simplify (desirable in a *schema*) and the need to compare very different moral systems, with the result that it will satisfy neither the theologian nor the physician.

To be more precise: "chastity" designates absolute chastity; "copulation" designates either the "conjugal chastity" of moral theology or intercourse as understood in physiology. The two facets of masturbation are coordinated, since the theologian makes no distinction between them but prefers the broader concept of "voluntary pollution."

It is well to note that chastity does not figure in the treatises on moral theology, in so far as it is not subject to its legalism. It nonetheless remains the ideal in relation to which the theologian legislates against sins and classifies them. It is the traditional method; in 1601, it is that of Benedicti in *La Somme des péches;* in 1753-1755, that of Alphonse of Ligouri in his *Theologia moralis;* in 1938, that of R. P. Héribert Jone in his *Précis de théologie morale catholique* [*Brief Summary of Catholic Moral Theology*].

23. Let us clarify by saying that, if only acts in conformity with nature cannot be sinful, it is only by reason of conformity with the rules prescribed by the theologians.

24. "if the root of the fascicule gathers all its powers into itself, if the whole system moves, as it were, in reverse, as happens, I believe, in the case of the man who meditates deeply, of the fanatic who sees the heavens open up, of the savage who chants in the midst of the flames, in states of ecstasy, in voluntary or in involuntary derangement . . ." (*Le Rêve,* pp. 349-50).

25. "Isn't there anything to be done for him?—Nothing.—So much the better, for he loaths treatment.—And so do I" (*Le Rêve,* p. 286).

26. "If the process begins at the sensuous tip of the branch which nature has destined to the pleasure of love and to the propagation of the species, the image of the beloved will be aroused as a result in the root of the fascicule. If this image, on the contrary, is first aroused at the root, the tension at the sensuous tip, the effervescence and discharge of the seminal fluid will be the result" (*Le Rêve,* p. 360).

27. A comparison with the account of the same anecdote by Voltaire will leave no doubt whatsoever about Diderot's intention: "not too long ago it was affirmed that in Brussels a rabbit had been responsible for a hen's producing a half-dozen baby rabbits" (*Dictionnaire philosophique,* art. "Dieu," cited by P. Vernière, *La Suite,* p. 382, n. 2). Diderot even claimed that his "infamous" rabbit was polygamous.

28. *Mémoires*, ed. Vernière (1966), p. 133.

29. A hope clearly expressed in 1753, in *De l'interprétation de la nature*: "Instead of worshipping the Almighty in the actual creatures of nature, they prostrated themselves before the phantoms of their imagination. If someone, held back by prejudice, doubts the soundness of my approach, I urge him to compare Galen's treatise on the various uses of the parts of the human body with Böorhaave's physiology, and his with Haller's. I invite posterity to compare what the latter offers in the way of both systematic and ephemeral conceptions, with what physiology will produce in the centuries to come" (pp. 237-38).

Prostitution and Reform in Eighteenth-Century England

Prostitution was widespread in eighteenth-century England.[1] Generally speaking, however, it was accepted as a fact of life, as something to be tolerated and accepted rather than abolished. Instead of seeing the prostitute as a sinner, as had the religiously oriented writers of the sixteenth and seventeenth centuries, eighteenth-century reformers regarded her more as a victim. Undoubtedly, this grew out of the mounting concern to reduce unnecessary pain and suffering in the eighteenth century. It resulted also from lessening concern over the virulent epidemic of syphilis that had hit Europe in the sixteenth century. Though venereal disease remained widespread, it was probably less virulent, and the fears aroused by the realization of the dangers both of venereal infection to unborn children and infants and of the third stage of syphilis did not occur until the later nineteenth century.

Sex was also beginning to be studied, although not quite as dispassionately as were other subjects.[2] The eighteenth century saw the beginnings of the pathological model of sexuality: Samuel Tissot equated all nonreproductive sexuality with illness.[3] Prostitution, however, was not included in this discussion, and most of the concern expressed over prostitution by the writers in the last half of the eighteenth century was economically based. The eighteenth-century reformer saw the prostitute as a victim of her economic situation; at the same time reformers recognized that prostitution for many was an economic necessity.[4] Inevitably, the failure to find any economic solution to prostitution made it difficult for reformers to advance any solution. Although they saw the prostitute as a victim, they continued to view her from an eighteenth-century masculine middle- and upper-class perspective.

❖

Much of eighteenth-century writing about prostitution in England concentrated on London, where prostitution was widespread.[5] London, by far the largest city in Great Britain, had no important industry, yet it acted as a magnet for people from all over the kingdom. Its population of approximately 500,000 in 1700 had reached nearly 900,000 in 1800, more than ten times the size of its nearest British rival. Its working citizens engaged in tasks that were busiest when the London social and governmental season was in full swing and usually just survived for the rest of the year. Many were employed as tailors, seamstresses, shoemakers, laundresses, coach makers, shopkeepers, builders—all seasonal occupations. Even the domestic servant, probably the largest class of employee, was in part dependent on the London season.[6] A significant portion of the population was either unemployed or unemployable, anxious to do almost anything for money. As F. A. Wendeborn wrote in 1791: "There is no place in the world, where a man may live more according to his own mind, or even his whim, than in London."[7] Wealth, even more than gentle birth or public service, was the touchstone that separated the classes; everything was available to those who had money. Inevitably, the lot of the poor was hard, harder in London than anywhere else because of its administrative defects and its rapid population growth.[8]

The eighteenth century was also a man's world. What constituted right or wrong was defined primarily in male terms. Women were measured in terms of their usefulness to men. Inevitably, women were divided into the good and virtuous—those whom one married—and the rest. Prostitutes, the bulk of the "rest," were ubiquitous, since no standards of virtue were imposed upon the male. Prostitutes plied their trade at public shows and feasts, churches, plays, parks—wherever there was likely to be a crowd. Each economic level of society had its own class of prostitutes, who ranged from the most exclusive to those who had no choice. For the rich man without a mistress there were upper-class houses, guides to which still exist. A *List of the Sporting Ladies,* dating from about 1770, is full of the double entendres to which males so often resorted when speaking of prostitutes:

> Miss Rattletrap, from Pall-Mall, London, is calculated for first rates; the rider must be very careful of her, as she starts at full speed. Price 15s. Bank notes taken, if good, but objects to paper currency in general. May be heard of at the Bagnio, Catch-all Lane.

> Miss D. G——Y intends visiting the Races as usual; she is a strapping wench, and from her experience and high training, is possessed with every charm to render an Amour with her delightful. Her figure is handsome, has good eyes, and a melodious voice; is well legg'd and her dress decent. May be spoken with in the Fisher Row. She allows gin and peppermint in the room, and includes all charges at 10s 6d.

> Marston Nancy of long standing in this town, has been some time in the country for her health, but returned from the races only, in prime order; she requires to be used gently, as she is very irritable; and having lately taken fresh instructions in the *pugilistic art,* from the celebrated B——K and B——r, at Friske, will be apt to treat her customers roughly—gets drunk and is quarrelsome in the evening. Price 2s 6d. May be met with after dark in St. Clement's.[9]

A more complete list of prostitutes, *Harris's List of Covent Garden Ladies,* also aimed at the wealthy, was published almost yearly. A 1788 list included such individuals as:

Miss B——rn. No. 18, Old Compton Street, Soho
Close in the arms she languishingly lies,
With dying looks, short breath, and wishing eyes.

This accomplished nymph has just attained her eighteenth year, and fraught with every perfection, enters a volunteer in the field of Venus. She plays on the pianofort, sings, dances, and is mistress of every Maneuver in the amorous contest that can enhance the coming pleasure; is of the middle stature, fine auburn hair, dark eyes and very inviting countenance, which ever seems to beam delight and love. In bed she is all the heart can wish, or eye admire, every limb is symmetry, every action under cover truly amorous; her price is two pounds.[10]

A persual of the list indicates indirectly why some women might have turned to prostitution. For example, Miss H–rd–ye of No. 45, Newman Street "borrows her names from her late keeper, who is now gone to the Indias, and left her to seek support on the wide common of independence." Many of the girls were rather young. Miss L–v–r, No. 17, Ogle Street, Queen Ann-Street East, is described as a young "nymph of fifteen." Others were probably younger.[11]

Prostitution was a popular subject for writers of the time, particularly for satirists, who employed prostitution to make fun of their contemporaries, to make moral points, or simply to arouse their readers. The anonymous *London Bawd* included chapter headings such as "How a Citizen Went to a Bawdy-House for a Whore, and the Bawd Helpt Him to His Own Wife."[12] The equally anonymous *Prostitutes of Quality* was what might today be called a gossip sheet.[13]

An English tract signed by a Father Poussin and said to have been written originally in French combines a moral point by its title, *Pretty Doings in a Protestant Nation*, with a pornographic one by its examples. Included in the tract is a sample letter alleged similar to the kind that various nobles sent their mistresses after a drinking bout or when a friend was in need of consolation:

August 23, 1734

Dear *Molly*

On sight hereof permit the Bearer, to immediately enter a Pair of Holland Sheets with you; let him have Ingress, Egress and Regress to your Person, in such manner as for him shall seem meet, for the space of twenty-four Hours, and no longer, and place it to the Account of

Your Kind and Constant Keeper
Edmund Easy

King's Arms Tavern
Four in the Afternoon
P.S. Child, go through all your Exercises and Evolutions, as well for your own as my Credit.[14]

Still others, though tongue-in-cheek, were conceived as exposés and condemnations of the social conditions of the time. The Reverend Martin Madan who, before his conversion by John Wesley, had been a man about London, wrote a short pamphlet entitled *An Account of the Triumphant*

Death of F. S.: A Converted Prostitute Who Died April 1763, aged 26. This recounted the story of a girl who was reduced to poverty in spite of her genteel education. To support herself she turned to the stage, then to needlework, and finally to prostitution; only at prostitution did she do well. The woman then repented, became a farm worker, lost her job when the season was over, was reduced to beggary, became ill and died.[15] Madan clearly implied that prostitution was one of the few ways a woman on her own could support herself, and that society, rather than the prostitute, was to blame.

Venereal disease, which had been of such concern in earlier centuries, was not absent from the eighteenth century; it was accepted simply as a fact of life. A good example of this is James Boswell, who reported in 1762 that he had vowed not to have anything to do with whores because he was concerned about his health. His intellectual rationalization, however, was not equal to his sexual desire, and he, like so many of his male contemporaries, picked up a girl on the Strand. He reported he went with her "with intention to enjoy her in armour," that is, with a linen prophylactic sheath (or possibly one made from animal intestines), but she had none with her (prostitutes usually furnished them to their customers). As a result, he just "toyed with her."

> She wondered at my size, and said if I ever took a girl's maidenhead, I would make her squeak. I gave her a shilling, and had command enough of myself to go without touching her. I afterwards trembled at the danger I had escaped. I resolved to wait cheerfully til I got some safe girl or was liked by some women of fashion.[16]

He soon returned to the subject, reporting on 14 December that he had been in London for several weeks without ever enjoying the delightful sex. All around him, he added, were all kinds of good hearted ladies "from the splendid Madam at fifty guineas a night, down to the civil nymph with white-thread stockings who tramps along the Strand and will resign her engaging person to your honour for a pint of wine and a shilling." He was unhappy that he lacked the money to pay for the higher-class prostitute and feared the diseases carried by the common prostitute (pp. 83–84).

Ultimately he became involved with an actress, Louisa, who demanded fifty pounds. Unable to meet her price, Boswell began courting her in an effort to get her to lower it. Louisa, for her part well accustomed to dealing with men like Boswell, managed to borrow two guineas from him. She put off going to bed with Boswell for more than a month, after which he proudly reported on 12 January 1763 that "five times was I fairly lost in supreme rapture. Louisa was madly fond of me; she declared I was a prodigy, and asked me if this was not extraordinary for human nature" (pp. 138-39). Though Boswell indicated that he was "somewhat proud" of his performance, he was most proud that he had only paid eighteen shillings for his "recreation." His initial success was followed by several other meetings, but he soon began to lose interest in Louisa, particularly after 20 January, when he found he had an infection on the "member" of his body "sacred" to Cupid (pp. 149, 155-62).

> What! thought I, can this beautiful, this sensible, and this agreeable woman be so sadly defiled? Can corruption lodge beneath so fair a form? Can she who professed delicacy of sentiment and sincere regard for me, use me so very basely and so very cruelly? (pp. 155-56)

After being treated by a surgeon, Boswell went to Louisa's in order to confront her with his infection. Louisa confessed that some three years earlier she had had a venereal infection but stated that she had not been bothered by it for fifteen months. She added that she had not been with a man other than Boswell for some six months. Not certain that Louisa had given him the disease, Boswell left, but upon consideration he became convinced that she had. He then asked her to return his loan of two guineas for the cure and on 12 February, after some delay, Louisa did so (p. 187).

Popular fiction also dealt with prostitution matter-of-factly, though sympathetically. Daniel Defoe's *Moll Flanders* (1722), is just one example. Her story emphasizes the economic aspects of prostitution cited by Madan. Moll had few options, since her mother had been transported to the New World as a felon when Moll was an infant of eighteen months without family or friends to care for her. Befriended by a band of gypsies who later deserted her, she became a ward of the local parish. At fourteen she was taken into the service of a kindly woman who treated her as one of her daughters; unfortunately, her eldest son did not regard Moll as a sister. Ultimately, Moll survived a whole series of adventures as indicated in the original title of the work: *The Fortunes and Misfortunes of the Famous Moll Flanders, Who was Born in Newgate, and during a Life of Threescore Years, besides her Childhood, was Twelve Years a Whore, Five Times a Wife (whereof once to her own Brother), Twelve Years a Thief, Eight Years a Transported Felon in Virginia, at last grew Rich, liv'd Honest, and dy'd a Penitent. Written from her own Memorandums.*

Another of Defoe's heroines, Roxana, of *Roxana; or, The Fortunate Mistress* (1724), could be classed as a courtesan; that is, she moved at higher levels of society, had good manners, was well dressed, and was both more seductive and more insincere than the forthright Moll. Roxana, like Moll, lost her virtue at an early age, but she was more successful in selling herself to the rich and renowned, reasoning that since nature had given her a beautiful body with agreeable features, both of which aroused men, there was no reason why she should fail to make use of them to her own best advantage once she found it necessary to prostitute herself.

A far more detailed description of the life of the prostitute can be found in John Cleland's novel *Memoirs of a Woman of Pleasure* (1748-49). Fanny's tale of woe also emphasizes an impoverished background. She was born of very poor parents in a small village near Liverpool; both parents died of smallpox when she was fifteen. She was then induced to move to London by a scheming friend who deserted her when they reached the city. Left on her own, Fanny applied for employment at the home of a Mrs. Brown, who, unknown to her, was the operator of a bordello. Her initiation into sexuality was through a lesbian experience in the brothel, whereupon she was sold to a lecherous merchant. Though he failed to seduce her, she soon lost her maidenhood to someone else and entered a brothel, this time willingly. She next managed to inherit a large fortune by giving assistance to an old man and after a variety of other sexual adventures married a handsome young man and became a great lady. The story differs from *Roxana* or *Moll Flanders* in its explicit but "chaste" description of the sexual act. Cleland continually hints at the ugliness and squalor of the prostitute's life but never really delves into it.[17]

Yet another view of prostitution is presented by Samuel Richardson in *Clarissa*: a passage describes prostitutes gathered about the bed of a dying "sister." Richardson presents them as having just risen from their nocturnal beds, faces streaked with paint, skins wrinkled, hair stringy; they are slipshod, stockingless, and range from a "blooming nineteen or twenty" to haggard, well-worn strumpets of thirty-eight or forty. Prostitution might seem unattractive after reading this, but the alternatives Richardson portrays also are not particularly attractive, since the virginal Clarissa, raped by her lover in a brothel, wastes away and dies. The problem facing Richardson and others was prostitution's alternatives; and if the death of Clarissa is an example of the economic rewards of virtue, many might well opt to imitate Fanny, Roxana, or Moll.

If fiction can be used as evidence, prostitution was closely linked with poverty, and it was not only tolerated but advocated by much of the upper orders as essential for protecting good women from the promiscuous male. Though prostitution might be an evil, it was necessary. Society had to tolerate it to avoid greater evils. To change matters proved difficult, since the law tolerated and even encouraged prostitution. The common-law attitude was summed up in the 1705 case of *Reg. v. Pierson*, in which the judge wrote that "this indictment is merely solicitation of chastity which is a spiritual offence and not enquirable or punishable at common law."[18]

Though prostitution itself could not be outlawed, some of its abuses could be controlled, particularly if they infringed on the prerogatives of the ruling class. This was done through the use of such terms as "vagrancy" or "public nuisance." Sir Edward Coke had written that a

> brothel or common bawdy-house is a form of disorderely house, the keeping whereof is a public nuisance not only in respect of its endangering the public peace by drawing together dissolute and debauched persons; but also in respect of its apparent tendency to corrupt the manners of both sexes.[19]

Actual laws on the subject, however, were almost unenforceable until Parliament in 1751 passed the Disorderly Houses Act, which, however, was applicable only in the London area. To further limit enforcement, the law stipulated that constables were allowed to initiate prosecution only when the existence of a bawdy house, gaming house, or other disorderly house was brought to their attention.

> And whereas by reasons of the many subtle and crafty contrivances of persons keeping bawdy houses, gaming houses or other disorderly houses, it is difficult to prove who is the real owner or keeper thereof, by which means many notorius offenders have escaped punishment; be it enacted that any person who shall at any time hereafter appear, act or behave him or herself as master or mistress, or as the person having the care, government or management of any bawdy house, etc., shall be deemed and taken to be the keeper thereof, and shall be prosecuted and punished as such, notwithstanding he or she shall not in fact be the real owner or keeper thereof.[20]

The original act was for three years, and it was made perpetual three years later.[21] It was only selectively enforced, however, more to contain and control than to eliminate prostitution. In reality it functioned as a zoning law, preventing houses of prostitution from contaminating the more desirable residential districts.

Further than this Parliament was unwilling to go, although it received many suggestions, many of them taking into account the economics of the time. Perhaps the most elaborate was that put forth by Bernard Mandeville, the physician and satirist best known for *The Fable of the Bees; or, Private Vices, Public Benefit* (1714). One of his lesser works was a 1724 pamphlet entitled *A Modest Defence of Public Stews*.[22] Mandeville believed that the greatest evil attached to prostitution as it then existed in London was the spread of disease to innocent spouses and children. His solution was the establishment of public brothels, since public whoring was "neither so criminal in itself, nor so detrimental to society as private whoring" (pp. 1-2). Unregulated prositituion, he proclaimed, led to increases in illegitimate births; it alienated the affections of wives and husbands, tempted people to live beyond their income, debauched married women, warped virtue, and ruined young virgins. These evils, however, were not intrinsic to prostitution, only to the "abuse and ill management" of it. All could be eliminated by better regulation, namely through the establishment of public brothels.

> The mischief of Man does in this Case is entirely to himself; for with respect to the Woman, he does a laudable Action, in furnishing her with means of subsistence, in the only, or at least most innocent way that she is capable of procuring of it. (pp. 9-10)

Mandeville worked out his plan in great detail. He proposed that a hundred or more houses of prostitution be set up in London to house a total of two thousand women, with a proportionate number of houses to be set up in every city and market town in the kingdom. Each house was to hold twenty women working under the direction of a matron and was to be established in association with an infirmary with at least two physicians and four surgeons in attendance for regular inspections. Supervising organized prostitution would be a body of three commissioners who were to redress the complaints of both the women and their clients. Each house was to have four classes of prostitutes, selected according to beauty or other qualifications, each group having a different price. The first or lowest class of prostitutes would number eight women whose fee was to be half a crown (two and a half shillings); the second class in each house would consist of six women who would charge a crown; the third class of four women were to be paid half a guinea; and the fourth class of two women, reserved for "persons of dignity," would cost a guinea. Medical inspection of women would be paid for by a tax on the public brothels. To protect the morals of minors, no children would be admitted into the house. Pregnant prostitutes would be removed in order that delivery of their children take place in a better environment. If, after parturition, the mother elected to return to the brothel, the child was to be sent elsewhere.

Mandeville argued that the adoption of his plan would prevent boys from masturbating, cut down "too frequent" or immoderate enjoyment of intercourse (by the rather high prices), protect against venereal disease, halt the debauching of modest women, and eliminate a host of other evils present in unregulated prostitution, which he enumerated in great detail. Women already practicing the trade would supply the houses; if the supply became insufficient there would be an increase in private prostitution, which would soon enable authorities to restock the public brothels. Mandeville also argued for the importation of foreign prostitutes into England, which would help keep English girls moral and at the same time satisfy people's curiosity about foreign girls without having to go abroad. He concluded that public brothels would not encourage "men to be lewd," but, on the contrary, would encourage them only to exercise their lewdness in a proper place (pp. 12-26).

Mandeville proposed simply to make things more efficient, and though this was a theme of prostitution reform well into the nineteenth century, most proposals for reform were more concerned with the women involved. It is obvious that the obstacle faced was simply what to do with women currently engaged in prostitution. One of the most controversial answers was put forth by Martin Madan, already mentioned, who in 1780 raised a storm of opposition with the publication of *Thelypthora; or, A Treatise on Female Ruin*. Madan, probably in jest, proposed the adoption of polygamy as an antidote to prostitution. As Madan saw it, polygamy was a major improvement over adultery, which he felt to be deserving of capital punishment. Polygamy was an expedient for some and an absolute necessity for others if more serious sins were to be prevented. Moreover, polygamy was only in keeping with the biblical injunction that required a man to keep, maintain, and provide for "the woman he seduces."[23]

At least nineteen pamphlets answered Madan's proposal,[24] and from the nature of the literature it appears that the average English writer much preferred prostitution to polygamy. Some of Madan's critics argued that polgamy would not solve the problem of prostitution, since a man might well continue to lust after women even though he had several wives. Others argued that rather than eliminating prostitution, polygamy might encourage it, because in order to support his wives a polygamist might encourage them to sally forth on the streets to sell themselves.[25]

Between the two poles of more efficient government regulation of prostitution and the adoption of polygamy were other proposals. Much of the difficulty with any serious discussion of the problem of prostitution is that those most articulate about the "immorality" of the "lower classes" belonged to the upper classes, which adhered to the double standard not only between the sexes but between the orders. Lower-class women were often considered fair game for young gentlemen, though many of them protested the unwanted attentions thrust upon them. The rich man often kept a mistress for his own pleasure as well as for the pleasure of his friends, but this was separate and distinct in his mind from ordinary prostitution. Several upper-class London prostitutes such as Fanny Murray, Kitty Fisher, Nancy Parons, Kitty Kennedy, Grace Dalrymple Eliot, and Gertrude Mahon became famous, patronized by the great and the near great. Their patrons never conceived of them as posing any problem either to public morals or to public order.[26]

If polygamy was not to support women otherwise unable to support themselves except through prostitution, then what other alternatives were there? It is in this area that eighteenth-century reformers failed almost totally, mainly because their alternatives were so unattractive. Many of the would-be reformers showed sympathy for the prostitutes' plight, arguing that they were not to be blamed for their condition, often having become prostitutes only after being deceived by hypocritical men. If women could find gainful employment or a husband, they would leave prostitution.[27]

John Campbell, who used the pseudonym of M. Ludovicus, thought that one way to protect girls from being recruited into prostitution was to establish a Foundling Hospital for young girls and other females.[28] Others advocated the establishment of Magdalen Houses, where women leaving the "trade" could be afforded training for employment while learning "habit and industry" so that they could ultimately make their way in the world without resorting to prostitution.[29]

But what kind of gainful employment should the girls be taught? This posed a problem. John Fielding, brother of the novelist Henry Fielding, and with him cofounder of the first police system in London, formed a detailed plan to rehabilitate prostitutes. Fielding became concerned because he believed the high crime rate in England, particularly in London, was due to the existence of large numbers of foundling children. Boys became thieves from necessity, while their sisters became "Whores from the Same Cause."[30] In his investigation of London prostitutes, Fielding found that large numbers of them were under eighteen and many of them only twelve or thirteen. Prostitution was their only means of survival. To give orphaned female children alternatives, Fielding proposed a "Public Laundry," that would:

> preserve the deserted Girls of the Poor of this Metropolis; and also reform those Prostitutes whom Necessity has drove into the Streets, and who are willing to return to virtue and obtain an honest livelihood by severe industry. (p. 49)

To establish the laundry he proposed a public subscription. The laundry was to be inspected periodically by a board of lady visitors. Fielding wanted his girls to learn as well as to work: part of his plan called for teaching girls under twelve to read and those between twelve and sixteen the housewifely tasks of knitting, cooking, and so forth; only those over sixteen were to work in the laundry, helping to support themselves until they were married (pp. 52–53).

Though Fielding's scheme could well have been challenged for its naiveté, opposition usually came from other directions, indicating the kind of difficulties that faced any efforts to change society to even a slight degree. Most of Fielding's critics were upset both by his "charity" toward the prostitutes and by the fact that his scheme provided education for the lower classes. Many social critics were convinced that rather than coming from economic deprivation, prostitution stemmed from girls' being spoiled by the "false good nature of their superiors." It was argued that too many good society women gave their servant girls cast-off clothing, which soon led these girls to putting on airs, and it was just such pretenses that led to prostitution. Even the severest critics, however, felt that repentant prostitutes ought to be given asylum, although any who refused to work were to be beaten or transported to the penal colonies. It was only by such a "due mixture of mildness and severity" that England could eliminate the great "enormity" of prostitution that had so long infested its streets.[31]

Saunders Welch, while sympathetic to Fielding, criticized him for ignoring bawdy houses. He also questioned whether the laundry concept would ever attract sufficient backers to be practical. Instead, he urged the erection of a "hospital" by public subscription to hold prostitutes until they repented. To encourage donations he wanted to give everyone who subscribed five pounds the title of governor for life.[32] Jonas Hanway, another sympathetic critic, also felt that Fielding's idea of a laundry was inadequate. He proposed a factory for manufacturing carpets, adding that the Turks had found that carpet weaving was a way to keep harem women busy and that what worked in Turkey for wives would work in England for prostitutes.[33] Such a factory would enable the prostitutes to work for

> their benefit, that they may be the farther removed from temptation; and next for our own sake that by their labor they may repay the husbandman and manufacturer for their food and raiment, and ease the community by supporting themselves by their industry.

Hanway believed that one of the major causes of prostitution was the obligation of girls to furnish a dowry when they married. Since many girls in the lower classes could not afford dowries, they turned to prostitution as an alternative to marriage. As a partial solution he urged that the English royal family give a number of poor girls dowries on occasions such as the birth of an heir to the crown (pp. 16–23).

Hanway was especially concerned about those citizens who felt that any steps to alleviate prostitutes' conditions would be against the will of God. Prostitution, to these people, carried "its own affliction" for acting contrary to God's law; and since the afflictions were God's will, the "order of

Providence" should not be counteracted. The clinching argument in favor of Hanway's case was that good Protestant countries such as England could not lag behind the Catholic countries of Europe, where several Magdalen convents had been established to reclaim the female transgressors.[34]

One result of such agitations was the establishment of the Magdalen Charity Hospital in London, which opened 10 August 1758. The facility was dedicated to the reform and rehabilitation of penitent prostitutes, but it was a far cry from Fielding's laundry. In fact, the Magdalen Charity Hospital more resembled a prison than a hospital: fixed daily regimens, uniforms, cell confinement, and constant control. The average woman was incarcerated for several years. Increasingly, however, its residents were not prostitutes but rather women (and girls) who had been "seduced" under the promise of marriage. It was perhaps for this reason that the hospital could claim a high success rate in reforming prostitutes; in reality the rate was not very high.[35]

✳

Eighteenth-century writers increasingly began to look at prostitution as an economic, not a moral, problem. Although this allowed would-be reformers to propose alternative solutions, most were not particularly realistic. Basic to all schemes was the assumption that prostitution was essentially a woman's problem; this ignored the fact that the prostitute could not have survived without a male clientele. Though Fielding, Welch, and others recognized that economic survival was an important factor in prostitution, their alternatives were not particularly attractive in theory, and, if the Magdalen Charity Hospital is any example, even less attractive in practice. By concentrating on the lower-class prostitute, they also ignored the women who served the middle and upper classes. To them prostitution was a class problem. To go beyond this would have required not only a reorientation of their thinking but a reorientation of society as well, something no one was willing to contemplate.

In sum, eighteenth-century reformers, all of them men, looked upon prostitution both from a male point of view and with their own class bias. Sex was regarded as a commodity to be purchased if necessary, to be taken freely if permitted. It was a buyer's market. Casanova, for example, cast aside the expensive Madame Prote in St. Petersburg for Zaire, whom he bought from her father for one hundred rubles to do with as he wished.[36] Boswell, who did not want to pay the fifty pounds demanded by Louisa, courted her in order to get her to lower her price, which she eventually did. Obviously women were not equal to men but rather were toys that could be bought and sold. Though women who played their cards right could acquire fame and fortune, ending up as mistress to the king or to other powerful individuals, few did so. Many young girls adopted these glamorous women as models, but in prostitution almost none of the successful courtesans started from the bottom of the social heap and worked their way up. Most of those who started at the bottom remained there. Though their lot was not particularly happy, it is not clear that the lower-class prostitute was necessarily much worse off than was the lower-class wife, nor that the upper-class prostitute did not have many of the privileges of the upper-class wife. Prostitution was one of the few ways a woman could make it on her own, and if she had intelligence, sophistication, talent, and the right contacts, she could go far. Most failed because they lacked the contacts. Often a woman's family pulled strings to make her mistress to a powerful man, since from this position she could do much in return.

Eighteenth-century reformers seem to have been motivated by real concern for the poverty-stricken prostitute. As such, they laid the groundwork for nineteenth-century efforts to curtail prostitution. They were, however, handicapped in their own efforts toward reform, since they adhered to the double standard and to the existing class structure. Although they proposed various solutions, few were put in place, since to do so would have required some reorganization of society and the place of women within it. Perhaps if eighteenth-century reformers had known the full horrors of syphilis or the implications of gonorrhea in the pregnant female, as they did in the nineteenth century, they could have mounted a public crusade. As it was, though their concern was real, their drive to change things lacked the crusading zeal of moving either against sin, as an earlier generation had done, or against the horrors of unrestrained sexuality, as the nineteenth century did. Women themselves had not yet organized enough to mount their own efforts. Though in the long run the secularization of discussions about prostitution looms important and was a necessary first step, eighteenth-century critics of existing conditions could offer no effective solutions to the basic problems they perceived.

Vern L. Bullough
State University College at Buffalo

NOTES

1. For a further discussion of this see Vern L. and Bonnie Bullough, *Prostitution: An Illustrated Social History* (N.Y.: Crown, 1979). For a more detailed bibliography see Vern L. Bullough, et al., *A Bibliography of Prostitution* (N.Y.: Garland, 1977). See also Paul-Gabriel Boucé, ed., *Sexuality in Eighteenth-Century Britain* (Manchester: Manchester Univ., 1982).

2. A good example of dispassionate discussion is David Hume's account of incest. See, for further amplification, Peter Gay, *The Enlightenment: An Interpretation*, vol. 2, *The Science of Freedom* (N.Y.: Knopf, 1969), pp. 199–200 and passim. Gay emphasizes, as does this essay, the unconscious acceptance of many assumptions in spite of enlightened discussion.

3. *Onanism; or, A Treatise Upon the Disorders of Masturbation*, trans. by A. Hume (London: J. Pridden, 1766). See also Vern L. Bullough, "Sex and the Medical Model," *Journal of Sex Research* 11 (1975): 99–116, rep. in Bullough, *Sex, Society and History* (N.Y.: Science History Publications, 1976), pp. 173–85; Vern L. Bullough, *Sexual Variance in Society and History* (Chicago: Univ. of Chicago, 1978); and for a slightly different view, Michel Foucault, *The History of Sexuality*, trans. Robert Hurley (N.Y.: Pantheon, 1978).

4. This supposition would be hard to document directly, but I base it upon Olwen Hufton's argument that begging and prostitution, as well as smuggling of salt, were not uncommon means of adding to family income ("Women and the Family Economy in Eighteenth-Century France," *French Historical Studies* 9 [1975]: 1–22).

5. In general, crime of any kind was more likely to be an urban affair; as far as women were concerned, extralegal or illegal activity was in the 18th c. an urban pheonmenon. See J. M. Beattie, "The Criminality of Women in Eighteenth-Century England," *Journal of Social History* 8 (Summer 1975): 80–116.

6. See J. Jean Hecht, *The Domestic Servant Class in Eighteenth-Century England* (London: Routledge and Kegan Paul, 1956).

7. *View of England towards the Close of the Eighteenth Century . . .*, 2 vols. (London?: 1791), 1:257.

8. Basil Williams, *The Whig Supremacy: 1714–1760* (Oxford: Clarendon Press, 1942), pp. 124–25. See also Dorothy Marshall, *English Poor in the Eighteenth Century* (London: G. Routledge & Sons, 1928).

9. *List of the Sporting Ladies* (London?: c. 1770), a 36″ × 18″ broadside rep. in *Venus Unmasked*, comp. Leonard de Vries and Peter Fryer (N.Y.: Stein and Day, 1967), pp. 31–32.

10. *Harris's List of Covent Garden Ladies; or, Man of pleasure's kalendar, for the year, 1788. . . .* (London: H. Ranger, 1788). The title page indicates that directories for other years were still available. There is an extract of this in de Vries and Fryer, *Venus Unmasked*, pp. 186–89.

11. *Harris's List*, passim.

12. *The London-Bawd with Her Character and Life Discovering the Various Subtile Intrigues of Lewd Women*, 4th edn., (London: John Willim, 1711). The copy in the British Library is incomplete.

13. *The Prostitutes of Quality; or, Adultery a-la-mode. Being Authentic Memoirs of Several Persons of the Highest Quality* (London: J. Cook and J. Coote, 1757).

14. *Pretty Doings in a Protestant Nation: Being a View of the Present State of Fornication, Whorecraft and Adultery, in Great Britain . . .* (London: J. Roberts, 1734), p. 18.

15. (London: Z. Fowle, n.d.). This is an 8-p. pamphlet in the British Library.

16. James Boswell, *London Journal: 1762–1763*, ed. Frederick A. Pottle (N.Y.: McGraw-Hill, 1950), pp. 49–50.

17. Cleland was pensioned by Parliament not to write any more erotic novels. Cleland's work was not readily available to the American modern reading public until fairly recently unless smuggled into the U.S. from Paris. The first American edn. was by Olympia Press in 1962; this was followed by a Putnam edn. in 1963.

18. *Reg. v. Pierson*, 2 Raym. 1197 (1705).

19. *Institutes of the Laws of England*, part 3 (London: E. and R. Brooke, 1797), p. 204.

20. Disorderly Houses Act, 25 Geo. 2, c. 36.

21. 28 Geo. 2, c. 19, s. 1.

22. *A Modest Defence of Publick Stews; or, An Essay Upon Whoring, as It is Now Practis'd in These Kingdoms* (London: A. Moore, 1724), pp. 1–10.

23. *Thelypthora; or, A Treatise on Female Ruin, in its Causes, Effects, Prevention, and Remedy; Considered on the Basis of the Divine Law*, 3 vols., 2d edn. (London: J. Dodsley, 1781), 1:xxi–xxii.

24. E.g., see *Martin's Hobby Houghed and Pounded; or, Letter on Thelypthora* (London: J. Buckland, 1781), James Penn, *Remarks on Thelypthora* (London: 1781), and *Remarks controverting Martin Madan's Thelypthora* (n.p., c. 1781).

25. See Richard Hill, *The Blessings of Polygamy Displayed* (London: J. Matthews, 1781), pp. 38–39.

26. *Prostitutes of Quality*.

27. E.g., see M. Ludovicus [John Campbell], *A Particular but Melancholy Account of the Great Hardships, Difficulties, and Miseries, That Those Unhappy and Much-To Be pitied Creatures, The Common Women of the Town, Are plung'd into at this juncture. The Causes of their Misfortunes fully laid down: and the Bad that too much Rigour against them will produce* (London, 1752), pp. 6–16.

28. Ibid., p. 27.

29. *Thoughts on the Plan for a Magdalen House* (London: James Waugh, 1758).

30. *An Account of the Origin and Effects of a Police . . . To which is added a Plan for preserving*

those deserted Girls in this Town, who become Prostitutes from Necessity (London: A. Millar, 1758), p. 32.

31. Saunders Welch, *A Proposal to Render Effectual a Plan to Remove the Nuisance of the Common Prostitute from the Streets of this Metropolis. . . .* (London: C. Henderson, 1758), passim.

32. Ibid., p. 25.

33. *Letter V. to Robert Dingley, Esq.: Being a Proposal for the Relief and Employment of Friendless Girls and Repenting Prostitutes* (London: R. and J. Dosley, 1758).

34. *Letters Written Occasionally on the Customs of foreign nations in regards to Harlots. . . .* (London: John Rivington, 1761), p. 13.

35. Stanley Nash, "Prostitution and Charity: The Magdalen Hospital, a Case Study," *Journal of Social History* 17 (1984): 617–28.

36. *The Memoirs of Jacques Casanova de Seingalt,* trans. Arthur Machen (N.Y.: A. & C. Bon, 1932), 5:513–16.

The Properties of Libertinism

꧁꧂꧁꧂꧁꧂꧁꧂

> Thus are wickedness and libertinism called a knowledge
> of the world, a knowledge of human nature.
> *Sir Charles Grandison* (2:17)

Should we abandon the term "libertinism"? Scholarly usage varies so widely that we begin to doubt whether there ever was a single libertine movement or attitude; anachronism, imprecision, and ambiguity further erode our confidence in the term. Nevertheless, because the concept of libertinism is clearly central to a discussion of illicit sexuality in the eighteenth century, we ought to sharpen our sense of what is involved in using it. This essay will explore some of the semantic inconsistencies of both modern and eighteenth-century usage, and then gather materials for the larger question: how can we construct a history of libertinism?

Apart from denoting some combination of irreligion and sexual rampancy, libertinism appears to be a nebulous concept defined by the interests of the individual scholar. The major French and Italian historians of libertinism confine themselves to the first half of the seventeenth century, placing *les derniers libertins* in the reign of Louis XIV; and their focus is on the defiance of organized religion rather than on illicit sexuality. French *dix-huitièmistes*, in contrast, normally apply "libertinisme" and "libertinage" to the erotic fiction of the Régence and to the sexual activities of literary characters, notably in Laclos and Sade. The most thorough German study of libertinism confines itself to France in the sixteenth and seventeenth centuries, and accords only a small role to literary texts, whereas English scholarship tends to apply the term to literature, frequently narrowing the period to the later seventeenth century. Even within this more limited frame, assumptions about the nature of libertinism—its scope and period of efflorescence, and its relation to other movements—vary widely and are often contradictory.[1]

One plausible scheme is offered by David Foxon, the leading bibliographer of pornography: he traces the libertine mode, originated by Pietro Aretino, from its first major flourishing in the 1650s to the publication of John Cleland's *Memoirs of a Woman of Pleasure* in 1748-49, and suggests a parallel between clandestine sexual literature and the intellectual and anticlerical movement that Europeans understood by "Libertinism."[2] Other English specialists apply the term to the Restoration (1660-1700), or narrow it to a specific decade (the 1670s) or author. In studies of a single author "libertinism" may be still further restricted: recent critics of the Earl of Rochester, for example, find that his poems *contain* elements of libertinism (defined rather crudely as the simplest expression of fleshliness and sensory gratification), but that they are transcended or undermined by some distinctly nonlibertine attitude—a sense of contradiction, perhaps, or a distrust of the body, or even an excessive physicality. But there seems to be no consensus on what defines these countervailing features; lines which for one critic embody antilibertine "Augustan" or "humanist" values strike another critic as the essence of "true libertinism."[3] These scholars agree, however, on the areas to which libertinism can be confined—the circle of Théophile de Viau in the 1620s, the court of Charles II in the 1670s. Readers of eighteenth-century fiction, on the other hand, would find it hard to withhold the term "libertine" from Richardson's Lovelace or Laclos' Valmont, both more thoroughly dedicated than any seventeenth-century rake to Machiavellian means and Hobbesian ends—power, glory, and solitary predation. For the Marquis de Sade, indeed, libertinism had barely started by the end of the seventeenth century and was only timidly realized in such mid-eighteenth-century works as d'Argens' *Thérèse philosophe*: Sade defines it as a combination of lawless obscenity and the denunciation of religion, consciously and systematically pushed to its farthest limit.[4]

These different chronological and conceptual restrictions reflect different theories of how libertinism relates to the prevailing *mores*. For some, it vanishes with the rise of the controlled politeness of Versailles; for others, it reaches its apogee there.[5] For some scholars libertinism develops into aristocratic neo-Epicureanism and polite gallantry, and the refined libertine of the late seventeenth century blends into the *honnête homme*: indeed, the main proponent of this view, Maximillian Novak, argues that English libertinism of the 1690s is "part of the general philosophy of the Enlightenment," and that it included the cultivation of discretion, emotional control, and romantic love. Others, however, deny this extension of the term: they establish a fundamental opposition between neo-Epicureanism and *honnêteté* on the one hand and libertinism on the other.[6]

Historians of the eighteenth century may likewise contrast the genuine sexual Enlightenment of their chosen period with the savage libertinism of the seventeenth century, which intended to shock rather than to liberate. Roy Porter, for example, finds a world of difference between "Enlightenment" naturalism, hedonism, and quasi-religious cultivation of sexuality, apparently diffused throughout eighteenth-century English society, and the abrasive, repressed "sexual libertinism" of the small Restoration court circle. Porter opposes Rochester ("still a Puritan at heart") to a typical late-eighteenth-century figure like Erasmus Darwin, for whom sexual love was the supreme happiness and "the cordial drop in the otherwise insipid cup of life;" but the contrast is less convincing when we recognize that Darwin borrows his idea, and even his phrasing, directly from Rochester himself.[7] We should not suppose that troubled and deliberately shocking forms of sexual display died with Charles II, or that hedonism, naturalism, and a fascination with Priapic religion did not flourish among the seventeenth-century *libertins érudits*. Some scholars, indeed, trace an even longer tradition of "libertine naturalism" that runs from classical antiquity to Montaigne and flourishes in successive portrayals of Héloise up to the time of Pope.[8] A further complication is provided by Lawrence Stone: in his major study of English sexuality he confirms the relaxation of morals during the Restoration and eighteenth century with an abundance of evidence; but rather than contrasting the libertine and Enlightenment stages, as Porter does, he traces a single "Rise of Libertinism" throughout the period and limits the Enlightenment's influence. In a more recent statement Stone restricts the applicability of "Enlightenment" still further; one of the striking enigmas of English history, he suggests, is that the ingredients of the Enlightenment— including sexual libertinism—developed in England in the seventeenth century, but failed to reach critical mass in the eighteenth century.[9]

Underlying these questions about the nature and development of libertinism are two different approaches to the history of ideas, one expansive, or maximalist, the other restrictive, or minimalist. The former depicts libertinism as a broad movement of sensibility, evolving towards cultured hedonism and incorporating the ideals of rakish vitality, psychological honesty, and a fair-minded assumption of combative equality between the sexes. The latter imposes sharp distinctions between the genuine libertine and the more agreeable aspects of the late-seventeenth-century mentality; it limits the duration, typicality, and influence of libertinism, and seeks to deny altogether its hegemony in English Restoration literature. Each approach, though based on sound intuition, runs the danger of being over-selective and of over-simplifying contemporary usage. The maximalist can blend libertinism entirely into *honnêteté*, obscuring their vital but always problematic relationship, and may even suggest that libertinism shares the ideals of romance—whereas "romance" was almost universally opposed to libertine eroticism.[10] The minimalist suspicion of unfounded generalization, admirable in itself, may lead to overzealous whittling of essential libertine characteristics: it is agreed that Epicureanism must be distinguished from libertinism, or that "extravagance" disqualifies a stage character from being a genuine libertine; but for many contemporary witnesses, sympathizers and critics alike, these were qualities definitive of the libertine.[11] Nor can libertinism be happily pruned back to its simplest form; it is constituted, not by a naive faith in sensuality and desire, but by internal contradiction and a troubled and complex history.

✳

Libertinism had been neither established within firm boundaries nor fixed by precise synonyms and antonyms. Seventeenth- and eighteenth-century usage varied as much as that of twentieth-century critics and historians. The libertine is sometimes interchangeable with, and sometimes distinguished from, the Priapean, the spark or ranter, the roaring blade, the jovial atheist, the cavalier, the sensualist, the rake, the murderous upper-class hooligan, the worldly fine gentleman, the debauchee, the beau, the man of pleasure, and even the "man of sense."[12] No one criterion is sufficient to define "libertinism," and it is certainly not a simple synonym for illicit sexuality. We would hesitate to call Samuel Pepys a libertine, busy as he was with "jupes" and "mamelles"; a proper stage libertine might even place him in the opposite category of "sneaking lechers"—that band of Puritans, City husbands, and covert masochists who bring out by contrast the frankness and openness of the rake-heroes themselves.[13] A figure such as Colonel Charteris, at the other extreme, might also be excluded; though he made no secret of his priapism, he lacked the wit and finesse associated with the true libertine. It is difficult, however, to determine the exact point at which the libertine becomes the fine gentleman, or the exact proportions in the volatile compound of disgusting debauchery and desirable urbanity, of extravagance and sense. Novak has concluded that, in comedy at least, the "libertine element" of the 1670s gives way to the "man of sense" in the 1690s. But in the 1670s Rochester's circle already refer to themselves as "men of Sense and Understanding" and as natural members of the "World"; and in the late 1690s Sir Richard Blackmore protests that "the *Man of Sense* and the *Fine* Gentleman in the Comedy" is indistinguishable from "a *Finish'd Libertine*."[14] These discrepancies suggest that "libertine" confounds neat boundaries and enjoys a paradoxical relationship to the social ideals of the "World," shifting with the observer's preoccupations.

It may be objected that such conceptual ambiguities are marginal and that in the ordinary parlance of the eighteenth as well as the twentieth century a libertine is simply a womanizer, a cocksman. When Boswell, pausing from his "high debaucheries" to analyse the character of a friend, notes that "I am more of a libertine [than he]," his meaning is surely unmistakable. It is equally clear when Michel Foucault describes the author of *My Secret Life* as "a kind of traditional libertine."[15] But the commonsense core usage conceals a more complex semantic history. Even when we set aside the original technical meaning (released from slavery under Roman law), English, French, and Dutch usages divide into three main branches: "libertine" may be a largely pejorative term for dissolute sexuality, a neutral or even agreeable description of airy freedom in behavior or writing, and—prior to and concurrent with these—a religious attitude.

The religious meanings of "libertinism," grouped under a single heading by the *Oxford English Dictionary,* actually refer to two quite distinct phenomena, the mocking denial of the truth and relevance of Scripture, and the intensification of spirituality among radical Protestants.[16] These movements have little to do with one another—*pace* the apologists of middle-of-the-road Anglicanism—but each is related, in a fascinating yet elusive way, to the world of sexuality. Calvin, for example, accuses the antinomian "Spiritual Libertines" of glorifying casual sexual liaisons under the name "spiritual marriages" and of being "carried away by their own libidos" while claiming to experience an ecstatic return to the paradisal state, where good and evil vanish and *le sens naturel* takes over.[17] Samuel Butler exposes a similar illusion among the Restoration rakes, who turn themselves into negative images of the Puritans they have just deposed, as if they "had no other Way but Sin and Vice / To be restor'd again to *Paradise*."[18] Pascal likewise equates the animalistic naturalism of the *libertin* Jacques Des Barreaux, a proponent of "sense" and an influence on Rochester, with the false "angelic" desires of contemporary mystic devotion: each is a futile attempt to escape the painful contradictions of the human condition.[19]

However tantalizing these shadowy correspondences between the spiritual and the sexual, we should recognize that there is no necessary connection, much less identity, between the religious and secular applications of "libertinism." The word refers, not to a single entity with different facets, but to three distinct movements of thought or clusters of attitudes: religious ("spiritual") libertinism, philosophical libertinism (the combination of antireligious skepticism and scientific materialism studied by René Pintard), and sexual libertinism. In England, the last of these meanings had already come to predominate during Shakespeare's lifetime. Nevertheless, we should recognize the symmetry between the extremes of sexuality and spirituality noted by Calvin, Butler, and Pascal; and we can perhaps detect the powerful covert influence of religious intensity shaping the activities and attitudes of the English sexual libertine. We may even see a reciprocal influence on the self-definition of some radical religious innovators.

Milton, for example, defending the Christian "Liberty" of erotic delight in marriage against the "license" of riotous extramarital sexuality, acknowledges their affinity-in-opposition; he recognizes that the "brood of Belial"—his term for the freemasonry of fornicators apparently well established in London by the 1640s—will be delighted by his divorce tracts, "see[ing] so great a strength of Scripture mustering up in favour, as they suppose, of their debausheries." This scandalous but evidently significant group of readers presented a special danger for Milton, since he himself had been branded a "Libertine" by critics of the divorce tracts—an accusation misguided but understandable. Both Milton and the Sons of Belial, I argue elsewhere, give a supreme importance to Eros, he in a uniquely intense vision of marriage, they in "unbridl'd and vagabond lust without pale or partition."[20] The enthusiastic sect of Ranters took this identity of opposites even further and adopted sinful manners as a sign of special grace, proving by oaths and fornications that for them good and evil had become a merely imaginary distinction. Both the extravagant prophet of the 1650s and the extravagant Town Gallant of the 1670s thus "deny that there is any essential difference betwixt Good and Evil." One Ranter adopted a Cavalier coiffure and preached that there was no heaven except sexual enjoyment; another described the service of God as "perfect freedom and pure Libertinism."[21]

At the other end of the social and doctrinal scale, Rochester was called an "Enthusiast in Wit" and a "Martyr to Sin" by his friends and retainers.[22] Deeply internalized religious motives can often be detected in the debaucheries of Rochester's contemporaries and imitators, too. Sir Charles Sedley and the future Earl of Dorset simulated the Eucharist before an enraged crowd, washing their penises in wine, distributing excrement to the "congregation," and preaching in mock-scriptural tones about their own sexual virtues. One of the frolics of the Earl of Wharton (who was later to become Viceroy of Ireland, much to Swift's disgust) included defecating on the altar of a church.[23] And Boswell, no less "a libertine," seems also to have associated the religious and the salacious: he experienced an overwhelming urge to lead the minister of the New Kirk past the scene of his first sexual conquest in London, and an equally irresistible impotence with his mistress Louisa that lasted for the precise hours of Sunday morning service.[24] One need hardly mention the frenetic blasphemies of the Marquis de Sade.

Even if we cannot prove a direct connection between these widely divergent religious and social extremists (though Rochester's conversion is closer to spiritual libertinism than to conventional piety) we can certainly classify them as antinomian. Libertines are not anarchists, since they believe in laws to govern "the rabble"; for themselves, however, they claim a special privilege or grace which allows them, or even compels them, to break those laws. The same is true of an eighteenth-century fictional libertine such as Richardson's Lovelace, who rejoices in the war between "tame spirits" and "us mad fellows as are above all law, and scorn to sculk behind the hypocritical screen of reputation." This makes him "not a sensual man, but a man of spirit."[25]

A history of libertinism should thus begin by recognizing the instability and complexity of the semantic field. Alternate meanings, like the religious, may influence the drift and implication of what was never a precisely delimited concept; or they may appear, like the foundations of ancient buildings during a drought, under extreme and critical conditions. With due caution, then, we may establish a maximalist conception of libertinism, in which the rebellious display of illicit sexuality is linked, by latent associations and ghostly companionships of language, to the religious and moral systems it purports to reject.

*

I would not want to overstate the religious dimension in libertinism; certainly not every wild rake was a devout believer led astray by the profligacy of his age. But the religious analogy does provide a useful model for deciphering the mental processes of the libertine; it may even throw light on the problems of definition and chronology that have divided scholars. Blasphemy, for example, evidently depends on a core of emotional belief glowing within a mantle of intellectual doubt; a secure and conventional believer has no need for blasphemy, and a true atheist has no reason for it. If Cassius really were the Epicurean he claims to be, he would not brave the storm bare-chested, daring the nonexistent gods to strike him down. The same game, in an extreme and therefore particularly visible form, is played by Sade's libertine heroes. The somewhat tamer rakes of Restoration England may be seen as blasphemers in two senses. Not only do they mock Scripture and the liturgy, and thus attest to the importance of the religion they pretend to despise, but they are also social blasphemers, rebelling against the rules of upper-class civility even though it is precisely those rules that give them the license to be uncivil. Religious antinomianism, likewise, paradoxically enforces the law that it sets aside and intensifies the concept of sin that it appears to negate: if sin were not so overwhelmingly serious there would be no miracle in the divine grace that absolves the elect from a concern with it; experiencing sin "as no sin" may thus give reassurance to the radical Calvinist perpetually in doubt of his own election.[26] Libertines may be seen as secular antinomians, not simply above the law, but deeply in need of the law to guarantee their privileges and to fuel their emotional rebellion. They confirm in the very act of infraction.

Libertine rebelliousness is a kind of dramatic testing procedure, like a child's testing of the boundaries of parental tolerance. It flourishes in areas of ambiguity and doubtful authority, along the uncertain boundary of two value-systems—ethical propriety and aristocratic license. The Restoration rake defined himself by his frolics and heroic debauches—

> Whores attack'd, their Lords at home,
> Bawd's Quarters beaten up, and Fortress won,
> Windows demolisht, Watches overcome,
> And handsome ills by my contrivance done.[27]

Would they be punished by the authorities, as was Sedley for his obscene display; or would they be pardoned by an indulgent king or dazzled beau monde? Punishment would reassure the libertine of a stable world of proprieties, statuses, and boundaries; impunity would reinforce his own power to soar about convention. Would the police enforce the law and kill the upper-class hooligan in self-defense, as happened in Rochester's frolic at Epsom, or would they sacrifice legality to social deference, as they did when Lord Wharton, the defecating viceroy, smashed up a woman's house with a gang of his friends? (In a dizzyingly paradoxical phrase, the constable was reported to have been "so civil as not to secure them.")[28] The child analogy is almost literally true in the case of the fatherless Rochester, who repeatedly provoked the king to the point of exercising sovereign wrath, only to melt the royal displeasure and rescind the order of banishment with some irresistible witticism. As he reiterates in his love poetry, stable affection may prove a mere phantom, but conflict—"Love rais'd to an Extream" by pain and doubt—"can ne'er deceive."[29]

The Restoration libertines were thus particularly fascinated by the oxymoronic conjunction of the civil and the rude. Their entertainments are "handsome ills," and their literary ideal is either to melt the fair sex with "Songs and Verses mannerly obscene" or to cut down jilts and rivals in verses that combine revolting filthiness with "almost lacy precision."[30] Mrs. Willis, the lady honored by Lord Wharton's demolitions, was told in perfectly manicured verse that "Her belly is a bag of turds, / And her cunt a common sewer."[31] Sexuality is a particularly rich area for this deliberately cultivated dissonance of moral and aesthetic values. In sexual relations, as in few other areas of potential transgression, there prevailed a deep uncertainty as to which of two criteria applied: the model of law, which ruled on the bastardies and fornications of the lower orders and controlled the wives of the middle and upper classes, or the social norms of the beau monde, which allowed the gentleman his pleasures (and indeed required him to gain the reputation of a cocksman) while keeping the belle strictly within the bounds of chastity. It is perhaps this ambiguous, liminal condition, even more than the obvious physical pleasures—which are often disparaged as "slimy drudgeries" or wearisome "obligations"—that attracts the libertine to the *mundus sexualis*.[32]

It may be objected at this point that my characterization of the libertine applies only to the narrow circle of Charles II, to the "merry gang" and to a few tearaways in the next generation such as Wharton. Roy Porter may therefore be right to distinguish the easygoing Enlightenment of the eighteenth century from the frenetic libertinism of the court rakes, still "Puritans at heart" and still trying to invite the thunder of an indulgent and "disengaged" Father, a secularized *deus absconditus*. Perhaps, too, a profound gulf does separate the libertine 1670s from the refined neo-Epicurean 1690s, as some historians of drama suggest. Perhaps Addison and Steele's moral revolution dug a trench between the old century and the new, and perhaps the growth of Enlightenment hedonism in the age of Fanny Hill and James Graham, Porter's principal witnesses, took England farther still from the uneasy obscenity of the Restoration era.[33]

Porter's delightful sketch of a nation of rococo fornicators is considerably more attractive than other simplifications of the eighteenth century, but it is still a simplification. The evidence may be selected and interpreted in a different way to reveal a complex, divided culture with many strands of continuity from seventeenth-century libertinism. The characters of Restoration drama and their supposed real-life originals continued to serve as exempla for the young man about Town. The most fully developed of these characters, Dorimant in Sir George Etherege's *Man of Mode*, was condemned by Steele as a proper role model for the young gentleman of the new age, but a serious critic like John Dennis could find in him a perfect embodiment of social breeding and the perennial effervescence of youth; and Fielding's Tom Jones uses Dorimant as a synonym for the wild-oats stage of the hero's development—Sophia's beauty could "fix a Dorimant, a Lord Rochester."[34] The young Boswell aspired to be a stage rake or a court wit of Charles II's time in his "high debaucheries," though he outstrips his models, ironically, in revealing his own egotisms, obsessions, and buried tensions—particularly when he confuses the sexual drive with the struggle against the secular and religious Father. Perhaps Scots Calvinism left a deeper mark than the Church of England could inflict, a century after the Puritan Revolution; whatever the explanation, Boswell does not support Porter's thesis of an evolutionary progress away from libertinism.

Literary evidence for the demise of libertinism is again rather inconclusive. Portrayals of the libertine character actually increase, and though their intention is generally critical, they clearly express fascination as well as disapproval. Clandestine and obscene sexual writing does not die out, but evolves like any other branch of literature; new genres arise, such as the genital tale, the mock-proposal, or the Miltonic pastiche, but old genres also persist—erotic lampoons, for example, continue at least through the reign of William III, and new ones appear in posthumous editions of Rochester even in the 1760s. Libertine pornography continued to be imported and prosecuted spasmodically, as it was in the seventeenth century. When Cleland's *Memoirs of a Woman of Pleasure* appeared it was regarded as highly scandalous, despite its genteel diction and marital conclusion. Porter points out, in support of his vision of relaxed Enlightenment, that the book was favorably reviewed in a widely read magazine; but that review refers only to a bowdlerized version, and was in any case written by the publisher himself. Another favorable notice of Cleland suggests an old continuity as much as a new tolerance. The *Memoirs* are compared to Nicholas Chorier's *Satyra Sotadica* (1660), on the grounds that in both works the elegant style redeems the wildly sexual subject-matter; the critic thus chooses the masterpiece of seventeenth-century libertinism to justify Cleland's work. These terms were themselves borrowed from a 1707 encomium of Rochester, which praises the Earl for having managed, like Petronius and Chorier, to "give merit to lewdness"—that is, to articulate and control the oxymoronic combination of the "mannerly" and the "obscene."[35]

To generalize about moral tone and development is a difficult task for the historian; how, for example, can one place a figure like Sir William Temple, who appears variously as the old-fashioned romantic Cavalier, the new refined Epicurean, or the gross womanizer who boasted to Swift of "his amours, and extraordinary abilities that way, which had once upon a time very nearly killed him"?[36] One should expect the genuine bearers of continuity to be figures such as Temple, *halve-libertijnen* as the Dutch would call them, amphibious men who moved freely between the demi-monde and the politest circles, and for whom libertinism was a sort of dressing-up box of rakish attitudes and gestures. The monomaniac, perfect, demonic libertine, probably always an imaginative construct, continues to develop throughout the eighteenth century in the world of the imagination—from Thomas Shadwell's *Libertine* to Lovelace, Valmont, the self-projections of Sade, Coleridge's meditations on Shadwell, and Kierkegaard's on Don Giovanni. It is a sublime procession; meanwhile, the real history of libertinism continues in the tempered "social libertinism" of the drawing room and *la ruelle*.

Eighteenth-century polite society developed unevenly; its ideas of decorum—the essential ingredient in a libertinism that simultaneously violates and upholds propriety—varied not just by decade or social class, but as it were geographically, from household to household and from location to location. Ancient "liberties," like the foul speech permitted to Thames watermen and their respectable passengers, survived, and new places of license, like the masquerade, the gentleman's club, or the assemblies of the "Modish Rakes," were established; alongside these developed the new politeness of the drawing room, the self-conscious elimination of indelicacy called for by Addison and Steele.[37] No doubt eighteenth-century London could seem a vast machinery of sexual gratification that contemporaries did not hesitate to call libertine; but it was above all a bewildering mass of contradiction, and it is misleading to select any one strand as typical of the whole. If the fully fledged libertine is devoted, in Milton's phrase, to "vagabond lust without pale or partition," then the social libertine respects the pales and partitions that society has constructed to allow the coexistence of lust and respectability; he knocks against them, playing a milder version of the Restoration testing game.

When Richardson's Pamela—herself typical of one branch of eighteenth-century politeness—visits the Theatre Royal, she stumbles painfully across a "partition" that a more worldly, amphibious woman could negotiate with ease. She is shocked at the contradiction between the noble tragic role of Andromache (in Ambrose Philips' adaptation of Racine), and the hilariously lewd epilogue delivered by the actress who played her, Anne Oldfield. Pamela's sensitive but somewhat prudish refinement—she is also shocked by the supposedly respectable Steele—is just as typical of eighteenth-century sexual attitudes as is the easy eroticism that Porter emphasizes. What horrifies her is not so much a new Enlightenment freedom as a pure survival of the libertine element in Restoration drama, sealed into a repertory tradition. She is particularly disturbed because as Andromache grows ever more specific about the nocturnal abilities of her late husband, the men in the audience triumphantly challenge the women to reveal their understanding of the double entendre—precisely as Bellinda and Lady Brute had described the London theatre of the 1690s in Sir John Vanbrugh's *Provok'd Wife*: "the pleasure this gave the men was equally barbarous and insulting; all turning to the boxes, pit and galleries, where ladies were, to see how they looked."[38] Thus the occasion makes the ordinary male theatre-goer, together with those ladies not afraid to acknowledge the jest, into "half-libertines." Their enjoyment has many characteristics of the genuine libertine spirit, supposedly vanished generations before: the cynical assumptions about female virtue and the gentleman's right to assault it, the politely aggressive testing game, the pleasure in forcing blushes, and the delight in the power to shock.

This incident is slender in itself, but it is only by patient accumulation of such small details that an accurate picture of eighteenth-century sexuality can be built up. Above all, such a picture should not diminish the contradictions inherited by those who attempt to preserve libertine traditions—by Boswell, for example, who defines himself as "a libertine" and yet condemns his friend Belle de Zuylen when she proposes identical freedoms for herself, as a "frantic libertine." (Only in fantasy can a Fanny Hill enjoy "libertine pleasures" and yet reconcile "all the refinements of taste and delicacy with the most gross and determinate gratifications of sensuality.")[39] This double emphasis, on contradiction and continuity, could allow us to move beyond the methodological dilemma that divides current scholarship, by generating a cautiously maximalist history of libertinism that nevertheless respects the paradoxes and shortcomings that nourish the minimalist view.

James G. Turner
Northwestern University

NOTES

1. For 17th-c. studies, cf. René Pintard, *Le Libertinage érudit dans la première moitié du XVIIe siècle* (Paris: Boivin, 1943); Giorgio Spini, *Ricerca dei Libertini: la teoria dell'impostura delle religioni nel Seicento italiano* (Rome: Editrice Universale de Roma, 1950); Gerhard Schneider, *Der Libertin: zur Geistes- und Sozialgeschichte des Bürgertums im 16. und 17. Jahrhundert* (Stuttgart: J. B. Metzler, 1970); Hugh M. Richmond, *Puritans and Libertines: Anglo-French Literary Relations in the Reformation* (Berkeley and Los Angeles: Univ. of California, 1981); Joan E. DeJean, *Libertine Strategies: Freedom and the Novel in Seventeenth-century France* (Columbus: Ohio State Univ., 1981)—the last offering a bizarre formalistic definition of libertinism that excludes the sexual completely (pp. 23-4). For 18th-c. studies, cf. Ernest Sturm, *Crébillon fils et le libertinage au dix-huitième siècle* (Paris: A. -G. Nizet, 1970); Philippe Laroch, *Petits-maîtres et roués: évolution de la notion de libertinage dans le roman français du XVIIIe siècle* (Quebec: Presses de l'Universitaire Laval, 1979); *Laclos et le libertinage*, ed. René Pomeau, Actes du colloque du bicentenaire des *Liaisons dangereuses* (Paris: Presses Universitaires de France, 1983).

This essay is principally concerned with examples from the English-speaking world, which will be documented as they arise; it also follows the English convention of treating the decades after 1660 as if they belonged to the 18th c.

2. *Libertine Literature in England, 1660-1745* (New Hyde Park, N.Y.: University Books, 1965).

3. Cf. David Farley-Hills, *Rochester's Poetry* (London: Bell and Hyman, 1978), pp. 30, 183; *Spirit of Wit: Reconsiderations of Rochester*, ed. Jeremy Treglown (Oxford: Basil Blackwell, 1982), pp. 10-11 and 17-18 (Barbara Everett, "The Sense of Nothing"), 52-54 (John Wilders, "Rochester and the Metaphysicals"); *Restoration Literature: Critical Approaches*, ed. Harold Love (London: Methuen, 1972), pp. 167-71; Maximillian E. Novak, "Margery Pinchwife's 'London Disease': Restoration Comedy and the Libertine Offensive of the 1670's," *Studies in the Literary Imagination* 10, no. 2 (1972): 6, n. 19 (the last two citations refer to Rochester's "Letter from Artemisia in the Town to Chloe in the Country," lines 40-65, and it is Novak who refers to "true libertinism"). The 19th-c. critic Frederic Harrison, far from separating libertinism and humanism, refers to the "libertine humanism" of the Renaissance (*Oxford English Dictionary*, s.v. "Libertine" B.4); a similar connection is made in Dale Underwood's *Etherege and the Restoration Comedy of Manners* (New Haven: Yale Univ., 1948), still the standard account of libertinism for English readers (cf. Novak, *William Congreve* [N.Y.: Twayne, 1971], p. 42).

4. Sade's contemptuous review of his predecessors is discussed in Barry Ivker, "Towards a Definition of Libertinism in Eighteenth-century French Fiction," *Studies on Voltaire and the Eighteenth Century* 83 (1970): 221-39.

5. Cf. Pintard, passim; Sir Richard Steele, *Spectator,* 139; John Dryden, "Defense of the Epilogue" (1672), interpreted as an expression of libertine values by Novak, "Margery," pp. 4-5.

6. Novak, *Congreve*, pp. 42-44; "Margery," p. 4; Robert D. Hume, "The Myth of the Rake in 'Restoration' Comedy," *Studies in The Literary Imagination.* 10, no. 2 (1972): 29-30, 41, 45. Hume's dichotomies are sometimes qualified—the seeds of refinement are latent in the "polite rake" of the 1670s (p. 30)—and sometimes absolute—"The rise of the neo-Epicurean school of thought drove the serious libertine out of business" (p. 48).

7. "Mixed Feelings: The Enlightenment and Sexuality in Eighteenth-century Britain," in *Sexuality in Eighteenth-century Britain*, ed. Paul-Gabriel Boucé (Manchester: Manchester Univ., 1982), pp. 3-4; cf. Rochester, "Letter from Artemisia," lines 44-45. Peter Gay assumes a similar opposition between libertinism and Enlightenment in *The Englightenment: An Interpretation*, Vol. 2 (N.Y.: Knopf, 1969), pp. 201-03.

8. E.g., *Alexander Pope: Eloisa to Abelard, with the Letters of Heloise to Abelard in the Version by John Hughes (1713)*, ed. James E. Wellington (Coral Gables: Univ. of Miami, 1965), pp. 126-27, cited in Jean H. Hagstrum, *Sex and Sensibility: Ideal and Erotic Love from Milton to Mozart* (Chicago: Univ. of Chicago, 1980), p. 127.

9. *The Family, Sex and Marriage in England, 1500-1800* (London: Weidenfeld and Nicholson, 1977), pp. 528-45; "The New Eighteenth Century," *New York Review of Books*, 29 Mar. 1984, p. 42.

10. E.g., Virginia Ogden Birdsall, *Wild Civility: The English Comic Spirit on the Restoration Stage* (Bloomington: Indiana Univ., 1970), pp. 32-39; Sarah Wintle, "Libertinism and Sexual Politics," in *Spirit of Wit*, ed. Treglown, pp. 133-65; Novak, "Margery," p.4 and passim. Jane Barker makes an interesting and detailed defense of romance in the preface to *Exilius, or, The Banish'd Roman: a New Romance* (London, 1725): her revival of literary romance is a conscious attempt to reestablish "Heroick Love" and thereby help those who wish to be happy in marriage; romance is absolutely opposed to the current monopoly of "Interest and loose Gallantry," and to "that Deluge of Libertinism which has overflow'd the Age" and produced "many unhappy Marriages and unkind Separations" (fols. A2-v).

11. Hume, passim; cf. Novak, "Margery," pp. 9, 15-17.

12. Cf., among other, Thomas Shadwell, *The Libertine* (London, 1675); Edward Ward, *The Libertine's Choice, or, The Mistaken Happiness of the Fool in Fashion* (London, 1709); Mary Davys, *The Accomplish'd Rake, or Modern Fine Gentleman* (London, 1727); David Trotter, "Wanton Expressions," in *Spirit of Wit*, ed. Treglown, pp. 116, 127.

13. Hume quite rightly distinguishes the "Polite Rake" from the "Debauch": indeed, the distinction between the true, reflective voluptuary and the mindless sensualist is absolutely central in all libertine writings. Hume then mistakenly categorizes the Debauch[ee] with the "sneaking" fornicator, however (p. 38).

14. James Sutherland and Sir Richard Blackmore, cited in Hume, pp. 27, 54; Henry Bulkeley, letter to Rochester, in *The Letters of John Wilmot, Earl of Rochester*, ed. Jeremy Treglown (Oxford: Basil Blackwell, 1980), pp. 124-27; Rochester, "Satyr [against Mankind]," lines 98-111. Unless otherwise stated, all citations from Rochester's poetry will be from *Poems*, ed. Keith Walker (Oxford: Basil Blackwell, 1984).

15. James Boswell, *London Journal, 1762-1763*, ed. Frederick A. Pottle (N.Y.: McGraw Hill, 1950), pp. 231-32; Foucault, *History of Sexuality*, trans. Robert Hurley (1978; rep. Harmondsworth: Penguin, 1981), pp. 21-22.

16. *OED*, s.v. "Libertine," A.2a, 2b, B.2; Henry More quoted in ibid., "Libertinism," 1. Two of the quotations in the last entry (Burnet and Hartley) actually refer to sexual immorality and should be under "Libertinism," 2.

17. *Treatises against the Anabaptists and against the Libertines*, trans. and ed. Benjamin Wirt Farley (Grand Rapids: Baker Book House, 1982), pp. 263, 279-81, 306; *Commentarii in quinque libros Mosis*, 2nd edn. (Geneva, 1573), commentary on Gen. 2:9.

18. *Satires and Miscellaneous Poetry and Prose*, ed. René Lamar (Cambridge: Cambridge Univ., 1928), p. 42.

19. *Pensées*, Lafuma 410 (Brunschvicg 413); cf. Dustin H. Griffin, *Satires against Man: The Poems of Rochester* (Berkeley and Los Angeles: Univ. of California, 1973), pp. 176-79.

20. Milton, *Complete Prose Works*, ed. Don M. Wolfe, et al. (New Haven: Yale Univ., 1959), 2:225. For Milton's reputation see Christopher Hill, *Milton and the English Revolution* (1978; rep. N.Y.: Penguin, 1979), pp. 109, 131, and cf. 315, 453; my own discussion of Milton is forthcoming in *One Flesh: Paradisal Marriage and Sexual Relations in the Age of Milton* (Oxford: Oxford Univ.).

21. Laurence Clarkson, in *A Collection of Ranter Writings from the 17th Century*, ed. Nigel Smith (London: Junction Books, 1983), pp. 180-82, 161-75 (and esp. p. 169 — "sin hath its conception only in the imagination"); *The Character of a Town Gallant* (London, 1675), p. 9; E. Stokes, *The Wiltshire Rant* (London, 1652), passim, describing Rev. Thomas Webbe; Abiezer Coppe, in *Ranter Writings*, ed. Smith, p. 86, and cf. p. 99, where "loosenesse and libertinisme" clearly have some sexual connotation. Tobias Crisp, in some ways an antecedent of the Ranters, declared that "to be called a libertine is the most glorious title under Heaven" (quoted in Christopher Hill, *The World Turned Upside Down: Radical Ideas during the English Revolution* [1972; rep. Harmondsworth: Penguin, 1975], p. 186).

22. *Rochester: The Critical Heritage*, ed. David Farley-Hills (London: Routledge, 1972), pp. 37, 46.

23. Pepys, *Diary*, ed. Robert Latham and William Matthews (Berkeley: Univ. of California, 1970-1983), entry for 1 July 1663; Anthony à Wood, *Athenae Oxoniensis*, ed. Philip Bliss (1813-20; rep. N.Y.: Burt Franklin, 1967), 4:731, and *Life and Times*, ed. Andrew Clark, Vol. 1 (Oxford: Clarendon, 1891), pp. 476-77; V. de Sola Pinto, *Sir Charles Sedley, 1639-1701: A*

Study in the Life and Literature of the Restoration (London: Constable, 1927), pp. 61-67, 307-09; John Harold Wilson, *Court Satires of the Restoration* (Columbus: Ohio State Univ., 1976), pp. 293-94.

24. *London Journal*, pp. 236, 117; when he is in church, conversely, Boswell makes "plans for having women" (p. 54, and cf. pp. 68, 227).

25. *Rochester: The Critical Heritage*, ed. Farley-Hills, p. 82; Rochester, "Satyr," line 219; Novak, "Margery," p. 18; Richardson, *Clarissa Harlowe*, Everyman edn., 2:23, 147. Harold Love defines the libertine as more an anarchist than a sensualist (*The Penguin Book of Restoration Verse* [Harmondsworth: Penguin, 1968], p. 27).

26. Clarkson, in *Ranter Writings*, ed. Smith, p. 180.

27. Rochester, "The Maim'd Debauchee," lines 33-36. Gangs of morally-outraged Puritan apprentices as well as drunken noblemen smashed the windows of brothels—another interesting convergence of the religious and the libertine.

28. Wilson, *Court Satires*, p. 293.

29. " The Mistress," lines 25-32.

30. Rochester, "The Maim'd Debauchee," line 36; "An Allusion to Horace," line 61 (referring to Sedley). Peter Porter refers to the lacy precision of "On Mistress Willis" in *Spirit of Wit*, ed. Treglown, p. 63.

31. "On Mistress Willis," lines 19-20; the attributon to Rochester is not certain. I have modernized the text of this citation to assist comprehension.

32. Cf. Rochester, "Song" ("Love a Woman! y'are an Ass!"), lines 5-8; Richard Ames, *A Satyrical Epistle* (London, 1691), p. 5.

33. Porter, "Mixed Feelings," passim; cf. Robert Hume, pp. 29-30 and passim. David Hume characterizes Charles II as "disengaged" in *The History of England*, ch. 60.

34. Steele, *Spectator*, 65; Dennis, *A Defence of Sir Fopling Flutter* (London, 1722); Henry Fielding, *Tom Jones*, 18.12. For an earlier (1690s) example of Dorimant functioning as a synonym for the dangers of the Town, see Novak, "Margery," p. 22; for letters to the *St. James's Journal* using the pseudonym Dorimant, ascribed to Pope on no solid evidence, see M. Ellwood Smith, "Four Hitherto Unidentified Letters by Alexander Pope," *PMLA* 29 (1914): 239-47.

35. Porter, "Mixed Feelings," p. 12; Foxon, pp. 57-58; William Rider, *An Historical and Critical Account of the Lives and Writings of the Living Authors of Great-Britain* (London, 1762), p. 16; *The Miscellaneous Works of the Right Hon. the Late Earls of Rochester and Roscommon* (London, 1707), fol. B6v.

36. Irvin Ehrenpreis, *Swift: The Man, His Works, and the Age*, Vol. 1 (London: Methuen, 1962), pp. 111, 120. Temple is evidently the model for Novak's characterization of the neo-Epicurean libertine, as suggested by the inclusion of a love of gardens among his refinements (*Congreve*, p. 43)

37. Ward uses "Modish Rake" and "Libertine" interchangeably, and constructs an elaborate argument for sexual promiscuity on the grounds that it would be "Ill Manners" towards God to refuse the blessing of Gen. 1:27 (*Libertine's Choice*, pp. 6, 15). Other moralists, too, assume that libertinism is enhanced rather than diminished by the increase in social refinement (e.g. James Wright, quoted in Novak, *Congreve*, p. 45), and Richardson is clearly concerned that "libertinism" and "a knowledge of the world," i.e. *le monde*, have converged (epigraph).

38. Richardson, *Pamela*, The Second Part, Everyman edn., pp. 253-54 and cf. 255-56; Philips, *The Distrest Mother* (London, 1712), epilogue by Eustace Budgell; cf. Vanbrugh, *The Provok'd Wife*, ed. Curt A. Zimansky (Lincoln: Univ. of Nebraska, 1969), pp. 62-63. Note that in Rochester's paradigmatic praise of Sedley his "Songs and Verses mannerly obscene" arouse desire *"without* forcing blushes" ("An Allusion to Horace," lines 61-63, italics mine).

39. Boswell and Cleland, quoted in Porter, "Mixed Feelings," pp. 18, 24 n. 32 (Porter recognizes in this note, though he does not give it weight in his main argument, that Boswell was "deeply troubled" by the conflict of sexuality and Christianity).

Between the Licit and the Illicit:
the Sexuality of the King

> More deadly than armaments, Licentiousness has engulfed us in
> vengeance for the conquered world. (Juvenal, *Satire* 6, 11. 292-93)

At eleven o'clock on 21 January 1793, in a silence heavy with fear mixed
with hatred, awe, and horror, the head of Louis XVI fell severed on the
Place de la Révolution—one of those complex historical events whose
implications and consequences are given deep and systematic study, but
all too often from a narrow perspective. The historical significance of the
king's execution has thus been long debated from countless points of
view, yet there may be factors still to be analysed, especially from our
newer vantage of historical psychology.[1]

I propose to focus on the metamorphoses undergone by the image of
the king in order to understand how his executioners and jailers could
dare lay hands on the Lord's anointed.[2] How, since the advent of Louis
XV, could public opinion have turned about so radically from reverential
adulation to bitter contempt? Most historians have attributed this to the
faults and incapacities of Louis XVI, Marie-Antoinette, and their entou-
rage, even to the diminished magnificence of his court and to his relatively modest style of life; yet we might better look back to the much
longer reign of Louis XV for the causes of the people's disenchantment
with the monarchy.

The increased burden of taxation along with the repeated military and
diplomatic setbacks of his reign were, no doubt, important factors,
though France had never been more prosperous. Neither the king nor his
ministers, moreover, showed much talent for political leadership. All of
this was not unprecedented, however, and had never before caused such a
profound loss of respect for the monarchy itself. We know that in matters
of public opinion realities count less than how they are perceived; and in
this case there seems to have been a catalytic factor at work which, in
modern terms, we might call the *sexuality* of the king.

Libido had rarely been lacking on the French throne. If anything, the
exercise of power seemed only to intensify its activity. Louis XV, to be
sure, long remained faithful to his wedded wife: Marie Leczinska was
pregnant eighty months during her twelve years of marriage, bearing ten
children. Even if, as several reports maintain, she may have been the one

to repulse him, he eventually tired of one so constantly in childbirth and began to cast his eyes on the many beauties who graced the court.

Most of the nobles close to the monarch actively sought privileges and pensions, their income being quite inadequate to support their ostentatious style of life; and the king was the supreme source of all favors. With the resigned consent, even the active complicity, of many a husband, the king could therefore promote an ongoing rivalry between the women who vied, by every device, to be noticed, chosen and finally "déclarée" by the master in exchange for substantial rewards. Louis thus succeeded in realizing the ultimate of fantasies, turning the court into a gigantic seraglio devoted to satisfying the lust of the prince and his favorites. So, at least, was it viewed by the impoverished and excluded nobility in the provinces.

Everyone knew the intrique, the court being an ingrown and transparent milieu of courtiers who knew one another all too well, and infested with spies to boot. The king, moreover, having to rely on numerous intermediaries, not all of whom could keep their mouths shut, could hardly hide his multiple affairs. The extent and duration of his often spectacular maneuvers were all the more widely remarked as news travelled further and more rapidly than in previous reigns. There were, of course, exceptions: one recalls the anecdote wherein Voltaire, then finding refuge at Senones, had to explain to the venerable Dom Calmet who Mme de Pompadour was. But from the time when Mme de Châteauroux, third of the Nesle sisters, became the king's favorite, no further doubt was possible: by his very manner and constant need for amorous change, Louis XV not only showed himself to be a true Bourbon but set out on a path that, in recent times, only Henry IV and Louis XIV had dared to pursue so openly. The former's assasination in the prime of life, however, had turned him into a martyr in the public's eye while the latter eventually renounced his youthful pursuit of pleasure and settled down to a devoted marriage.

Louis XV, however, never changed, thus posing a major problem. Given his admitted lack of interest in political affairs, he could only be considered as someone constantly obsessed with fresh erotic conquests and, later on, as a lascivious old man. This made it difficult to maintain the public image of one in whom the three roles described by Louis Marin as essential to a sovereign coexisted—the roles of human being (corporal), legal entity (political), and, finally, sacramental figure (symbolic).[3] In Louis, did not this humano-politico-religio trinity not risk destroying itself from within by the growing excess of one of its elements? By showing himself to be all too human, would the sovereign not lose his subject's respect for the ineffable mystique of his power?

By the eighteenth century, the kings of France were heirs to a long tradition of veneration earned by their right Christian ancestors from the time of Charlemagne. The tradition and consecration by the Church conferred on them an almost hallowed awe, even faith in their power to heal the sick by their touch. Such deeply rooted, popular myths die hard: yet the day was coming, especially in a climate of enlightenment, when the king's mantle of quasi-divinity would easily fall, and it was Louis XV himself, by his manner of life, who unloosed it.

At his accession upon coming of age in 1722, Louis was the object of ardent adulation, drawing over two thousand sufferers from all over Europe simply to obtain his healing touch. The hopes for renewal were all the more intense after the interregnum of a despised regent. So the disappointment was severe when Louis left the responsibilities of Government to Fleury and began to be seen as a "roi fainéant" (do-nothing king).[4] It wasn't until he was refused absolution, however, and was thus denied Communion at Easter in 1739 because of his affair with Mme de Mailly that his royal image was seriously tarnished in the popular mind. Then a series of further scandals, culminating in the long ascendancy of Mme de Pompadour, provoked increasingly violent attacks on the king's behavior and prestige, though much of the people's hatred was directed more at the mistresses than at the master.

Mme de Pompadour, for nearly twenty years Louis' companion— confidante and counselor as well as mistress—was frequently attacked in the most base and bitter terms, not only by the Jesuits and the pious, sustained by the Dauphin and Marie-Josèphe de Saxe, but by unseated ministers of state like Maurepas and d'Argenson, by officials exasperated with the favorite's capricious demands, and by aristocrats who balked at having to kowtow to a "petite bourgeoise" and carped incessantly about her reputedly base origins. Even Choiseul, though in debt to her for his own rise in status, spoke of her with cold indifference, even with disdain, in his *Memóires*. The masses hated her especially for the extravagances which raised their taxes and overstrained the national budget, and they blamed her for debasing the king. She whom they called a "whore's bastard" was accused of leading the king by the nose, of ruling in his place, of selling royal favors to satisfy her passion for building: "That low-born slut / Rules him with insolence, / And she's the one who hands out / Honors for sale" (*Chansonnier*, 7:136). In this climate of opinion it was easy to blame Mme de Pompadour for every political, economic, and military failure, especially since, as the center of a large coterie, she soon began to make and unmake ministers and generals and to meddle in the daily affairs of state. Thus the expulsion of the English Pretender, linked by many contemporaries with the collapse of French diplomacy, provoked pamphlets of unprecedented virulence:

> Oh, Louis, your subjects in abject defeat,
> Have respect for Edward, captive without a crown.
> E'en in shackles, he's a king; what are you
> >   upon your throne?
> At the feet of Pompadour, I've seen your
> >   scepter fall.   (*Chansonnier*, 7:141)

What, after all, could one expect from a sovereign forgetful of his promises, a monarch who neglected his wedded wife, publicly scorned the sacrament of marriage, and lived with a despicable woman, herself married to another?

It was, in fact, during the ascendancy of Mme de Pompadour that rumors arose concerning the king's sporadic impotence and his occasional amorous embarrassments. Earlier, at the birth of the Duc d' Anjou, 5 August 1730, the "chansonniers" (popular political and social satirists) had glorified, in their jocular way, such a prolific king:

> Vertubleu! What a man, what a man, what a man!
> Vertubleu! What a man is our good king!
> Father of five children,
> At twenty years of age!   (*Chansonnier*, 5:219)

The populace found in this a certain Gallic verve which looked upon virility and fecundity as the mark of the real man. After 1745, however, the tactless indiscretions of his favorite let the public know that the "man" was not infallible

> Adorable Etiole,
> I'd go from pole to pole
> To admire your charms;
> But it would be, I swear
> (The whole world's whispering it)
> To make love, believe me,
> Better than does the king;
> What an insult! what a gibe!
> Could one fizzle out for you?   (*Chansonnier*, 7:53)

Choiseul, it is said, tried to reduce the influence of the dangerous Mme d'Esparbès by lying to the king that she had indiscretely revealed lapses in his sexual potency. From then on, Louis, without passing for an outright impotent like Maurepas, was considered sick, a pervert needing recourse to dangerous expedients and strange refinements to attain his pleasure. One is reminded of the episode in Mme du Hausset's *Mémoires* in which the Duchess of Brancas throws into the fire the aphrodisiacs used by Mme de Pompadour to satisfy her royal lover. By other such indiscretions we know the intimate behavior of Louis with some of his more ephemeral conquests. Dufort de Cheverny reports in his *Mémoires*, for instance, that a certain Mme de P ____ fell sincerely in love with the king. She wrote to him and obtained a rendez-vous at the palace. No sooner was she introduced into the royal bedchamber than Louis appeared and, without a word, began to take peculiar liberties with her. Then, telling her to undress, he suddenly left to perform the ceremony of his public "coucher." On his return, he was unable to satisfy her and sent her packing half naked at three in the morning, angry and humiliated.[5] Such boorish behavior could justify harsh judgment of the sovereign. One should, however, take into account that, thanks to his rank and reputation, he'd grown accustomed to making easy conquests even if, at times, he paid dearly for them. So, as Mme du Hausset remarked, "He was firmly persuaded that all women were ready to cede to his every whim. He thus simply assumed that they were in love with him."[6] Such misadventures were, nevertheless, far from rare and were food for gossip at the court. Dufort de Cheverny, for one, reports that the pretty Marquise de

Séran obtained 100,000 écus and a house in exchange for her favors, "though it was affirmed that by a quirk of fate the king earned his money very badly" (*Mémoires*, 1:260). The youthful "superman" was on his way to becoming something less than a man.

It was at this period, above all, that the tales of the king's debauches took on almost mythic proportions. Since Mme de Pompadour no longer shared the royal bed after the death of her daughter, Alexandrine-Jeanne, in 1754, the sovereign fell back on the available bourgeoises and aristocrats of the court, supplemented by the very young girls procured, for the most part, by his valet-intermediary, Lebel.

Louis arranged two small rooms near the palace chapel where, under the cloak of anonymity, he held what today would hardly be called debauches. It was also about this time (1755) that, through a bailiff of the Châtelet, he acquired the "Parc-aux-Cerfs" (Deer Park) which he regularly frequented in the disguise of a nameless Polish nobleman, a close relative of the queen. The existence of this house, soon known to the whole court, incited the most fantastic rumors. In his *Fastes de Louis XV*, Bouffonidor calculated as follows: the whole layout included the beaters of the hunt, the intermediaries, the "sultanes" themselves, their domestics, personal care, clothing, jewelry, etc., even money to raise their bastards, adding up, according to his estimate, to at least a million for each of the favored. At the rate Bouffonidor supposed—two new candidates a week or a thousand in ten years—the total expenditures for the Parc-aux-Cerfs would have come to a billion, a sum which any present-day historian familiar with the modest furnishings of the rue Saint-Médéric would find laughable. But it is not the realities which count since his contemporaries were convinced that the king was despoiling the treasury for his orgies.

The monarch's sexuality thus became an unavoidable element in French political thinking; and it is there, no doubt, that one must look for the origin of the people's growing scepticism of all the attempts at fiscal reform and budgetary economies which marked the last years of the *ancien régime*. The king's known expenditures, those the people suspected, and especially those they imagined opened breaches no amount of taxes could hope to repair.

Mme de Pompadour's death in 1764 left a place to be filled in the king's intimate circle. Everyone knew that he needed a trusted mistress in whose company he could shed his mask. Better than any other example, the frantic competition thus provoked gives a clear picture of what the morals and the morale of the court had come to. Virtually every woman entered the lists to win the coveted title, and countless were the husbands who pressed their wives to throw themselves at the king in hopes of substantial advantages. These rivalries only added to the conflicts already raging between the various cliques striving for political power, and we know how the triumph of a hitherto unknown contributed to the downfall of Choiseul and his supporters.

The rise to favor of Jeanne Bécu de Vaubernier, Countess Du Barry, unleashed a new torrent of insults and accusations justified, in contemporary eyes, by her sordid origin (illegitimate daughter of a defrocked monk) and reputed past (low-grade prostitution). The king, nevertheless, succeeded in "presenting" Mme Du Barry officially to the court, lodged her close to himself, covered her with jewelry, built her the château of Louveciennes, thus confirming and further aggravating the behavior which, step-by-step, transformed the world's most splendid monarch into a senile old man vainly groping after trivial pleasures:

> See the first among all kings
> In the skirts of such a wench,
> As once a single silver piece
> Your mistress could have made,
> With endless lewd devices trying
> To activate his antique workings.
> (*Chansonnier*, 8:205-06)

> [Regardez le doyen des rois
> Aux genoux d'une drôlesse,
> Dont jadis un écu tournois
> Eût fait votre maîtresse,
> Faire auprès d'elle cent efforts
> D'une façon lubrique,
> Pour faire mouvoir les ressorts
> De sa machine antique.]

As for Louis, he was well satisfied with his "queen of the bed." He vaunted the beauty of her breasts and described to his friends the new amorous techniques she was teaching him. Contemporary reminiscences clearly depict the prevailing climate of a waning reign: the administration carried on of its own momentum, the ministers dealt with day-to-day affairs, while the king scarcely involved himself in political matters. Everyone was waiting for the inevitable crisis which loomed ever closer. And all the while the festival and "petits soupers" proliferated at Versailles. Those courtiers who had accepted the new mistress continued to dance on the volcano, and the Du Barry woman, surrounded by her favorites, the Duc de Richelieu, Terray, Maupéou, and d'Aiguillon, gradually extended her power over men and events:

> Who'd imagine that a clique,
> In the teeth of all critique,
> Could turn a wanton, public whore
> Into a brand new potentate?
> Who'd ever think that, without shame,
> Louis would give up the helm
> To such a bitch, and let
> Founder the imperiled ship of State?
> (*Chansonnier*, 8:252-53)

For sometime, now, the king no longer ventured into Paris where, as police reports warned him, he'd not be safe. The popular enthusiasm at his accession in 1723 was now but a distant memory, and a bitter one, too, for those who had lived through it in their youth. After centuries of steady expansion, the France of Louis XV had suffered defeats and the ravages of religious conflicts. She had lost extensive territories and had ceded supreme power in Europe to the English. The throne was up for auction. The prelates of the Church kept mum while waiting for the end. The aging king's twilight grew even dimmer; and, at his death, a host of epitaphs stressed the one trait which, to his contemporaries, summed up his paltry personality:

> His shameful aims at last achieved,
> Louis closed his long career.
> Wail, you knaves; weep, you tarts;
> You've lost your royal father. (*Chansonnier*, 8:320)

Louis was not, to be sure, the only eighteenth-century Frenchman to have kept mistresses or to have lived in sin. But he was the king, and in that capacity faced obligations he was incapable of fulfilling. To the monarch he gave the image of an incurable libertine, and he left the monarchy a vacuum, a defenseless space to be conquered. The decline had begun, and nothing could now arrest it.

✳

All theoretical reflection on the licit and the illicit in matters of sex under the *ancien régime* is beset with difficulties. The distinction between what is permissible and what is forbidden—permitted by whom? why forbidden?—assumes the existence of a frontier; but analysis of the texts soon reveals a fluctuating boundary, unclear, permeable, changing with circumstances and with each individual case. The legal and the customary, the need, the desire, the categorical imperative, and, among theologians, the consideration allowed to human frailty, all play their part. That dividing line is to the sexual what the present is to the past and future: without dimensions, it is the meeting point of two realms, that imaginary point at which quantities change their sign; what is permitted on one side, what is forbidden on the other.

Is there, in fact, a legitimate use of the body or, more precisely, of the genitals? The answer seems to be positive, namely the "increase and multiply" of the bible. But in reality nothing is that simple. If countries of the Protestant persuasion hastened to discard the exaltation of virginity, it was not so among the Catholics. There were plenty of good souls in eighteenth-century France to glorify purity, chastity, and an ascetic life devoted to God; but it is generally understood that such a way of life is the province of exceptional beings. If, for the great majority, the licit practice of sex is allowed only in marriage and for procreation—a practice not only *allowed* but *ordered* (in both meanings of the term) by the word of God— then all transgressions of the laws promulgated by Church and State and applied by the courts should be subject to punishments accepted by society as a whole. Yet we know that nothing of the sort prevailed. The immorality indulged in by many nobles and rich bourgeois, which usually entailed living apart from their wives, is evidenced by the symmetrical layout of so many aristocratic residences. This, as well as the semiofficial prostitution, tolerated and even regulated by the police, shows that society allowed its members a certain license, as is also evidenced by the generally accepted practice of taking care of foundlings, most of whom were born out of wedlock.[7]

True, it was the custom for Lentan voices to be raised against the sins of the flesh and the moral laxity of the times, but their echoes did not linger long and who really paid them much attention anyway? Tradition, moreover, tended to draw the line much less strictly for sovereigns and for the highly placed in general than for the ordinary run of morals. Nor can this be attributed simply to the complacent attitude of courtly writers. Bouffonidor, for instance, who was hostile towards the king, wrote in his *Fastes de Louis XV*, "If a prince would draw the evil of decency over the pleasures which help him to carry the crushing burden of government, he'd deserve the people's indulgence and the silence of those around him."[8] In the same vein, Mme du Hausset in her *Mémoirs* quotes from a letter whose author, identified only as a counselor of parlement, observes that, "It's right for the master to have a friend and confidante like all of us, such as we are."[9] Under the euphemistic language the same evidence appears: the king and those important personages who are placed above the common condition have a right to a special morality. The author of the *Fastes de Louis XV* gives this a quasi-physiological explanation, which he applies to Choiseul, whose extramarital adventures and appetite for women were well known:

> the Duke de Choiseul has again been reproached for an excessive love of pleasure. Yet only mediocre people can bear constant work without relieving it with those dissipations which renew one's strength and organic functioning. So, granted the need for such recreations, what matter if one chooses women, gardening, good food, or the fine arts, or even combine them all, so long as one is physically up to it? (Bouffonidor, *Fastes*, 1:45)

If, then, debauchery was accepted in the 1780s as a necessity of State, one must still ask why Louis XV failed to benefit ten years earlier from the indulgence which, by what we have already observed, seemed accorded to him. We can here only venture answers whose confirmation would require long and profound research concurrently into private correspondence, recollections of contemporary witnesses, and police reports which informed those in power, probably quite accurately, of the real feelings of the public. That which transpires from such sources is that the king's transgressions were both qualitative and quantitive. One lost count, according to the usually anonymous satirists, of the number of victims offered up to the sovereign's lust, of the young girls wrenched from parents' arms to be thrown to the maniac and perverted desires of the master of Versailles—legends historians have long laid to rest. It would doubtless have been enough for the king to have limited his choice of mistresses to the ladies of the court for public opinion to grant him the same toleration as was accorded to so many other monarchs. What appeared intolerable was the absolute scandal denounced by Bouffonidor along with a host of other pamphleteers:

> What a spectacle it is to see the king mired in indolence and vice, wasting the treasure of the State to load a vile prostitute with all the trappings of a

queen, multiplying taxes to satisfy his mad fantasies, and letting his subjects dance to the whims of a nitwit! What a sight to see a hairdresser's wench become the object of the monarch's loving and fawning attentions, to see him surrender the most precious objects for her caresses! What a spectacle to see a chancellor of France having to address an upstart courtesan as "cousin"—one raised by sheer chance to the highest possible station yet whose youthful favors had been lavished on every coachman and groom of the capital. (Bouffonidor, *Fastes*, 1:99-100)

A prostitute transformed into a queen, coachmen and grooms the equals of the king, a monarch wallowing in filth and slime, here the world's hierarchical order is already turned upside down. The outrage of the pamphleteers must not make us forget that around 1770-80 such developments seemed quite plausible, even commonplace. It was Edmund Burke who drew the lesson from this line of thinking when he described, much later, those October days when "the baker, his wife, and their little apprentice" were dragged from Versailles to Paris. In such circumstances, he concluded, "a king is but a man; a queen is but a woman; a woman is but an animal, and an animal not of the highest order."[10]

By thus letting show the man under the monarch's robe, and by acting this role so fully, Louis XV, an enigmatic Janus to his subjects, did not exactly prepare the Revolution, but he sapped the foundations of the monarchy, and undermined them lastingly. He rendered fragile that imposing statue fashioned over centuries by the centralization of power. The king's sex, that fabulous phallus, was one of the major instruments of *political* subversion in France towards the end of the *ancien régime*.

It still remains to examine the question of public opinion to which I have often referred. Short of being able to pursue the exhaustive research just mentioned, I have relied on an intentionally limited corpus: the recollections of several contemporaries like Dufort de Cheverny, Choiseul, Mme du Hausset, and Buffonidor, and on the popular songs included in the Clairambault-Maurepas collection. These sources are, to be sure, tainted by an evident aristocratic bias or even, in the case of Choiseul, with the rancor of a cashiered retainer; for not all composers of satirical ditties were of humble extraction. Their versification, at least, shows a certain literary formation. Nonetheless, the narrow sociological base of our sources need not render our conclusions unduly misrepresentative since we know that the peasantry, by far the largest part of the population, had, with rare exceptions, no access to culture or even to literacy, and thus left no enduring record of their opinions of the sovereign.[11] In rural communities the king was probably a mysterious personage. His lavish life, his intimate circle, his mistresses, took on a quasi-mythical aura, distantly perceived, distorted or clouded by the vagaries of oral transmission. In such a case, and if one accepts that the catalogues of grievances of 1789 were themselves produced by local notables, it must be admitted that the ony trustworthy documents are those referred to here. They even acquire a certain "objectivity" in so far as, despite a variety of nuance, they agree on the essentials, and all pronounce the same severe condemnations. It is clear, however, that their very existence leads us to inquire still further into the importance and role of the elites in the rising tide of discontent, in the provocation and development of the revolutionary process. But that is another story.

Translated by
Michael Murray

Jean-Pierre Guicciardi
Université Paris VII

NOTES

1. See Jean-Marie Goulemot, "De la Polémique sur la Révolution et les Lumières et des Dix-huitièmistes," *Dix-huitième siècle* 6 (1974): 235-42. As early as 1924 Marc Bloch explored the role of the irrational and the vast differences in the state of psychological understanding between the Middle Ages and the end of the *ancien régime*: *Les Rois Thaumaturges* (rep. Paris: Gallimard, 1984).

2. François Furet and Denis Richet have argued that "The Revolution was not caused only by economic and social conditions, but also by anecdotes, scandals, and accidents" (*La Révolution française* [Paris: Fayard, 1973], p. 45).

3. See *Le Portrait du roi* (Paris: Editions de Minuit, 1981).

4. Ernest, Raunié, *Chansonnier historique*, 10 vols. (Paris: A. Quantin, 1879-82), 6:110.

5. Dufort de Cheverny, *Mémoires*, 2 vols. (Paris: Plon-Nourrit, 1886), 1:261-63.

6. See the author's edn. of the *Mémoires* of Mme du Hausset (Paris: Mercure de France, 1985).

7. In 1566 the ordinance of Moulins obligated parishes to take care of their own illegitimate foundlings, and the royal edict of 1670 created the Hôpital de la Couche for their care. Abandoning children was not discouraged, and no questions were asked of the parents.

8. *Fastes de Louis XV . . .*, attr. to Bouffonidor, 2 vols. (Ville-franche, Veuve Liberté, 1782), 1:34-35. "Bouffonidor" is probably a pseudonym.

9. See note 6.

10. *Reflections on the Revolution in France* (London: J. Dodsley, 1790), p. 114.

11. On the question of the witness of the peasantry, see Jean-Marie Goulemot's introduction to his edn. of the *Mémoires* of V. Jamerey-Duval (Paris: Sycomore, 1981).

The Sublimations of a Fetishist: Restif de la Bretonne (1734–1806)

By the last third of the eighteenth century in France, the concept of *libertinage* had evolved from its earlier association with free thought to a much more specifically sexual radicalism. In a sense, this change reflected the general rise of individualism and self-awareness, but its effects were not uniformly positive. Peter Nagy has shown that while the new libertinism freed some, it enslaved others: it dehumanized sexual relationships and removed from the desiring subject all need to show genuine feeling toward the object of desire.[1] Paradoxically, at a time when Rousseauistic sensibility was revaluing emotion, the libertine countercurrent redefined the self in narrower physical and egocentric terms. Celebrated rakes such as the Comte de Richelieu and the Prince de Conti gave a public lead; ignoring the responsibilities traditionally associated with their rank, they rode roughshod over social and moral conventions. The *philosophes* warned against unbridled self-interest but, like Diderot, found it difficult to draw a line between legitimate self-expression and the duties of all men to their neighbors. The liberty semantically implicit in libertinism, however, proved to be an increasingly attractive proposition. As the *ancien régime* drew to a close, a preoccupation with explicit eroticism emerged as a cipher for a wider, conscious subversiveness. Thus may the French Revolution be said to have been sexual long before it became openly political.

The evolution of the new eroticism is a large subject that exceeds the limits of this essay,[2] but the parameters of what may be described as systematic sexuality would seem to lie at one end with Casanova's personal rejection of taboos (sexual freedom as a proper part of the total self) and, at the other extreme, with the Marquis de Sade's equation of sex and power. In historical terms, the life of Restif de la Bretonne reflects the swing from mild revolt to erotic dictatorship. Until the 1780s, he remained close enough to philosophical optimism to argue that since nature had made him, nature was answerable for his excesses. From around 1785, however, his moderation steadily degenerated into sexual totalitarianism. While Sade's obsessions were heavy with philosophical implications of a general nature, Restif's fantasies were hermetic, enclosed, and eternally personal. He moved away from the real world into a private universe; for this reason, he is much less interesting as an historical phenomenon than as a "case." He is most profitably viewed as he viewed himself: as an outsider who responded less to external stimuli than to the bidding of his unstable psyche. Of course, no man stands outside history. Yet the most rewarding approach to Restif continues to be one that examines the relationship between his writing and his life,[3] especially as regards his sexuality.

Few readers have failed to be struck by Restif's obsessive concern with his sexuality. In 1912, Dr. P.-J.-L. Charpentier suggested tentatively that Restif "was mentally unstable, his condition being characterized by hypomania, an underlying paranoia, mythomania (with daughter fixation), erotomania and sexual perversions."[4] If this diagnosis now seems overstated, Restif's self-analysis, while more revealing, is no more reliable. In *Monsieur Nicolas* (1794–97), Restif wrote that he had been conceived in a "warm embrace" and explained that his temperament was "consequently formed of three parts water for each part of the other elements."[5] His heart was "constituted in such a manner that I had a compelling need for the love or at least the friendship of a woman . . . ; without women, I was nothing, a creature lacking in vigor, energy, dynamism, in short, a creature without soul" (3:78–79). He claimed that his life was full of "erotic incident" (4:598) and to prove this point drew up *Mon Kalendrier* (1789) in *Monsieur Nicolas* (4:507–5:101), which he filled with the names of women who had found him irresistible. "Elise made me a happy man," he wrote with fine disdain, "and I made her a mother: the slate is clean" (4:619). Unforewarned, the reader may be forgiven for concluding that Restif was an energetic womanizer. In reality, he approached the opposite sex with diffidence and was unable to sustain satisfactory relationships with women. He remained sexually active until the time of his near-fatal illness ("love and all that goes with it have been quite beyond me since 1795"),[6] but his unpublished *Journal* reveals that his loves were bought in the Palais Royal or the brothels of Paris.[7] Occasionally he could be objective about himself: "I did what engravers do when they draw an unfinished building. I set things out as I would have liked them to be."[8] Women were necessary to him, he said, "if not in reality then at least in prospect. . . . If I had my way, I would see women only in my dreams and that would be enough: but we cannot choose what dreams we have."[9] Yet as author he was able to supply himself with waking dreams, which he did. His sexual exploits are the result of his fathomless capacity for fantasy.

Not all of his wishful thinking was negative, however, for some women figured in nobler dreams. His mother is always cast as the perfection of womanhood, just as Mme Fournier, the wife of his first employer at Auxerre, survives as the virtuous Mme Parangon. To the end of his life he idealized Jeannette Rousseau, his first love, to whom he had never spoken, and turned Mme Filon, a shopkeeper with whom he had never exchanged a word, into the Filette of his dreams. His illusions fitted too snugly to be put at risk by contact with reality, but the persistence of his idealism reveals less of his fear of women than of the distorting power of his imagination. With another part of himself he exploited women as sexual objects, but even the women who prompted his unhealthy dreams were inadequate. With time, Restif displaced reality by redesigning the female body.

The Restif woman is clearly visible in the engravings that began appearing in his books in 1777.[10] Under his supervision, the artist Binet created what Restif called in *Monsieur Nicolas*, "la femme féïque," a word coined to describe a tiny-waisted, globular-breasted, and long-legged sylph whose feet are smaller than her hands, a point on which Restif insisted. His interest in the female foot predated "la femme féïque" and provides the best example of his distortions, which are quite clearly externalizations of inner compulsions. In *Le Pied de Fanchette* (1769), he not only exploited this taste in fictional terms but added a learned appendix on the subject. But it was not merely the foot that interested him. Whereas his physical descriptions of women tend to be perfunctory ("pretty little face," "graceful arms," etc.), he lingered over their shoes. *Mon Kalendrier* is particularly rich in such details. It was, he explained in *Monsieur Nicolas*, Agathe Tilhien, "a pretty peasant girl from Sacy, dark-haired and trim, with shoes invariably fastened by a piece of blue ribbon, who gave me my first notion of what a pretty foot was like. I liked seeing hers, and it would have given me pleasure to handle and kiss her shoes; whereas I felt nothing but loathing for the shoes worn by men and old women" (4:510). He preferred a "pretty foot" in green or pink shoes. The heel had to be high—one of his objections to the French Revolution was the disappearance of fashion shoes and "the abomination of low heels"— and the shoe had to be new and clean. It was his habit to follow women who wore pretty shoes, though he rarely spoke to them. He kept an eye on cobblers' shops and ordered copies of shoes he had seen, sometimes buying a pair that pleased his imagination, and—in imagination—sometimes engineering situations in which he was invited to fit the pretty foot into the pretty shoe. His interest was much more than a literary theme: it was a firmly rooted fetish. His daily diaries reveal even more clearly than his stories that he was a shoe voyeur, a shoe stealer, and a shoe collector. Restif used shoes in his oranistic rites as a patent sexual stimulant. For instance, the 854th *Inscripcion* reads: "As I left, I spied the pretty Maris girl, at a quarter past one, in the rue Saint-André, wearing black shoes and a white dress; voluptuous legs; next, the Lambert woman; then the dark girl from the rue des Noyers; then a pretty foot in the rue Saint-Hyacinthe; then the Richer woman, bis emiss[io]."[11] Restif went on to develop a theory that justified his weakness, "parvum pes, barathrum grande," by which he meant that a small foot was an indication of sexual openness.

Although it is possible to detect elements of masochism in Restif's fetishism, it was fairly harmless. His attraction to incest, however, exhibited in his first novel,[12] was to spill over from fiction into real life. During the 1780s, incest appears with increasing regularity in Restif's stories and novels and is very marked in *L'Année des dames* (1791–94).[13] No accident, this development coincided with the beginnings of his sexual relations with his elder daughter, Agnès. After separating from his wife in 1784, Restif lived with his two daughters in a state of some tension. Agnès had married and left the sadistic Augé, but now, except for long periods that she spent in the country, was the object of her father's sexual attentions. Between April 1788 and early 1791, Restif's *Journal* carries notations that, though disguised by Latin and anagrams, are quite unambiguous: "Senga pleno cno à 4 h. et demie, habillée, chaussée, dans son alcôve," "Senga m'a refusé," "benè futua Senga," and so on. When Agnès was away, Restif fell back on fetishistic rites (12 April 1789: "Déchgé dev. Mar[ion] en voy. les soul. de Senga; boit orangeade") and from early 1791, her shoes replaced her person. Many entries from the *Journal*—"souls d'A 6 livres," "Emis. sem. in calc. Sengae," "Agn. 2 pes [of shoes] 14 livres,"—testify to Restif's union of fetishism and incest.[14]

After Agnès' final departure, Restif found his younger daughter, Marion, no less sexually arousing, although considerably less accommodating. As opportunities for incest disappeared, Restif found compensation in a paternity fixation of astounding proportions. His fiction had often paid attention to the relationship between father and daughter, as in *Adèle de Comm**, ou, Lettres d'une fille à son père* (1772), and although the closeness of brother and sister is stressed in both *Le Paysan perverti* (1776) and *La Paysanne pervertie* (1784), Restif felt easiest when cutting a paternal dash. In *La Dernière avanture* (1783), it is not mere sentiment that explains his fondness for the treacherous Sara's calling him "papa" and why he in turn called her "ma fille." In the collections of stories that began with the forty-two-volume work *Les Contemporaines* (1780–85), he returned many times to sexually stimulating situations involving fathers and daughters, such as the brothel client who discovers that the girl for whom he has paid is his lost child. Many of these tales are semi-autobiographical accounts of old affairs that result frequently in the birth of a daughter (and rarely a son); at a rough count, Restif claims to have fathered in this way around 250 female offspring. This is, of course, highly suspect; although most of his early fiction, such as the first "époques" of *Monsieur Nicolas*, are reasonably balanced, from the late 1780s the trickle becomes a flood, and our suspicions become certainties. Approximately three-fourths of the women remembered in *Mon Kalendrier* bear him daughters. *La Drame de la vie* (1793), yet another autobiography presented as a vast theatrical saga, dwells on his affairs and his paternities. It is as though Restif were no longer in charge of his imagination.

What is new in the books written at this time, is his insistence that many of the women he had loved in his recent past were daughters of women he had loved in his youth, so that his loves acquired a comforting continuity in time. To some extent, his "daughters" were doubtless an unconscious expiation of his guilt feelings, but it is obvious that he also pursued them quite consciously. Thus in *Le Palais royal* (1790), he elaborated a theory of "resemblances" which flattered his obsession: if a face, a foot, or a tone of voice reminded him of a woman he had once loved, he concluded immediately that here was the daughter of that old love. With time, the process diversified. Rose Bourgeois, whom Restif had loved in the 1760s, now turns out to have been the daughter of a child sired by his own father; Rose had therefore been his own half-sister and a most satisfactory union of paternity fixation and incest. Virginie, the heroine of *Le Quadra-génaire* (1777), is now revealed as the daughter of Restif and Mme Lallemand, and the Sara of *La Dernière avanture* proves to have been his own daughter after all. As time passed, the flimsy line between reality and imagination disappeared completely. In 1797 he calmly informed an admirer, Mme Fontaine, that Mme Filon the shopkeeper had been his own child: "Filette was a daughter of Louise and had her grace and beauty."[15]

It should not be thought, however, that Restif foundered on pleasantly dreamy fantasies. His paternity fetish was intimately linked to his sexual performance. Rousseau bundled his bastards off to the Foundling Hospital; Restif went looking for his in the Palais Royal. While a few of the "daughters" we meet are respectable married women, most are represented as having become whores from necessity. In *Monsieur Nicolas,* he explains that their mothers had been poor and "the majority ensured that their children repaid the costs of their upbringing! Oh yes, I regret it! but I could not prevent it, for I had no money and, besides, would not have recognized them if I'd met them" (4:250). In a passage quite remarkable for its egocentricity, Restif lingers over the terrible acts they had been required to perform by vicious men before adding that he was not so depraved that he had not sought them out on the streets of paris:

> I was obliged to mingle assiduously in their company if I was to tell which were my children by the thermometer of my heart. For without it, recognizing them would not have been possible. . . . So when I came across a beautiful girl who did not make me feel sick with her flat heels but who, on the contrary, struck me as childlike and pleasing, I would examine her features closely and soon discover the talisman in them. (4:250–51)

Clearly, every whore tasteful enough to wear pretty shoes was a potential daughter, though what happened next with Adèle, Bouton de Rose, and others mentioned in the *Journal* could be described as a family reunion only in the Restivian sense. Foot fetishism, paternity fixation ("childlike"), and the impulse to incest meet here in a magical ("talisman") and instinctive ("the thermometer of my heart") unison.

Restif's fetishes outlasted his unsatisfactory dealings with Agnès because the perfect form of his imagination was much more satisfying than the reality of its expression. He derived increasing pleasure from recreating his sexual practices in the controlled environment of his writing. His obsessions loom larger in his books as time passed. They are noticeable even in *Les Nuits de Paris* (1788–94), in which the shoe follower, while describing the September Massacres, lingers over four episodes of incestuous rape. In *L'Année des dames,* a twelve-volume collection of tales, his fascination with unusual sexual arrangements is even more clearly marked. In several stories such as numbers 93 and 203, a young woman marries an hermaphrodite, while in number 53 another marries her brother-in-law. But it is incest that dominates his mood, though a number of tales also involve a degree of sadism: number 114 shows Geneviève (an evocation of one of Restif's sisters) cruelly abused, and in number 578 a group of Indians are tortured by white settlers. Incest, which he occasionally defends perfunctorily but normally retails with obsessive satisfaction, moves from strength to strength in the books that followed, nowhere more so than in *L'Anti-Justine* (1798).[17]

Restif claims to have written *L'Anti-Justine* as a counterblast to the pernicious Sade, whom he called "scoundrel," "execrable author," "vivisectionist." The work was to have been in seven or eight parts, but though only two were printed, what has survived of Restif's grotesque scenario is enough to reveal how far he had retreated into his private fantasy world. The work is a succession of graphic descriptions of both the sexual exploits of Cupidonnet/Restif with his mother, his sisters, and his daughters and of their encounters with priapic refugees from Restif's other books. In attempting to out-Sade Sade, he claims a useful purpose: to reinstate sensuality within marriage. In reality, he simply exploits a convenient framework for expressing a number of fantasies ranging from sadism and incest to petty spite. Clearly, he derived immediate pleasure from inventing scenes in which he is both actor and observer and which do nothing to justify his claim that "sweet sensuality" is preferable to mere genital contact. He does insist, however, that "if incest figures here, it is simply intended to counterbalance the corrupt tastes of the Libertines and the appalling cruelties which Sade employs to excite them" (1:4). Although his moral pretentions are absurd in this context, Restif had long since been prepared to defend incest on social and scientific grounds. In *Le Nouvel Abeilard* (1779), for example, he had argued that the incest taboo had originated under historical circumstances that no longer applied.[18] Pressured by his fantasies, he was now prepared to go much further. In a stray page from the unpublished and now lost *L'Enclos et les oiseaux*,[19] he made incest a desirable social goal:

> Our children grow around our table, like olive saplings: it is a means of promoting peace and concord to marry our children to each other. . . . To require all men to behave mechanically and follow the same path is the way of a clever despot. When the French Republic was established, I would have wished its instigators had turned it into mankind's finest achievement by leaving men quite free to marry their mothers, their sisters, and their daughters (provided, of course, that the latter were wholly and freely consenting).[20]

His apology for incest is intellectually weak, however; his imagination was too strong. He lived it first with Agnès in real life and then through his books, where it was experienced more intensely. *L'Anti-Justine* shows us an hallucinatory world that is both a travesty and a perversion of human reality. In his last books, *Les Posthumes* (1802) and *L'Enclos et les oiseaux*, the distortions become the new reality, the starting point for a new application of the social and political principles central to his reforming purpose. In Restif's last fiction, politics and sexuality come together in a combination that provided the answers to his quest.

Les Posthumes, begun in 1787, is an immense, rambling novel dominated by the wizard Multipliandre, who is omnipotent, immortal, and clearly a

Restivian doppelgänger. His creator uses him to pay off old scores—he imposes Restif's political solutions on the whole of Europe—and turns him into the voyeur-agent of cerebral, erotic acts of a clearly unhealthy nature. When his work on Earth is finished, he journeys to the planets, much as Victorin had explored the southern archipelago in *La Découverte australe* (1781). Multipliandre creates perfect societies from chaos and chooses their leaders for the strangest reasons. In one such state, young Jacobé comes into his own:

> It was the Cobbler's craft which made him great in the land. . . . He made shoes and anyone who wanted to be shod had to beg with due humility. . . . In his fitting room, he gave audiences with nothing less than the greatest aloofness and solemnity. . . . The Governor gave his eldest daughter to Jacobé, who had asked for her hand, in exchange for a pair of hobnailed boots.[21]

When Multipliandre has brought cobbler-kings and wisdom to the universe there would seem little more to do. But this is to ignore the obsessive tenacity of his creator, who now embarks on the "histoire future du duc Multipliandre." The duke marries twelve shepherdesses, who give him many children; all grow up in a community based on the "general confraternity" recommended in Restif's most fully considered social statement, *L'Andrographe* (1782). By the time he is thirty-six, Multipliandre has 232 children. When he is one thousand years old, he is the master of a vast empire populated almost exclusively by his descendants. When he reaches the age of three thousand, the social structures, values, and inhabitants of the new world are literal images of its ruler. Multipliandre/Restif has become God.

Les Posthumes marks the convergence of Restif's sexual aberrations. The authoritarianism (essentially a sadistic impulse) of his early schemes for social reform here approaches megalomania. When his narrator aims "a little bomb weighing between three and six pounds" at Frederick-William, who asks in terror who it is that deals with him thus, the answer "Justice" comes out of a cloud. "Someone is bound to protest," remarks the narrator, "that this tone is unsuitable, that it is despotic. I was a slave for many years and there is no one more despotic than an unfettered slave" (2:40). It is as though Restif, his judgment weakened by age and infirmity, consciously shook off his last restraints and now felt free to do to the world what he had done in his books to Sara, Virginie, and the rest. The latent autocratic stance of his earlier utopias emerges as a new literal political paternalism.

Even this was not his last word. His imagination continued to be haunted by the figure of the *enclos*, an enclave in which he felt safe and in which his sexuality could be expressed freely. The concept was firmly rooted in his psyche; he tells us in *Monsieur Nicolas* that he had written a poem in 1749, in which as a reward for services to the state he was installed in a walled enclosure near Sacy in the company of twelve beauties of his choosing (1:304). The poem was entitled "Mes douze travaux" and the nature of his labors is clear. He had exploited this literary theme on many occasions. In his first novel, *La Famille vertueuse*, a number of bloods build an *enclos* to which they transport their kidnapped mistresses (3:249–58). The utopian "Bourg d'Oudun" described in *Le Paysan perverti*, like the cooperative of the tenth "Contemporaine" or even the "Parthénions" that house his reformed prostitutes, are so many retreats and withdrawals. By the late 1780s, however, the *enclos* had acquired even more obvious sexual overtones. In *Le Palais royal*, a progressive aristocrat marries thirteen wives to illustrate not merely the case for polygamy but also the delights of sequestered sexual gratification.[22] In the same way, the "curé patriote" (who is a "curé multiplicateur" and an anticipation of Multipliandre) endows a number of convents occupied by women whom he fertilizes indefatigably in the cause of population (3:159–66). There are many subsequent variations on this theme, prominent among which are his accounts of the colonial settlements so rich in sexual possibilities.

The *enclos*, which may be seen as the womb, was not Restif's only obsession. In 1798, prompted by Cazotte, who had asked him what he would do if he could relive his life, Restif conceived the idea of the *re-vie*. He lost interest in his "real" life, of which he had written so compulsively, and set out to rewrite his past as it should have been. The result was the now lost *L'Enclos et les oiseaux*, which he planned in six or eight volumes. He had given a taste of his relived lives in *Les Posthumes*, which, supplemented by the surviving odd pages of *L'Enclos et les oiseau*, provides a clear idea of his intentions. Thus the second *re-vie* in *Les Posthumes* shows the young Monsieur Nicolas settled in an estate at Sacy, where he marries Jeanette Rousseau amid scenes of popular acclaim (4:322–35). But the union of *enclos* and *re-vie* led him beyond mere wishful thinking. The link had been established in *Les Posthumes*, in which Dulis/Restif is made master of yet another estate at Sacy. In twelve years, he fathers 6,000 children, who multiply incestuously and populate a new city, Dulisbourg, which is hailed as "the capital city of philosophy" (4:304–14).

L'Enclos et les oiseaux turns Restif's twin obsessions (fear of reality, symbolised by the *enclos*, and incest) into an expression of the will to dominate: here at last is he able to possess the world, past and future. The fabulously wealthy hero makes his son immortal by means of a potion called "spermaton." His plan is to "renew the human race through his son . . . and to repopulate the Earth progressively." He acquires a vast enclave that includes Sacy and with a team of eagles (the birds of the title) destroys those who oppose him. The eagles ferry in 366 girls over whom the Immortal has "a power greater than that of all kings and princes." Each evening a new bride tells her mother's story; and since these mothers are Rose Bourgeois, Victoire, and the stars of *Mon Kalendrier*, Restif may luxuriously relive adventures that had never matched his expectations. Since Restif is invariably both the father of the wives of the Immortal and also the Immortal himself, the permutations of incest defy analysis.

The population (made in Restif's image) multiplies and the *enclos* expands. The rest of humanity is kept outside its walls and withers away of natural causes to which the superior enclosed race is immune. But this is only the beginning, as he says in *Monsieur Nicolas*:

What is truly novel in this Work, is the rapid spread of the Immortal's race over the entire surface of the globe, and the history of its manners and language extending over ten, twenty, thirty, a hundred, a thousand, a million, a hundred million years. The reader will see how the Author, who is personally acquainted with the Immortal, has been able, with his help, to peer into the future as far as the end of time or of the individual existence of our planet. (6:611)

L'Enclos et les oiseaux was no longer the expanded metaphor that *La Découverte australe* had been: it had become a new and more satisfying reality. The world at last had become Restifocentric and as faultless as its creator, who had now eliminated all friction between himself and the actual.

    L'Enclos et les oiseaux was to have been Restif's most triumphant utopia. It is in fact his most wretched. It does not invalidate the principles of *L'Andrographe*, but it springs from narrow, cramped obsessions. It is a book that excludes more than it includes. What it offers is not a vision of a paradise for all but a glimpse of a world in which only Restif would feel at home. His inadequacies have become omnipotence. Fraternity and benevolent paternalism assume an appalling literalism, and deviant sexual practice acquires the moral authority of custom. There are few more graphic insights to be had of the oneiric yet perversely logical workings of a disordered mind.

    Restif's last novels are so much fungus growing on the failed idealism of a decomposing personality. Yet their very excesses enable us to see clearly how many of his broader philosophical ideas, not to mention his fiction, were inspired by a specifically sexual impulse. The process is very obvious in the evolution of his utopianism, which may be interpreted as a withdrawal from the world and more precisely as a receptacle for his wayward eroticism. But the same psychological determinants are detectable in his "scientific" explanations of the working of the universe. Developing the old distinction between active and passive matter into an unambiguous sexual tension, he argued that God, in whom all things are contained, is hermaphroditic. God, the Center of Centers and Sun of Suns, creates lesser suns and planets: the former are male; the latter, being "passive," female. The rays of our "active" sun fertilize the Earth, which contains the matrices of an infinite variety of life-forms. Every material form is either male or female, and the function of each is to seek out the other. Thus acid is male and alkali female. The mechanics of literary creation are subject to the same law: "I would have you know that when a beautiful woman inspires a work of art, she discharges the functions of the male; and the Author conceives, carries, and gives birth."[23] It was on the same philosophical ground that Restif denounced the fashion that required men to affect dandified sytles and women to dress as Amazons. He believed that such blurrings of traditional gender patterns were both blasphemous (only God is an hermaphrodite) and an immediate threat to social order: current fashion undermined the family both by making women less attractive and by the encouragement it gave to homosexuality. Thus Restif was prepared to view any number of intellectual issues in terms of sex. If he denounced homosexuality and celibacy, it was fundamentally because they denied true sexuality. If in economics he was a populationist, it was because a populous nation encouraged the procreative drive. If he reformed prostitution, it was because he had an inexhaustible interest in the making of children.

Restif's ostensible purpose in writing was to improve the world, and as a witness to his age he has his place in the evolution of late eighteenth-century *libertinage*. But at a deeper, personal level, he wrote not merely to explore his self but also to redesign the world to accommodate it. His fantasies annihilated the facts of existence and projected him into a superreality where desire and fulfillment met. The *enclos* was the ultimate haven in which he could be what he was. He was not the enterprising seducer of his self-image but a mythomaniac racked by a Jansenist conscience, a man undone by a diminishing sense of the morality of his actions. He felt no remorse for producing his many "daughters" and in life never once suggested that his relationship with Agnès was wrong. Writing was a form of practical therapy; release was found in the workings of his imagination. In this sense, a remark made by Mme Oursillame in *Le Drame de la vie* might well pass for a Freudian slip: "Oh, what a man! what a man! As many children as books, as many books as children!"[24] The daughters were inventions and the books were real, yet both were figments of his imagination. If books and daughters can be equated in this way, then it is clear that for Restif writing was a sublimated sexual activity.

David Coward
University of Leeds

NOTES

1. *Libertinage et révolution*, (Paris: Gallimard, 1975). See also Marilyn L. Horowitz, "The Attitude of Cruelty in Late Eighteenth-Century French Fiction," unpub. Ph.D. diss. (City Univ., New York, 1978).

2. For a brief discussion of how the theme of *libertinage* has been applied to *Liaisons dangereuses*, see my "Laclos Studies," *Studies on Voltaire and The Eighteenth Century* 219 (1983): 289–330.

3. This is the approach of Pierre Testud, *Rétif de la Bretonne et la création littéraire* (Geneva and Paris: Droz, 1977).

4. *Restif de la Bretonne. Sa perversion fétichiste. Thèse pour le doctorat en médecine* (Bordeaux, 1912), p. 92. (Throughout, translations are the author's.) For other analyses, see Charpentier, "Restif de la Bretonne, étude psycho-pathologique," *Hippocrate* (1934): 577–604; Dr. Louis, "Un romancier fétichiste," *La Chronique médicale* (June 1904); J. Avalon, "Restif de la Bretonne, fétichiste," *Aesculape* (Apr. 1912); and especially M. Heine, "La vieillesse de Rétif de la Bretonne," *Hippocrate* (Sept. 1934): 605–33. Dr. Louis Barras took the view that Restif

was not a true fetishist; his conclusions were supported in a preface by John Grand-Carteret (*Le Fétichisme: Restif de la Bretonne, fut-il fétichiste?* [Paris, 1913]).

5. *Monsieur Nicolas; ou, Le coeur humain dévoilé*, 6 vols. (Paris: Pauvert, 1959), 1:6.

6. *Lettres inédites de Restif de la Bretone* (Nantes, 1883), p. 16. The letter is dated 30 Apr. 1797.

7. Bibliothèque Nationale nouv. acq. fr., 22.772. For an excellent introduction to this MS, see Pierre Testud, "Le *Journal* inédit de Rétif de la Bretonne," *Studies on Voltaire and The Eighteenth Century* 90 (1972): 1567–93.

8. *Memento* (Arsenal Library, Bibliothèque Nationale 12.469), fol. 89.

9. *La Malédiction paternelle*, 3 vols. (Paris, 1780), 2:506.

10. See J.-C. Courbin-Desmoulins, "Les femmes féïques de Binet," *L'Oeil* 81 (Sept. 1961): 22–31.

11. *Mes Inscripcions*, ed. Cottin (Paris: Plon, 1889).

12. *La Famille vertueuse*, 4 vols. (Paris, 1767), 4:230–67. See on this theme Testud, *Rétif de la Bretonne*, pp. 616 ff.

13. See Pierre Testud, "Du conte moral au conte total: *L'Année des Dames nationales* de Rétif de la Bretonne," *Studies on Voltaire and The Eighteenth Century* 228 (1984): 321–36.

14. B.N. nouv. acq. fr., 22.772.

15. *Lettres inédites*, p. 48. Louise had "inspired" Restif during the early 1770s.

16. *Les Nuits de Paris*, 16 vols. (Paris, 1788–94), 16:386–94.

17. *L'Anti-Justine; ou, Les délices de l'amour*, 2 pts. (Paris, 1798).

18. *Le Nouvel Abeilard*, 4 vols. (Paris, 1779), 4:85–86n.

19. For an account of this title, see Pierre Louÿs, "Un Roman inédit de Restif," *Revue des livres anciens* 1 (1913): 87–94, and Heine, "La Vieillesse de Restif." J.-C. Courbin–Desmoulins' catalog notes prepared in 1961 for the Paris bookseller Rousseau-Girard describes a letter dated 1800 in which Restif speaks of his plans for *L'Enclos et les oiseaux* (*Restif et son oeuvre: le monde de Restif* [Paris: Rousseau-Girard, 1961], pp. 38–40). Restif himself provided a long summary of it in *Mes Ouvrages* in *Monsieur Nicolas*, 6:609–12). *L'Enclos* may be lost, but Restif's intentions are more than clear.

20. Quoted in Heine, "La Vieillesse," p. 625.

21. *Les Posthumes*, 4 vols. (Paris, 1802), 2:320.

22. *Le Palais royal*, 3 vols. (Paris, 1790), 3:86–103.

23. *Ingénue Saxancour; ou, la femme séparée*, 3 vols. (Paris, 1789) 3:135.

24. *Le Drame de la vie* (Paris, 1793), p. 956.

Sodomitical Subcultures, Sodomitical Roles, and the Gender Revolution of the Eighteenth Century: The Recent Historiography

The history of sodomy in the eighteenth century is not simply the history of repression. It encapsulates the history of all of society. It can provide a key to unlock the mysteries of the history of gender, sexuality, individual identity, human society's relationship to the physical world, and even (it has been claimed) the mysteries of the rise of modern capitalism. It remains however, a history that has just begun to be written, centering, so far, on three themes: the nature of governmental repression, the organization of sodomitical life, and the meaning for gender of the presence or absence of a specific sodomitical role.

The first articles dealing with the history of sodomy appeared in standard historical journals a mere ten years ago. They have come out of at least three intellectual milieus. Some historians who set out to study crime, deviance, and witchcraft have collected and tried to interpret the sodomy trials they found among their materials. Others began with the history of the family and then turned to the history of sexuality, and so of homosexuality. Some historians, as participants in the Gay Liberation movement, have gone looking for their roots. And increasingly, and perhaps most promisingly, the historians of gender have begun to see the importance of the topic. Some of us, of course, have taken up the topic for a combination of reasons. It is, alas, still possible to write an article such as David Rollison's and to have it published in 1981 in a journal of the distinction of *Past and Present*, in which the story of a charivari directed against a man for sodomizing a boy in 1716 is discussed, with singular obtuseness, from every angle of property, of ideology, and of popular as opposed to elite culture—is discussed, in short, in all the terms provided by the dominant male heterosexual culture—but never in the obvious and blinding light of the history of sodomy.[1]

Rollinson's failure is especially disappointing since he had available to him a rare form of documentation from a period in which Mary McIntosh had previously proposed that a major cultural shift in these matters had occurred. Rollison's evidence was a series of letters between local agents in Gloucestershire and their landlord in London in which the incident and the local reaction to it were discussed from a number of angles. Less fortunate, most historians have as a principal source, especially in England, the accounts of the trials of men for sodomy and attempted sodomy. These trials, of course, can be counted, and some historians have been tempted, with varying degrees of caution, to use a statistical series as a means of relating sodomy to the general history of society. It is a somewhat doubtful method; rashes of trials could be brought on by quite fortuitious circumstances. But some proposals worth considering have been made.

The earliest such series for a European society has been constructed by Guido Ruggiero and is discussed in his new book on Venetian sexuality in the fourteenth and fifteenth centuries. This may seem a great way from the eighteenth century, but I hope eventually to show its relevance. Ruggiero shows that there were a mere eleven convictions for sodomy in the twenty years from 1348 to 1369, but that one hundred years later, between 1448 and 1469, there were 110 convictions, or ten times as many. From this Ruggiero argues that whereas there had been only a rudimentary sexual underground in the fourteenth century, there was by the fifteenth century an open homosexual subculture. He notes further that while in the fourteenth century primarily couples or individuals were prosecuted, in the fifteenth century groups were also arrested and prosecuted and some of the prosecuted individuals were noblemen. Ruggiero argues that this sodomitical milieu was part of a wider illicit sexual subculture in which prostitutes were pursued, pornography was written, and nuns were seduced in ever increasing numbers. This illicit milieu, the obverse of the respectable sexual milieu tied to marriage and childbirth, became a major aspect of western civilization before it was modified in the twentieth century by the changing role of women. According to Ruggiero, sodomy was more severely prosecuted than any other sexual crime; since the incidence of sodomy prosecutions increased as those of other crimes declined, it is likely that Early Modern Europe experienced a sodomy paranoia paralleling the witch-burning craze.[2]

Alan Bray, by contrast, uses the absence of large numbers of trials to argue that there was in early seventeenth-century England *no* homosexual subculture. He argues from this statistical paucity a number of other things as well, to all of which I will return when I consider Mary McIntosh's thesis on the history of sodomy in the eighteenth century, which employs literary rather than statistical evidence.[3]

Some six historians—William Monter, D. A. Coward, Arthur Gilbert, A. D. Harvey, Anthony E. Simpson, and Michel Rey—have used a statistical series as the peg on which to hang an argument about the history of sodomy. Monter's study of Geneva in the sixteenth, seventeenth, and eighteenth centuries, when it was a city of from 12,000 to 20,000 people, shows that seventy-five people were tried for sodomy, but that sixty-five of these cases occurred before 1700, only *five* cases were from the eighteenth century. From this he has argued a number of points. First, although large Italian cities of at least 60,000 people had well-developed homosexual subcultures from the High Middle Ages, it was not possible for a northern European city to support a homosexual subculture with a population of less than 100,000, and it was not really until the seventeenth century, when the great capital cities of the north began to surpass 200,000 people, that in them appeared continuous, well-developed homosexual subcultures. Second, sodomy was punished with greater severity than was any other crime except, perhaps, infanticide. Third, the repression of sodomy was most intense in the sixteenth and seventeenth centuries, when prosecutions for witchcraft were also at their peak; sodomy, like witchcraft, was often confused with heresy in a period when intense religious zeal was fueled by the Reformation and the Counter-Reformation. By contrast, in the eighteenth century there were few prosecutions because an enlightened judiciary would not put men to death for sodomy.[4]

D. A. Coward has similarly argued that in eighteenth-century France, especially in Paris, there were only a handful of executions for sodomy. This contrasted sharply with the previous two centuries, when the Parlement of Paris (as Alfred Soman has shown) executed seventy-seven men for sodomy between 1565 and 1640. Coward, however, does not explain the eighteenth century's mildness in terms of philosophical enlightenment. He makes instead a somewhat arcadian proposal, namely, that in the eighteenth century there was a widespread confusion of sexual roles, in contrast to our own sharp contemporary gender differentiations; he even suggests a collective unconscious urge to androgyny. If this was so, presumably it was a condition that did not exist before or after the eighteenth century. Coward does document that the police, less benignly, kept close watch on sodomites, to the point of maintaining registers of suspects. From these and other documents Claude Corouve, Monter, and Michel Rey have maintained that there was present in Paris from at least the 1720s, a well-developed sodomitical subculture.[5]

Michel Rey has more systematically studied the same Paris police records that Coward used. Few men may have been executed, but the police were well informed. First offenders were often let off, but there was no real consistency in punishment. Police arrested men not only for the commission of actual sodomy but also for being in certain places at certain times or for conversation—any of which might establish that an individual was a sodomite. Thus Rey states that it was increasingly a taste or disposition that was punished and that from the 1740s the word *pederast* rather than *sodomite* came to be used as a descriptive term. Similarly, from the 1740s police ceased to question individuals about the sin of sodomy. Instead, they were concerned that public decency not be violated by sexual acts in public places, that sexual relations between social classes be limited, especially as it was being recognized that sodomy was not only an aristocratic vice, and finally, that adolescent males be protected from corruption by adult pederasts. This last point is important. It may be that in France it was age rather than effeminacy that determined sexual subordination. Rey does document considerable effeminacy of the new eighteenth-century variety. Nonetheless, the concern over adolescents both points to the emergence of a tripartite division of the male world into men, sodomites, and boys and shows that adolescence was being recognized as the time in which the formation of sexual identity occurred.[6]

The English in the eighteenth century, in contrast to the French and the Genevans, were far more bloody-minded about sodomy, as Gilbert, Harvey, and Simpson show from three different statistical series. Arthur Gilbert has studied the courts-martial for sodomy in the British navy over the course of the eighteenth and early nineteenth centuries. The evidence is fascinating, and the sexual language recorded is especially vivid. Gilbert found that in wartime, such as during the wars of Queen Anne's reign, the Seven Years' War, and the Napoleonic Wars, there were many trials and executions; in peacetime, by contrast, there were few trials and no executions. His speculations lead him to conclude that these trials were a way of displacing anxiety in times of extreme stress. As he puts it, "Being soft on buggers was somewhat analogous to being soft on Communists in our own day, or soft on witches in an earlier time." He speculates that there may have been an actual increase in sodomy as men of different backgrounds were thrown together and sought through sexuality to affirm life in the face of death. But he also suggests that sodomy made gender definitions ambiguous, whereas the navy prided itself on simple and direct distinctions. Sodomy and the breakdown of order thus became identified in the minds of naval commanders. Finally, he suggests, the anal associations of sodomy were especially disturbing to a Christian society that saw defecation as a persistent reminder of man's fate and his association with the animal world and as a sign of his ultimate death and probable damnation. Gilbert also claims that civilian society similarly acted out its anxiety in wartime, offering as evidence the scandals and raids on the London homosexual subculture in 1810. But he is hard pressed to place the prosecutions of the 1720s into this schema, and so he sweeps them away into a footnote.[7]

A. D. Harvey, who raises questions about the details of Gilbert's statistical findings and too abruptly dismisses Gilbert's suggestions on the symbolic meanings of anal sex, bases his own paper on government statistics of the number of executions for sodomy in England in the first thirty-five years of the nineteenth century. At least sixty men were hanged for sodomy in that period. While there had only been three such executions in London in the second half of the eighteenth century, in the generation after 1804 there was an execution nearly every year. Harvey explains this wave of executions by examining class and gender relations in the eighteenth century. He suggests (on the basis of the Kinsey Reports) that homosexuality is especially prevalent among the lower middle class and in towns and that in the eighteenth century both towns and this class had grown in size. The increase in executions might therefore be explained partly by an increase in the incidence of the behavior. He also suggests that there was a massive reinforcement of gender stereotypes in the eighteenth century; for example, men felt a need in conversation to boast of their sexual prowess with women. The statistical argument's difficulty is that there certainly had been more executions for sodomy in the early than in the latter part of the eighteenth century and probably as much gender stereotyping and urban growth before 1750 as after 1750; yet the number of executions for sodomy declined for a half century after 1750. In short, Harvey must try again.[8]

Antony Simpson has counted the trials for rape and for sodomy at the Old Bailey in London. He finds the treatment of rape to have been lenient and the treatment of sodomy comparatively severe. From 1730 to 1785 most charges of sodomy concerned acts attempted and committed with adolescents; this is similar to Michel Rey's findings for Paris. But from the 1780s the number of cases increased, while prosecutions were now for consensual acts between adult males that often had been performed in public. On this last point, Simpson's material again coincides with Parisian evidence. A second legal action—of blackmail for sodomy—grew in numbers and was made a capital crime. From these series Simpson argues that among working men in London a new code of gender identity had emerged that made manly virtue the basis of masculine domination and defined that virtue in terms of the avoidance of sodomy. It may well have been so. Both Harvey and I have already suggested something along this line. Simpson, however, begins his series in 1730, ignoring cases from the 1720s and before; consequently, his placing of the emergence of the new manly code in the late eighteenth century is probably mistaken.[9]

Gilbert, Harvey, and Simpson do raise an interesting point, if Bray is right in finding as few trials and executions in the early seventeenth century as he does. The point is that England experienced its sodomy paranoia not in the fifteenth, sixteenth, and seventeenth centuries, when witches were also being prosecuted, but in the eighteenth and early nineteenth centuries, when the English elite, at any rate, had given up all belief in witches. It begins to look like another argument for the peculiarity of the English, and Monter has almost suggested as much in the revised version of his paper. Dutch historians save the day and restore the English to the human race by showing that in the three years between 1730 and 1732 Holland experienced a sodomy scare in which 276 men were executed, which matches anything in previous European history.[10] It thus appears as though England and Holland, the two most modernizing societies of the early eighteenth century, were also the two to experience the most intense waves of sodomy prosecutions. Some will rush in to point out that these were both Protestant countries, but then so was Geneva; and to the great Casanova's eye, Protestant England and Catholic France and Spain were all of a piece in this matter when compared with tolerant Italy, which apparently had long since put its Renaissance terrors behind it. Italy also had, however, slipped from its position of technological and economic dominance between the fifteenth and the eighteenth centuries. In short, it may be possible that David Greenberg and Marcia Bystryn's argument that the late nineteenth- and twentieth-century stigmatization of homosexual behavior is a consequence of competitive capitalism and bureaucratic organization is applicable to the societies of Early Modern Europe.[11]

It would be overhasty, however, to use comparisons of Renaissance Italy with early eighteenth-century France and Holland to leap to the conclusion that sodomy was, relatively speaking, the same phenomenon throughout the Early Modern period if not, indeed, between the twelfth and the eighteenth centuries. Stopping us from making that leap is Mary McIntosh's suggestion that an important reorganization in homosexual behavior and its meaning occurred in England in the late seventeenth and early eighteenth centuries.[12] It is a theme with which in our different ways McIntosh, Bray, and I have each tried to deal; we have each based our findings on the evidence of literary sources and the interpretation of particular cases rather than on statistical series. It is clear that those historians who rely primarily on the interpretation of statistical series have tended to ask three interrelated questions: first, whether sodomitical behavior was organized into an urban subculture; second, what the effect of such behavior was for the enactment of gender roles among those who engaged in it and among those who did not; and third, how such behavior was used to construct an overall symbolic universe and to deal with issues of life and death, of man and nature, and of witchcraft, heresy, true religion, science, and enlightenment. These three questions arise naturally out of Western European taboo against all homosexual behavior; a taboo that Derek Bailey, I, and John Boswell, have each maintained was part of Western European tradition since its independent emergence in the twelfth century.[13] The taboo and its attendant questions of interpretation must, in their eighteenth-century habitation, be considered in the light of McIntosh's proposal.

In 1968, in a brief but pithy essay, Mary McIntosh made the following interpretation: all theorizing that began by seeking the causes of homosexuality was doomed to fail, since it asked the wrong question. Instead, it was essential to see that the homosexual is a deviant role created by society and that it serves the same end as all deviant roles, of keeping the rest of society law abiding. In modern societies that recognize a separate homosexual role, it is presumed that homosexuals are exclusively or predominantly homosexual in feelings and behavior, that they are effeminate in manner, personality, and preferred sexual activity, that sexual desire plays a role in all their relations with other men, and that they will be attracted to boys and young men and aim at their seduction. McIntosh argued that there were societies in which homosexual behavior in men did not require any special role. Even in contemporary Western society the presumption that men are exclusively heterosexual or homosexual in desire and action is belied by the statistics of actual practice. Finally—this is the issue crucial to my paper—she maintained that the role of the effeminate, exclusively homosexual male did not appear in Western society until the late seventeenth and early eighteenth centuries, when such individuals can first be documented in the London sodomitical subculture.[14]

I took McIntosh's distinction between homosexual behavior and the homosexual role as a point of departure in my study of the London sodomitical subculture of the 1720s. I sought to show that Western society in the eighteenth century was unique in neither allowing homosexual behavior nor providing for any approved homosexual role. Other world cultures allowed adult men to take the "dominant" role in homosexual acts without stigmatizing them in any way or denying them access to women. But males who took the passive role were allowed to do so only if in either the temporary status of boy or adolescent or the permanent adult status of tranvestite. In other words, the distinction between males as active and females as passive ruled all sexual acts whether between the same or opposite genders, because the passive male was always conceived of as being female, either from a permanent transvestite condition or from the temporary adolescent condition characterized by slight, hairless bodies. The Western inability to accept these worldwide distinctions seems to have arisen from a Christian taboo first clearly enunciated in the twelfth century. It seemed likely, therefore, that since I could find clear evidence both of homosexuality among European males between the twelfth and the eighteenth centuries, usually in an urban setting, and of descriptions of these males as effeminate, that McIntosh could not be right in thinking that either effeminacy in sodomites or the construction of an urban sodomitical subculture could be phenomena appearing for the first time in late seventeenth- and early eighteenth-century England. To give weight to this position, I claimed that the published evidence for the cities of Renaissance Italy and Reformation Geneva documented urban sodomitical subcultures.[15]

My position as to the enduring presence of urban sodomitical subcultures between the twelfth and the eighteenth centuries has been accepted by some and disputed by others: I would wish to modify it in two important respects. Arthur Gilbert is, in some ways, my most radical sceptic, since he doubts that there was a continuous subculture even in London in the eighteenth century. He may be correct in the sense that it flourished more in some years than in others, but it is impossible to think that known places of sodomitical rendezvous ever disappeared in eighteenth-century London. William Monter, in his revised essay on Geneva, has disagreed with my reading of his earlier presentation. He insists that in a city the size of Geneva it would have been impossible for the consistory not to have known of and destroyed the presence of a homosexual subculture. In private correspondence, however, I returned to the case of Pierre Canal, which I thought would prove my point; I asked Monter whether Canal demonstrated if not the presence of a *subculture* then at least the presence of a safe sodomitical *network*. Here was a man who, after his first homosexual experiences as a student in Italy, carried on a bisexual life in Geneva for five or six years; none of his lovers ever gave him away, and he only gave himself and them away when under torture for another crime in 1610 he confessed his sodomy and accused twenty other men. Monter has replied that it is apparent that "there were places and men who were 'safe' even in a place like Geneva."[16]

Stephen Murray and Kent Gerard have come partly to my support in a paper surveying the published evidence for the prosecution of sodomy in Europe between the thirteenth and the seventeenth centuries. They have found considerable material from towns of various size, involving both large groups and individuals, for Germany, France, England, Switzerland, Holland, Spain, and Italy. They conclude that "during the fourteenth, fifteenth, and sixteenth centuries, a variety of ruling elites found searching out homosexual relations an effective means of extending social control [and] distracting the frustrations of restive and occasionally riotous masses." They state further that this does not dismiss my hypothesis but that there is an unacknowledged problem of explaining the sudden prominence of *effeminate* sodomites in the early eighteenth century.[17]

Wayne Dynes and Warren Johansson, in a commentary on Richard of Davizes' description of homosexual relations in London in 1192, have made a number of interesting points: Johansson shows that Richard distinguishes between passive and active males, while Dynes has proposed a distinction between a subculture in which individuals have "a subjective sense of belonging to a particular group set apart from the rest of society" and an "objective pattern of same-sex networking that has generally arisen in urban settings—outdoor and indoor meeting places; 'semiotics' and other non-verbal gestures and tokens of recognition; consorting with other outcasts such as prostitutes, entertainers, beggars, and soothsayers."[18] This is certainly a distinction worth making, that is, whether the persons in a network have, as a consequence of the network, a sense of separate identity. In the case of eighteenth-century London it can probably be shown that the network gave such an identity to only a few.

It is necessary also to make a distinction of scale between the networks of small towns and the subcultures of large cities. An unexpected arrest could reveal such a network in Geneva in 1610 or Windsor in the 1690s, Exeter in the 1780s or Warrington in 1806. Bath, in the eighteenth century, according to Polly Morris, had nothing like London's subculture, but it did have "its own topography of sodomy; safe-fields, pick-up streets."[19] Kent Gerard hopes to show active sodomitical networks in eighteenth-century Dublin, York, Bristol, Exeter, and Norwich. Sodomitical life in these provincial towns, however, was insufficient for the public parks and taverns of London, Paris, or Amsterdam, while Venice had produced long before the eighteenth century what Ruggiero has called a subculture. Thus Monter is probably right in saying that the amount of public activity was greater in southern than northern cities before the seventeenth century. It is also probable that the sodomitical life of London, Paris, and Amsterdam in the early eighteenth century was conducted on a scale that not even the cities of Renaissance Italy had known.

The principal supporter of McIntosh's position, and therefore my most serious critic (though it has been criticism very discreetly and collegially expressed), has been Alan Bray, and it is to a consideration of his book that I now turn.[20] Bray goes to great pains to read the early seventeenth-century evidence in such a way as to deny the existence of a sodomitical subculture in London, although he does not always make clear that that is what he is doing. Along the way, however, he makes a number of highly interesting comments on the satirical and linguistic evidence, as well as a number of less cogent ones on the sodomy trials. He begins with the point that the words "sodomy" and "buggery" were general terms that might refer to relations with a man, a woman, or an animal. However defined, sodomy was often seen as the final step of a sexual sinner after rape, adultery, and incest. Sodomites were classed also as part of an infernal trio of "sorcerers, sodomites, and heretics," and were not viewed, therefore, as exclusively sexual persons. Sodomy was only one, if the gravest, of the sexual disorders to break out when marriage (the bulwark against debauchery) was ignored. Bray also points out that the word "effeminacy" was in the early seventeenth century similarly protean, sometimes used to describe cross-dressing boys but also to describe men who had become weakened through excessive sexual contact with women. To be a sodomite or effeminate in the early seventeenth century was therefore to be debauched, but such debauchery might be displayed indifferently towards males and females. For these reasons it is hard to understand why Bray dismisses as worthless the descriptions of the young man about town who was to be found with his mistress on one arm and his catamite on the other. It seems to me a likely description of which actual examples may be found; as McIntosh herself says of Pope Julian II, it is only the later theory of exclusive attachment to one gender that leads us to discount descriptions of European men as having male lovers and female mistresses simultaneously. Michel Rey mentions a number of cases of bisexual deviance, and Natalie Davis has criticized LeRoy Ladurie for anachronistically labeling a man whose sexual life included both boys and girls as a homosexual. Before 1700, this may well have been the pattern of those men who deserted what Ruggiero has called the sexual milieu of marriage for the milieu of libertinism and debauchery.[21]

It seems that Bray denies the bisexual libertine to provide a precedent for dismissing another, to him more embarrassing, part of the satirical observations, that the sexual world of London was a world apart from the rest of England as far as whoredom and sodomy were concerned. London's size dwarfed all other cities, but it depended on a flow of immigrants from the countryside and its rate of illegitimacy was no higher than elsewhere (it was actually much lower than many places).[22] But C. S. Fischer has shown that the modern city can shelter and support equally both a stable, conventional majority and deviant subcultures whose deviancy is reinforced by the experience of urban life.[23] The same may well have been true for early seventeenth-century London. Bray does admit (in footnotes) that London's records hold a relatively large number of sodomy cases in comparison to the records for the rest of the country. He circumvents this obstacle in two ways. First, the grounds on which the London cases were brought were similar to those elsewhere: the use of violence, the complaint of a boy or his parents. The same is true, however, of most London cases in the eighteenth century, when Bray agrees that there was a subculture. Second, there were few cases—about one a year—and justices were far more interested in heterosexual immorality. Unfortunately, the same is true for most years in the eighteenth century. The incidence of sodomy cases in eighteenth-century legal material is different from that of the early seventeenth century in only one, very significant, respect: there were, in a handful of years, mass arrests, when large numbers of sodomites, singly and in groups, were rounded up. It is likely, therefore, that there was more sodomy in London than elsewhere in the early seventeenth century and that people recognized this. When one adds the evidence for boy-prostitution in London that Bray reports honestly is there for the whole century, it becomes very likely that in early seventeenth-century London there was a sodomitical network or subculture that perhaps, because it was not as large as it later became, because policing was not as effective as the Societies for the Reformation of Manners later made it, and, most of all, because sodomy with men was not yet conceived of as excluding sex with women, was not attacked in the early seventeenth century in the way it occasionally was in the eighteenth.

On the other hand, Bray is probably right to presume that male homosexual contact outside of London was made through neighborhood and household ties. But surely it is absurd to argue from this that since there were relatively few prosecutions for sodomy and the age of marriage was late then homosexuality existed "on a massive or ineradicable scale." It is far more likely, when one considers the expressions of horror against sodomy, to conclude that there were few prosecutions because there was very little sodomy. It is hardly safe to conclude that if men marry late and premarital sex is difficult then they will turn to each other. It seems much more likely that in a Western Christian society, they will sublimate, take to drink, or riot in the streets, pulling down the whorehouses, as London apprentices were wont to do.

Nevertheless, despite these strictures, I would now agree with McIntosh that a profound shift occurred in the conceptualization and practice of male homosexual behavior in the late seventeenth and early eighteenth centuries. It was a shift caused by the reorganization of gender identity that was occurring as part of the emergence of a modern Western culture. It left behind the pattern of homosexual behavior that had been produced by the emergence of a traditional Western European culture in the twelfth century. In that older pattern, the debauchee or libertine who denied the relegation of sexuality to marriage had been able to find, especially in cities, women and boys with whom he might indifferently, if sometimes dangerously, enact his desires. In the modern pattern, most men conceived first of all that they were male, because they felt attraction to women, and to women alone. Gender differences were presumed therefore to be founded on an ineradicable difference of experience: men did not know what it was like to desire men, and women did not desire women, though in the minds of men, and perhaps of women, too, the latter was less so. In this culture the sodomite became an individual interested exclusively in his own gender and inveterately effeminate and passive. A man interested in women never risked becoming effeminate as he had once done, since there was never a chance that he might passively submit to another male. In this world it was no slander to say that a man was debauched or a whoremonger—it was a proof of his masculinity—and such cases disappeared from the courts, but adult men could not tolerate a charge that they were sodomites. Adolescent masturbation, often practiced as a group male activity, was outlawed on medical grounds, and by the early nineteenth century sodomy itself was being categorized as a mental disease. By about 1800, the London house of correction, recognizing perhaps the difficulty of achieving full adult heterosexuality under the trying conditions of prison life, had set up separate wings for boys, for men, and for sodomites.[24] It is also likely that in naval vessels at sea (as a close reading of Gilbert's *Africaine* evidence would show) one would have found by 1816 a similar set of distinctions among men who engaged in sodomitical acts. Michel Rey has found in Sade a related tripartite division of man, woman, and sodomite.

However, the distinction that I proposed in 1977 between the illicit relations of adult men who found each other in the urban subcultures of Europe and the licit sexual relations in the rest of the world of men with boys or transvestites was a valid one. It was a distinction already made by Geoffrey Gorer (unknown to me) in an undocumented essay.[25] What I could not see in 1977 was that Europe before 1700 was closer to the rest of the world than it was after. The European libertine before 1700 was still a sinner, although he might not have lost masculine status by having his boy on one arm and his whore on the other. Sodomy before 1700 was still the worst of sexual sins and passive sodomy the most unmanly of acts. Historians who propose models of sexual development, whether they do so for the early seventeenth century (like G. R. Quaife) or more for the early eighteenth century (like J.-L. Flandrin), cannot afford to ignore the central role of sodomy.[26] But even a great philosopher might find it difficult (as does a poor historian) to see all the connections: so that Bentham, might, in an unpublished manuscript, mock the alarm of his contemporaries over sodomy while taking for granted the alarming consequences of onanism.[27]

Randolph Trumbach
Baruch College, CUNY

NOTES

1. "Property, Ideology and Popular Culture in a Gloucestershire Village, 1660–1740," *Past and Present* 93 (1981): 79–90.

2. *The Boundaries of Eros* (N.Y.: 1985). For a legal study of Venice in the 15th and 16th cs. there is now also P. H. Labalme, "Sodomy and Venetian Justice in the Renaissance," *Legal History Review* 52 (1984): 217–54.

3. *Homosexuality in Renaissance England* (London: 1982). B. R. Burg, *Sodomy and the Perception of Evil: English Sea Rovers in the Seventeenth-Century Carribean* (N.Y.: 1983), is a book that must strike a historian as an instance in which evidence sufficient for a 15-page article has been stretched to book length by the use of possible but unprovable analogies with 20th-c. material. The author himself does not offer it as a work of history. Other historical work on the period: Caroline Bingham, "Seventeenth-Century Attitudes toward Deviant Sex,"

Journal of Interdisciplinary History 1 (1971): 446–72; A. G. Craig, "The Movement for the Reformation of Manners, 1688–1715," unpub. Ph.D. diss. (Univ. of Edinburgh, 1980), chap. 11; J. H. O'Neil, "Sexuality, Deviance, and Moral Character in the Personal Satire of the Restoration," *Eighteenth-Century Life* 2 (1975): 16–19; J. R. Dubro, "The Third Sex: Lord Hervey and his Coterie," ibid. 3 (1976): 89–95.

4. "Sodomy and Heresy in Early Modern Switzerland," *Historical Perspectives on Homosexuality*, ed. S. J. Licata and R. B. Petersen (N.Y.: 1981), pp. 40–53. This article was published simultaneously in the *Journal of Homosexuality* 6 (1980–81). It is a revised version of "La sodomie à l'époque moderne en Suisse romande," *Annales: E.S.C.* 29 (1974): 1023–33. I criticized the original version in my "London's Sodomites: Homosexual Behavior and Western Culture in the Eighteenth Century," *Journal of Social History* 11 (1977): 9–11. Monter claims that my criticisms are mistaken (*Historical Perspectives*, p. 51, n. 6), but a comparison of his two versions will not quite show that, and he has in correspondence (as noted in this essay) further acceded to my point than he has yet done in print. See also Monter, *Ritual, Myth and Magic in Early Modern Europe* (Brighton: 1983), pp. 62, 69, 117–18, where he cannot quite decide whether the men burnt at the stake were homosexuals or sodomites. He is at work, apparently, on the Spanish Inquisition and its treatment (among other matters) of sodomites. On this last topic, see Bartolomé Bennassar, ed., *L'Inquisition espagnole XVᵉ–XIXᵉ siècle* (Paris: 1971), pp. 339–69.

5. "Attitudes to Homosexuality in Eighteenth-Century France," *Journal of European Studies* 10 (1980): 231–55; Alfred Soman, "The Parlement of Paris and the Great Witch-Hunt," *Sixteenth Century Journal* 9 (1978): 36.

6. "Police et sodomie à Paris au XVIIIᵉ siècle: du péché au désordre," *Revue d'histoire moderne et contemporaire* 29 (1982): 113–24; and "Sexual Ambiguity and Definition of a Particular Taste: Male Relationships, from the End of the Middle Ages to the French Revolution," *Among, Men, Among Women: Sociological and Historical Recognition of Homosocial Arrangements* (Amsterdam, 1983, Conference Proceedings). The latter essay is more revealing than the first. (I am grateful to Kent Gerard for sharing with me his copy of these proceedings and for a great deal of other bibliographical assistance.) For further work on 18th-c. France, see Claude Courouve, *Les Gens de la Manchette, 1720–1750*, (Paris: 1978), a pamphlet; "Aspects of Male Love in the French Language," *Gay Books Bulletin* 7 (1982): 13–14; "Sodomy Trials in France," ibid. 1 (1979): 22–23; "The Word 'Bardache,' " ibid. 8 (1982): 18–19; and *L'Affaire Lenoir-Diot* (Paris: 1980) (which last I have not seen).

7. "The *Africaine* Courts-Martial: A Study of Buggery and the Royal Navy," *Journal of Homosexuality* 1 (1974): 111–23; "Buggery and the British Navy, 1700–1861," *Journal of Social History* 10 (1976–77): 72–98; "Sexual Deviance and Disaster during the Napoleonic Wars," *Albion* 9 (1977): 98–113; "Sodomy and the Law in Eighteenth- and Early Nineteenth-Century Britain," *Societas* 8 (1978): 225–41; "Conceptions of Homosexuality and Sodomy in Western History," *Historical Perspectives*, ed. Licata and Petersen, pp. 57–68.

8. "Prosecutions for Sodomy in England at the Beginning of the Nineteenth Century," *Historical Journal* 21 (1978): 939–48.

9. "Masculinity and Control: The Prosecution of Sex Offences in Eighteenth-Century London," unpub. Ph.D. diss. (N.Y. Univ., 1984). I am grateful to Dr. Simpson for allowing me to consult this.

10. The Dutch material is extensive and growing, but because of my linguistic inability I do not pretend to control it. But see, *inter alia*, L. J. Boon, "De grote sodomietenvervolging in het gewest Holland, 1730–1731," *Holland* 8 (1976): 140–52, translated in English as "A Witch Hunt: The Sodomy Trials in Eighteenth-Century Holland, 1730–1731," (unpub. paper, 1979); "Those Damned Sodomites: Public Images of Sodomy in the Eighteenth-Century Netherlands," *Among Men, Among Women* (Supplement 2), pp. 1–7; D. J. Noordam, "Homosocial Relations in Leiden (1553–1811)," ibid.; and Theo van der Meer, *Der Wesentlijke Sonde van Sodomie en Andere Vuyligheeden. Sodomietenenvervolgingen in Amsterdam, 1730–1811* (Amsterdam: 1984). Adrian Meerman has helped me with the last. Kent Gerard of the Department of Anthropology, University of California at Berkeley, has prepared an extensive bibliography of Dutch writing on this subject. Some of the work is now published in English in this issue of *Eighteenth-Century Life*, and more will be forthcoming in a special issue of the *Journal of Homosexuality* on sodomy in Early Modern Europe, ed. by Gerard.

11. "Capitalism, Bureaucracy and Male Homosexuality," *Contemporary Crises* 8 (1984):

33–56; and "Christian Intolerance of Homosexuality," *American Journal of Sociology* 88 (1982): 515–48.

12. "The Homosexual Role," *Social Problems* 16 (1968): 182–92, reprinted in *The Making of the Modern Homosexual*, ed. Kenneth Plummer (London: 1981), in which there is further discussion, especially by Plummer and Jeffrey Weeks. I discussed McIntosh in "London's Sodomites," pp. 9–11; 27, n. 17.

13. Bailey, *Homosexuality and the Western Christian Tradition* (London: 1955); Trumbach, "London's Sodomites"; Boswell, *Christianity, Social Tolerance, and Homosexuality* (Chicago: Univ. of Chicago, 1980).

14. McIntosh, "Homosexual Role."

15. Trumbach, "London's Sodomites."

16. Gilbert, "Conceptions of Homosexuality"; Monter, "Sodomy and Heresy"; letter, Monter to Trumbach, 22 Oct. 1982.

17. "Renaissance Sodomite Subcultures," *Among Men, Among Women*, pp. 183–96.

18. "London's Medieval Sodomites," *The Cabirion and Gay Books Bulletin* 10 (1984): 5–7, 34.

19. "Sexual Reputation in Somerset, 1733–1850," unpub. Ph.D. diss. (Univ. of Warwick, 1985), chap. 8. I am grateful to Dr. Morris both for allowing me to see this and for a number of stimulating conversations.

20. *Homosexuality in Renaissance England*.

21. Rey, "Sexual Ambiguity"; N. Z. Davis, "Les conteurs de Montaillou," *Annales: E.S.C.* 1 (1979): 66–68.

22. Roger Finlay, *Population and Metropolis* (Cambridge: 1981), 148–50.

23. *To Dwell Among Friends* (Chicago: 1982).

24. Parliamentary Papers, *Third Report from the Committee on the State of the Police of the Metropolis* (London, 1818), pp. 12–13, 37, 50, 76–77, 85, 87–88, 164–65, 168.

25. *The Danger of Equality* (London: 1966).

26. See my reviews, of G. R. Quaife in *Journal of Interdisciplinary History* 11 (1981): 532–35, and of J.-L. Flandrin, in *Annals of Scholarship* 2 (1981): 125–28; see also my *Rise of the Egalitarian Family* (N.Y.: 1978), pp. 281–84, for an argument about the role of sodomy in the formation of gender identity in modern man.

27. Louis Crompton, ed., "Jeremy Bentham's Essay on 'Pederasty,' " *Jour. Homosexuality* 3 (1978): 383–405; ibid. 4 (1978): 91–107. Bentham's essay raises the interesting question of the relationship between modern individualism and attitudes toward sodomy. Wayne Dynes discusses this ("Privacy, Sexual Orientation and the Self-Sovereignty of the Individual: Continental Theories, 1762–1908," *Gay Books Bull.* 6 [1981]: 20–23); but the question of privacy told against the licitness of sodomitical acts, which were often performed in public or semipublic places (for which see Rey and Simpson, above, and E. J. Bristow, *Vice and Vigilance* [London: 1977]).

The Priest, the Philosopher, and
Homosexuality in Enlightenment France

Modern study has defined sexuality mostly in terms of norm and perversion, model and deviance. In response to this dominant discourse, which gives itself out as medical truth and moral rule, a challenging discourse accepts the category, sexuality, but nevertheless considers sexuality in terms of freedom and repression. Either mode of discourse, however, makes homo- and heterosexuality mirror notions. Whatever the limits of some of Michel Foucault's analyses, and of this taste for paradoxes, we can credit him both with pointing out the inadequacy of contemporary categories to explain attitudes and practices of past centuries and with freeing ourselves from moral oppression. To Foucault, although industrial, or bourgeois, society appears to have led a great crusade against sex (with all the real suffering this has meant for individuals), nevertheless it has attributed to sex the means of expressing individual truth, as in an outpouring of emotions which express the speaker's honesty, thus making sex the source of power and pleasure. Therefore, one should renounce both the "repressive hypothesis" and, in order to escape the dominant discourse, renounce the very category, *sexuality*.[1] Classical antiquity showed how to use the body's pleasures without polarizing them as homo- or heterosexual. Although Greek literature addressed the debate between love for women and love for boys, the conceptual couple that organized Greek moral life was composed of active and passive halves. The homosexual was not opposed to the heterosexual; rather active man was opposed to the three possible figures of passivity in classical thought: woman, slave, and adolescent. Ethical difficulty stemmed only from the fact that the adolescent was a future adult, that he was only provisionally passive. Hence the classical literary and philosophical focus on pederasty.[2]

The classical age with which we are concerned did not recognize the word "homosexuality" but did recognize the legal notion of sodomy—an act of varied anal contact or penetration of a man, woman, or beast. In life as lived, however, the issue at stake was not sodomy but social privilege. Sodomy was permitted in the upper classes and often came under the provisions of the law only when sexual partners did not belong to the social elite. Sodomites were burnt to death on the Place de Grève in Paris as late as the middle of the eighteenth century, yet trial records show that aristocratic privilege was equivalent to immunity; it entailed the right to deviant behavior.[3] Such behavior could be claimed by an aristocracy that was characterized by its privilege. Here the operating category was libertinism, the morals of which deviated from the generally accepted norm. Don Juan and Casanova may have slept with boys on occasion, but they were, above all, libertines. Their refusal of monogamous love assumed the appearance of a sequence of transient adventures with females. A few male partners on the seducer's list in no way altered the nature of his libertinism. Alongside these legal and practical configurations of sodomy and libertinism, we can see the theoretical postulates that made homosexuality the object of debate between defenders of religious orthodoxy and philosophers of the Enlightenment. Homosexual desire and pleasure created a gap between divine order and nature, between a transcedent principle to which religion refers and an immanent principle with which encyclopedic morals profess to be content.

The supporters of religious tradition, such as Father Lafitau and other missionaries, often cited pagan and primitive cultures to show the inadequacy of natural morals and the necessity of revelation. Ancient philosophers may have reached the acme of purely human wisdom, and some American Indians may have lived in the innocence of nature; both, however, yielded to their passions: Socrates loved Alcibiades, and American Indian males sometimes mated with each other. They lacked divine law. European orthodoxy easily rejected every form of deviance as a result of historical otherness (antiquity) or geographic difference (the East, the New World, Africa), which Christian apologetics traduced as a cause-and-effect relation between ignorance of Christ and unorthodox practices.

The terms used to designate what was not yet conceived as homosexuality are symptomatic. "Philosophical sin" is mentioned as if it were characteristic of the philosophers who, from antiquity to scholarly libertinism, either did not know or disregarded the certitudes of faith. The phrase is used by Edmond J. F. Barbier in 1726, by Montesquieu in 1728.[4] Others speak of "nonconformity" or "nonconformism." In the article, "Nonconformité," the *Dictionnaire de Trévoux* takes it up in 1732: "Some call love for boys the sin of non-conformity"; and in the outline of one of his dramas Diderot introduces one character as "somewhat non-conformist."[5] The same phrase also means religious heterodoxy; the vocabulary is party to the polemic that condemns the libertinism of ideas as leading to the libertinism of manners and vice versa.[6] The theologians who examined the dramatic case of young Christians kidnapped by Berbers were pleased to note that their Moslem ravishers converted them to Islam before corrupting them sexually.[7] In these polemic texts, the modern notions of hetero- and homosexuality are obscured by those of religious orthodoxy and heterodoxy.

Even when defenders of Christianity insist on the turpitude of pagans, savages, and other unbelievers, they know they cannot draw too firm a line between divine law and worldly reality. Though emphasizing the inadequacy of nature in relation to grace, they cannot admit that nature should be left wholly to itself or to the hold of evil in complete ignorance of the divine truth that must be implicit everywhere until revelation makes it explicit. Nature is the place of human corruption; nevertheless, it shares in divinely ordained law. Nature must also exemplify the blindness of non-Christians and their eventual involuntary submission to Christianity. Nature is both the opposite and the intimation of grace. Sexual nonconformity, condemned in the Bible, thus cannot be admitted in the natural world, where it is called a sin against nature or unnatural (*antiphysique*) vice.[8] Such is the attitude of Father Joseph-François Lafitau, who undertook to compare the manners of American Indians with those of the ancient Greeks and Romans. According to Lafitau, the custom of "peculiar friendships" was common to America and antiquity. Law condones those pairs of friends. Lafitau admits that such friends are often lovers, but denies that law could ever legitimate homosexual relationships:

> For though the Greeks were subject to monstrous vices which have become but too common everywhere, vice nevertheless, whatever it may be, always carried with it a withering character of shame which makes it seek darkness even among the utmost Barbarians themselves. This reason is more than enough to convince us that if the one among vices which is most hateful and most revolting to reason had been attached to such kinds of friendly connexions, those rulers would have been wary of bringing it into honor.[9]

Thus, the laws of pagans and savages can be but the deadened echo or the rough sketch of Christian law. Homosexual practice, although attested to, must remain condemned and unnamed, designated only by periphrases and superlatives: "The one among vices which is most hateful."

The French Enlightenment attempted to laicize morality and, therefore, opposed the monopoly on virtue claimed by Christianity. The nature they referred to is either a normative principle that replaces divine order or a principle of reality that accepts the world's contradictions. In the former, homosexuality remains an unnatural but social, not religious, sin. In the latter, it is accepted. Voltaire's deism is not, however, a mere reproduction of the Christian position; nor is Diderot's materialism an advanced recognition of homosexual difference. The two philosophers' attitudes are more complex, but we are concerned only with analyzing textual strategies.

In Voltaire's *Dictionnaire philosophique*, there is an entry entitled "Amour nommé socratique" ["So-called Socratic love"]. The preceding entry recognizes the ambivalence of human love, which is both less happy than animal love (which does not know moral complications and the dangers of venereal diseases), and more happy, because it is amplified by feeling and perfected by social refinement. Such is the contradition of a nature that prescribes that sexes should unite but makes this union potentially dangerous. This ambivalence is also at work in "So-called Socratic love":

> How could it happen that a vice which, if it were general, would destroy the human kind, and which is an infamous offence against nature, should however be so natural? It seems to be the last degree of deliberate corrup-

tion and yet it is commonly shared by those who have yet had time to be corrupted.[10]

Voltaire starts objectively, recognizing homosexuality as a fact; yet immediately he confines it to one particular situation, adolescence, where it is favored by social factors such as education segregated by sex. This step in the development of sexual identity is also explained as a consequence of the discrepancy between the maturation of male and female. To Voltaire, sexual passion is stronger in man than in woman; this allows him to ignore lesbian love and to circumscribe the homosexual phenomenon within adolescent male illusion. But at this point Voltaire rediscovers traditional discourse, and the entry resumes the arguments we have noted in Lafitau. The peculiar loves of ancient Greece and Plutarch's commentary on them cannot be an official theory and practice of homosexuality. They have become so only by overindulgence. Society can neither tolerate nor legitimate this kind of love: "No, it does not pertain to human nature to make a law which contradicts and outrages nature, a law which, if literally observed, would annihilate mankind" (p.20). Nature can err but momentarily; it remains a norm and a reference to which human laws, in their diversity and contradictions, are but many variations. All of Voltaire's examples reduce homosexuality to pederasty, or, more exactly, to a relationship between young men. So Socrates could not love Alcibiades physically: "It is as certain as ancient science can be that Socratic love was not an infamous love; the very name of love has deceived us" (p. 20).

Once philosophy is cleared of blame, suspicion turns against its accusers. Voltaire does not miss the opportunity of a few anticlerical allusions. If homosexuality belongs to antinature, it is closely connected with the morals of mortification, with Christian morals. Murky friendships can be accepted in secondary schools; they become guilty only when the teachers take it upon themselves to seduce their pupils, or when segregation of the sexes is protracted beyond adolescence, as in monasteries. To charge Greek city-states with legitimizing the love of men for each other is to charge the Society of Jesus with advocating pederasty because "two or three young Jesuits lead a few schoolboys astray" (p. 20). To his attack on Jesuits, in 1769 Voltaire adds to the *Dictionnaire philosophique* a satirical reference to his enemy, Abbé Desfontaines, who "was about to be cooked on the Place de Grève for misusing some little chimney-sweeps who swept his chimney" (p. 21).[11] The purpose of natural morals is the free blooming of the individual and his or her sexuality, according to the principle that individual pleasure does not run counter to social order. Sexual pleasure is in accordance with the common interest as soon as it becomes procreative. It is not yet procreative in the period of male "running-in," but it cannot remain unproductive after this. In condemning homosexuality Voltaire does not propose legal repression but rather moral condemnation. Unnatural sin must be brought back to its right proportions: "Punishment must be proportional to the offence" (p. 21). The stakes on the Place de Grève are obscurantist; but if one may let sodomites live, one must not make life too easy for them.

Voltaire's scant tolerance of homosexuality contrasts sharply with Diderot's point of view. No doubt as an individual Diderot was as capable of homophobic banter as was Voltaire. He mocks Fréron's and Frederick the Great's tastes as much as Voltaire mocks those of Desfontaines.[12] The morals he presents in his theatre are apologies for the family and the procreating, husbanding father. Yet his philosophical reflection led him to conceive of nature as a fluid mass of animated substances and of man himself as a fleshly being tormented by pulsions. No finality or stability is possible in the universe or in human physiology. If even a temporary balance is established, it is at the price of waste and excess. Survival of the human species is assured only in the plentiful desires and pleasures that go beyond mere reproductive sexuality. In *Le Rêve de D'Alembert* and its continuation, the *Suite de l'entretien*, Diderot unfolds a visionary picture of this universe in which the essential differences between male and female are blurred.[13] Drifting in the huge ocean of matter, bodies are in a constant flux; they meet, penetrate each other, change. The frontier between animality and humanity is blurred, as in the case of the orangutan in the Jardin du Roi and Cardinal de Polignac who, on the other side of the bars, thinks of baptizing it (*Suite*, p. 103). The barrier is equally ambiguous between man and woman; desire impels one body toward the other. Nature is a mad prodigal, and we happy parasites of the great cycle of reproduction enjoy at its expense. "Man is perhaps but woman's monster, or woman man's monster," suggests Docteur Bordeu (*Rêve*, p. 57).

Just as the mingling of species is a natural reality that the materialist must take into account, so are disturbances in male and female functions. Diderot cautiously refuses to approve publicly homosexuality or masturbation (see T. Tarczylo's essay in this volume), but he recognizes that the philosopher can accept no argument against them. Far from limiting homosexual desire to minor causes, Diderot expands the range of its possible origins. The *Suite* ends with a question put by Mlle de l'Espinasse: "Where do those abominable tastes come from?" Bordeu replies: "Everywhere from the abnormal nervous systems [*pauvreté d'organisation*] in young men and from decaying of the brains [*corruption de la tête*] of old men. From the lure of beauty in Athens, the scarcity of women in Rome, the fear of the pox in Paris" (p. 104). Physiological causes and social arguments are presented by turns. A positive reason, the lure of beauty, crops up in the middle of negative explanations. Unlike the medical discourses of the nineteenth and early twentieth centuries that searched for an explanation of homosexuality,[14] Diderot presents human sexuality as polymorphous. Physical and affective life unceasingly overflow the small "norm" of heterosexual monogamy.

Homosexuality appears in the young as well as in the old, among the savage and civilized worlds alike. A reader of travelogues, Diderot ponders the "unnatural taste" of American Indians.[15] Like his character Bordeu, he multiplies possible explanations: the hot climate, the moral and material condition of women, or the conformation of genitalia. This last point breaks down the traditional argument that considered the complementarity of male and female organs as the mark of a strict procreative finality. Diderot retorts that two Indian men may have more in common than a man and a woman on that continent; finally, he adds a notion that totally transforms the conception of sexuality, turning it into a principle of pleasure in everlasting quest of itself: at the origin of unnatural taste one would find "the oddness that leads in everything to uncommon pleasures," "the quest for a wantonness more easily imagined than explained." Just like Bordeu's deontological caution above, allusion and preterition qualify the audacity of the wording. But Diderot's point is clear: at the heart of human desire there is a well-established pulsing dynamism that no norm can satisfy, since it thrives on the infinite diversity of form. One can no longer even speak of homosexuality in the singular.

Is the Indian's unnatural taste identical to the Parisian sophisticate's foible for dressing up? Diderot never had a high opinion of Marivaux, yet he borrows from Marivaux's theatre the art of playing with taboos and identities in a comedy he sketched and entitled *Le Train du monde; ou, les moeurs honnêtes comme elles le sont* (1759). A young love-crossed girl dresses up as a man. As a little knight she is pursued by three women and a "somewhat non-conformist man" and enjoys multiplying ambiguous situations (4:344). At both extremes—primitive savagery among the sturdy Indians and worldly refinement among the Parisian fops—the only reality of sexual norm is statistical. Homosexual desire is now both a fact of nature and a fact of society. Religion suppresses it and portrays it negatively, as Diderot shows in the passion that Suzanne Simonin induces in the mother superior of the convent of Arpajon in *La Religieuse* (written 1760, published 1796).[16] But it can also appear wholly positive in the Greek antiquity that often served Diderot as a model. There passions unfolded in a sense of patriotic devotion. Individual and public life were never separated from their physical dimension.

Whereas a tradition that culminates with the Marquis de Sade focused ancient homosexuality on the debauchery of Rome's decline, Diderot evokes Nero's marriages with his freedmen only fleetingly in the *Essai sur Sénèque* (1778) and does not allow himself to be fascinated by the Priapic festivals of the twelve Caesars (13:385). The antiquity that aroused his admiration was auroral, a land of physical and moral energy, where the relationship of man with man was one component of the prevailing heroism. He contradicts the edulcorated, normalized, and Christianized Greece of the schools with his knowledge of ancient texts. Plato's love was not platonic love, and the "Composition" entry of the *Encyclopédie* ends with the description of an assembly of venerable men fascinated by the eloquence and charms of a young libertine called Alcibiades (3:553). In the city-state male nudity was a pivot of both public and artistic production.

In the *Salons*, Diderot brings up this idea several times. Beauty, like patriotic devotion, consists of sexual desire. In discussing the painter Jean Baptiste Deshays in the *Salon de 1763*, Diderot draws a parallel between Christian scripture and ancient mythology, comparing their respective aesthetic resources. Christianity is superior as concerns the tragic: it can rouse fanaticism, madness, and crime, all of which are inspirational subjects for great painting.[17] But when it comes to pleasure and enjoyment, writes Diderot, the pagan paradise has the better of its Christian analogue:

> There is no comparing our saints, our apostles, and our sadly ecstatic virgins with those feasts on Olympus where virile Hercules, leaning on his club, amorously beholds fragile Hebe, where the master of the gods, intoxicating himself with the nectar poured brimful by the hand of a young boy with ivory shoulders and alabaster thighs, makes the heart of his jealous wife swell with spite. (5:420)

Desire is not divided into homo- and heterosexuality; it is homage to beauty, whatever its sex. In a work by Jean-Honoré Fragonard submitted two years later—"Le Grand Prêtre Corésus s'immole pour sauver Callirhoé"—this beauty becomes more androgynous. The subject is a pagan priest, taken with hysteria like a bacchant, who must sacrifice the young woman with whom he is in love. He is surrounded by acolytes, one of whom particularly attracts every look. In this painting, male beauty nearly eclipses the beauty of the young victim. A homosexual fragrance pervades the description of the "undetermined sex" of this priest and his aides, those "kinds of hermaphrodites" (6:198). The *Essai sur la peinture* that accompanies the *Salon de 1765* reverts to the parallel between paganism and Christianity, between a religion that glorifies the body and one that suppresses it. Ancient man was able to perceive in his fellow creatures Thetis' feet or Venus' bosom, Apollo's shoulders or Ganymede's "rounded buttocks":

> When the assembled people enjoyed themselves beholding naked men in public baths, gymnasiums, public games, there was, without their suspecting it, in the tribute of admiration they paid to beauty, a blended hue of the sacred and the profane, I do not know what bizarre mixture of libertinage and devotion. (6:284)

Better than Tahiti, where sexuality remains subordinate to procreation, Greece becomes a utopian model of liberated bodies. Diderot begins to dream of a similar sexualization of Europe. We, too, could be taken by curiosity and desire for naked men. But how to mention it? It is difficult to confess, even to his best friend, Sophie Volland: "Once in the public baths among a number of young men, I noticed one of astonishing beauty, and I could not help drawing near him" (5:666).[18] Acknowledging this desire would transform Western society and religion. Diderot is unafraid of writing the New Testament anew after the pagan model: the Virgin Mary would first be praised for her physical beauty and the archangel Gabriel for his fine shoulders. The nuptials at Cana would resemble the feasts on Mount Olympus: "Christ half soused, somewhat non-conformist, would have surveyed the bosom of one of the bridesmaids and St John's buttocks, uncertain whether to remain faithful to the apostle with the chin shaded by light down" (6:287).[19] The scene is quietly blasphemous. The whole of Diderot's work cannot be reduced to this one glorification of ancient bisexuality, but one must recognize the recurrence of this theme in Diderot.

The Enlightenment hesitated between secularization of traditional thinking and more radical rethinking. The same hesitation pervaded libertine and pornographic fiction. Most novels in this vein cast suspicion or ridicule on homosexual, and sometimes even on heterosexual, sodomy. Few are those that integrated it with a free development of the pleasures of the body. Sade made sodomy the principle of his eroticism, yet he remained within the framework of a tragic vision of sexuality that involves both traditional religious condemnation and philosophical discourse. Since Diderot's audacity used the ancient model and is voiced in the *Salons*, we should also investigate neoclassicism as both an aesthetic movement and a political reality at the end of the eighteenth century. Homosexual passion inspired the work of Johann Winckelmann, who saw in pederastic desire the origin of artistic achievement in antiquity and who proposed Greek art as a model for the Europe of his time. Neoclassical painting included numerous pairs of Achilles/Patroclus and Apollo/Hyacinthus or Apollo/Cyparissa,[20] and Anne-Louis Girodet magnified male beauty in the features of Endymion. Bodies tend toward androgyny, and the scandal of homosexual mating is extenuated by the growing effeminacy of male forms.

In France, the neoclassic aesthetic assumes a political dimension in its opposition to rococo, the symbol of the *ancien régime*. It inspires a revolution characterized by a concern with virile heroism. Although the French Revolution decriminalized sodomy and removed legal proscriptions from private life, leaving consenting adults free to do as they liked with their bodies, the dominant discourse remained homophobic.

The ancient war tactic of questioning the manners of one's opponents inspired a passage that may serve as a conclusion. Anacharsis Cloots, a German, was attracted to Paris by the French Revolution. "A speaker for the human kind," he portrayed himself as mankind's apostle. His writings decried antihomosexual slander, resuming Diderot's materialistic arguments. "All that is can be neither against nor out of nature," Bordeu remarked in *Le Rêve de D'Alembert* (p. 100). "Nothing is antiphysical in the physical world," Cloots confirms.[21] The laws of nature, cited in the arguments of those who oppose homosexuality, turn against them. The desires nature rouses in human bodies escape moral judgment just as do electrical phenomena. Cloots' first conclusion thus quietly admits physical affairs between men:

> Eh! because Achilles loved Patroclus; Orestes, Pylades; Aristogiton, Harmodius; Socrates, Alcibiades, and so on, were they the less useful to their country? People speak much about nature without knowing it, fix its limits at random; they do not know or ignore that it is impossible to thwart it.
>
> (p. 124)

As did Diderot, Cloots argues that homosexual passion can prompt political heroism (as in the case of Aristogiton and Harmodius, who murdered the tyrant of their city-state); but Cloots adds a second conclu-

130

sion that undermines the first when he explains that sexual sublimation is still the best way of serving one's country: "The Revolution takes up all my leisure time, and we need all our vital spirits for such a beautiful cause" (p. 125).

The France of 1793 was not to be the Greece of Diderot's fantasies, but the philosophy of the Enlightenment took several steps toward an undramatizing of sexuality. Before the nineteenth-century fixation on medical and moral conceptions of homosexuality, the Enlightenment helped to conceive a polymorphous *body of pleasure* which replaced the *body of glory* of theology.

Translated by
Nelly Stéphane

Michel Delon
Université d'Orléans

NOTES

1. Michel Foucault, *Histoire de la sexualité*, vol. 1, *La Volonté de savoir* (Paris: Gallimard, 1976), passim.

2. Ibid., vol. 2, *L'Usage des plaisirs* (Paris: Gallimard, 1984), pp. 207-48.

3. Ludovico Hernandez, *Les Procès de sodomie aux XVIe, XVIIe et XVIIIe siècles* (Paris: Bibliothèque des curieux, 1920).

4. Pierre Nouveau, "Le péché philosophique ou de l'homosexualité au XVIIIe siècle," *Arcadie* 254 (Feb., 1975): 77, and Pierre Peyronnet, "Le péché philosophique," *Aimer en France, 1760-1860*, ed. Paul Viallaneix and Jean Ehrard (Clermont-Ferrand: Faculté des lettres, 1980), p. 471. See also David A. Coward, "Attitudes to Homosexuality in Eighteenth-century France," *Journal of European Studies* 10 (1980): 231-55.

5. *Le Train du monde; ou, les moeurs honnêtes comme elles le sont*, in Diderot, *Oeuvres complètes*, ed. Roger Lewinter, 15 vols. (Paris: Club français du livre, 1969-73), 4:346. Unless otherwise indicated all further refs. are to this edn. See also Claude Courouve, *Vocabulaire de l'homosexualité masculine* (Paris: Payot, 1985), pp. 162-66. Diderot describes the character as follows: "insinuant, doux, flatteur, caché, mystérieux, silencieux, ironique, avec l'accessoire de son goût" (4:355). This description is interesting as a stereotype of the homosexual.

6. See Gerhard Schneider, *Der Libertin. Zur Geistes– und Sozialgeschichte des Bürgertums im XVI. und XVII. Jahrhundert* (Stuttgart: Metzler, 1970).

7. Guy Turbert-Deloff, *L'Afrique barbaresque dans la littérature française aux XVIIe et XVIIIe siècles* (Geneva: Droz, 1970), pp. 95-99.

8. See Michel Delon, "Du goût antiphysique des Américains," *De l'Armorique à l'Amérique de l'Indépendance, Annales de Bretagne* (1977): 317-28, and "Corps sauvages, corps impurs," *Dix-huitième siècle* 9 (1977): 27-38.

9. *Moeurs des sauvages américains comparés aux moeurs des premiers temps* (Paris, 1724; rep., Paris: Maspéro-La Découverte, 1983), p. 178.

10. *Dictionnaire philosophique*, ed. Raymond Naves & Julien Benda (Paris: Garnier, 1967), p. 18. A description of Enlightenment philosophers' opinions on homosexuality is presented by Jacob Stockinger, "Homosexuality and the French Enlightenment," in *Homosexualities and French Literature: Cultural Contexts/Critical Texts*, ed. G. Stambolian and E. Marks (Ithaca and London: Cornell Univ., 1978), pp. 161-85.

11. In *Candide*, Cunégonde's brother's homosexuality is linked to his being a Jesuit and an aristocrat, which expresses traditional prejudices.

12. In the poems, "Parallèle," "Petit dialogue entre Marmontel et Collé," and "A Monsieur ou Madame Fréron," *Oeuvres*, 10:863, 866 & 868.

13. *Le Rêve de d'Alembert*, ed. J. Varloot (Paris: Ed. Sociales, 1962).

14. See J. P. Aron and R. Kempf, "Canum more," in *Le Pénis et la démoralisation de l'Occident* (Paris: Grasset, 1978), pp. 45-78.

15. "Fragments politiques échappés du portefeuille d'un philosophe," *Oeuvres*, 10:86.

16. See Georges May, *Diderot et "La Religieuse,"* (New Haven and Paris: Yale Univ., 1954).

17. See M. Delon, "La beauté du crime," *Europe* (May 1984): 73-83.

18. Letter of 24 July, 1762.

19. See "Essai sur la peinture," 7:388.

20. See, for example, paintings by Jacques-Louis David, Jean Broc, Jean Perrin Granger in *De David à Delacroix: Le Peinture française de 1774 à 1830* (Paris: 1974), pp. 340 and 360, and *Le Néo-classicisme français* (Paris: 1974), p. 32. This aspect of neoclassicism has been studied by Jean Molino, "Le mythe de l'androgyne," *Aimer en France*, pp. 401-11.

21. A. Cloots, *Ecrits révolutionnaires: 1790-1794, ed. Michèle Duval* (Paris: Champ libre, 1979), pp. 124-25. An example of an antihomosexual political pamphlet is *Dom Bourgre aux Etats généraux* (Paris, 1789), attributed to Restif de la Bretonne.

The Pursuit of Homosexuality in the Eighteenth Century: "Utterly Confused Category" and/or Rich Repository?

"Sodomy—that utterly confused category," Michel Foucault claims in a characteristically perceptive aside in the *History of Sexuality*.[1] How can we begin to understand "la sodomie," Foucault wonders, when we have no authoritative history of sexuality and no anthropology of gender identification, and, others will add, when we have no history of repression or anthropology of desire. That "la sodomie" is still confused today is crucial to my thesis, as is the recognition that the annals of homosexuality represent one of the richest untapped archives in our period.

In my understanding, sodomy—anal penetration of either sexual partner—is merely one of a number of homosexual practices and cults ranging from restrained platonic friendship and ordinary "clubbability" (sometimes called homoerotic or homosocial) to diverse forms of transvestism and anatomical penetration (sodomy or buggery). An intelligent phylogeny could also reverse the classification and create definitions to argue that all homosexual practices are forms of a larger group that ought to be labelled "sodomy." Given my sole criterion that sodomy necessarily involves anal penetration, the first approach is preferable, for any number of homosocial practices and cults between members of the same sex obviously do *not* include anal penetration. Indeed, the entire history of same-sex friendships would be altered if the second approach were adopted. Yet no matter how sodomy is defined—whether as Foucault's "la sodomie confusée" or as some other variety—no one ought to diminish its taxonomic riddles or pretend that literary historians can plunge into a discussion of the so-called "facts" and bibliographical treasures without some identification of the phylogenic problem. The subject requires some type of philosophical overview ranging from definitional aspects to matters of value judgment in research. Despite at least a decade of serious research on homosexuality and the eighteenth century, our approach today to the subject is only minimally scientific. We discuss laboratory as well as psychoanalytic approaches; such concepts as homosocial behavior, homophobia, and misogyny have entered the daily vocabulary of almost all working scholars. Yet in these dialogues there remains a sense that the identity of the scholar-critic is as crucial as the surface discussion because the subject is so emotionally charged. By "utterly confused category," Foucault seems to have captured an essential fiber of the ideological tissue of the discourse about homosexuality, and he has a point. But there is another matter as well to be considered: the vast amount of material waiting for the scholar who pursues it.

Homosexuality created a rich literary heritage in the Enlightenment, the omission of which renders serious discussion of sexuality primitive. This is not merely because the eighteenth century represents a crucial turning point. Vice and scandal worried the British authorities then because they were perceived for the first time to be endemic rather than merely courtly, aristocratic, or—still worse—foreign. But the literary record vis-à-vis homosexuality and homosocial behavior is crucial in other ways as well: for better understanding of the authors whose lives we think we fully understand, and for a deeper sense of the cultural milieu in which they wrote. This record may be no more trustworthy as a reliable source for social history—especially such puzzling matters as whether the incidence of overt homosexual behavior was increasing or was merely perceived to be on the rise—than for legal or economic history.[2] The literary record may ultimately prove a slippery handle to unlock the mysteries of gender stereotypification and societal repression in the eighteenth century. But reliable or not, the literary record is too rich to omit, and this is my main point here.

My purpose is therefore exploratory, not definitive. I want to open rather than close terrains, to suggest fields for further research. If I cannot disagree with Foucault about the confusion he appears to have found everywhere in the discussion of sodomy, I have no solution of my own, and I do not pretend to know anything the social historians—especially those whose essays accompany this one—do not. But I want to chart some of the landscape of homosexuality in the Enlightenment.

I

Before World War II, discussion of this topic was widely tabooed, and a critic in 1800 would have been unable to isolate the six categories developed below,[3] merely having been able to select references from diverse types of written material and, if brave, to generalize about the trends they represented. More recently—in the last decade—the whole discussion of homoeroticism has been usurped, if not hijacked, by the feminists. The feminists have triumphed in this usurpation as a consequence of genuine intellectual curiosity, as well as their good fortune in meeting with no significant resistance from their male counterparts who in most cases have been relieved that the women have taken on this burden—the black albatross most men would rather not confront. Moreover, we take for granted by now a book like Lillian R. Faderman's *Surpassing the Love of Men: Romantic Friendship and Literature between Women from the Renaissance to the Present* (New York: Morrow, 1981), yet often without realizing that no equivalent for men exists. What is even more extraordinary is the sense that such a book—if it *did* exist—would create shock and offense in those very circles where male homoerotic subcultures thrive today: among teachers of all types, lecturers, and the vast world of meta-academics. Furthermore, by now it has become evident that we need some type of model, or paradigm, if we are to discuss this subject historically; but no scholar has put forward one that coherently explains texts and historical events and patterns of behavior, let alone that takes account of the texts in which these events and patterns of behavior are encoded. Perhaps one of the greatest and bravest imaginative leaps occurred before World War I when it became evident that literature contained a rich field for an understanding of the homosexual condition.[4]

Since then, particularly in the last two decades, scholarship has marched forward at such a pace and has diversified into so many areas— literary, historical, sociological, political—that it is hard to know how they tie together. Studies of gender differences and the histories of sexuality on which these gender discussions are often based represent no exception. The stumbling block is that scholars have presented isolated "facts," whose significance can barely be evaluated without a model or framework in which to contain, and then interpret, the history of sexuality at large.

These dilemmas notwithstanding, I urge scholar-critics to scrutinize my six categories as a tentative model for investigating eighteenth-century literature of all types, for there remains now a widespread, growing consciousness that superb primary materials exist and await study. How to study them is admittedly puzzling. The question can only be further complicated by cowardice and prudery, still further by pretension.

No one sensible could possibly consider the writings of Irvin Ehrenpreis or Maynard Mack cowardly or prudish, but even they—the best biographers of Swift and Pope—have remained rather reticent about the frequently homoerotic correspondence and friendship of these men; so, too, for others of the Scriblerian circle, especially John Gay, who never married and whose psychological attachment to the older, if occasionally paternal, Pope merits more attention than it has received.[5] These men were probably *not* homosexual (certainly there is no evidence of genital activity), but they were homosocial and homoerotic by any definition, and their biographers might wish to adopt a less reticent attitude toward their sexuality. The Swift who, in *Polite Conversations*, playfully writes in the character of Mr. Neverout that according to lore "he who hates Women, suck'd a Sow," is not merely exercising his agile pen but dipping into misogynistic lore for the purposes of wit.[6] The fact nevertheless remains that the sexuality of even some of the greatest writers of the time has been circumvented; and the reason cannot be owing entirely to semantic confusion over the terms "homosexual," "homoerotic," and "homosocial," which will always stand in better need of demarcation.

Even in the last few decades there has been an almost universal reticence to contemplate these definitions. When Frank Manuel suggested that Newton may not have been primarily heterosexual, the Newtonian establishment attacked him as if he had uttered the unthinkable.[7] Newton was uninterested in women; he once challenged Locke on the absurd grounds that Locke consciously set out to ruin him by distracting him with female sensuality: "You endeavoured to embroil me with women & by other means."[8] Manuel merely wondered if Newton's romantic attachment to Fatio de Duillier ought not to be considered. But the Newtonians would have none of it. They abused Manuel's psychohistory and argued that he was projecting his own interest in psychoanalysis; they charged that he wrote with no more evidence than John Barth did in *The Sot Weed Factor* when, in chapter 3, Ebenezer is told by the ingenuous Burlingame that he had "once nearly [been] raped" by Isaac the sodomite,[9] (it seems not to have occurred to most critic-scholars that Barth may have done research before casting Newton in this role). They refused to contemplate Newton's psychic depressions and relationships with his young male prodigy, viewing these as disgusting irrelevancies, approaches not to be seriously contemplated in the pure, if primarily male, world of Newtonian scholarship.

Other instances—valid and spurious—abound. When Handel replied to his sovereign's question about "the love of women" with a solecism about having no time for anything but music, George II apparently was satisfied;[10] it is surprising that Handel's recent biographers should leave the matter there in this post-Freudian age.[11] No one should suggest that Handel was homosexual without evidence, or even that his behavior was more homosocial than the norm for the age (difficult as this norm is to gauge): the point is rather that Handel's biographers have overlooked their subject's sexuality for reasons they never explicitly state. One can understand if a critical or thematic study of Handel's music should consider the composer's sexuality extraneous; yet biography, even when judged by the most puritanical criteria set out in the eighteenth century, has the duty to reveal the whole truth about the subject's life with at least a modicum of dispassionate objectivity. Although Pope assured Joseph Spence, perhaps recklessly, that "Addison and Steele were a couple of H——s,"[12] Addison's most recent student, Edward Bloom, objects: not because he can discredit Pope's testimony but because he believes it unthinkable, and he and Lillian Bloom continue to maintain that it is unthinkable without explaining why.[13] Edward Bloom has not even been willing to discuss Addison's *Guardian* 154 within the context of early eighteenth-century homoeroticism.

When Isaac Kramnick recently dared to open the matter of Burke's homosexuality, he was savaged for broaching the subject.[14] His understanding of conservatism may have been defective, as several reviewers noted, but surely he was justified in discussing Burke's sexuality in psychoanalytic terms. And though the evidence does not support their position, most scholars of our period continue to talk about the children of Pope's arch-dunce, Colley Cibber, as if they were heterosexual.[15] Even the lurid Cleland has escaped detailed analysis and exploration: Peter Sabor and Peter Wagner, the editors of two recent editions of *Memoirs of a Woman of Pleasure*, both published in 1985, say very little about the famous homosexual episode—only that Fanny despises homosexuals, that Cleland caters to middle-class contempt for sodomy, that Cleland himself was charged with being a sodomist—rather than interpret the episode in any depth. These are lost opportunities in view of the scene's length and Cleland's rich literary devices reflecting social attitudes and fantasies then current about the illicit sexual practices of sodomists. Only Thomas Gray, who probably *was* exclusively homosexual, especially in his attachments to his Cambridge pupil Charles Victor de Bonstetten, has found, in Jean Hagstrum, a sympathetic student.[16] Paul Fussell wisely has endorsed Hagstrum for the courage to uncover "Gray's powerful but frustrated homoeroticism" and has mandated that as a result of this orientation "Gray's biography needs a fully modern rewriting."[17] This is true, but Fussell and Hagstrum have been practically solitary in their open-mindedness. In all these desiderata (even in Fussell's euphemistic designation "homoerotic" when Gray was so clearly homosexual) one wonders if the discussants really mean homosocial, homocentric, homoerotic, homosexual, or sodomitical. One also wonders whether "homoerotic" is preferred because it sounds less offensive, less extreme, or whether a case of homoeroticism rather than of homosexuality can be substantiated.[18]

II

Among the most vexing questions about a valid approach to this material is the semantic one, but semantic ambiguities of "sodomy"—as merely one category of homosexuality—turn out to be fewer than the taxonomic quandries. The eighteenth-century significance of sodomy includes heightened legal persecution and transformations in its typology, stereotypification, symbolism, and iconography, as well as new social arrangements of its practitioners.[19] Circa 1700 the *word* "sodomy" denoted a large class of sinners; unlike the *category* sodomy (Foucault's "la sodomie"), it poses fewer problems for interpretation than does the larger class of homosexuality. Yet by the middle of the eighteenth century, the word "sodomy" was still "hard" for most users, the concept even harder. An anonymous author commenting on the practice understood it but insisted it still had no name: "It [i.e. homosexuality today] is yet without a Name: What shall it then be called? There are not Words in our Language expressive enough of the Horror of it."[20] According to the terminology of the time, "sodomites" may or may not have been "homosexuals." The evidence is ambiguous. The homosexual sodomite was a penetrator of males, unlike the larger class of sodomites, who may have committed any number of sexual and nonsexual "crimes." A synonym for bugger (derived from *boulgre* or *bougre*, apparently a Bulgarian),[21] "sodomite" was an extreme and opprobrious form of condemnation designating religious blasphemy, political sedition, and even satanic activities including demonism, shamanism, and witchcraft.[22]

Several historians have surveyed the legal history of sodomy in Europe, an historical record that poses problems for conceptualizing its eighteenth-century status, especially in England.[23] The sodomy acts of 1533 were the first to punish sodomy by hanging; the rest of Europe had no such laws. For three centuries these acts remained on the books but were rarely enforced. The homosexual liaisons of James I—possibly unknown outside the court—relaxed the sense of oppression in England because the court was, and remained well into the seventeenth century, the center of homosexual activity. But opinion turned when the second earl of Castlehaven was exposed. His "sodomitical compulsion" with men *and* women resulted in a set of trials in the 1630s that called attention to the acts of 1533 and "to all those practicing the unnamable."[24]

Yet if history is a set of checkers, as more than one historian has argued, with alternating trends representing different squares, the trend turned again in the Restoration when libertine ethics at court and elsewhere permitted homosexuals to flourish. The evidence is not hard to find. The earl of Rochester's *Sodom; or, The Quintessence of Debauchery*—certainly written by him despite the continuing scholarly skepticism that denies him authorship[25]—provides a clue to the treatment homosexuality could be given in a play. In this work, King Boloxinon, Prince Prickett, and Borastus the Buggermaster General, have converted the court to sodomy. Rochester weaves the plot into a dramatic fantasy rather than serving it up as a satire of the court's sexual practices. By the end, Heaven punishes all Sodom's devotees and restores the court to heterosexual norms. Rochester's play was unusual, even in its time; yet by the end of the seventeenth century it was becoming evident to many observers that whatever its geographical origins, the widespread practice of sodomy had now been transplanted to English soil. Thus do the 1699 reprints of the 1632-33 trials of Lord Castlehaven make clear; so, too, Daniel Defoe's conventional speculation that even if sodomy's "original home" had been in Turkey or "the Torrid Zone of *Italy* / Where Blood ferments in Rapes and Sodomy," sodomy was now an English and altogether genuinely "Gothic" vice.[26] These vices and diseases must be viewed, of course, within the context of national deseases then believed to afflict particular peoples; the Dutch disease, the French disease, the Italian disease, and so forth. Even so, a perception of transmigration and transplantation was developing vis-à-vis sodomy—the notion that it was an international phenomenon afflicting men, and boys, in many countries.

III

Chronological surveys and legal histories of this type are benign enough; they barely offend the academic establishment. Only when favorite authors are involved do prudery and cowardice seem to be offended. This is why I am persuaded that if prudery and cowardice can somehow be averted, the interests of truth will be better served. With this goal in mind the following six categories should be tried to see what results they produce. The six have another advantage: synchronicity within a fundamentally diachronic approach. That is, their use makes unnecessary a discussion of traditional genres (poetry, drama, the novel, travel, autobiography, espistolary forms, history, etc.) since the categories permit "literature" to be *any* writings.

The six categories are these, and it is apparent at once how interesting it would be to compare them with the varieties of female homoeroticism in the eighteenth century:

1. the school experience comprising students, teachers, cults of friendship;
2. the ironic-aesthetic tradition: Romantics, Aesthetics, Decadents;
3. the democratic tradition from Whitman and Edward Carpenter to our own time;
4. the Anglo-Saxon, Teutonic tradition: the "German myth," Johann Winckelmann to Thomas Mann;
5. theoretical apologies: Wilde's *De Profundis*, André Gide's *Corydon*, Christopher Isherwood's *Christopher and his Kind;*
6. the scientization of the homosexual: medical-legal developments.

By "the school experience" I designate the broad cults of friendship and "love" in which students and teachers engaged. This phylogeny is the most crucial of the six because most English homosexuals who have written the records on which social and literary history is necessarily based had their first awakening here. School was viewed by them as the purest period of their lives; for students it often meant first love, for teachers the possibility of fulfilling a lifelong dream. Necessarily apolitical for those involved in it, although hardly classless or lacking in ideological dimensions, the school category is essentially an English phenomenon because of the important role schools played in the development of British society. Its significance for both homosexuality and sodomy can hardly be overstated.[27] Through this category we begin to comprehend why Lord Byron—no heterosexual—could declare of John Clare, his schoolboy chum, that "I have always loved him better than any male thing in the world."[28] The school experience remains a constant throughout time. It permits us to understand not only eighteenth-century homosexuality but also central themes in Isherwood's *Christopher and his Kind*, the candid account of university "friends" who flee to Berlin to search for their true sexual identity, and D. H. Lawrence's *White Peacock* and *Women in Love*, both of which deal with the initiations through schoolsport and adolescent intimacy into "a higher love," called by H. Montgomery Hyde "the love that dared not speak its name."[29]

I find no evidence that an ironic-aesthetic tradition in relation to homosexuality existed in the eighteenth century. The romantics—not merely Byron and his circle—must be credited with its discovery. In imaginative literature this version of homosexual representation thrives on distance between the writer and his thematic subject. Often taking the form of irony and not infrequently based on principles of art for art's sake, this category attempts, as Wilde would later say on the witness stand, "to reveal art while concealing the artist."[30] As such, it refrains from sentimentally extolling, as Lawrence did, those *rites de passage* into "the love that dared not speak its name." Instead it invokes initiation, while distancing itself through irony, satire, and parody. Chronologically, the category commences with the romantics and culminates in *fin de-siècle* decadence: especially in art forms produced by the circles of Walter Pater,

J. K. Huysmans, and others of the French aesthetes, such as Théophile Gautier and Gustave Moreau. It was transformed by the often androgynous and bisexual "Bloomsburians": those "decadents" especially despised by Lawrence because they would not, or could not, construe "Greek love" seriously. The pages of *Tristram Shandy*, it is true, do contain allusions to St. Booger who presides over "all those saints at the back side of the door of purgatory" (7.43) and his tribes (7:43);[31] to "well-hung" families outside Shandy Hall (5:17);[32] to "two men's nine-pin-alleys" (3:40); and to a soldier, within Le Fevre's story, who is "harrassed, perhaps, in his rear today;—harrassing others tomorrow" (6:7)—priapic images not so arcane to Sterne's largely male readership as to disguise his playful attitude to the subject, even his possible distancing. But Sterne appears to be practically solitary in this approach (compared, for example, with Tobias Smollett, discussed below)—so solitary that one wonders what, if anything, should be made of his exception.

The third category embraces the democratic bonding of men and women on the frontier. Singlehandedly named by Whitman, though hardly his invention, the idea of democratic bonding was transplanted to England by Edward Carpenter, the early Socialist.[33] Fundamentally political and classless, it conceptualizes socialistic mankind in sexual utopias and demonstrates how sexual equality cuts away from all other considerations. This is the category we now associate *faute de mieux* with "gay lit": that vast ocean of magazines and books that now line bookshops everywhere. Its democratic origins on native American soil should not cause wonderment, as Leslie Fiedler implied in his perceptive study, *Love and Death in the American Novel*.[34] Geography and setting are crucial here: the Edenic frontier, the unpredictable future rather than a retrievable past, the possibility of genuine sexual equality. As Carpenter explained when he returned to England, on the American frontier sexuality arises not from particularity but from bonding: that curious activity practiced in factories and on farms that conjoins people of the same sex into new sexual arrangements. So far as I can tell, this version of bonding was unknown to the world of Dryden and Defoe, Gray and Johnson. Bonding then existed in practice but was unnamed; and there is good reason to believe, as Foucault and others have suggested, that things must be named before they can appropriate a life of their own. At least the written record is silent about this type of bonding.

The fourth grouping is not remote from the Enlightenment. It isolates the Teutonic tradition and its creation of a German myth based on the physical superiority and extraordinary self-sufficiency of the white-skinned, blue-eyed, blond-haired, Aryan male. Modern German literature abounds with examples of these idealized males.[35] Extending at least from the time of Ludwig of Bavaria and Nietzsche in the 1840s, it continued to gather momentum in Wagner, Stefan Georg, and Thomas Mann, and is thematically reflected in the English literature of the early part of this century. Ideologically retrograde in its extreme male chauvinism and radical antifeminism, it has no precise counterpart in the world of the Enlightenment for reasons owing to the political development of modern Germany. Teutonic homosexuality is often linked to German militarism—especially fascism and nazism—and thrives on the playing fields of German schools as well as in the camps and barracks of fascist military life. This is the category about which Hans Mayer, the German Jewish Marxist critic, has written so brilliantly in *Outsiders*, especially in part 2, "Sodom and Gommorah," where Mayer comments that the eighteenth-century origins of the German myth remain to be researched.[36] Mayer is accurate: in view of the inadequate documentation of the circles that gathered around both the homosexual Winckelmann in Rome (Anton Mengs, the comte de Caylus, Cardinal Albani, et al.) and Pietro Metastasio in Vienna (where he was court poet), Mayer's caveat comes as no surprise.[37]

The fifth and sixth categories, theoretical apologies and scientization, are more recognizable to us in the late twentieth century. Biographical apologies, unusual in the time of Wilde and Gide, are now commonplace. Yet eighteenth-century equivalents do not exist except for Voltaire's candid, if disarming, discussion of "amour Socratique" in "L'anti-Giton, à Mademoiselle Lecouvreur" and in article nineteen ("De la sodomie") of his *Dictionnaire philosophique* where he, like G. B. Beccaria later on, begs for toleration.[38] These discussions in Voltaire and Beccaria are neither apologetic nor autobiographical, and they differ so much in tone from the treatment Wilde and Gide provide that it is surely inaccurate to lump them together. In the century since the 1890s, these apologies appear as a transformed genre: the "secret," no longer capable of the blackmail it could prompt in the 1880s or 1890s, is no longer the point; the irrevocable and dire consequences of the "secret" are what count.

The scientization of the homosexual is a late nineteenth-century development grounded in post-Darwinian zoology and developed primarily for forensic reasons. To be certain, there are abundant "scientific" (anatomical) discussions of hermaphrodites in the Renaissance and "medical" dialogues about onanists in the Enlightenment.[39] Seventeenth- and eighteenth-century dissertations are permeated with discussions about the physiological characteristics of eunuchs; one does not need to read beyond Pierre Bayle to see how many authors commented on the matter. And the "philosophic," if seemingly secular, idea that excessive masturbation was the chief cause of homosexuality flourished throughout the eighteenth century. Lady Mary Wortley Montagu, perhaps anticipating Simone de Beauvoir, even ventured the naughty notion that the races of mankind contained not two but three sexes: men, women, and "Herveys."[40] The pre-Darwinian scientific world, however, had no coherent secular concept of the homosexual except as onanist, hermaphrodite, or mad masturbator.[41] The noble savage was neither homosexual nor passionately homosocial, and although masturbators and sodomists were often differentiated—as the anti-onanist campaigns of the time demonstrate—there remained no clear sense of whether homosexuality was a disorder of mind or body, or whether it was curable. Gideon Harvey, a vocal, if controversial, member of the College of Physicians in London during the Restoration, seriously believed that whatever the "natural" cause of homosexuality might be, cure could be found in "Heterogeneous minerals"; towards this magnanimous end he described his "Grand Hermaphroditic Cure."[42] Others thought that diet, or climate, was responsible for the aberration. In the 1740s, Johann Wolfart disagreed:[43] legally and medically trained, he believed that any anatomical variations evident in sodomites were irrelevant; genital activity—penetration—was what counted, and this bore no relation to the size or texture of genitals.

Real hermaphrodites continued to intrigue the Restoration and eighteenth century as a type of sodomite *manqué*. Newspapers published quasi-scientific reports and letters about them, as in the series of "Observations on Hermaphrodites" run in the *Gentleman's Magazine* (vol. xvi, beginning in February 1744); physicians and obstetricians speculated about their origins before and during birth, as Dr. James Parsons did in his very open-minded *Mechanical and Critical Enquiry into the Nature of Hermaphrodites* (1741) and William Smellie in his famous *Collection of Preternatural Cases* (1766); and writers exploited the public's confusion by casting hermaphrodites into the role of sinners born to commit crimes. Thus the minor novelist Richard Griffith named one of the children in *The Triumvirate* (1742) merely "Hermaphrodite," who, as a baby, no curate will baptise, no doctor cure; and the now elusive writer Pierre Henri Treyssac de Vergy composed *Memoirs of an Hermaphrodite,* published in English in 1772, which thrive on a heightened sense of scandal ordinary heterosexuals cannot enjoy. Yet the eighteenth-century debates reveal that no one then was certain whether hermaphrodites were really sodomites at all: that is, whether they inherited a somatic stain, in the blood or nerves, which inevitably led them to commit buggery, or if—for reasons having nothing to do with anatomy—they participated in a more general type of sin only marginally associated with sodomy. Some eighteenth-century doctors were more moderate, believed that homosexual proclivity and activity arose from what we would call psychological, rather than physiological, conditions. Other physicians viewed the aberration as merely one of a large class of "Nervous diseases," a view Smollett, himself medically trained, picked up in *Roderick Random*, as we shall see, when Surgeon Simper assures Roderick that Captain Whiffle's "disorder was entirely nervous."[44] From about 1660 onward, then, an abundance of views saw the sodomite as an extreme sinner, a cousin of Cain, but none produced a coherent model to explain natural anatomical and physiological types. The two decades after 1859 washed away much of this tradition: from 1860 to 1880 a new phylogenetic "type" emerged; variously labeled "urning," "androgyne," "uranian," or "third sex," this type was developed especially by the speculative Darwinian energies of such bona fide medical doctors and lawyers as Richard Krafft-Ebing and Karl Ulrichs, who published as "Numa Numantius."[45] Before the Darwinian revolution there was no notion that sodomites could be, as Ulrichs boldly claimed in 1868, an evolving species that was diminishing in numbers because it had been unable to "survive among the fittest" and select itself out over the centuries.[46] All this elaborate phylogeny has little counterpart in the world of the eighteenth century. Only now and again, as in Lady Mary's classification, are there echoes of "another sex." As the Swiss Protestant Dr. Samuel Tissot quickly learned in his antimasturbation campaigns, educated people were willing to believe that onanism caused insanity; it was, therefore, not difficult to persuade them that male sodomitical penetration represented a far more extreme version of physical and mental derangement.

IV

If the six categories and the phylogeny they apply appear crude in the abbreviated form in which they appear here, they nevertheless adumbrate the shapes of the eighteenth-century literary discussion. These categories may not be helpful in every case, for example, when pondering in a particular passage or literary work, whether we are in the presence of one or another type of homosexual or homoerotic character; for the varieties ranged from Restoration male libertines, like Rochester and the rakes of his circle, who were drawn to women as well as boys, and who considered anal penetration a final act of defiance, to the newer school of rakes vividly described almost a century later in the anonymous *Satan's Harvest Home* (1749)—see the discussion below—and who sodomitically relished female, and even male, whores but who could not abide being kissed by other men. There were also those, especially in schools and among the clergy, who were primarily homoerotic but who remained anything *but* libertine: men who were at best homosexual in the Platonic sense—that is, homoplatonic—and who romantically idealized same-gender friendships. All three varieties flourished at different times and in different places during the epoch, and it is impossible to say which was more representative of the age. What is clear is that schools—especially English schools—continued to be breeding grounds for all these varieties, and in this sense the first grouping—the school experience—is most genuinely present in the period. The literary "kinds"—poetry, prose, and drama—reveal why. By the eighteenth century the idyllic "Greek" pastoral, populated with pretty shepherds disguised in the attire of the opposite gender, and popular in the Renaissance, had died out.[47] The representations of homosexuality on the stage now appear as objects of disgust: creatures to condemn rather than Arcadians to celebrate. Seventeenth-century plays were permeated with characters disguised in the dress of the other gender, falling in and out of love with one another and playing the role of "the other." Homosexuality sometimes looms large as an *idée fixe* among these figures (Dryden's Dorax in *Don Sebastian*), but the school experience is barely represented. Whatever homosexuality exists as a theme in this body of drama, it is not of the sort designated by the school experience. That will come later, in the next century. Gone too from eighteenth-century drama are the single-sex couples commonly found, if disguised in dress, in Caroline and Restoration plays. These are replaced by the effeminate "Fribbles" (Garrick's *Miss in her Teens*) and "French Dukes" (Buckingham's *Tragedy of King Henry IV of France*), of eighteenth-century plays. The point is that the latter characters, whether merely homoerotic or homosexual, have met in schools and awakened to "the dangerous love" early in their lives.

In real life, in London's amusement parks and places of diversion, things were not very different. Eunuchs and castrati could readily be seen, as Thomas Southerne had suggested in the prologue to *The Spartan Dame* (1720); indeed, the English craze to import them from Italy seems to have reached a peak by the 1730's, as Hogarth's satires suggest and as the meteoric career of Farinelli, the most successful castratus in England, makes evident. The anonymous author of *A Ramble through London* (1739) captures an essence of this new jumble in his subtitle: *A conversation between a Sodomitical Baronet, a Bawd, and the Author, on a Bench in St. James's Park*, and the social history of London in the 1720s indicates that Londoners were more terrified by the Italian menace—as sodomy was then often conceptualized—than ever before.

The confusion of genders and stereotypes was further scrambled after the 1720s at masquerades and balls, in carnivals and fairs, places where liberty and license could flourish with impunity. It is impossible to fix a date to the perception that homosexuality in England was in the eighteenth century more apparent than ever before, but by the 1720s voices from different quarters begin to chant a similar strain. There is a veritable litany about the "new vices" of "the town," or, in the words of one author who remains anonymous, *A Hell upon Earth, or, The Town in an Uproar . . . Occasion'd by the late Horrible Scenes of . . . Sodomy, and other Shocking Impieties* (1729). Earlier the outcry had been directed at the stage as a spawning ground for this detestable breed, but in the 1720s, the fields for breeding had diversified. William Lee, the Whig lawyer, remarked on the numbers of sodomies in London in his *Considerations upon Street Walkers* (1727); and Henry Fielding commented in the next year on the ambiguity of the genders in masquerades.[48] Christopher Pitt, the celibate recluse who lived in Dorset, also noted in his poem "On the Masquerades" that homosexuality was flourishing in "the town" under the cover of costume: "New ways and means to pleasure we devise, / Since pleasure looks the lovelier in disguise."[49]

Except for Smollett's detailed representation in chapters 34 and 35 of *Roderick Random*, this homosexual subculture was not realistically represented in *literary* texts, however, except as easy targets for abuse. There exist a few exceptions, and these naturally call attention to themselves. Enlightenment travel literature, for example, often depicted young British male travelers in search of Teutonic types: the accounts of Lord Hervey's Algarotti at different courts well describe the significance of the court in relation to the school.[50] In fiction the court and the school divided the empire of homosocial cults, even though the latter was probably undergoing greater social transformation than the former. As social historians now recognize, schools were the place where adolescents first awakened to the "demon hovering,"[51] those sexual urges encouraged by extreme male bonding. By the eighteenth century the British school, comprising public schools as well as the two universities, was an ancient institution that thrived on male isolation. Magazines like *The Student; or,*

The Oxford and Cambridge Monthly Miscellany warned students about "the dangers of friendship between men";[52] *The Faithful Narrative of the Proceedings In a late Affair* . . . (1739) proved what the dangers could amount to when "a Sodomitical Attempt" was made by an older Fellow on one of the students.[53] In all these affairs, real as well as imagined, historical as well as literary, male bonding in schools was crucial. Its result was radical female isolation and a complex pattern of male friendship codes instilled by years of male bonding.

The church was only slightly less important as a breeding ground. English boys who awakened to their sexual difference by intimate bonding were often drawn to the clergy precisely because it offered them, in adulthood, shelter and refuge from the disappointments of the outside heterosexual world. This may be why so many homosexual students, at least in Britain, were attracted to the posts of schoolmaster, private tutor, and chaplain. No one to my knowledge has compiled lists of homosexual clergymen in the period; if it could be compiled—a big if—the long list would be permeated with familiar as well as unfamiliar names. John Kidgell, William Douglas' chaplain, was almost certainly homosexual; no other explanation exists for the degree to which he was distrusted and considered "dissolute and dishonest" by his contemporaries.[54] He may have been corrupt, but corruption alone could not have brought such opprobrium on him. In all ages the homosexual has been viewed suspiciously as an object evoking distrust and horror; yet the annals of eighteenth-century life brim over with corrupt men, and few of them are referred to in the tones that attach to the homoerotic Kidgell. Wardens of colleges—like the one at Wadham in Oxford, already mentioned—and reverends in parishes were distrusted more so than the supposedly innocent youths left in their charge. Yet the essential psychological factor was the awakening while at school: a moment of discovery the boy-man never forgot.

"England's wealthiest son," William Beckford, shows a varied pattern.[55] He never attended school and craved the forbidden fruits he was prevented from enjoying: exclusively homosexual, for the rest of his life he became fixated on pink-cheeked schoolboys. Beckford transformed these compulsive object choices into dreamy landscapes both at Fonthill where the second earl of Castlehaven had lived before he was executed for sodomy, and in such sexually charged gothic tales as *Vathek* (1786). The fixation guided Beckford's monolithic drive and compelled him to satisfy a powerful homosexual urge that remained insatiable for much of his adult life. His pursuit of sixteen-year-old William Courtenay, whose father threatened to bring suit against Beckford if he continued his pursuit, resulted in Beckford's flight to the Continent. His escape, like Wilde's, is less significant than is his homosexual psychology: it thrived on imagined loves of the type Beckford knew to be common in England's finest schools.

Horace Walpole's boyhood circle serves as another example of this pattern; and it shows us how far academic propriety has extended into our own century. This circle included Walpole, Gray, Richard West

("Favonius"), and Thomas Ashton; only Ashton married but it was a dismal marriage from the start. The group was somewhat homoerotic at Eton; pairs of lovers dubbed "The Quadruple Alliance" had formed. Even the discrete biographers of Walpole have indicated as much.[56] But care was taken, even by the best of these scholars—especially Wilmarth Lewis, who underwent an extensive Freudian psychoanalysis[57] and who certainly knew better than to pretend that Walpole was heterosexual—to suppress discussion of the group's sexuality. More recently, a non-academic London lawyer suggested a redating of Gray's "Elegy Written in a Country Churchyard."[58] His admittedly controversial hypothesis, supported by the local geography of the various churches (including Burnham and Stoke Poges), was thrown out of court because it dared to suggest that the elegy may have been originally written with Walpole in mind: as a memento mori to the "dead love" of the two friends, Gray and Walpole.

The poet of *Pleasures of Imagination* (1744) offers another curious example. Samuel Johnson wrote that Mark Akenside's "ardour of friendship" with the English lawyer Jeremiah Dyson had few parallels.[59] Dyson eventually left his wife and children to live with Akenside, whom he set up in a fashionable townhouse in London and upon whom he lavished large sums for life. Dyson was at least homoerotic, although the extant evidence suggests that Akenside was exclusively homosexual. Further evidence shows that Akenside and Dyson were members of a homoerotic club of young libertines, also frequented by John Wilkes and Baron d'Holbach while all were students at Leiden.[60] The libertine ethics of the period tolerated homoerotic behavior, but the biographers of these figures remain silent on the matter. There has been no modern biography of Akenside; had there been one, I wonder if the truth about Akenside would have been suppressed. Like Akenside, the dramatist Samuel Foote was thoroughly narcissistic; although less obviously homosexual than Akenside, his homoeroticism is patent. His modern students, however, have not delved into the matter, not even into his misogyny.

The leap from real boys attending real schools to fictional youths attending fictional schools is not great. English fiction reveals many types of homoerotic friendships and arrangements and offers the open-minded critic new avenues of exploration. In fiction some rather interesting, if still misunderstood, transformations of youthful sexual energy abound, giving rise upon occasion to new codes of ethics. For example, Peregrine Pickle's circle at Winchester and Oxford, led by the monogamous Tom Pipes, engages in too many pranks and stratagems for the contemporary post-Freudian reader not to notice their degree of narcissism and autoeroticism.[61] Here the clue is not ethics but evil, especially its sexual undertones. The activities of these seemingly harmless boys are not, of course, necessarily homosexual, but they reveal the homoerotic dimensions built into Smollett's narrative content.

Peregrine Pickle is merely one of several midcentury English novels that contain descriptions of the transformations of homoerotic friendships in English schools. The theme extends to other prose forms in the decades following the appearance of Smollett's novel. A 1761 *Treatise on the Use of Flogging in Venereal Affairs*, apparently written by John Henry Meibomius (originally Meiboom or Mayboom), assures the reader that schoolboys flagellate each other for sexual excitement. "Strike with more nerve," one boy requests; in Meibomius' "Black School of *Sodomy*" names are doled out according to "the laws of the whip," with some students "call'd learned Students in the Science of Debauchery," others *"flogging Cullies."*[62] The parlance of the time must have invented dozens of names to disgrace those charged with the vice. But there can be little doubt that flogging also served as a temporary "cure" for the pubescent passions that naturally arose in these schools. The anonymous *Venus School Mistress; or Birchen Sports*, a 1788 London prose tract verging on hard pornography, seems to be a school equivalent of Nicholas Venette's earlier *Conjugal Love*, the century's most popular manual of sex.[63] In a sober tone the author declares that flogging has prevailed as a substitute for sodomy among schoolboys (pp. 22-23, 105, 139).

V

If boys bonded in English schools, they were not much older when they bonded at sea and in the field. Eighteenth-century military bonding may not correspond entirely to Whitman's sexual bondings on the American frontier, but similarities do exist. On ships the "hammock system," which consisted of close sleeping quarters and intimate sharing of facilities, played havoc with adolescent sexual desire, although everyone involved, those in command as well as the victims of desire, seems to have known how great the risks were.[64] Offenses were doled out for minor infractions even more severely than would have been the case for identical offenses in civilian society. Court records show a high degree of guilty verdicts in court martials based on sodomy—about 70 percent of those actually tried—although it was common knowledge that sodomy was rampant at sea (Gilbert). Surgeon's apprentices were taught before sailing how to search for "obliteration of the radical folds around the anus" as evidence of penetration.[65] Such instruction was deemed necessary because it produced the most convincing evidence in court. Almost every year, it now appears from printed court records, the public could read in newspapers about the court martials for sodomy, a trend that culminated in the sensational investigations of a handsome young sailor who fell victim to evil forces aboard the HMS *Indomitable* in 1797 (which so intrigued Melville), and of Captain Bligh and his mutineers on the HMS *Bounty* nine years earlier. Many reasons for the mutiny on the Bounty were suggested in court; none was so offensive as the charge of sexual sadomasochism.[66] It may be accurate to suggest although impossible to prove that, so far as military life is concerned, sodomy flourishes more during war than during peace. If the suggestion (based on printed records comparing the decades of peace with those of wartime) is valid, the reason may be that as the British navy suddenly expanded during war, men of different nationalities and backgrounds were brought together in more cramped quarters. The temptations were therefore all the greater, while space was at a premium. Furthermore, if sex affirms life in the face of imminent death on the battlefield—as the early twentieth-century German sexologist Magnus Hirschfeld has contended in his *Sexual History of the World War*[67]— this fundamental psychological reality may indicate that the flourishing of sodomy on eighteenth-century seas and fields partook of a larger share of Whitman's male bonding than has been imagined.

Smollett seems to have thought so in *Roderick Random* (1748). Set in the Carribean Sea en route to Cartagena in the province of Bolivar, Columbia, the moment of military action is 1741, eight years before the publication of *Satan's Harvest Home*, a treatise that dealt with "Reasons for the growth of Sodomy" in England.[68] In this decade the British public's mood grew intolerant, as war in Europe and a shift in the moral climate at home combined to cast suspicion on all foreigners. Cleland's *Fanny Hill*, rich in homosexual contents, and *Satan's Harvest Home* capped the decade; and the trial of Richard Spencer, who was convicted in 1749 for merely *hoping* "to commit the horrible Crime of Sodomy," instilled reinvigorated fear among those who may have thought they could follow in his footsteps.[69] During this all-important decade, the material pertaining to homosexuality is so diverse that one wonders exactly what it meant then—say in 1749—to call someone a "sodomite," and to what degree the label was a commonplace for attacking foreign nationals or those of a different religion. Any number of passages written in the 1740s can be cited to show that its meaning is often empty. But Smollett, himself a Scots "foreigner," was sensitive to these developments, all the more vigilant because although he had witnessed great medical reforms while serving in the British navy, he had seen no improvement in morals. Indeed, the disparity between the two realms—medical and moral—appeared excessive to the young, impressionable Smollett while at sea. One means of coping with the discrepancy was the fictive creation in *Roderick Random* of a flamingly homosexual, but nevertheless high ranking, naval officer who embodied precisely this medico-moral disparity.

On board ship, Random, still a teenager, as was Smollett when he set out to Jamaica in the Cartagena Expedition in 1740, develops epidemic fever from a lack of ventilation. While recovering, Random is summoned to bloodlet Captain Whiffle (chap. 35); here Random witnesses an altogether new phenomenon: a homosexual military confederation. The ensuing portrait of Whiffle-the-sodomite, powdered, perfumed, and dressed in clothing so stereotypic that it must have been archetypal in the 1740s, is well worth deciphering since it may represent the first authentic description of the enduring male homosexual stereotype in modern culture. The portrait is even more extraordinary in that it places the stereotype at sea rather than in the town, theater, school, or court.

Captain Whiffle is "a tall, thin, young man" (p. 194), whose name and physique as well as mode of dress suggest female fickleness and insubstantiality. As such, he embodies the anatomical archetype and effeminate dress described at length in *Satan's Harvest Home*, which devotes a chapter to each of these subjects—in the first case to demonstrate that "men of a tender Constitution" are particularly prone to homosexuality; in the latter, to a detailed discussion of "The Effeminacy of our Men's Dress and Manners, particularly their Kissing each other." As Smollett introduces Whiffle the narrative pace changes abruptly from the rapid intensity often associated with Smollett to a slower and more descriptive mode: "a white hat garnished with a red feather, adorned his head"—the red feather ridiculously flamboyant for a naval captain and indicating aberration—"from whence his hair flowed down upon his shoulders, in ringlets tied behind with a ribbon" (pp. 194-95). Smollett anticipated the warning about dress that *Satan's Harvest Home* put forward a few months later. Her Majesty's naval code then permitted long hair, but "ringlets" in men, too epicene a sign for the British authorities, were forbidden. Whiffle's "coat, consisting of pink-coloured silk"—pink is the important detail—"lined with white, by the elegance of the cut retired backward, as it were, to discover a white sattin waistcoat embroidered with gold" (p. 195). This attention given to the "backward cut" could only depict a fop or—something worse. But there is more: the waistcoat is "unbuttoned at the upper part, to display a broch set with garnets"—red again—"that glittered in the breast of his shirt, which was of the finest cambrick, edged with right mechlin" (p. 195). These are genuine, imported fabrics, and Smollett's specificity shows how the red garnet brooch glitters in the center of Whiffle's pink and presumably hairless chest. "The knees of his crimson velvet breeches"—red again—"scarce descended so low as to meet his silk stockings, which rose without spot or wrinkle on his meagre legs" (p. 195). Again and again Whiffle's slender physique denotes his female gender identification. *Satan's Harvest Home* offered the innocent public clues toward identifying sodomites by the detection of "enervated effeminate Animals" with a "thin, crazy Constitution" whose flamboyant dress suggested they had "sucked in the Spirit of Cotqueanism from . . . Infancy" (p. 49). Whiffle wears "shoes of blue Meroquin"—like the Belgian "mechlin," this Moroccan leather is imported—"studded with diamond buckles, that flamed forth rivals to the sun!" (Again, *Satan's Harvest Home* noted that "the low-heel'd Pump" when adorned with jewels "is an Emblem of their [i.e. the homosexuals'] low Spirits" [pp. 49-50]).

Smollett's portrait is a riot of color—pink, red, and gold—calculated to elicit shock and revulsion among both male and female readers, even those thoroughly acquainted with the representation of the fop in Restoration drama. In the combination of decadent colors and jewels, Smollett anticipates Wilde in the famous chapter 11 of *The Picture of Dorian Gray*. "A steel-hilted sword, inlaid with figures of gold, and decked with a knot of ribbon . . . fell down in a rich tossle" and "equipped his side." Most offensive is "an amber-headed cane" that "hung dangling" from his presumably limp and equally thin wrist (p. 195). "But the most remarkable parts of his furniture were, a mask on his face, and white gloves on his hands, which did not seem to be put on with an intention to be pulled off occasionally, but were fixed with a ring set with a ruby on the little finger of one hand" (p. 195). The red ring on the pinky is a telling detail, as revealing today as it was in the eighteenth century. Roderick's revulsion is intensified by his observation that the ring is complemented by another jewel "on that of the other;" although without performing an exhaustive study of literary wrists and little fingers in literature before the 1740s we do not know to what degree Smollett is original in assembling these details into perhaps the first composite picture of the male homosexual, there can be no doubt about his intentions. By the effeminate, if grotesque, caricature he calls "Whiffle," Smollett intended to satirize a type he despised both as a young man and throughout his life, and he took extraordinary care to make certain that his first composite picture omitted no detail of physique, appearance, mannerism, gesture, gait, costume and smell.

Smollett's homosexual confederacy takes possession of the ship in this atmosphere, revealing how intuitive the novelist was to focus on the homosexual's attraction to clothing. "In this garb" Whiffle appears "surrounded with a crowd of attendants, all of whom, in their different degrees, seemed to be of their patron's disposition" (p. 195). Smollett knew, of course, about the representations of French and English fops; here he wishes to expand further on their epicene tendencies. The abrasive Smollett, who recoiled at the mere notion of homosexuality, nevertheless perceptively observed the banding together of homosexual types as well as the different degrees of their homosexual persuasion. Smollett is unable to discover toleration for his confederacy, and he hardly anticipates the liberation of homosexuals found in modern fiction, but he does not view the banding together of the confederacy in terms of extremes: as a black-and-white heterosexual or homosexual disposition. Once his imagination, probably buttressed by observation of real homosexuals in London, set to work, it produced vivid scenes like this. Smollett's pioneering presentation triumphs because it appeals to all the reader's senses, especially the visual one, as well as provides realistic detail. Even the olfactory figures in: not for nothing was he later satirized as Smelfungus. When Whiffle and his tribe take possession of Random's ship "the air was so impregnated with perfumes, that one may venture to affirm the clime of Arabia Foelix"—the remote, decadent Arabia upon which Smollett, the satirist of soft primitivism, often seized for an example of effeminacy—"was not half so sweet-scented" (p. 195).

Elsewhere I have suggested that "Smollett was not the eighteenth-century Laurel and Hardy of homosexuality; he was not attempting what *La Cage aux folles* has tried so successfully in our time: to neutralize a painful subject by trivializing it."[70] The portrait of Whiffle and his confederates in *Roderick Random* shows why. Smollett's aim is neither to neutralize nor to trivialize but to heighten by detailed description. Considering his deep satirical bent, especially in this first novel, it should not be surprising to find the sketches of Whiffle the captain, Simper, his limp-wristed private surgeon, and their effeminate *valet-de-chambre* Vergette (in French, a clothes brush, but also a pun on *verge:* a very small penis) to be caricatures bordering on the grotesque. There can be no doubt that Smollett intended to expose and ridicule: the extremity of Whiffle's foppishness and "nervous" feminine constitution attest to that, as do

Smollett's earlier and later descriptions of the "pathics" (usually passive sodomites) he finds everywhere in "the town." Later in the novel Roderick is nearly seduced by Earl Strutwell, part of another homosexual coterie, who frequently squeezes his hand and shows him "uncommon . . . fondness" (pp. 307-09). *Satan's Harvest Home* cautioned readers to beware of this symptom as preeminent among those indicating a "sodomitical type." In a chapter on "The Effeminacy of our Men's Dress and Manners," the author warns that " 'tho many Gentlemen of Worth, are oftentimes, out of pure good *Manners,* obliged to give into it [i.e. squeezing of the hand]; yet the Land [England] will never be purged of its *Abominations* till this *Unmanly, Unnatural* Usage be totally abolish'd: for it is the first Inlet to the detestable Sin of *Sodomy*" (p. 52). Strutwell actually kisses Random; and his "great kindness and familiarity" (p. 308) extend well beyond the boundaries of ordinary manly conduct.

Strutwell's impassioned discourse on the spread of homosexuality in England is so well informed, if antithetical to what must have been Smollett's personal beliefs, that one wonders to what extent the subject was being publicly discussed while Smollett was composing. There can be no doubt, in light of the evidence, that the topic was discussed: war, the domestic, political scene, and suspicion of foreigners intensified the impression of widespread homosexuality. The only question is how widely. A year before publishing his first novel, Smollett had ranted in his early Juvenalian poetic satires *Advice* and *Reproof* against "pathic" deviants. In *Roderick Random* he invents a whole repertoire of homosexual characters and scenes and comments on the subject at large, as in this quasi-comic, quasi-serious, disquisition delivered by Earl Strutwell:

> The best man among the ancients is said to have entertained that passion [homosexuality]; one of the wisest of their legislators has permitted the indulgence of it in his commonwealth; the most celebrated poets have not scrupled to avow it at this day; it prevails not only over all the east, but in most parts of Europe; in our own country it gains ground apace, and in all probability will become in a short time a more fashionable vice than simple fornication.—Indeed there is something to be said in vindication of it, for notwithstanding the severity of the law against offenders in this way, it must be confessed that the practice of this passion is unattended with that curse and burthen upon society, which proceeds from a race of miserable deserted bastards . . . And it likewise prevents the debauchery of many a young maiden, and the prostitution of honest men's wives; not to mention the consideration of health, which is much less liable to be impaired in the gratification of this appetite, than in the exercise of common venery, which by ruining the constitutions of our young men, has produced a puny progeny that degenerates from generation to generation: Nay, I have been told, that there is another motive perhaps more powerful than all these, that includes people to cultivate this inclination; namely, the exquisite pleasure attending its success. (p. 310)

However ironically intended, this is a sweeping survey of mid-Georgian beliefs, ranging from endorsement by the Greeks to commentary on the legal, economic, and social status of homosexuality at midcentury, and, finally, to Strutwell's pronouncement that its devotees worship it because of "the exquisite pleasure attending its success." Strutwell's summary may not be representative of a large segment of the British aristocracy in the 1740s, a decade I suggest is crucial in England for the perception that sodomy was spreading rapidly; it nevertheless provides a clue to the common charges of the time. Smollett was such a keen observer of the customs and mores of "the town" that it is not surprising to find him dwelling on the matter at such length. He may also have harbored personal reasons now lost to time. His sense that sodomy is fundamentally an aristocratic pollution, as depicted by Strutwell, continues in *Peregrine Pickle*. Here chapter 49 is devoted to the attempted illicit intercourse of an Italian Marquis (Italy being the specific place "Where Blood ferments in Rapes and Sodomy")[71] and a German baron who attend Akenside's "Dinner in the Manner of the Ancients" and who are caught before they can penetrate one another.

Smollett's reason for such harsh treatment of sodomites remains unclear, but whatever the origin of his attitude, homosexuality continued to evoke his fiercest whip. It may be that the radically antiluxurian Smollet saw in sodomy the most pernicious form of the soft primitivism he despised. Alternatively, if one adopts a more psychoanalytical perspective, it is possible that he himself had been the victim of homosexual overtures when he first arrived in London in the summer of 1739 as a poor Scot of only eighteen. Neither of these suggestions is capable of proof; but Smollett, unlike Richardson and Fielding, is explicit about homosexuality.

On the other hand, the poet Charles Churchill writes out of a perception that the spread of sodomy "everywhere about the town" is but an emblem of the debauched times. In "The Times" he sees homosexuality everywhere and seems persuaded that almost every Englishman is somehow a "Slave of SODOM." Debauchery and corruption, he intimates, have progressed as far as they can; yet with typical poetic license he invokes a mythical time "ere masquerades debauch'd" and "warbling eunuchs fill[ed] a Licens'd Stage."[72] Rampant sodomy is one of the signs that "the town" has been transformed into an Anglo-Saxon Gomorrah populated by a homosexual subculture flourishing in all social classes. Both Smollett and Churchill dwell on the centrality of place; it is important to notice that however confused a category Foucault's "la sodomie" may be, in England it remains a phenomenon thriving especially in London, "the common shore of Paris and of Rome,"[73] that is to say, the common sewer partaking in all the vices of the two great cities of the Continent. This is why Smollett's various episodes are *geographically* so revelatory. If the jewel-studded Whiffle appears at sea and the brocaded Italian marquis and his stunning German baron dine in Paris, for Churchill it is not necessary to travel abroad to find sodomy. There is a surfeit in town and at court.

VI

Minor writers at midcentury bear out Churchill's intuition. At least since the end of the seventeenth century, when William III and his alleged "catamite" Joost van Keppel, later the earl of Albemarle, had crossed over from Holland, the English court gathered a reputation as one of several European centers of aristocratic homosexual license.[74] William's allegedly unnatural attachment to Keppel elicited remarks far and wide; commentary seems to have reached a peak in 1692, when the king began to grant lands to his Dutch favorites. Anti-Dutch sentiment, already high in England, exploited the intimacy of William III and Keppel to stir up memories of the Anglo-Dutch wars, thereby capitalizing on the homoerotic symbiosis of the two as a tool of political propaganda.[75]

The court remained a focus of homosexual gossip down through the eighteenth century, although the theaters and their adjoining dens of real and imagined lewdness soon rivaled the court. If a royal court is anything, it is a hierarchical oasis where every vassal knows the lord he serves. Here sworn favors and secret pledges flourish in diurnal rhythm better than in other zones because the demarcations of sway and power are so finely drawn. It is therefore not surprising that much literary treatment of homosexuality in this period should be set so preponderantly at court. Homosexual scandal thrived here, as it also did in the contemporaneous literature of escape that located the entanglements in imaginary courts. The rare *Love-Letters between a certain late Nobleman and the famous Mr. Wilson* (1723) recount how the wealthy earl of Sunderland kept Beau Wilson, a colt-like "stud," decked out in sartorial splendor.[76] Both men had affairs with women, yet together they flourished as secret lovers until Wilson was killed in a duel. Real men whose masculinity was challenged also flourished or fell at court: Pope, like Lady Mary, reduced the hermaphroditical" Lord Hervey to a third sex that was neither male nor female but, ridiculously, an "Amphibious Thing."[77]

The literary record is permeated with accounts of the "real" and "imaginary" intrigues of sodomites at court. The further southward in Europe one traveled, the more sodomitical intrigue seemed to thrive; at least this is the suggestion of the comte de Mirabeau—in real life Honoré Gabriel Riquetti—who worked his way from Paris to the court at Berlin. From Berlin he wrote an anonymous *Secret History of the court of Berlin*, which was permeated with allegedly true accounts of the male liaisons he found there as well as the all-male orgies of Frederick the Great.[78] Homosexual links also appear in Simon Berington's obscure, if imaginary and utopian, *Memoirs of Sir Gaudentio di Lucca* (1735), the story of an aristocratic Tuscan youth who wins the hearts of myriad ladies by endearing himself to their men. Berington—about whom almost nothing verifiable is known except his dates (1679-1755) and Catholic origin—claims to have "copied the history from original manuscripts in St. Mark's Library in Venice"; but the assertion in the preface may be nothing more than literary convention.

Moving further southward, Count Gorani revealed a flourishing homosexual culture in Rome, describing how boys of all social classes, but especially of the lower classes, thrived among courtesans and aristocrats.[79] Nor was the church spared from these revelations. An anonymous Dutch traveler who wandered in the Mediterranean for years produced *Intrigues Monastiques, ou l'Amour Encapuchonné* (The Hague, 1739), which describes some of the homosexual activities of the clergy. Joseph Spence records that he came upon the "real history" of Metastasio, the greatest opera librettist of his time, while in Italy.[80] According to Spence, Gravina, the unequivocally homoerotic Italian poet-critic, heard the eleven-year-old Metastasio playing music impromptu in the streets of Rome. On a whim he adopted the urchin as "son" and lover; nine years later he left the now twenty-year-old Metastasio a small fortune to set himself up as a librettist. Metastasio recognized his own sexuality; he gravitated to the court not only because of his vocation, but also because the court offered him economic security and sexual license. Apparently by choice he spent the next fifty years as court-poet in Vienna, enjoying the favors of younger men who now courted him.[81]

Italy and Austria were favored literary settings, perhaps because sodomy actually thrived better there, but if the record reveals anything, Turkey existed in a class of its own. Its exotic location and mythic image gave rise in Western Europe to tales of Ottoman homosexuality that have no parallel in any European country. From these myths, we, like our nineteenth-century forebears, inherited the notion of the homosexual "Turkish baths," a phrase that continues to be invoked in some parts of the English-speaking world. Angerius Gislenius, known as Busbecq or Busbequius, was a sixteenth-century Romanian diplomat whose letters and travel books continued to be translated into English and reissued in the eighteenth century. Busbecq traveled widely throughout Turkey on diplomatic missions, recording customs and manners he found, including social arrangements between the sexes and the way in which the institution of the Turkish baths encouraged diverse sexual practices.[82] Busbecq's travels were read in translation by the author of *Satan's Harvest Home*, who claims to have discovered much information there about "the Game of Flatts," which was played by the "sodomitical Turks" (chapter 5)—a game whose rules are best withheld in a scholarly discussion like this one. Yet, if without conducting more research it is impossible to know to what degree Busbecq's *Travels into Turkey* fed into preexisting British myths about Turkish sodomy, there can be no doubt that Turkey and Italy were the two places of greatest appeal to English authors interested in the growth and spread of sodomy.

In England, diverse cults of homosexuality flourished according to different laws in the city and at court. Ned Ward described London's "molly clubs" and their habitués.[83] There is little doubt that by the time the London Spy, as Ward was called, was writing at the turn of the century, a homosexual network, of whatever size, had developed around itself a protective subculture. If court records constitute good evidence, this subculture was living in relative peace with the law. Social historians continue to debate the precise origins and development of this subculture, as does Randolph Trumbach in this issue, but no scholar I have read doubts its existence by the early eighteenth century. The ephemera of the time also provide clues. Such diverse, if now virtually obscure, works as the anonymous *Learned Dissertation upon Old Women, Male and Female* (1720), the equally anonymous *Character of the Times Delineated design'd for the Use of those who mourn in secret for the Iniquities of the Nation* (1732),[84] the Reverend Thomas Newcomb's *The Manners of the Age . . . Written with a Design to expose the Vicious and Irregular Conduct of Both Sexes* (1733),[85] Father Poussin's religious and political attack entitled *Pretty Doings in a Protestant Nation: Being a View of the Present State of Fornication, Whorecraft . . . in Great-Britain* (1734), and the anonymous *Tricks of the Town laid open; or, A Companion for country gentlemen . . . to dissuade him from coming to town* (1755), all comment on the spread of "sodomy." The author's identity must be borne in mind. It is significant, for example, that Father Poussin, "a Priest Regular of the Order of S. Dominick" according to the title page of his *Pretty Doings*, who "resided six and thirty years in Great Wild-Street, near Drury-Lane," considered him to be "An Inhabitant of this ancient *Sodom*" (p. 37) called London. The details of the subculture remain vague, but by the 1720s or 1730s there was a growing perception that homosexuality in England was on the rise.

The sociological laws of the group seem to have resembled those of other "criminal" subcultures: flourish but never get caught. By the 1730s, the network of male pimps and prostitutes who haunted the bagnios and brothels around Covent Garden was thriving, as was its Dutch counterpart in the narrow lanes behind the tree-studded Voorhout in The Hague. Both English and Dutch networks were moored to the upper-class homosexuals who made the enterprise economically possible. In Holland, it was the sudden detection of this network in 1730 that prompted the Dutch massacres, which now have been called the first mass genocides of homosexuals in Western Civilization—exaggeratedly, in my view, as only two hundred men were executed.[86] The circumstances of detection were predictable: a large network of homosexual prostitutes was uncovered, which implicated aristocrats, diplomats, doctors, lawyers, clerics, and lower-class boys. After a few Calvinist judges in Groningen decided to enforce existing laws and sentenced the alleged ringleaders to death, panic set in. Those who could fled the country; the less lucky, or less affluent, were executed. Shock waves rippled throughout Europe wherever similar networks existed. Whether genocide or not, the English newspapers provided daily "Accounts of the Proceedings against the *Sodomites* in that Country,"[87] and Kent Gerard, Department of History at Berkeley, has compiled an unpublished archive that demonstrates that in Britain these newspaper reports totaled more than two thousand within a period of less than two years. If, as Defoe's narrator suggests in the opening paragraphs of the *Journal of the Plague Year*, the Dutch had exported the great plague of 1665 to England, the Hollanders were now exporting another type of plague; perhaps less lethal in the epidemiological sense, but much more morally repugnant.

London's sodomites also constitute some of the best evidence that the city at midcentury was an emblem of throbbing chaos and catastrophe. Homosexuals, both rich and poor, figured into the Whig commercialism by a kind of applied Mandevillian principle of "private vices" as "public virtues"; and the patent existence of the subculture substantiated every prediction of the doomsday seers by acting as living proof that the apocalyptic end must be near. Terry Castle has demonstrated how one segment of this underworld flourished at masquerades, a unique atmosphere of liberty and license that provided homosexuals with the anonymity they craved.[88] But license also flourished in all-male clubs and societies, in Ranelagh which was a perfect cruising ground, and in such brothels and bagnios as Hummums in Covent Garden. It remains to be shown by scholars that in millenarian and apocalyptic literature this perceived growth—I continue to stress that it may only have been perceived, not genuine—is equated with disaster. The year 1750 produced many poems like Benjamin Stillingfleet's pensive *Thoughts occasioned by the late Earthquakes* (1750); in all these, the suggestion is made that the spread of sodomy has been a primary cause of imminent disaster. Poems like *Sodom's Catastrophe . . .* (1748) are clearly of the mode; but there remains a considerable, if ephemeral, literature of catastrophy rife with references to homosexuality, waiting to be tapped.[89]

Perhaps the retreats of the rakes to Medmenham Abbey and other secluded gothic spots haunted by Dashwood's Hell-Fire Club should also be explored in this context, as should the diverse forms of homoeroticism practiced by some of its "gentlemen" members. The Medmenham Monks remain the best known of these protomale groups whose satanic Black Masses clearly cultivated the profane.[90] But there were other groups that resembled the "profane clubs" now decried anew by the author of *The Character of the Times Delineated* and resembling the Guinea and Baller's clubs of Rochester's days.[91]

England at midcentury had any number of phallic clubs whose members reenacted the rites of Priapus; some of these, like the Tuesday Club, engaging in group masturbation.[92] Even in the falsely imagined "puritanical" colonies across the ocean, men's clubs partly given over to dubious sexual practices had started up, but the ones in England and France were more numerous and notorious. Several, modeled on the occasionally phallocentric activities of the group that gathered around the wealthy, eccentric, French antiquarian and archaeologist the comte de Caylus, indulged their homosexuality secretly.[93] Others seemed to be imitations of Prince Condé and his boys and flirted with homosexuality but never extended themselves so far. The villa of Cardinal Albani in Rome, which Caylus visited, was an unrivaled nervecenter for combined antiquarian and homosocial activity. In the unique atmosphere of this Roman villa many homosexual aesthetes, in addition to Winckelmann, the bisexual Mengs, and the homosocial Richard Payne Knight, discovered their artistic and erotic sides conjoined. Some day the story of the group's activities will be told in English: its cult of Antinous that flourished among homoerotic men bonding together in exile and the fawn's head Caylus kissed each night before going to bed. Pisanus Fraxi, the nom de plume of the erudite Victorian bibliographer Henry Ashbee Spencer, could write that "Paris was at that time [1750s] infested with clubs of pederasts, and sodomy was very generally practised by men of all classes."[94] It remains to be demonstrated to what extent the same generalization can be made of London or Edinburgh in the middle of the eighteenth century. The literary record must not always be trusted, but if it counts for anything, it is evidence of a growing perception that vis-à-vis homosexuality London was becoming, in Johnson's words, "the common shore of Paris and Rome."

The ties between such secret societies and the sequestered groves of gothic fiction are too obvious to be labored. Both thrive in dark, melancholic haunts located far from the clear light of day; in both an awful secret, usually based on a deviant sexual past, hovers near the foreground threatening to tear everything asunder. Yet the writers of this gothic fiction, even Horace Walpole, have not been viewed precisely in this light. Walpole, the father of gothic fiction, was patently homocentric and did little to conceal his propensity among his intimates. Monk Lewis, as Matthew Lewis became known for his popular gothic tale *The Monk*, was also homocentric. His fiction, like Walpole's, thrives on a blend of the gothic and the phallic.[95] No biography of Lewis spells out his homocentric psychology, but anyone familiar with the facts of his life and the autobiographical transformations of it into his work must concur that Lewis' imagination, and probably his inner mental life, was anything but heterosexual.

Prisons have been described as gothic haunts of a type. The affinity is imperfect, but there is some truth in the similarities between the cloistered dungeons of Otranto and the real cells of Newgate or the King's Bench.[96] At least Lord George Germain, formerly known as Lord George Sackville, thought so when he described a colonial prison to one of his correspondents. Like many homoerotic men of the time, Germain had married, but he was preponderantly homocentric and thrived in the all-male world of the overseas British militia. His reckless colonial policy contributed to the American Revolution in an indirect way. And while there is no evidence whatever that a heterosexual Germain would have blundered less or been less corrupt, it nevertheless remains true that we owe something, however small, in our revolutionary heritage to a homosexual British commander of the armed forces.[97] Yet most literary historians have omitted discussions of prisons, madhouses, and monastic retreats as breeding grounds for homosexuality; indeed, the prison has been viewed as anything but a sexual zone. The lacuna is not insignificant in view of the rich extant archive—prison literature, religious confessions, memoirs of the mad—these sequestered places have nurtured. In my bibliographical researches I have found no eighteenth-century prison memoirs of the quality of Wilde's *De Profundis* or monastic diaries prying open the secret sexual practices of the Church in the way that numerous Anglo-Catholic writers in the nineteenth century did,[98] but a more extensive search could produce results.

VII

No one needs to search far into the ocean of eighteenth-century travel literature to recognize that the grand tour could be a disguise for the "erotic tour"—homosexual as well as heterosexual—and that men could yearn to travel on foreign roads to seek out foreign boys. A collaboration between private tutors and their tutees that has no exact contemporary counterpart could exist in this complex arrangement.[99] Even the travels of the young Walpole and Gray suggest this, although they probably did not leave England to search for boys. The story of their falling out in Florence need not be retold here, but there can be no doubt that romantic attachments were involved. It is even possible, although now nearly incapable of proof, that their impasse, passed off as financially based, was caused by jealously over a sexual rival.[100]

So much has been written about the grand tour that a false impression arises that all has been said. Nothing could be further from the truth; in the homosexual domain the search has not even begun. Prudery, cowardice, and reticence have combined to deter scholars. Yet this is one field of investigation where the extant annals await to be tapped if only the scholars will dig in.

A single example suffices. In the Manuscripts Division of the British Library is the unpublished correspondence of Andrew Baxter, a minor Scottish Enlightenment philosopher who left his wife and children in Edinburgh and migrated to Holland.[101] He brought young male Scots students to Utrecht and Leiden, supervised their studies at the universities there, and acted as private tutor and moral mentor (fol. 9). Although married and a father, Baxter was deeply homoerotic; even when viewed within the linguistic conventions of the time, the language of his letters to these students overflows with erotic asides and gestures. Baxter especially lavished attention on those males who reciprocated his "sighs" and "kisses." The group lived in close quarters, sharing beds and bedrooms, falling in and out of love, enjoying the sense of Dutch sexual libertinism in the relaxed aftermath of 1730. Certainly by the time Baxter and his students arrived in the 1740s, there was no longer talk of repression or panic at the thought of a recurrence of the executions of 1730-31, although these massacres had not been forgotten. Their letters adumbrate the point about the erotic or homosexual grand tour. Here are found exhortations to adolescent sexual love, as well as sworn fidelity among "brothers." The group linked up with an affiliated homosocial club in Leiden that included LaMettrie, Akenside, and d'Holbach.[102] Baxter, the fatherly figure of authority, encouraged homoerotic love: his letters are explicit. His effusions were reciprocated by John Wilkes, the radical political figure who was then a sexually permissive student living in Leiden. Baxter confessed to Wilkes: "Never man was thought so much upon by another, I dare say: tho' a woman perhaps may. This [passion] is all a Riddle—No 'tis Literal Passion."[103] A "Riddle" this version of homoerotic love may have been; it did not prevent all those involved—Baxter, Wilkes, Akenside, d'Holbach, over a dozen Scots—from sobbing and kissing when departing one another.

The sexual adventures of missionaries and religious travellers are sometimes equally frank. Allen Edwardes has written a biography of Robert Clive, the British diplomat and explorer, which is, as Edwardes' subtitle indicates, effectively "a Sexual History of the Conquest of Hindustan."[104] But Clive was also the great sexual nabob of the Indian subcontinent. Some of Edwardes' primary sources are hidden in remote nooks of the world; it is not easy to check and verify them all.[105] Corroboration notwithstanding, Clive's "conquest" was sexual, partly homosexual. Clive went out to India in 1756, and according to his own manuscript diaries, which survive in the privately controlled Powis and Orms manuscript collections in England, Clive committed sodomy on dozens of natives in orgies that today seems scarcely credible. The anonymous *Intrigues of a Nabob . . . or, Bengall the Fittest Soil for the Growth of Lust* (1773) fictionalizes Clive's exploits and chronicles his pelvic penetrations.[106] While in Paris Clive claims to have been initiated into the Secret Order of Sodomites: "La Sainte Congrégation des Glorieux Pédérastes." But even his French adventures among the *confrérie de sodomie* seem tame in comparison to those he had in India. Like Father Ricci in Manchu China, Jesuit missionaries in India were curious about the homosexual practices purported to exist there. They forwarded abundant materials for inclusion in the voluminous *Lettres édifiantes et curieuses, écrits des missions étrangeres par quelque missionaries de la Compagnie de Jesus . . .* 34 vols. (Paris, 1717-74), which were suppressed at home, thereby curbing knowledge about these customs. The missionaries hardly emulated Clive's aggressive sexuality, but they were unabashedly curious about the exotic sexual practices of the Orient, in Jonathan Spence's words, curious about "the Men of Sodom" who thrived there.[107] The 1743 *Travels of the Jesuits into various Parts of the World*, a much abridged and expurgated version of the massive *Lettres édifiantes*, may be less rich in explicit homosexual detail but nevertheless confirms that sodomy was practised in Manchu China and occasionally practised between traveling Jesuits and the Chinese. European authors writing in the seventeenth century about Oriental sexual mores continually claimed to have been shocked by the practices of adultery, whoredom and sodomy (heterosexual sodomy as well as homosexual) they saw flourishing there. The seventeenth-century works of Frans Caron, Bernardus Varenius and Arnoldus Montanus, for example, are permeated with these descriptive accounts, as are the eighteenth-century ones of Giovanni Francesco Gemelli-Carreri and George Psalmanazar.[108] Caron's narrative of his travels to Japan seems to have been the source of many of the later accounts (except for Varenius), since the stories he tells are repeated in later works, as is his citation of a passage in Romans I. 27: "God has given them [i.e. these heathens] up to shameful passions. Their women have exchanged natural intercourse for unnatural, and their men in turn, giving up natural relations with women, burn with lust for one another; males behave indecently with males, and are paid in their own persons the fitting wage of such perversion."[109] All these authors probably wrote with a European audience distinctly in mind and tailored their accounts so the narratives would prove exciting to readers at home; even so, there was probably some grain of truth in the accounts of the homosexuality they claimed to have witnessed in the Orient.

The homosexual exile, typified by John Addington Symonds, had not yet come into his own as he would in the nineteenth century. Symonds, the Victorian historian of the Renaissance, fled from England to Italy, where he could satisfy his need for men of other social classes. There he became the archetype of the romantic homosexual exile, managing an international clearinghouse that coordinated correspondence and kept people in touch.[110] I have found no evidence of a similar homosexual clearinghouse kept by any Englishman in Italy in the previous century, when, before the advent of the railroads, travel between Britain and the Continent was more precarious. But the overseas British community in Florence, Venice, and Rome flourished during the eighteenth century, and some lesser Enlightenment counterpart to Symonds may have thrived there. As Sir Harold Acton has shown, libertinism and license flourished among these exiles as it could not at home.[111] Walpole, again, remains one of the best sources for the development. He followed the career of the Baron Poellnitz and ruthlessly picked the brains of his faithful correspondent, Horace Mann, for information about the *ruspanti* of Florence.

Walpole seems to have intuited the erotic tour, as well as the grand tour. He wrote to Mann that while traveling about from court to court Poellnitz "had fallen in love with all the Princes . . . on the earth."[112] While young and incredibly handsome Poellnitz had been admitted in 1731 to the court of Gian Gastone, the last prince of the Medici. Poellnitz recounts how he first discovered Gastone "sitting upright in Bed, accompany'd by several Lap-dogs, with nothing on but a Shirt without Ruffles, and a long Cravat about his Neck."[113] Gastone was by this time a decayed manic depressive who had never recovered from a heterosexual marriage into which he himself claimed he ought never to have entered.[114] Gastone's only solace lay in the infamous *ruspanti* named after the *ruspe* with which these local and foreign creatures were paid to divert him. Poellnitz recounts that the *ruspanti*'s business is "to attend the Great Duke whenever he send so for them at Dinner or Supper; 'tis said their Number consists of above four hundred, and that they cost his Royal Highness 80,000 Crowns *per Ann*" (2:133). Sodomy was a usual practice here. "They wore no Livery," Poellnitz claimed when he was there, "nor are they clad alike, and they are only known by their Locks, which are long and sensuous." Smollett's Whiffle and Strutwell would not have discovered themselves too estranged here. The *ruspanti* have now been identified by name,[115] and constitute a unique phenomenon in the annals of eighteenth-century homosexual practice: almost four hundred men and women reenacting the practices of the *Satyricon* and *Arabian Nights* morning, noon, and night.

Further southward, in Rome, Cardinal Albani also attracted many Englishmen, although life in and about his villa in no sense resembled the bacchanalian orgies of the last of the Medici in Florence, or the phallic rites Sir William Hamilton claimed to have found remnants of in Isernia in Naples. At Albani's villa, Richard Payne Knight, whose Sicilian journal has only recently been discovered and whose sexuality remains in question, first came upon the idea of composing a "sexual history of Priapus."[116] His work, building on the theories of Hamilton and Townley, and the banned *Recherches sur l'Origine, l'Esprit et les Progrès des Arts de la Grèce*

(1785), became the first extensive treatment of phallic symbolism, an Enlightenment landmark in the development of sexual symbols. Unique in any language, Knight's book, like d'Hancarville's *Recherches*, initiated a wave of writing that carried on for several decades, culminating in such derivative treatments as Jacques Antoine Dulaure's *Gods of Generation: a history of phallic cults among the ancients and moderns*. Knight was only one of several homoerotic men attracted to Albani's magnificent surroundings near the heart of symbolic Rome. But for every Knight or Winckelmann gathered at Albani's villa, there must have been other homoerotic Europeans whose accounts do not survive. Personal sexuality, manner of homoerotic bonding, and neoclassical retrieval commingled significantly in this epoch. No one ought to suggest that the archaeological discoveries of the period, conducing to a neo-Hellenism, were homosocial or homosexual *in origin*—that would be going too far. Thus far, however, the neo-Hellenism of the eighteenth century has been discussed apart from its sociological contexts, apart from its homoerotic basis, and I am suggesting that the sexual arrangements of the grand tour, as well as the research trip, are so complex that neoclassical retrieval and sexuality should no longer be considered separately.

But Johann Winckelmann, the greatest aesthetician of his age, has not been lost to time. On the contrary, Wolfgang von Wangenheim has recently reconstructed the most credible biography of the man to date.[117] An inveterate traveler who considered himself a permanent exile, Winckelmann was also a sexual exile for whom the annual ritual of travel southward represented a series of symbolic acts embracing his aesthetic and sexual desire as well as pilgrimage to Rome the Sacred. Like the "Shropshire poet" A. E. Housman, whose patterns of sexual exile resembled those of Symonds in Venice,[118] Winckelmann could not be his sexual self on his native German heath. But the double standard and double life eventually took their tolls, and he was not to live to the ripe age of Housman. Winckelmann died at age fifty in a cheap hotel room in Trieste on 8 June 1768, knifed by a young hustler who may or may not have been homosexual and whose name was merely Arcangeli. As Hans Mayer has suggested, the "condition of Sodom" for these homosexual exiles of the eighteenth century was as geographical as it was spiritual.[119] The heavenly City of Sodom for them was eternally Italian, or at least Mediterranean, however impermanent a "Sodom of the Soul" it may have been.

The literature of travel is no doubt both the least explored terrain and the one that will yield, paradoxically, the greatest riches for the understanding of homosexuality in the eighteenth century. Its resources have not even been estimated, let alone tapped[120] Traveling sodomites in courts, spas, and inns, as well as among sharpers, gamblers, and prostitutes have never been studied. Yet even when this huge reservoir is tapped, the data will require a theory or model, Foucaldian or other, to contain it.

The stumbling block is the relation of these widespread practices of homosexuality to the specific act of sodomy, which obviously also flourished during the period, and the forms of homophobia and repression that continued to resist them. In a sense the difficulty is twofold because of a dialectical relation implied by the activity and its response. Today a further impediment seems to persist: the models of gender identification and sexual stereotypes provided by the social historians, on whose work literary historians necessarily build. Even casual scrutiny of the social historians' discussions contained in this volume demonstrates their differences. There is little agreement about a basic model relating gender identification, subcultures, and socioeconomic determinism of this large class of homosexual and homoerotic people, who run the gamut from aristocratic libertines who flirted with homoeroticism, to hardened sodomists like Castlehaven, and—in the next century—Beckford and the Warden of All Souls of Oxford, who made an avocation out of debauching his Wadhamites (*The Faithful Narrative*).

VIII

The problem I have put forward in this essay is simpler: whether the mere existence of an "obviously confused category"—to echo Foucault—ought to deter scholars from exploring the field, in view of the immensely rich materials available. I hope by now it is patent that I see no contradiction. I recognize that the social scientists have performed research on this topic for a brief period only, and that their research stands on the verge of a breakthrough. Yet this brief duration has inevitably taken its toll: has caused disagreement among its practitioners and instilled confusion into our conceptualization of the matter—in brief has placed a natural limitation on the research they have thus far generated. But merely because confusion continues to reign among the social scientists is no reason for others to remain idle. Twenty years ago prudery and cowardice were factors; today only vestigial reticence survives. But it would be a shame to procrastinate further in the name of an inadequate social science that is still incapable of providing incontrovertible frameworks and models, or more specifically, because the sociology of human bonding and the history of same-gender friendships remains unwritten.

Even more fundamentally, empirical research into the available materials is now necessary in much desired theoretical models. Stated otherwise, the social scientists cannot perform their work in this domain—homosexuality in the eighteenth century—without consulting the annals of literature, conceived in the broadest possible terms. The record of literature is not, to be sure, entirely trustworthy, but it cannot be overlooked. Ultimately, the social scientists may generate new models of conceptualization proving that the literary record of the Restoration and eighteenth century is grossly distorted. This development of the future will not be surprising: imaginative literature has often diminished or enlarged the lens of reality. Literature broadly conceived nevertheless remains one of the most sensitive barometers—however inaccurate its measurements and distorted its antennae—of the climate of opinion and feeling in an age.

G. S. Rousseau
University of California, Los Angeles

162

NOTES

1. Vol. 1: *An Introduction* (London: Penguin, 1978), p. 101. For reasons of space, my discussion is limited to male homosexuality, although the reader will discover, very soon, that discussion of homosocial behavior also abounds everywhere in my treatment. I am grateful to my distinguished colleague, Prof. Peter Thorslev, as well as Robert Adams Day, for commenting on this essay, even if its remaining imperfections are entirely my own.

For the purposes of clarity my working definitions are these:

sodomy—anal penetration of either sex (i.e., homosexual or heterosexual sodomy) not necessarily with personal homosexual involvement;

homosexuality—an umbrella term to designate all forms of homosexual behavior, including homosexual sodomy and the activities of pathics;

homoerotic—referring to male-oriented friendship not necessarily oral or genital;

homosocial—referring to relations which are less than homoerotic friendship, thus a weaker form of homoerotic behavior;

homocentric—male oriented, male centered, male dominated.

Of these working definitions the term "homosexual(ity)" is problematic and anachronistic. Homosexuality is a late nineteenth-century concept denoting a psychological frame of mind that exists independent of action, and a general orientation that may or may not correlate to specific patterns of behavior. A homosexual, in this sense, primarily describes a mental set rather than a prescribed course of action or predisposing bio-anatomical conditions. But the eighteenth century had no such concept of homosexuality, and nowhere in this essay do I claim it did. It is therefore evident that a title reading "The Pursuit of Homosocial Arrangements in the Eighteenth Century: 'Utterly Confused Category' and/or Rich Repository?" would have been historically more precise, especially since a portion of my discussion is clearly not about those who were called sodomites—i.e., those in the eighteenth century who had sexual relations with other men—but about males who were in varying degrees homoerotic and homosocial, whether passively (the mid-century's constant reference to pathics) or actively. Yet I have permitted the anachronism to remain for a number of reasons, ideologically explosive though the concept homosexuality is today. Not least of these reasons is my aim to convey to readers that I attempt to survey a broad spectrum here: not merely those who actually engaged in sexual acts with another person of the same sex, but also those who were homoerotic and who cultivated the homosocial dimensions of friendship. Also, I have tried to reach a broad readership that does not consist exclusively, I presume, of historians of sexuality, and which may be as interested in this wide repertoire of same-sex relations as in the more extreme sodomitical ones. An alternative usage was the umbrella phrase "homosocial arrangements"—a cumbersome literalism presenting its own hurdles, if not of anachronism then of misleading implications for a late twentieth-century readership, among which is the remote sound of the phrase and the unfortunate suggestion that those involved were "arrangers"—consciously arranging something. On balance, the roadblocks created by such a literalism are as formidable as the use of the anachronistic noun "homosexual"; and ultimately less confusion arises for contemporary readers by use of the familiar noun and adjective "homosexual," so long as readers are warned well in advance that the noun, especially, is an anachronism. Still, the reader who wishes to avoid this interpretative crux can eradicate all traces of the anachronism by substituting "homosocial arrangements" for every use of "homosexual," and can also substitute the noun "sodomite," provided it is clear that the concept sodomy in the eighteenth century was itself very much in flux, as I show—so much so that by the end of the century it had rather different connotations from those at the beginning.

2. Much of this essay deals with the perception in 18th-c. sources that homosexuality was on the rise, not with my own perception that it was.

3. The first four of these categories were Thorslev's before they were mine and he hopes to develop them at a future time; the last two are mine. Any genuinely historical discussion of the subject today is inadequate without taking account of them: for support of this attitude see the five position papers in *The Boston Colloquium: The Gay Science, Philosophical and Scientific Perspectives on Homosexual Research* (forthcoming, 1987); and it was epistemic distinction that Foucault believed was lacking in the historical discourse about sodomy.

4. See Magnus Hirschfeld, *Berlins drittes Geschlecht* (Berlin: n.p., 1905).

5. See Ehrenpreis' excellent biography, *Swift: The Man, His Works, and The Age*. 3 vols. (London & Cambridge; Methuen & Harvard Univ., 1962-83), and Mack's numerous biographical studies. Mack avoids the subject when discussing Pope's romantic temperament in a review essay of George Sherburn (ed.), *The Correspondence of Alexander Pope*, 5 vols. (Oxford: Clarendon, 1956), *Philological Quarterly* 36 (1957): 394—95; and his more recent *Alexander Pope: A Life* (London: Yale Univ., 1985) does not advance understanding of the dilemma of Pope's sexuality. The best book about Gay remains Patricia Spacks' *John Gay* (N.Y.: Twayne, 1965), which is silent about Gay's sexuality.

6. In *The Prose Works of Jonathan Swift*, ed. Herbert Davis, 9 vols. (Oxford: Blackwell, 1957), 4:165.

7. *A Portrait of Isaac Newton* (Cambridge: Harvard Univ., 1968), and *Times Literary Supplement*, (1973): 615, 644, 692, 749, 779. See also the discussion of Newton's narcissistic relation to Fatio in J. E. McGuire, "Newton and the Demonic Furies: Some Current Problems and Approaches in The History of Science," *History of Science* 11 (1973): 40-45; McGuire's essay is an analytic review of Manuel's psychobiography of Newton.

8. *The Correspondence of Isaac Newton*. Vol. 3: *1688-1694* ed. H. W. Turnbull (Cambridge: Cambridge Univ. Press, 1961), p. 280; the letter has been interpreted by Brian Easlea in *Witch Hunting, Magic and the New Philosophy* (Sussex: Harvester, 1980), p. 245.

9. Garden City: Doubleday, 1960, p. 23.

10. Quoted in Walter Serauky, *Georg Friedrich Händel: Sein Leben, Sein Werk* (Basel: Barenreiter, 1956), p. 612.

11. See Walter Newman Flower, *George Frideric Handel: His Personality* . . . (N.Y.: Scribner's, 1948), pp. 85, 177; R. A. Streatfield, *Handel* (N.Y.: Da Capo, 1964), p. 305.

12. *Observations, Anecdotes and Characters*, ed. James Osborn, 2 vols. (Oxford: Clarendon, 1966), 1:80.

13. *Times Literary Supplement* (5 Sept. 1980): 963; (19 Sept. 1980): 1039.

14. *The Rage of Edmund Burke* (N.Y.: Basic Books, 1977), pp. 83-87. The negative reviews were many and were less based on Kramnick's misunderstanding of the basic nature of Burke's conservatism than on his application of psychohistory and Freudian psychology, especially Kramnick's analysis of the masculine and feminine principle in Burke's personality. See, for example, the reviews by Reed Browning, *Modern Age* 22 (1978): 105-08; Carl Cone, *American Historical Review* 83 (1978): 722-23, and F. A. Dreyer, *The Eighteenth Century: A Current Bibliography* n.s. 3 (1977): 180-01, who writes on p. 181: "What is particularly objectionable about Kramnick's argument, however, is that he has stated it in irrefutable terms. It is not merely argued that Burke is the champion of a Marxist aristocracy. . . . Also Burke is half-heterosexual and half-homosexual. . . , Kramnick's device for salvaging this nonsense is to conclude that Burke is ambivalent." "Ambivalence" is a primary tenet of Freudian analysis; therefore, given Kramnick's disposition to employ it, there is nothing inherently "pretentious," as Dreyer asserts, in Kramnick's application. The matter is rather that Dreyer is offended by Freudian psychoanalysis in the first place, and believes that Burke's reputation will be tarnished if it is applied to him.

15. Charlotte Charke, Cibber's youngest daughter, lived as a man for many years and involved herself in numerous lesbian affairs; see *A Narrative of the Life of Mrs. Charlotte Charke . . . written by herself* (London, 1755). The sexual lives of Cibber's children have not yet been told.

16. Jean Hagstrum, "Gray's Sensibility." In *Fearful Joy: Papers from the Thomas Gray Bicentenary Conference at Carleton University*, ed. J. Downey and B. Jones (McGill-Queen's Univ., 1974), pp. 6-19.

17. "Recent Studies in the Restoration and Eighteenth Century," *Studies in English Literature: 1500-1900* 15 (1975): 520.

18. The words are still so emotionally charged today that few scholars have been willing either to define them or to discuss their demarcations.

19. Useful studies include: Randolph Trumbach, "London's Sodomites: Homosexual Behavior and Western Culture in the 18th Century," *Journal of Social History* 11 (1977): 1-33; Philippe Ariès, "Réflexions sur l'histoire de l'homosexualité," in *Sexualités occidentales*, ed. Phillipe Ariès and André Bejin (Paris: Editions du Seuil, 1982), pp. 81-97; Eve K. Sedgwick, *Between Men: English Literature and Male Homosexual Desire* (N.Y.: Columbia Univ., 1985); and the essays by Arend Huussen, Michel Rey, and Trumbach in this volume.

20. [Argus Centoculi] *Old England: or, the Broadbottom Journal*, 2 June 1750. Centoculi is obviously a nom de plume.

21. The lexical history of the word is discussed in Reay Tannahill, *Sex in History* (Slough, Berks.: Hollen, 1980), pp. 285-87, and John Boswell, *Christianity, Social Tolerance, and Homosexuality* (Chicago: Univ. of Chicago, 1980), p. 284, n. 47.

22. E.g., see *A Short Treatise . . . Of the Sins of Sodomy . . . By a Learned Bishop in Ireland* (London, 1689), whose author uses "sodomite" to designate those who dress effeminately but who do not necessarily penetrate; for political uses, see *Sodom-Fair; or, The Market of the Man of Sin . . . to which is added, the history of adultery* (London, 1688), which attacks Papism under the guise of offering advice to "all Young English Papists, who intend to take Holy Orders, or Travel through Italy" (t.p.).

23. See E. J. Burford, *The Orrible Synne . . .* (London: Calder and Boyars, 1973), p. 139ff.; Tony Honore, *Sex Law in England* (London: Duckworth, 1978); and Susan Staves, *Players' Scepters* (Lincoln: Univ. of Nebraska, 1979), pp. xi, 261-62. Several cases are discussed in John Fortescue, *Reports of Select Cases in all the courts of Westminster-Hall* (London, 1748), and *Proceedings of the King's Commission of the Peace . . . for the City of London*, no. 6 [1749]: 127-29.

24. *The Trial and Condemnation . . . of Lord Castlehaven* (London, 1699), p. 23; see also discussion of it in Caroline Bingham, "Seventeenth-Century Attitudes toward Deviant Sex," *Journal of Interdisciplinary History* 1 (1971): 447-72.

25. The most definitive evidence will be put forth by J. W. Johnson in the *Princeton University Library Chronicle* 47 (1985): forthcoming.

26. *The True-Born Englishman: a satyr* (London, 1701), ll. 96-97. Italy continued to be cited as the true home of sodomy; for convincing evidence of the way it flourished there earlier, see Thomas Sterling, *Medieval Love Poems of Male Love and Friendship* (N.Y.: Garland, 1984). See, also, n. 71.

27. One of the best, if least researched, discussions of the subject remains Lawrence Stone's *The Family, Sex and Marriage in England, 1500-1800* (London: Weidenfeld and Nicholson, 1977), pp. 44-45, 516-18; but there is no equivalent, for the 18th c., of Ian Gibson's *The English Vice: Beating, Sex and Shame in Victorian England and After* (London: Duckworth, 1978).

28. Byron to Thomas Moore, 1 Mar. 1822, repeated on 8 June 1822, in *Byron's Letters and Journals*, ed. Leslie Marchand, 12 vols. (London: John Murray, 1979), 9: entries 91, 113, 120. For Byron's homosexuality, see Louis Crompton, *Byron and Greek Love: Homophobia in Nineteenth-Century England* (Berkeley and Los Angeles: Univ. of California, 1985).

29. *The Love that Dared not Speak its Name: A Candid History of Homosexuality in Britain* (Boston: Little Brown, 1970).

30. Quoted in H. Montgomery Hyde, *The Trials of Oscar Wilde* (N.Y.: Dover, 1962), p. 110.

31. The editors of the *Florida Edition of the Works of Laurence Sterne* (Gainsville, Univ. of Florida, 1984) do not comment on the possible homosexual implications of these passages; see 3:496, 473, 416.

32. Brushing aside "psychoanalytical criticism," let alone possible homosexual allusions in *Tristram Shandy*, the editors of the *Florida Edition* send the reader interested in this passage (3:367) to another source. I omit discussion of Yorick's complex erotic urges for reasons of space.

33. After a correspondence of several years, Carpenter visited Whitman in May 1877 and later that year brought back to England many of Whitman's democratic and sexual views about "the armies of those I love." (Whitman, "I Sing the Body Electric," l. 2, in "Children of Adam").

34. See Rev. edn. (N.Y.: Stein and Day, 1966), p. 366, and Dennis Altman, *The Homosexualization of America* (Boston: Beacon, 1982), pp. 69-71.

35. See Jeffrey Meyers, *Homosexuality and Literature, 1890-1930* (London: Athlone, 1977), pp. 42-57.

36. *Outsiders: A Study in Life and Letters* (Cambridge: MIT, 1982).

37. See note 117 below. Francis Haskell and Nicholas Penny are among the few authors who realize to what degree sexual otherness was involved in the neoclassical retrievals of the period *(Taste and the Antique* [New Haven: Yale Univ., 1981]).

38. *Oeuvres de Voltaire*, ed. M. Beuchot, 50 vols. (Paris: Lefevre, 1832), 14:5-9 and 26:275. Beccaria (1716-81) was professor of philosophy in Rome. He advocated toleration for homosexuals but not for heterosexual sodomists in his *Essay on Crimes and Punishments, translated from the Italian: with a commentary, attributed to Mons. de Voltaire* (London: J. Almon, 1767).

39. The anon. author of *Anecdotes pour servir à l'histoire secrète des Ebugors* (Amsterdam, 1733) promoted the idea that buggers were a species of hermaphrodite. No such notion is suggested in Gervaise de Latouche's fictional *Histoire de Dom Bougre, portier des Chartreux, par lui-même* (Paris, 1741).

40. The background of her observation, as well as the remark, is discussed in *The Yale Edition of Horace Walpole's Correspondence*, ed. W.S. Lewis, 48 vols. (New Haven: Yale Univ., 1937-1983), 17:274.

41. An exception is found in M. de la Croix, *Peinture des moeurs du siècle* (Amsterdam, 1777). In a chap. entitled "Lettre conjecture sur un troisième sexe," he suggests that there existed a third, neuter gender, which was probably hermaphroditical.

42. *Great Venus Unmasked* (London, 1676), p. 140.

43.. See Wolfart's *Tractatio juridica de sodomia vera & spuria hermaphroditi . . .* (Frankfurt, 1742). Much earlier, Jacques Duval, a professor of medicine in Paris, had linked hermaphroditism to effeminate behavior: *Des Hermaphrodits, accouchmens des femmes . . .* (Rouen, 1612). A century later Charles Ancillon wrote a liberal treatise entitled *Traité des Eunuques* (no place, 1707) arguing against all churches that eunuchs should be permitted to marry, at the same time the French physician Nicholas Venette begged for greater sexual licence within marriage. By 1700 or 1720 hermaphroditism had been wrenched from its exclusively theological stranglehold and viewed, intermittently, from a physiological and biological perspective, although its medical link to homosexuality is a nineteenth-century development. For hermaphrodites see Pierre Darmon, *Le tribunal de l'impuissance* (Paris: Sevil, 1979), pp. 53-56 and the same author's *Le mythe de la procréation a l'âge baroque* (Paris: J. J. Pauvert, 1977), pp. 161-184.

44. *The Adventures of Roderick Random* [1748], ed. Paul-Gabriel Boucé (Oxford: (Oxford Univ., 1979)., p. 198. Boucé's notes identify and address some of the issues of concern in this portion of the essay.

45. Ulrichs was well read in medicine and science, although he had studied jurisprudence. According to John Addington Symonds it was Josef Kaserer, a Viennese physician, who invented the term "urning" in 1862; see John Addington Symonds, *A Problem in Modern Ethics* (London, privately printed, 1881), p. 54.

46. See Karl Ulrichs, *Die Geschlechtsnatur des . . . Urnings* (Berlin, 1868); his collected works have recently been trans. by Michael A. Lombardi at Urania Manuscripts, Los Angeles.

47. These pastorals had described the love of Ganymede for other shepherds; see Richard Barnfield, *Affectionate Shepherd* (1594) and *The Shepherd's Content* (1595). The relation of neoclassical pastoral literature to passionate male friendships has been studied in Rictor Norton, *The Homosexual Literary Tradition: An Interpretation* (N.Y.: Revisionist, 1974).

48. Fielding treats the matter ironically *(The Masquerade* [1728], and *The Female Husband* [1746]).

49. In *The Works of the English Poets*, ed. Samuel Johnson, 72 vols. (London, 1790), 52:50-52.

50. His travels have been well surveyed by Robert Halsband in *Lord Hervey: Eighteenth-Century Courtier* (Oxford: Clarendon, 1973), pp. 272ff.

51. The phrase is John Chandos', in *Boys Together: English Public Schools, 1800-1864* (New Haven: Yale Univ., 1984), p. 284, who also astutely notes, on p. 303, that even in the nineteenth century "a sodomite was identified by his acts, not by the nature which caused them." For boys bonding in schools and their close sleeping quarters, see also Brian Reade, *Sexual Heretics: Male Homosexuality in English Literature 1850 to 1900* (N.Y.: Coward-McCann, 1971), pp. 10-51 and T. W. Bamford, *Rise of the Public Schools: A Study of Boys' Public Boarding Schools in England and Wales from 1837 to the Present Day* (London: Nelson, 1967).

52. 2 vols. (Oxford, 1750), 1:10-12, 18-19, 2:136-38.

53. The subtitle reads: *To which is prefix'd, A Particular Account of the Proceedings against Robert Thistlethwayte, Late Doctor of Divinity, and Warden of Wadham College, For a Sodomitical Attempt upon Mr. W. French, Commoner of the Same College* (Oxford, 1739). See also *College Wit Sharpened; or, A Head of a College with a Sting in the Tail* (London, 1739).

54. Gordon Goodwin, "John Kidgell," in Leslie Stephen, et al (eds.), *The Dictionary of National Biography*, 22 vols. (Oxford: Oxford Univ., 1922), 11:98.

55. See Boyd Alexander, *England's Wealthiest Son* (London: Centaur, 1962), pp. 108-17.

56. R. W. Ketton-Cremer, *Horace Walpole: A Biography* (London: Faber, 1946), pp. 35-37: W. S. Lewis, *Horace Walpole* (N.Y.: Pantheon, 1960), pp. 45-48.

57. W. S. Lewis, *One's Man's Education* (N.Y.: Alfred Knopf, 1967), pp. 226-28. Linda Colley is undoutedly right to comment (*Times Literary Supplement*, 1985: 1035) that Walpole "was almost certainly homosexual, though possibly passively so." Not unpredictably she was assaulted for this position by the male scholars entrenched in the Walpole Factory who have insisted, even after Lewis' death, on suppressing all discussion of Walpole's sexuality. For the response to Colley see *TLS*, 1985: 1207.

58. Peter Watson-Smyth, "On Gray's Elegy," *The Spectator* (31 July 1971): 171-74, who concludes (p. 171): "As Gray was, like Walpole, particularly devoted to his mother, it will surprise no psychiatrist that such a background produced a homosexual whose first and greatest love, I believe, was Horace Walpole." This interpretation stirred a controversy about Gray's sexuality in subsequent issues of *The Spectator*: see letter-columns in issues dated Oct. 9 (p. 523), Oct. 30 (p. 629), Dec. 4 (p. 826), Dec. 18 (p. 895).

59. *Lives of the English Poets*, ed. G. B. Hill, 3 vols. (Oxford: Clarendon, 1905), 3:414. The only discussion of Akenside's homosexuality I have seen is by William Ober, M.D., "Mark Akenside, M.D. Physician and Philosophic Poet," *New York State Journal of Medicine* 68 (1968): 3169, but see note 102 below.

60. Some of the club's correspondence is found in BL Add. MSS 30867, fols. 1-37.

61. Tobias Smollett, *The Adventures of Peregrine Pickle* (1751), chaps. 17-21.

62. John Henry Meibomius, *A Treatise on the Use of Flogging in Venereal Affairs* (London, 1761), p. 139, first published in 1639.

63. *The Mysteries of Conjugal Love Revealed* (London, 1712). Venette, a French physician who practiced medicine in New Rochelle, France, remains obscure.

64. See Arthur N. Gilbert, "Buggery and the British Navy, 1700-1861," *Journal of Social History* 10 (1976): 74-75. For a contemporary description of the hammock system, see Henry Meredith, *An Account of the Gold Coast of Africa* (London: Longman, 1812), pp. 58-60.

65. See Richard Wiseman, *Eight Chirurgical Treatises*, 2 vols., 5th ed. (London, 1719), p. 348, and Paulus Zacchius, *Quaestionum medico-legalium* (Leiden, 1726).

66. See Madge Darby, *Who Caused the Mutiny on the Bounty?* (Sydney: Angus and Robertson, 1965), pp. 80-81.

67. N.Y.: Panurge, 1934.

68. The author is obsessed with new gender arrangements and stereotypings, and remarks in the concluding lines of an inserted poem addressed to someone of the new third sex: "I stand amaz'd, and am at a Loss to know, / To what new Species thou thy Form does owe?" (p. 62).

69. *Proceedings of the King's Commission*, pp. 127-28.

70. G. S. Rousseau, "Threshold and Explanation: The Social Anthropologist and the Critic of Eighteenth-Century Literature," *The Eighteenth Century: Theory and Interpretation* 22 (1981): 149.

71. Defoe, "The True-Born Englishman," in F. H. Ellis, *Poems on Affairs of State: Augustan Satirical Verse, 1660-1714*. Vol. 6: *1697-1714* (New Haven: Yale Univ., 1970), p. 268. The country of supposed origin varied depending on England's political relations at the moment; Turkey, Italy, and France continued to be the main rivals. Bernard de Mandeville claimed that sodomy first arose in Italy when Pope Sextus V banished courtesans (*A Modest Defence of Public Stews* [London, 1724], pp. 7-8). Even the author of *Satan's Harvest Home* blames all homosexuality on Italy: on the Italian opera's corruption of the English stage; on the Italian "Masquerades, Ridotto's, and Assemblies", on the castrati and eunuchs imported into England, and on the new "kissing" among men in England that rivaled the worst behavior in Italy (pp. 52-57).

72. *The Poetical Works of Charles Churchill*, ed. Douglas Grant (Oxford: Clarendon, 1959), p. 398.

73. Johnson, "London. A Poem in Imitation of Juvenal's Third Satire," line 94.

74. For William III and Keppel's relations 1694-97, see Marion E. Grew, *William Bentinck and William III* (London: John Murray, 1924), pp. 224, 276-78, and G. S. Stevenson (ed. and trans.), *The Letters of Madame. The Correspondence of Elizabeth-Charlotte of Bavaria, Princess Palatine, Duchess of Orleans*, 2 vols. (London: Arrowsmith, 1924), 1:217. The curious friendship of Keppel and Matthew Prior, the perpetually unmarried poet-diplomat who was at The Hague during these years, requires further investigation.

75. John Dryden's translations of Persius' fourth satire, especially of the figure of Alcibiades, who prowls the streets at night with his "Guards" and who engages in unnamed

acts with his "Catamite," needs to be reconsidered in this light; *The Works of John Dryden*, H. T. Swedenberg, Jr., et al, eds. (Berkeley and Los Angeles: Univ. of California, 1974), 4:319 (1. 122), 317 (1. 85).

76. Printed by A. Moore, the only copy I have seen is in the Bodleian Library. See R. A. Day, *Told in Letters* (Ann Arbor: Univ. of Michigan, 1966), pp. 142-43, 225, 251.

77. "An Epistle to Dr. Arbuthnot," *The Poems of Alexander Pope*, vol. 4, ed. John Butt (London and New Haven: Yale Univ., 1969), p. 119 (1. 326).

78. *The Secret History*, ed. Oliver H. G. Leigh (Washington, D.C.: M. Walter Dienne, 1901), pp. 76-77, 179, 230; letters 18, 29, 33, 39, 45, 48.

79. Raoul Girardet, *Mémoires de Gorani* (Paris: Gallimard, 1944).

80. *Observations*, 2:556. Charles Burney, the musicologist, is silent about the liaison with Gravina.

81. See Amadeo Quondam, *Cultura e ideologia di G. Gravina* (Milan, 1968), pp. 43, 57, 259.

82. *Travels into Turkey* (London, 1744). For the sexual bonding of Turkish women at the Turkish baths, see pp. 146-47.

83. Edward Ward, "The Mollies' Club," *The History of the London Clubs* (London, 1709), pp. 28-29.

84. Sodomy is described on p. 14, "drunkenness and profane clubs" on p. 10.

85. Newcomb is disturbed by the ambiguity of the genders appearing everywhere at court and in the streets of London; see "Satire VIII," pp. 415-17.

86. Louis Crompton covers the Dutch persecutions of the 1730s in "Gay Genocide: From Leviticus to Hitler," in L. Crew, ed., *The Gay Academic* (Palm Springs: ETC Pub., 1978), pp. 67-91. For a contemporary account of these persecutions see Michael Lombardi, *Emanuel Valk: The Trial of a Gay Preacher in 18th Century Holland* (Los Angeles: Urania Manuscripts, 1984), which is based on the Dutch original, *Advys van Regtsgeleerden* (Utrecht: Pieter Muntendam, 1731).

87. Vivid accounts are found in *Applebee's Original Weekly Journal*, 20, 27 June; 4 July 1730, unpaginated.

88. "Eros and Liberty at the English Masquerade, 1710-1790," *Eighteenth-Century Studies* 17 (1983-84): 156-76 and "Matters not fit to be mentioned: Fielding's *The Female Husband*," *English Literary History* 49 (1982): 602-22.

89. Such earlier works as *King Satan* (1724) and *The Religion of Satan* (1736) deal with lust as a force of the devil, but do not predict catastrophe.

90. These phallocentric clubs have not been studied in any detail, but see D. P. Mannix, *The Hell-Fire Club* (N.Y.: Ballantine, 1959); Ronald Fuller, *Hell-Fire Francis* (London: Chatto and Windus, 1939); Louis Clark Jones, *The Clubs of the Georgian Rakes* (N.Y.: Columbia Univ., 1942); Robert Joseph Allen, *The Clubs of Augustan London* (Cambridge: Harvard Univ., 1933).

91. *The Character of the Times Delineated* (London: J. Wilford, 1732), pp. 10, 14.

92. I owe this reference to Peter Wagner, who has discussed these masturbatory clubs in *Eros Revived: A Study of Eighteenth-Century Erotica* (London: Secker and Warburg, 1985).

93. I have found no modern study of Caylus' circle, which included, at different times, Winckelmann, Mengs, and D'Hancarville (Hugues), author of *Veneres et Priapi* (Paris, 1771) and the lurid, if pornographic, two volumes, *Monumens de la vie privée des douze Césars* and *Monumens du Culte Secret des Dames Romaines*, both published between 1780 and 1784.

94. *Bibliography of Prohibited Books*, 2 vols. (N.Y.: Jack Brussel, 1962), 2:414-15.

95. See Louis F. Peck, *A Life of Matthew G. Lewis* (Cambridge: Harvard Univ., 1961), pp. 14-17.

96. See Michel Foucault's introduction to *Herculine Barbin: Being the Recently Discovered Memoirs of a Nineteenth-Century French Hermaphrodite* (Brighton: Harvester, 1980), pp. xiv-xvii, for the overlaps of the prison and the madhouse.

97. Alan Valentine, *Lord George Germain* (Oxford: Clarendon, 1962), p. 211.

98. David Hilliard, "Unenglish and Unmanly: Anglo-Catholicism and Homosexuality," *Victorian Studies*, 25 (1982): 181-210.

99. I have found no study of these arrangements between private tutors and their tutees; such authoritative works as William Mead, *The Grand Tour in the Eighteenth Century* (Boston: Houghton Mifflin, 1914), and Percy G. Adams, *Travelers and Travel Liars: 1660-1800* (Berkeley and Los Angeles: Univ. of California, 1962), are silent on these matters.

100. Lewis, *Horace Walpole*, pp. 45-48.

101. See Add. MSS 30867, fols. 8-45.

102. See G. S. Rousseau, " 'In the House of Madame Vander Tasse on the Long Bridge': A Homosocial University Club in Early Modern Europe," *Journal of Homosexuality*, XI (1986): forthcoming.

103. Add. MSS 30867, fol. 8. Wilkes presented Baxter with copies of Spinoza's works (fol. 9).

104. Allen Edwardes, *The Rape of India: A Biography of Robert Clive . . .* (N.Y.: Julian, 1966). By the time D'archenholz wrote *Picture of England* (Dublin, 1790), Clive's sexual reputation was well known.

105. See pp. 335-38 for the locations of Edwardes' manuscript sources.

106. I consulted an unexpurgated edition of *Intriques* in the Royal Library at The Hague; much evidence exists to support the idea that Clive's diaries are at least partly true. For Clive in the Parisian Order of Sodomites see *Intrigues of a Nabob*, pp. 71-72.

107. See Jonathan D. Spence, *The Memory Palace of Matteo Ricci* (New York: Viking Penguin, 1984), chap. 7, "The Men of Sodom." The 1743 *Travels of the Jesuits* is a translation sometimes attributed to John Lockman.

108. Respectively, Frans Caron, *Rechte Beschrijvinge van het machtigh koninghrijk Jappan* (The Hague: I. Tongerloo, 1662) which appeared in English translation in 1663 as *A True Description of the Mighty Kingdoms of Japan and Siam . . . now rendred [sic] into English By Capt. Roger Manley* (London: Samuel Brown, 1663) and which continued to be reprinted in the eighteenth century; Bernardus Varenius, *Descriptio Regni Japoniae* (Amsterdam: van Wijk, 1649); Arnoldus Montanus, *Gedenkenwaerdige Gesantschappen der Oost-Indische Maatschappij . . . aan de Kaisaren van Japan* (Amsterdam: Jacob Meurs, 1669), which was translated into English within a year by John Ogilby as *Atlas Jappannesis* (London: T. Johnson, 1670) and reprinted in 1745 as volume 3 of John Green's compilation, *A New General Collection of Voyages and Travels,* 4 vols. (London: Thomas Astley, 1745-47); George Psalmanazar, *Memoirs of * * * * commonly known by the name of George Psalmanazar, a reputed native of Formosa . . .* (London: T. Davis, 1764); Giovanni Francesco Gemelli-Carreri, *Giro del mondo,* 6 vols. (Naples, 1699-1700), excerpts of which were also trans. into English and included in vol. 3 of John Green's compilation just cited. Caron was awestricken by the amount of homosexuality he found in Japan. "Their Priests," he wrote, "as well as many of the Gentry, are much given to Sodomy, that unnatural passion, being esteemed no sin, nor shameful thing amongst them"; see C. R. Boxer, ed., *Francois Caron's A True Description of the Mighty Kingdoms of Japan and Siam. Reprinted from The English Edition of 1663* (London: The Argonaut Press, 1935), p. 43; see also pp. 23-24 for homosexual sodomy.

109. *The New English Bible* (Oxford and Cambridge: Oxford Univ. and Cambridge Univ., 1970), p. 192.

110. See vol. 3 of *The Letters of John Addington Symonds,* ed. Herbert M. Schueller, et al, 3 vols. (Detroit: Wayne State Univ., 1969).

111. Sir Harold Acton, *The Last Medici* (London: Macmillan, 1980); see also *Oxford, China and Italy: Writings in Honor of Sir Harold Acton on his Eightieth Birthday,* ed Edward Chaney, et al (London: Thames and Hudson, 1984).

112. *The Yale Edition of Horace Walpole's Correspondence,* W. S. Lewis, 48 vols. (New Haven: Yale Univ., 1937-1983), 22:343.

113. *Memoirs of the Baron Poellnitz,* 4 vols. (London, 1738), 2:130-33.

114. Sir Harold Acton, *The Last Medici* (London: Macmillan, 1980), pp. 211-13, 234-36.

115. Norman Douglas, *The Last of the Medici . . .* (Florence: privately printed by G. Orioli, n.d.), pp. 139-59.

116. *The Arrogant Connoisseur: Richard Payne Knight, 1751-1824,* Michael Clark, et al, eds. (Manchester: Manchester Univ., 1982) and G. S. Rousseau, "Homosocial Desire, Anticlericalism, and The Making of *The Worship of Priapus*," in Roy Porter and G. S. Rousseau (eds.), *Sexual Underworlds of the Enlightenment* (Manchester: Manchester Univ., 1986), forthcoming. Knight's history was *A Discourse on The Worship of Priapus* (London, 1786). His Sicilian journal (1777) was discovered by Claudia Stumpf in 1980 in Weimar.

117. Forthcoming, 1986. Many of von Wangenheim's conclusions about Winckelmann's homosexuality were anticipated by Hans Mayer in *Outsiders,* pp. 167-74.

118. See A. E. Housman, *The Scholar-Poet* (London: Routledge, 1979).

119. Mayer, *Outsiders,* pp. 167-71, 228.

120. Only Mayer has suspected how important this resource is (*Outsiders,* p. 218).

Sodomy in the Dutch Republic during the Eighteenth Century

The introduction of Calvinism in the emerging Dutch Republic seems to have had little effect on conceptions of morality. Legislation against sex crimes, for example, was little changed. The Reformed ministers were struggling for stricter observance of Calvinist norms of behavior; but in a society in which the Reformed church was not the state religion, the clergy's influence was necessarily less formal and less direct than in England or France. Synods asked for stricter legislation against such vices as inebriety, dancing, theatre, luxury, and other intemperances; but public authorities did not yield to these puritan tendencies. The Calvinist church, though privileged, had to rely on its own methods to induce change in attitudes and behavior of its members. This was effected by means of the discipline *(censura morum)* exercised by the local consistories and regional synods.[1]

Legislation on moral issues was gradually adapted to Calvinist norms, but this does not necessarily imply that it was stiffened or puritanized. In conformity with Reformed ecclesiastical dogma regarding the nonsacramental character of marriage, divorce was introduced, and civil marriage for dissenters was made a legal option in Holland after 1580. However, divorce was neither advertised nor otherwise promoted. Marriage for life remained the ideal alliance between man and woman.[2]

New "reformed" secular legislation was introduced; but no special attention to sex crimes can be traced. Adultery, prostitution, incest, sodomy, and bestiality continued to be considered particularly heinous crimes; it appears, however, that during the seventeenth century they were not singled out for punishment that was exceptionally severe by the standards of the day, which frequently imposed corporal and capital punishment.

If we are to single out the position and treatment of homosexuals for the purposes of this essay, one caveat must be stressed: as far as we know, the Calvinists did not develop a new vision of the phenomenon of sodomy. Calvinists considered it a sin and crime, *contra naturam*, as did the Roman Catholic theologians and criminalists before them.[3] As "natural," or as ordained by God, heterosexual intercourse was normally to be confined to marriage, where its end was procreation. Sodomy's origins as a grave sin are found in the traditional interpretation of the biblical events at Sodom and Gomorrah and the destruction of those cities by the wrath of God. Secular interference with the sin/crime of sodomy could be justified in a society in which the active, revenging hand of God was still expected and feared. Indeed, belief in magic and Satan still informed the average *outillage mental* of Dutch people, although witch trials were virtually nonexistent in Holland after 1600.[4]

People of the "world we have lost" avoided discourse about sodomy as either sin or crime. This avoidance makes it even more difficult for us to form an image of the real status of sodomy and homosexuality. The "unspeakable" crime *(crimen nefandum)* has left, by definition, little trace of itself. Nevertheless, historians, progressive or not, are looking for answers to such questions as: did homosexuality exist in this period? If so, how prevalent was it, and in what social groups? May we speak of a homosexual subculture during the seventeenth and eighteenth centuries? What did people mean by "sodomy," and what kinds of reactions did they have to homosexual and, especially, sodomitic, behavior?

An inquiry into Dutch criminal law reveals a certain degree of indistinctness in interpreting the concept of sodomy and therefore in using the term. The famous German *Peinlich Gerichtsordnung* (penal code) or Constitutio Criminalis Carolina of 1532, promulgated by Emperor Charles V—a criminal statute that gained authority among criminalists in the republic—assigned to the category of crimes against nature (article 116) intercourse between men, between women, and between humans and animals.[5] The Dutch laws on military discipline mandated capital punishment for "unnatural misuses"; and, in defining *sodomia,* commentators Petrus Pappus van Tratzberg and Gerhard Feltman alleged *expressis verbis* the German Carolina, though this statute did not use the term "sodomy."[6]

The same picture emerges from local and regional customary laws and statutes that contained provisions against the crime of sodomy. In fact, many laws do not contain any regulations on this topic at all. Death by burning was the usual prescription for sodomy: a practice confirmed without much comment by such prominent criminalists and commentators on Roman and common law as Joos de Damhouder (1507-81) and Antonius Matthaeus II (1601-54).[7]

From these sources alone it would be virtually impossible to answer our questions. Where "theory" fails, it seems appropriate to consult practice. Before the beginning of the nineteenth century criminal jurisdiction in the Dutch Republic was fragmented into hundreds of local and regional courts. Quantitative research into the incidence of a specific crime would be an enormous task, even supposing the series of criminal sentences to be complete and uninterrupted.[8] Moreover, as has been rightly stressed by Bert Oaks, court records must be handled with care when seeking information about sexual activities:[9] the historian is dependent upon the governmental and judicial policy of the moment in uncovering certain crimes; he or she will read, more often than not, a description of the prosecuted offenses as viewed by the judge or clerk; and so-called "confessions" may have been obtained by torture or other means.[10] In the case of trials against sodomites it even seems that some were burned along with their files. Even conceding the methodological problems that have to be solved by the historian's usual critical devices, criminal records can be a source of great importance. By studying them serially over a long period we can develop insight into the changing attitudes of peoples and governments towards deviant or abnormal behavior.

Modern serial research in Dutch criminal records before the eighteenth century is scarce, yet it seems justified to contend that sodomy was not unknown and was not unrecognized. Judicial proceedings were rarely instituted, however. What does this mean? Was sodomy rare or merely not manifest? From contemporary reactions and literature about the notorious mass persecutions of sodomites and homosexuals in general in Holland and Utrecht in 1730 and 1731, we know that perplexed spectators perceived sodomy as a completely new evil never before seen among them. Explanations given for this "new" phenomenon varied widely but stressed effeminate French cultural influences and general relaxation of morality. Panic spread, both among sodomites, who fled to escape death, and among Calvinist ministers and the judges themselves, who feared the wrath of God. We now know that accepting these perceptions would be to misinterpret the facts. First, before 1700 there were several capital sentences against sodomites: in 1629 in the town of Breda, Province of Brabant, against the painter Carel (or Daniel) de Lasco; in 1676 in Utrecht against a cooper's workman; and in 1686 in Amsterdam against a ship-boy. Serial research of the criminal records of the university town of Leiden has revealed five sentences for sodomy out of five thousand sentences during the years 1533-1700.[11]

Second, we find that courts or judges often ignored unambiguous evidence. In November 1702 the Court of Holland was confronted with a delinquent who made remarkable statements indeed. The suspect, twenty-five or -six years old, born at The Hague, had just arrived in the town, probably on leave from his military regiment. He told the judges that several persons, whom he named, had propositioned him at the Vijverberg to commit sodomy. Was he at this area of rendezvous for homosexuals by chance or on purpose? Was extortion his malicious intent? It seems that the suspect, Gabriel de Berger, assaulted and robbed three persons, of whom one was rescued by a strong coachman who delivered the suspect to the police and who gave evidence of the disorder of the victim's clothes at the time of rescue. The court, which had jurisdiction over the "Binnenhof" (now the House of Parliament) and over the neighboring Vijverberg, thus became involved.

From the files of this case it is evident that at first the court was alarmed by the accusations of de Berger against the sodomites he named. Although de Berger revoked his charges at some point during the preliminary examination, on 12 December, the court ordered a special interrogation, during which, on 10 January 1703, he gave information on the special signs by which sodomites could be recognized and on the places where they met in The Hague, and he confessed to having walked in female dress two days before his arrest.

The interesting point is that although the Court of Holland condemned de Berger to death, it did not condemn him for attempted sodomy or travesty. Capital punishment was imposed on 22 January for multiple assault and falsely accusing people of propositioning him to commit sodomy. In this case the attention of the authorities was drawn to a subculture of sodomitic behavior; that they did not pursue it indicates a lack of concern about sodomy in the begining of the eighteenth century.

From the many trials that occurred throughout the republic during the eighteenth century it is evident that there existed a kind of sodomitic or homosexual subculture, especially in the great cities, where networks of friends and clubs of men met regularly, presumably to seek sexual partners, apply their own rules of behavior, and play their specific roles. Many interesting features of this subculture have been brought to light by recent research into, in particular, the waves of persecution of 1730, 1764, and 1776.[12]

In 1730 the Court of Frisia was puzzled by the fact that homosexuals often seemed to give each other girls' names. The court informed the authorities of the neighboring province of Groningen of this custom. In 1764 the authorities in Amsterdam became aware of special places in the city where sodomites or homosexuals gathered, recognizing each other by specific signs. Arcades of the town hall, dark parts of the churches, and public urinals were all favorite meeting places. By the middle of the century there existed houses or taverns, so-called *lolhuysen,* where homosexuals met. Contacts were also sought in parks or in the theatre. Transient contacts were contrasted with intense love affairs and the lasting engagements of men who sealed "marriage" contracts with blood. A traveling Don Juan such as Zacharias Wilsma, who must have been paid for his services during the 1720s, seems as atypical as the couple who wrote ardent love letters to each other in the 1770s, for many of the prosecuted sodomites were married and had children. The social positions of those accused of sodomy varied widely; they formed a range of social statuses and occupations, from distinguished gentlemen to simple manservants.

Serial research of criminal court records in the republic during the eighteenth century provides evidence that before 1730 sodomy was only sporadically prosecuted, although it certainly was not an unknown phenomenon. After 1730 several waves of persecution occurred; isolated trials became more frequent until 1811. Three points should be noted: the definition of the crime of sodomy, the seemingly arbitrary penalties, and the scarcity of condemnations of women.

After prosecution of sodomites began in Utrecht in the spring of 1730, the town of Groningen and the provincial state of Holland proclaimed special statutes against sodomy. Apparently, the purpose of these new laws was to make it possible to prosecute those who had made themselves suspects by fleeing the country. The courts could condemn these suspects by default—an unusual procedure for that time. From the records it is evident that the crime of sodomy was defined narrowly. Capital punishment was to be applied only in cases in which the suspect had confessed to anal contact and to *ejaculatio in ano* with another man. This seems in accord with legal practice in England and France during the period.[13]

Capital punishment was imposed in only about 10 percent of the sentences. Prison terms of up to thirty or fifty years or banishment, sometimes in combination with corporal punishment, were the prescribed sentences for the large majority of cases. Fugitives were usually punished with "eternal" banishment. The death penalty and banishment for life were, until 1732, combined with the confiscation of the condemned man's personal property. Some suspects committed suicide while being held in detention.[14] (See table, *Criminal Sentences*.)

We know of very few cases in which women were prosecuted for lesbianism or tribadism: three women at Leiden in the seventeenth century and some twelve women at Amsterdam during the years 1792-98. (Indeed, romantic stories of brave young women who fought as soldiers or went aboard ship as sailors tickled public imagination.) Perhaps the fact that physical contact between women is more accepted in western culture explains why women remained largely outside the scope of criminal justice in these instances. Moreover, lesbians could not be implicated in the crime of sodomy as it was usually defined, which perhaps also explains the relatively light penalties conviction for lesbianism incurred; punishments were often due in part to other offenses of which they were also accused.

The last known imposition of the death penalty against sodomites was in 1803 in the little town of Schiedam, near Rotterdam. Six years later the first national criminal code, the *Crimineel Wetboek voor het Koningrijk Holland,* fixed life imprisonment as the most severe penalty for sodomy. Two years later, after the annexation of the Kingdom of Holland by Emperor Napoleon in 1810, the French penal code was introduced. The *Code pénal* did not fix penalties for the traditional sodomitic acts. A new chapter had begun.

Most contemporaries defined sodomy literally in terms of a sexual *act*. No other approach seemed justified as long as one wished to see in sodomy only the unmentionable sin or crime. Yet one finds traces of other opinions in some trial records after 1730. Particularly interesting in this regard is Rev. Andreas Klink, on whom the Court of Holland on 13 November 1759 imposed "eternal" banishment from the provinces of Holland, Zeeland, and Utrecht for sodomy. Klink, a Calvinist minister, had defended himself, saying in substance that his attraction to young men was proper by nature ("hem van natuure eijgen was"), because while his mother was pregnant she had a very strong desire for his absent father, a desire which he inherited in the womb from her. The lawyer Pieter Loens, who wrote a tract about the case, seems not to have been convinced by this explanation.[16] Yet one may venture to suppose that some of Klink's contemporaries empathized with him, interpreting their homosexual or homoerotic attraction to men as an inborn disposition.

Twenty years later we find a plea for tolerance towards sodomites in a tract written as a consequence of the wave of homosexual persecution in

1776. Anonymous, but attributed to Abraham Perrenot, the tract considered sodomites or homosexuals as infected by a disease that did little harm to society at large. Influenced by the enlightened ideas of the self-styled *philosophe* and criminalist Cesare Beccaria, Perrenot was of the opinion that the act of sodomy was a crime only if perpetrated with a boy under age. Perrenot rejected capital punishment, preferring a long prison term for convicted sodomites.[17]

During the seventeenth and eighteenth centuries sodomites were not persecuted in the Dutch Republic on the same scale and intensity as were heretics and witches elsewhere. Persecutions found a place, indeed, at a time when one would expect more tolerance, and they ended during a period when "Victorian" prudery announced itself.[18] But while the intro-

Legend

1) Provincial Court of Frisia 2) Provincial Court of Holland 3) District Court of Waterland 4) District Court of Wassenaar & Zuidwijk 5) Town Court of Brielle 6) District Court of Twente 7) District Court of Heerlen 8) Town Court of Zierikzee 9) Town Court of Vlaardingen 10) Town Court of Leiden 11) Town Court of Breda 12) Town Court of The Hague 13) Town Court of Amsterdam
NOTE: The total of 269 sentences includes cases of default; the Amsterdam numbers do not include the cases in which no definite sentence is recorded (1730-32, 33 cases; 1764-65, 61; and 1776, 16).

Sources

1) A. H. Huussen Jr., "Gerechtelijke vervolging van 'sodomie' gedurende de 18e eeuw in de Republiek, in het bijzonder in Friesland" ["Judicial Persecutions of 'Sodomy' during the 18th Century in the Republic, Especially in Friesland"] *Groniek, Gronings Historisch Tijdschrift* 66 (Jan. 1980): 18-33;   2-7) unpub. material collected by H. A. Diederiks, S. Faber, A. H. Huussen Jr., et al.;   8-9) unpub. material kindly put at our disposal by Dr. H. A. Diederiks;   10) D. J. Noordam, "Homosexualiteit en sodomie in Leiden, 1533-1811" ["Homosexuality and Sodomy at Leiden, 1533-1811"] *Leids Jaarboekje* 75 (1983): 72-105;   11) J. van Haastert, "Beschouwingen bij de criminele vonnissen van de schepenbank van de stad Breda uit de jaren 1626 tot 1795" ["Considerations on the Criminal Sentences of the Town Court of Breda during the Years 1626 till 1795"] and "Beschouwingen bij de criminele vonnissen van Bredase rechtbanken in de periode 1796-1811" ["Considerations on the Criminal Sentences of the Courts of Breda during the Period 1796-1811"] *Jaarboek van de Geschieden Oudheidkundige Kring van Stad en Land van Breda "De Oranjeboom"* 29 (1976): 56-106 and 35 (1982): 62-119, with unpub. material kindly put at our disposal by the author;   12) A. J. van Weel "De strafvonnissen van de Haagse Vierschaar in de periode 1700-1811" ["The Criminal Sentences of the Court of The Hague in the Period 1700-1811"] in *Die Haghe* (1984), pp. 134-189;   13) Theo van der Meer, *De wesentlijke sonde van sodomie en andere vuyligheeden. Sodomietenvervolgingen in Amsterdam, 1730-1811. [The Real Sin of Sodomy and other Lewdness. Persecutions of Sodomites in Amsterdam 1730-1811]* (Amsterdam, 1984).

CRIMINAL SENTENCES (269) IN SODOMY CASES, 1701-1811

	1	2	3	4	5	6	7	8	9	10	11	12	13
1730	8	12	—	—	—	—	—	—	1	21	—	—	12
1731	—	40	—	—	—	—	—	—	—	—	—	1	1
1732	—	—	—	—	—	—	—	—	—	—	—	—	1
1733	—	1	—	—	—	—	—	—	—	—	—	—	—
1734	2	—	—	—	—	—	—	—	—	—	—	—	—
1739/40	—	—	—	—	—	—	—	—	—	—	—	—	1
1741	—	—	—	—	—	—	—	—	—	—	—	—	3
1743	—	—	—	—	—	—	—	—	—	—	—	—	2
1746	—	—	—	—	—	—	—	—	—	—	—	—	3
1749	—	—	—	—	—	—	—	2	—	—	—	—	1
1750	—	—	—	—	—	—	—	—	—	—	—	—	2
1755	—	—	1	—	—	—	—	—	—	—	—	—	—
1757	1	—	—	—	—	—	—	—	—	—	—	—	—
1758	—	—	—	—	—	—	—	—	—	4	—	—	—
1759	1	1	—	—	—	—	—	—	—	—	—	—	—
1760	—	—	—	—	—	—	—	—	—	—	—	—	1
1761	—	—	—	—	—	—	—	—	—	—	—	—	1
1762	—	—	—	—	—	—	—	—	—	—	—	—	1
1763	—	—	—	—	—	—	—	—	—	—	—	—	3
1764	—	—	—	—	—	—	—	—	—	2	—	—	10
1765	—	—	—	—	—	—	—	—	—	2	—	—	4
1766	3	—	—	—	—	—	—	—	—	—	—	—	—
1768	1	—	—	—	—	—	—	—	—	—	—	—	—
1772	—	—	—	—	—	—	—	—	—	1	—	—	—
1774	1	—	—	—	—	—	—	—	—	—	—	—	—
1775	3	—	—	—	—	—	—	—	—	—	—	1	—
1776	—	1	—	—	—	—	—	—	—	2	—	3	4
1777	—	—	—	—	—	—	—	—	—	2	—	—	—
1778	—	—	—	—	—	—	—	—	—	—	—	1	—
1779	—	6	—	—	—	—	—	—	—	—	—	2	—
1781	—	—	—	—	—	—	—	2	—	—	—	—	—
1784	—	—	—	—	—	—	—	—	—	—	—	1	—
1789	—	—	—	—	—	—	—	1	—	3	—	—	—
1790	—	—	1	—	—	—	—	—	—	—	—	—	—
1791	—	—	—	—	—	—	—	—	—	1	—	—	2
1792	—	—	—	—	—	—	—	—	—	—	—	—	2
1793	—	—	—	—	—	—	—	—	—	1	—	—	—
1794	—	—	—	—	—	—	—	—	—	—	—	—	2
1795	—	—	—	—	—	—	—	—	—	—	—	—	3
1796	—	—	—	—	—	—	—	—	—	—	—	—	12
1797	1	—	—	—	—	—	—	—	—	—	—	2	5
1798	1	—	—	—	—	—	—	—	—	—	1	1	19
1799	—	—	—	—	—	—	—	—	—	—	—	—	3
1801	—	—	—	—	—	—	—	—	—	—	—	2	2
1802	—	—	—	—	—	—	—	—	—	—	—	—	1
1803	—	—	—	—	—	—	—	—	—	2	1	—	1
1804	—	—	—	—	—	—	—	—	—	—	—	1	1
1805	—	—	—	—	—	—	—	—	—	1	—	—	—
1806	—	—	—	—	—	—	—	—	—	—	—	—	1
1808	2	—	—	—	—	—	—	—	—	—	—	—	2
1809	1	—	—	—	—	—	—	—	—	—	1	—	6
1810	—	—	—	—	—	—	—	—	—	—	—	—	3
	25	61	2	—	—	—	—	5	1	42	3	15	115

Total 269

duction of the French penal code in 1811 may account for the ending of the persecution of sodomy as a crime, the persecutions from 1730 on are more complicated and difficult to explain.

It seems an established fact that the frequent demands for stricter observance of norms and prescriptions of morality were already put into practice in the 1720s (for example, prosecution of prostitution or adultery). By 1730 there seems to have emerged a stricter moral climate, voiced by "spectatorial," theological, and other writers, in which a radical new view on sodomites and on the sin/crime of sodomy was promulgated.[19]

The much-debated issues of the existence of a homosexual identity and of homosexual subcultures before the new medical observations of the nineteenth century cannot as yet be verified.[20] However, research in Dutch criminal records has brought to light some evidence both on contemporary self-perceptions, which point to a kind of homosexual awareness, and on groups that formed a kind of subculture: there were special meeting places in the open air and indoors; and homosexuals used peculiar mimicry, specific signs, love names, and a network of friends and contacts. A true sexual market existed all over the republic.

A final point emerges from the court records: the amount of physical distance between men seems, in this period, to have been less than in later periods. Guest and host, master and servant, and manservants among themselves often slept in one bed. It was undoubtedly the same group of people who both stressed the importance of maintaining a stricter moral code and who tried to impose their own notion of "privacy" and of physical distance on the lower strata of society. Certain intimate customs of sleeping together were increasingly perceived as uncivilized. From the end of the eighteenth century, the bourgeoisie worried about immoral situations in the houses of the working class and in the dormitories of prisons and workhouses. The cell, symbol of the smallest individual entity and space, seemed the best guarantee for disciplining—to refer to Foucault—body and soul.

Arend H. Huussen, Jr.
Rijksuniversiteit, Groningen

NOTES

1. L. F. Groenendijk, *De nadere reformatie van het gezin* [*Puritanism and the Family*] (Dordrecht: J. P. van den Tol, 1984); A. Th. van Deursen, *Het kopergeld van de Gouden Eeuw* [*Coppers of the Golden Age*], vol. 3: *Volk en overheid* [*People and Government*] (Assen: Van Gorcum, 1979).

2. Heinz Schilling, "Religion und Gesellschaft in der calvinistischen Republik der

Vereinigten Niederlande. 'Öffentlichkeitskirche' und Säkularisation; Ehe und Hebammenwesen; Presbyterien und politische Partizipation," in Franz Petri, ed., *Kirche und Gesellschaftlicher Wandel in deutschen und niederländischen Städten der werdenden Neuzeit* (Cologne and Vienna: Böhlau, 1980) pp. 197-250; Steven Ozment, *When Fathers Ruled: Family Life in Reformation Europe* (Cambridge: Harvard Univ., 1983).

3. Gisela Bleibtreu-Ehrenberg, *Tabu Homosexualität: Die Geschichte eines Vorurteils* (Frankfurt: Fischer, 1978) is silent on the topics of the Reformation, Luther, Calvin, etc.

4. Willem Frijhoff, "Prophétie et société dans les Provinces-Unies aux XVIIe et XVIIIe siècles," in Marie-Sylvie Dupont-Bouchat, Willem Frijhoff, and Robert Muchembled, *Prophètes et sorciers dans les Pays-Bas XVIe-XVIIIe siècle* (Paris: Hachette, 1978) pp. 263-362; Van Deursen, *Kopergeld*, vol. 4: *Hel en hemel* [Hell and Heaven] (Assen: Van Gorcum, 1980).

5. John H. Langbein, *Prosecuting Crime in the Renaissance: England, Germany, France.* (Cambridge Harvard Univ., 1974), pp. 165ff.

6. Peter Pappus van Tratzberg, *Articul-brief, waer bij eenige annotatien gevoeght zijn* [*Articles on Military Law, with Addition of Annotations*] 6th edn. (Groningen, 1681), pp. 9, 48; Gerh. Feltman, *Aanmerkingen over den Articulbrief ofte Ordonnantie op de discipline militaire* [*Commentaries on the Articles or Ordinances on the Military Discipline*] 3rd edn. (The Hague, 1716), pp. 17-18, 63-65.

7. Joos de Damhouder, *Praxis rerum criminalium* (1554; Antwerp, 1601; rep. Aalen: Scientia, 1978), cap. 98, "De peccato contra naturam"; Antonius Matthaeus, *De criminibus ad Lib. XLVII et XLVIII Digestorum commentarius* (Utrecht, 1644), pp. 460-61. On Matthaeus see Felix Schlüter, *Antonius Matthäus II. aus Herborn, der Kriminalist des 17. Jahrhunderts, der Rechtslehrer Utrechts* (Breslau, 1929), pp. 92-93.

8. Herman Diederiks, "Patterns of Criminality and Law Enforcement during the Ancien Régime: The Dutch Case," in *Criminal Justice History: An International Annual* I (N.Y., 1980), pp. 157-74.

9. Bert F. Oaks, " 'Things fearful to name': Sodomy and Buggery in Seventeenth-Century New England," *Journal of Social History* 12 (1978-79): 268-81.

10. G. R. Elton, "Crime and the Historian," in J. S. Cockburn, ed., *Crime in England 1550-1800* (London: Methuen, 1977), pp. 1-14.

11. On Leiden: D. J. Noordam, "Homosexualiteit en sodomie in Leiden, 1533-1811" ["Homosexuality and Sodomy at Leiden, 1533-1811"], *Leids Jaarboekje* 75 (1983): 72-105; and "Homosocial relations in Leiden (1533-1811)," in *Among Men, Among Women: Sociological and Historical Recognition of Homosocial Arrangements* (Gay Studies and Women's Studies Conference, University of Amsterdam [22-26 June 1983]); collected papers, Amsterdam Sociological Institute, University of Amsterdam [1983], pp. 218-23.

12. L. J. Boon, "De grote sodomietenvervolging in het gewest Holland, 1730-1731" ["The Great Persecution of Sodomites in the Province of Holland, 1730-31"], *Holland, regionaal-historisch tijdschrift* 8 (1976): 140-52; and "Utrechtenaren: de sodomieprocessen in Utrecht, 1730-1732" ["Utrechters: Trials against Sodomites in Utrecht, 1730-32"], *Spiegel Historiael, maandblad voor geschiedenis en archeologie* 17 (1982): 553-58; D. J. Noordam, "Homoseksuele relaties in Holland in 1776" ["Homosexual relations in Holland, 1776"], *Holland, regionaal-historisch tijdschrift* 16 (1984): 3-34.

13. A. N. Gilbert, "Buggery and the British Navy, 1700-1861," *Journal of Social History* 10 (1976-77): 72-98; R. Trumbach, "London's Sodomites: Homosexual Behaviour and Western Culture in the Eighteenth Century," *Journal of Social History* 11 (1977-78): 1-33.

14. Theo van der Meer, *De wesentlijke sonde van sodomie en andere vuyligheeden. Sodomietenvervolgingen in Amsterdam, 1730-1811* [*The Real Sin of Sodomy and other Lewdness. Persecutions of Sodomites in Amsterdam, 1730-1811*] (Amsterdam: Tabula, 1984), cases on pp. 86, 100, and—perhaps—178.

15. Noordam, "Homosexualiteit"; Van der Meer, *De wesentlijke*, pp. 137-47; Rudolf Dekker and Lotte van de Pol, *Daar was laatst een meisje loos: Nederlandse vrouwen als matrozen en soldaten. Een historisch onderzoek* [*Dutch Women as Sailors and Soldiers. An Historical Study*] (Baarn: Ambo, 1982).

16. Pieter Loens, *Regtelyke aanmerkingen omtrent eenige poincten, concernerende de execrable sonde tegens de natuur* [*Legal Commentary Concerning Some Points in the Case of the Abominable Sin against Nature*] (Rotterdam, 1760).

17. [Abraham Perrenot], *Bedenkingen over het straffen van zekere schandelijke misdaad*

178

[*Considerations on the Punishment of Certain Infamous Crimes*] (Amsterdam, 1777). On Perrenot and Beccaria see Noordam, "Homoseksuele," pp. 24-27.

18. A. D. Harvey, "Prosecutions for Sodomy in England at the Beginning of the Nineteenth Century", *Historical Journal* 21 (1978): 939-48.

19. Noordam, "Homosexualiteit,": 96; J. de Jong, L. Kooijmans, and H. F. de Wit, "Schuld en boete in de Nederlandse Verlichting" ["Guilt and Punishment during the Dutch Enlightenment"], *Kleio* 19 (1978): 237-44; Paul Kapteyn, *Taboe, ontwikkelingen in macht en moraal speciaal in Nederland* [*Taboo: Developments in Power and Morals, Especially in The Netherlands*] (Amsterdam: De Arbeiderspers, 1980); L. J. Boon, "Those Damned Sodomites: Public Images of Sodomy in the 18th Century Netherlands," in *Among Men, Among Women*, supp. 1, pp. 19-22. On the struggle against disorder in France, see Michel Rey, "Police et sodomie à Paris au XVIIIᵉ siècle, du péché au désordre," *Revue d'Histoire Moderne et Contemporaine* 29 (1982): 113-24, and his contribution to *Among Men, Among Women*, pp. 197-206.

20. See, for example, Stephen Murray and Kent Gerrard, "Renaissance Sodomite Subcultures?," in *Among Men, Among Women*, pp. 183-96; Jeffrey Weeks, "Discourse, Desire and Sexual Deviance: Some Problems in a History of the Modern Homosexuality," in Kenneth Plumner, ed., *The Making of the Modern Homosexual* (London: Hutchinson, 1981) pp. 76-111; Philippe Ariès, "Réflexions sur l'histoire de l'homosexualité," *Communications: Ecole des Hautes Etudes en Sciences sociale, Centre d'Etudes Transdisciplinaires (Sociologie, Anthropologie, Sémiologie)* 35 (1982): 56-67.

Parisian Homosexuals Create a Lifestyle, 1700–1750: The Police Archives

※ ※ ※ ※

Because of a lack of documents and studies, the actual practice of a homosexual lifestyle before the eighteenth century is little known. Those insights which are available, and even the definition of sodomy (including homo- as well as heterosexual acts), seem to suggest that for a long time sodomy implied neither a particular lifestyle nor inclusion in a clearly designated minority. Most often, moreover, an attraction to boys did not preclude other tastes. In respect to this matter, however, the police archives of the eighteenth century indicate, at the heart of the Parisian population, a transformation which had perhaps begun earlier at court: male homosexuality becomes a taste that sets one apart from other men, being seen both as a refinement and a source of particular identity.

Police sources consist, for the most part, of reports dictated by *agents provacateurs* paid by a specialized office, and by officers charged with overseeing those royal gardens open to the public. These reports contain abundant and valuable details about the daily lives of those arrested, because the agents, appropriately called *mouches*, encouraged those who approached them to give as much information as possible about their desires and acquaintances.[1]

The Geography of "la Bonnaventure"

For hours on end, police observers were on the lookout for those cruising for a sex partner. It is actually possible, from these reports, to reconstruct cruising routes in Paris. Most of the sites frequented are mentioned from the beginning of the century, and it is difficult to discern precisely the evolution of popular rendezvous sites just from the fragmentary evidence of police interest in the sites. The boulevards laid out along the lines of the former fortifications which girdled Paris are mentioned with regularity only beginning in the 1730s, but they are cited as early as 1714 in a log recording those booked by the police at the prison-hospital at Bicêtre.[2] Were there more homosexuals on those boulevards, or did the police simply send more staff to report them?

The use of meeting places was socially diversified. In principle, the archers allowed into the royal gardens only persons of quality, or at least those who dressed as such. The people arrested in the Tuileries, Luxembourg, or Palais-Royal gardens, or the Champs-Elysées, were thus mostly of the nobility or middle class, but included some master craftsmen, schoolboys, students, and household servants. These same groups frequented the streets, public squares, and river embankments; but there they could lose themselves in the mass of small shopkeepers, workers, and young tradesmen.

Like numerous heterosexual couples, or like prostitutes, homosexuals did not hesitate to engage in sexual relations in any places which were somewhat sheltered from view—and scarcely that at times—behind ramparts, in thickets or ditches, in alleys. In any case, dwellings offered little more privacy: walls were thin and doors could be opened quickly.[3] Few people had the means or inclination to obtain real privacy. In fact, all busy places (such as the Pont-Neuf or the fair of St. Germain) attracted those in pursuit of *la bonnaventure*.

Those who found public places too exposed had recourse to a tavern:

> Scouring the pathways, when he finds someone alone, he accosts him and asks him to go have a drink. He is always very careful to ask for a private room, anticipating the fulfillment of his infamous passion.

Caution had to be exercised with the proprietor and the waiters: "Since half of Paris was so inclined [homosexual], none of the innkeepers was unaware of the practice, and all were on their guard concerning such activities."[4] However, one who knew his way around could find complicitous owners; so in 1749, when homosexual encounters were multiplying, the police arrested twelve "sellers of wine" for *pédérastie*.

Rendezvous sites were kept under surveillance almost daily, with, so far as surviving archives can substantiate, increased intensity in spring and summer, on Sundays and holidays, and at certain times of day: a certain Renard "did not fail to come to the Luxembourg gardens looking for a pick-up (*pour y raccrocher*) from around ten in the morning until noon, and the same in the evening from seven to nine."[5] Most people seemed to circulate between 10 a.m. and 2 p.m., and from 8 to 10 p.m.

All these people had a singular perception of the city, directly related to the satisfaction of homosexual desires; but the majority of the places we have pointed out were equally well-known for female prostitution, which the police readily equated with the homosexual solicitation (the term *raccrochage* was used for both cases), even when there was no payment for sex: in short, all types of errant sexuality were pursued alike by the police, who had scorn for men who offered their bodies to other men, or whom they saw as satisfying a law of supply and demand. To complicate the situation further, certain nobles did systematically offer money, thus reproducing in their homosexual lives the master-servant model on which the society was founded.[6] Some of those propositioned had the courage or self-esteem to decline: "He refused to take . . . [the hundred halfpennies (*sols*)] because he was not doing it out of interest, but only for his pleasure."[7]

Cruising: a Brief Discussion of Methods

Making a pick-up was a trade (*métier*) whose techniques had to be mastered if one was to escape being considered a novice. In the eyes of certain practitioners, cruising distinguished homosexuals as a group similar to an important social configuration of the period: *la corporation*.

Methods of operation differed depending on sites, time of day, and conditions. During the day, at the Tuileries or the Luxembourg and in public walkways, the pick-up was carried out mostly by dialogue. "He asked what time it was"; he walked up "while asking me for a pinch of tobacco."[8] The conversation might continue for some time, touching first on mere pleasantries, then slipping into the topic of pleasures in general, before broaching any more specific pleasurable possibility. On the river embankments, on the streets or walkways at nightfall, or in pissoirs, the approach could be more direct. Certain people called attention to themselves by protracted circulating "in places where the infamous ordinarily hung out." The police were familiar with the codes governing these encounters: "having come up to me, making all the signals to me which these infamous types are accustomed to, in order to speak to me," or "having approached me, staring me in the face several times," or staring "with affectation," or "having pissed . . . in front of me several times—being one of the signals which all these sordid types have at their disposal." One might indicate his interest and attempt to create excitement by showing his penis: "I'm sure you prefer that to a pinch of tobacco." The *mouche* himself sometimes elicited a conversation: "As I was about to let flow, [he] asked me what time it was according to my cock (*vit*) and said that according to his it was high noon."[9] On the quais, one could relieve oneself (*faire ses nécessités*) and "expose oneself from the front and rear." These gestures in themselves were not unusual: only the ostentation which accompanied them identified homosexuals, and they were quickly followed by a question—"Do you have an erection?"—and a rapid reach to find out.

Without exception, each time violence occurred during solicitation or sex, nobles, particularly those in military office, were the aggressors. In 1725, the Count de la Tournelle was arrested n the Tuileries gardens "while he was leaning against a tree with said individual, forcibly coercing him and tearing his breeches in order to fondle him in a shameful manner." In 1724, in the same location, three gentlemen were arrested under similar circumstances. One of them, a brigadier general, "met an individual before whom he showed his penis outside his breeches, saying: "Let me fuck you" (*Attends que je te foute*). The three now seized the person encountered around the waist, more or less gently, but without his being allowed to refuse the offer. This sort of force also reappears in the noblemen's parties to which Deschauffours, a pimp (*proxénète*) and murderer burned in 1726, brought young boys who were given drinks before being molested.[10] Moreover, such sexual force rounds out the endless list of violent acts committed by the old, or military, nobility (*la noblesse d'épée*) against those whom they considered inferior.[11]

The police were not satisfied merely to observe pick-up techniques with a scientific eye; officials claimed to have caused adaptations in them. In 1748, two homosexuals known to him by sight followed a police agent along a quai and "stepped into a recessed area, a sort of gateway, where they showed themselves without speaking, a practice which certain of these infamous types have adopted recently, especially those who have been summoned before the lieutenant-general of the police."[12] It was a wise precaution to find out whether one was or was not dealing with a police agent; one exposed oneself in the ordinary way (as though urinating, etc.) without ostentation. Then the *mouche* had to become involved in order to catch his victim "in the act." The only other possibility was to make a report merely on suspicion. Thus the police, just as much as their quarry, influenced the "disorderly conduct" they were after.

Reactions and Hostility

Police sources provide some idea of opinion among ordinary citizens regarding homosexuals, for they present the reactions of those who had been approached unsuccessfully. In 1736, a man named P. Champ tried to "handle" a bather on the Pont-Neuf: "The young man pushed him away, trying to slap him, and saying, 'You dog, have you washed your hands,' and 'Are your hands clean?' " In 1738, a young man went to urinate behind the palings of the Tuileries. A man (L. Chaumont) joined him, fondling himself in front of him. The young man "began to shout at him, calling him: 'scoundrel'." In a cabaret in 1748 a man named Tranchant had placed his hands inside the breeches of another. The man would not let him do it; he told people about the attempt, and Tranchant was publicly reproached in the neighborhood.[13] "Dog," "scoundrel"— these mild insults could as easily have been addressed to an unsavory drunkard. The texts show the importance of the neighborhood; with the possible exception of some districts at the center of the city, Paris was still arranged like a series of villages where everyone knew everyone, and where the community oversaw the conduct of each of its members: communication between sexual deviants and their neighbors had not yet been severed. The neighborhood rebuked them as men who had gone too far, who had done something "dirty." They did not incur general hostility, but simply a silent reproach or a physical action such as might have repelled an intruder. In addition, such a deviant was perhaps viewed as not totally devoted to his passion, and therefore not "different," unlike the mason who, in 1723, was turned in to the police by a neighbor. He had a "bad reputation, having always in his company young men of the neighborhood whom he would lure to his home."[14] He had made the mistake of not considering the neighborhood. Not having hidden his activities discreetly enough, he was resented as a menace to public order who continued to seek his partners inside the delineated and watchful community.

It should be noted that in most such instances the police were not summoned. Faced with what it considered unacceptable behavior (and the same held for physical aggression or theft), to enforce good conduct the community used traditional instruments: neighborhood, parish, family, and professional scorn. Thus, in 1723, a man named F. Solle recounted how, in a tavern, he "had been caught by a waiter, who found them with their pants off and told his mistress, who in turn created an outcry."[15] Calling public attention to an act, singling out a black sheep, tarnishing a man's honor, branding him with infamy was apparently sufficient to preserve order in the community.

In 1737, four young men crossing the Pont-Neuf discussed in loud voices their previous evening and their past adventures: "They talked so loudly among themselves about their infamies that other people in the street admonished them for it."[16] Street life, at that period, allowed for such exchanges. Passers-by, not content with silent disapproval, willingly intervened in order to preserve respect for dignity and order. The later evolution of refined social decorum, the spread of the notion of private life, and the formation of a milieu reserved exclusively for sodomites all gradually established boundaries between homosexuals and the public's jurisdiction; and in the second half of the century systematic recourse to the district police commissioner appears to have become pervasive.[17]

Manifestations of Sexual Desire and Love

Trying to arouse a potential partner and determine whether he would be suitable, those who cruised among the *mouches* often expressed their desires; but their words present analytical problems as we attempt to discover how the eighteenth century made love. If sexual practices seem finite in number, the fantasies and taboos connected with them may seem infinite. But even now we have very few studies that allow for comparisons: how did people make love in the eighteenth century?

For certain years where files are numerous, it is possible to calculate the number and kind of homosexual propositions. For example:

Activity	1723	1724
active sodomy	11	24
passive sodomy	0	5
active or passive sodomy	9	20
fellatio	2	8
kissing	2	7

This limited table authorizes several observations. Two major categories stand out: active sodomy, and sodomy which is active or passive without preference; by contrast, exclusively passive sodomy appears infrequently. What accounts for this inbalance of preference? If it was particularly degrading to be sodomized, one would seldom have expressed this desire;

or else one would have done so while simultaneously expressing interest in sodomizing. The shame of passivity might have been founded on a rigid notion of the male and female sexual role. Is a man who screws another really "infamous"? Those who declared themselves exclusively active might have thought not. The marked effeminancy of the *assemblées* of homosexuals seems to confirm this, as do remarks made in 1738 by a male servant who wished to leave his master because the latter wanted to sleep with him although he had no money to pay for it. The servant, who fears being regarded as an *infâme*, speaks continually of his master in feminine terms, as "she," and speaks of him as a lewd woman.[18] At this time, those in whose interest it was to be seen as quite distinct from a sodomite depicted him as a man with an effeminate nature. In 1723, a servant out of work and married for three months, conversed as follows with a police agent in the Tuileries: "I asked him if he would allow me to screw him. He answered that he hadn't done that yet, but that he had screwed someone else occasionally, and that usually he only masturbated."[19] Other remarks indicate that though masturbation between men did not seem to present significant moral problems, nor did the fact of sodomizing someone, it was much more difficult to accept being sodomized.

The table above leads us to another observation: the infrequent mention of oral practices, which today appear common, even predominant. The kiss is perhaps mentioned only infrequently because it was so commonplace, though this is not at all certain. Kissing is a very old act in the West; however, it is even now not a universal erotic act, not being so in much of Asia, for instance. If we compare male sexuality of the eighteenth century with that of other societies, for example those of North Africa, we realize that there also sexual relations between men are rather frequent, with a clear distinction being made between active and passive roles, which hinders expressions of tenderness.

If the principal taboos in contemporary western societies seem to concern anal eroticism (as in *Last Tango in Paris*), this has not always been the case. In his study of Roman sexuality, Paul Veyne indicates that the ultimate abasement for Romans was fellatio; and in a study on homosexuality in court circles in the eighteenth century, Benoît Lapouge is also amazed at the apparent absence of the mouth as an erogenous zone.[20] For the eighteenth century, oral homosexual acts appear to have been seen as depraved or very wanton, in any case extreme. In 1738, a hustler, S. Fontaine, "says that he did it in all ways, *even that* if I wanted, I could consummate the act in his mouth." In 1748, J. Faver, a baker, was in love with an unresponsive water carrier, "which angered the witness all the more, since he desperately loved the said Vendreville, many times having kissed his genitals and even his anus."[21] In 1735, a hustler discriminated among the locations of homosexual acts: "I perform the act with my mouth, in the same way as with my ass when I see that a man is clean and doesn't smell of women." Similar expressions of digust for stinking (*puant*) female genitals, which were thought to cause venereal diseases more difficult to cure than those transmitted by men, are numerous: "He said that he hated women so strongly that he thought he saw the Devil whenever he saw them, and that if a married man touched him, he would just as soon have the plague."

In both 1723 and 1737-38, married men constituted one third of those arrested. They often hid their status while soliciting, however, either from fear of blackmail or of putting off their partner. Married couples did not, perhaps, lead such a self-contained emotional life as today, though marriage assured respectability. Gallimard, a lawyer in the Parlement de Paris, separated from his wife, declared in 1724 "that he had a wife but hardly ever made use of her, that his marriage was a stratagem, cover-up, and that he had not taste for women, that he preferred an ass to a cunt."[22] As the research by J. L. Flandrin and Philippe Aries, among others, shows, marriage and love were not commonly associated at that time.[23] All the passions, including love in various forms, were indulged in outside of the marriage bonds. Gallimard encountered a *mouche* on the Crescent in front of the Bastille and later testified "that he wanted very much to get to know me, and that we would live together, that he would pay for half of the room, that we would live together like two brothers, that we would drink and eat together."

The lifestyle proposed here is very standard: it is that of a companion, almost a brother, with whom one shares bread and daily life. It is an old, typically male arrangement. In 1725, a lackey related to a priest "that he had always encountered much difficulty in finding a friend with a good disposition, with whom he could have established a pleasurable relationship which might last."[24] The image of the couple is two-fold here: a pair of friends whose temperaments agree, with all the communication and sharing that this traditionally includes, and a "pleasurable relationship." The expression is ambiguous; it evokes rather more a relationship with a lover. At any rate, the emphasis on duration, always present in friendship, but associated here with the "liaison de plaisir," suggests what we today call "conjugal love"; and we know that until the end of the eighteenth century the relationship between spouses was commonly called "friendship."

A last example (1724)—but they are not very numerous in these reports, which, by their nature, record for the most part relationships of an ephemeral sort—documents the end of a relationship more lasting than a "liaison de plaisir":

> he had lived for six months with Abbé Candor, at that time the parish priest of Faverolles, in the diocese of Soissons . . . he passed himself off in the area as the man's cousin . . . they had amused themselves in every respect, and . . . he had only left this priest because he was too jealous, and because he loved a man as a lover loves his mistress.[25]

It would be unfortunate to conclude this section without pointing out the single gesture of tenderness which these police documents report. In 1748, a man spoke in the following manner about two lackeys whom he knew: "Duquesnel and Dumaine had been sleeping together for two years. They were unable to fall asleep without having mutually touched each other and without having performed infamous acts. It was even almost always necessary for Duquesnel to have his arm extended along the headboard, under Dumaine's head. Without that Dumaine could not rest."[26]

Congregations of Homosexuals

In 1706, the police officer who regularly inspected the general hospital of Bicêtre noted the presence of inmates who had congregated "in taverns in the St. Antoine district, where they committed the most foul abominations. In these groups Langlois was nicknamed the Grand Master; and Bertauld, the Mother in charge of novices."[27] The same essential characteristics of these meetings reappeared in the middle of the century: they most often took place in a tavern in a populous district, and the participants altered their identity by adopting surnames. These associations show a closing in of the group by imitating the court, a convent, or a secret society, and consequently affirm the necessity of an initiation in order to be admitted.

According to the reports, which are incomplete, this type of gathering appeared to increase, beginning in the 1730s. In 1748, one can count no fewer than eight taverns where groups of fifteen to thirty people gathered. The gatherings took place in the evening, with the shutters closed. The participants ate, danced, sang, seduced; they exchanged information, smutty stories, and obscene suggestions; but in several cases it is mentioned that they "did not commit the act on the premises," but on the road home after having paired up. Thus, in 1748, a man who tried to fondle a violin player was reproached by the assembly for his boldness.[28] The group established rules of civility. Other assemblies, more private and more sexual, are at times difficult to distinguish from—in the language of police ambiguity—"houses of disorder full of reprobates" (des bordels d'infâmes), though most often the meeting place had two rooms, one for socializing and one for sexual activities.

In the same year, 1748, several witnesses gave an account of a gathering held in a Parisian suburb, la Courtille, in the Fer à Cheval, a tavern, where a group was called "the locksmith's marriage" because they forcibly seduced initiates to perform infamous acts (faire des infamies) for the first time. Again in 1748, another witness described a similar ceremony: "This past summer, he found himself in several gatherings of people from la Manchette, either in la Courtille or at the sign of the Six Sparrows in the rue aux Juifs (in the central Marais district). In these assemblies the conversation is almost always in the same vein. Some members with napkins on their heads imitate women and mince about like them. Any new young man in their midst is called the bride (Mariée), and they all try for him. People pair off in order to touch and to perform infamous acts. Sometimes that also takes place after leaving the tavern."[29] In the marriage described here, the initiate (novice) is admitted into a family circle; however, he is not joined to one man but to a group who caress him in order to include him in it.

In 1735, J. Baron, a brewer, organized a dinner at his tavern: "The others approached us, embracing us and saying: Hello *Mesdames*. Baron arranged his hair with a woman's headdress which was black, like the hairdo of women at court. He placed pompoms in everyone's hair."[30] The word *Mesdames*, reserved at this time for women of status (*femmes de condition*), like the allusion to court styles, shows that within this group femininity, refinement, and aristocracy were closely linked to the drama of homosexual intrigue. This intermingling of terms reappears in the use of certain nicknames: *Madame de Nemours, Duchesse Duras, Baronne aux Épingles.*

Here follows the social class distribution of those arrested, during four years when documents are numerous:

	1723	1737-38	1749
nobility & gentry	8	17	28
craftsmen/merchants	20	63	129
servants	12	59	58
unknown status	4	7	19
totals	44	146	234

There is a proportional consistency in the distribution: and on the average, 14% were people of status; 48%, minor craftsmen and merchants; and 26%, servants. When arrested many people of uncertain social position declared themselves servants in order to avoid being classified with the lowly poor. However, these figures are only suggestive, as they are not complete.

According to testimony, the craftsmen/merchant group predominated in the assemblies, but it is not surprising that few nobles and important members of the middle class (*grands bourgeois*) were present, as they were moving in other social orbits. More surprising is the near absence of servants and persons of no social status, wretched immigrants from the provinces, beggars, and occasional prostitutes. The organized prostitution networks did not include the assemblies and catered more to the nobility or specific groups like the military. The assembly thus seems to have been a rather coherent social group of small merchants and tradesmen, which fantasized about the freedom of manners and the festivities of the court—as if, in order to fashion a transgressing identity and to become organized, some social demarcation was necessary.

The effeminacy and the politeness associated with these assemblies appear to extend into the streets in the course of the century. Certain members wore rouge and powder, colored ribbons, curtsied in a feminine manner and greeted one another as "Madame." Thus in 1737 a *mouche* was asked "whether there were any good lookers in the Luxembourg gardens." The obvious consciousness of belonging to a group is also attested to by the use of certain expressions: "There's somebody who looks like one. Let's split up and see what this sister is all about. That is an infamous term." When a boy did not seem to respond to advances, "they said to each other: Let's let him go, he doesn't understand Latin." In 1749, a master sculptor attended a gathering where he was asked if he would like to be a freemason. The characteristics of these assemblies caused certain people to shy away: though willing "to perform the act" they would not talk about it, and they rejected effeminacy. In 1748, a painter stated that "he withdrew from these gatherings because they were too scandalous. Several members imitated women and made gestures which showed what they were." He said he often replied to them, saying: "Can't you adopt men's mannerisms rather than women's?" The same year, a hardware merchant, J. B. Thomas, stated that he was angry at having gone to these assemblies at la Courtille, "because he didn't enjoy the company at all and because among those present were some who made propositions that were too licentious." In 1749, during a party of seven, where his acquaintances called him their aunt and assigned each other female first names, a second-hand clothing dealer exclaimed: "What! You are men and yet give each other women's names!"[32] These indignant participants seem to have been attracted momentarily by the warmth, relative security, and opportunities for enjoying themselves which these small groups offered; but they were unable to assume a public female role, which seems to have been the characteristic identity defined by these homosexual assemblies. They preferred to retreat to men who were more secretive and those who, from need, occasionally sold themselves in the shadowy anonymity of the usual pick-up spots.

Distinctions

During the same years, several educated people (such as a medical student and a priest) distinguished between ("those who think along those lines") and ("those who think differently") on the basis of tolerated and tolerant attitudes. Seen as a tolerated difference, homosexual desire was no longer merely a forbidden "passion," a sin whose very mention constituted a crime: it was felt to be a mode of thought. In the 1730s police texts reflect these changes, by replacing the word "sodomite" by "pédéraste." The first term is biblical and refers to divine prohibition of a sin, whereas the second more neutral term, which dates from the sixteenth century (and is not used here in its etymological sense signifying love of boys), refers to the ancient Greek ethos and designates here a man whose sexual desire is oriented exclusively towards other men. Does the change of wording in the police language indicate a greater acceptance of homosexuals and their subculture; or is the linguistic change insignificant? Similarly, what interpretation, if any, is to be made of the fact that beginning in the 1740s the police reports used another expression, which was to remain in use at least until the French Revolution: "les gens de la Manchette" or "les chevaliers de la Manchette," a reference to the aristocracy parallel, say, to the Knights of the Garter in England?

An answer to this question is suggested by the reports of the pederasty patrols (*patrouilles de pédérastie*) which circulated around suspected places during the second half of the century. On 1 October 1781, the inspector "charged with dealing with the pederasts" arrested on the streets "a peculiar individual whom the mob was chasing because of his indecent and characteristic dress (*costume*). . . . If ever an outfit, in every respect, was cause for suspecting an individual of pederasty, said Prainquet had assembled it all and the public judged him by it." Arrested again in the same outfit on 15 October at la Grève and "jeered at and hounded by the people," and arrested a third time on 20 October, he was finally locked up in the Petit-Châtelet for "obstinacy in dressing in an indecent manner, which is used only by the most dissolute pederasts." Though only seventeen and merely a cook's helper in the service of an army commissariat officer, he wore a dressing gown or frock coat, a cravat, a knot of hair at the back of his head, and a hat. What was indecent? What made the crowd recognize a pederast? Later, on 1 December, the inspector arrested an unemployed nineteen year-old on the street, "dressed in the most suspicious manner," that is, "dressed in a very long brown coat, with rosettes on his shoes, round hat, knotted hair, wide tie, and short hair around his ears. . . . Asked why he was dressed that way . . . [he] answered that his attire was nothing extraordinary, since all people of distinction dressed similarly in the morning."[33] These two young men sported sartorial refinement above their station, whereas for society in general and the police in particular the class hierarchy which delineated an entire social hierarchy had to be clearly visible, and was most obvious in clothing. But that is not sufficient to explain why they were immediately recognizable as homosexual. Two hypotheses, one linked to the other, are possible. First, to people of the lower class, a noble—powdered, pomaded, refined—was both elegant and effeminate; but that bothered no one as long as the mode of attire remained faithful to the specific superior social condition which its wearer represented. If someone lower on the social scale assumed this costume (and it should be asked whether the young age of the two men were not a factor), not only did he betray his social condition, but in addition, his effeminacy, by losing its accepted association with elegance and the upper class, became an indication of the wearer's real effeminacy. The crowd, the police, and the homosexuals themselves, all linked aristocratic refinement with effeminacy; and the wish to stand out by imitating the aristocracy must have been very powerful, judging from the perseverance of these young men despite the risks they ran.

During the entire eighteenth century, homosexual men tried to group on the basis of an exclusive and minority sexual desire—a phenomenon not exclusively French. Studies concerning England and Holland during this period arrive at similar conclusions.[34] Parallel with the image of the libertine lord who enjoyed sensual excesses, members of the lower classes created an identity involving a double deception: in gender (and thus in virility), and in social status. The adoption of an effeminate aristocratic mode of refinement was a social sin viewed more and more as the century wore on as an unnatural "passion" or "taste" which immutably characterized certain people. The report of 1765 (the only one in the archives consulted) speaks of the "crime against nature" (*crime anti-physique*). At the end of the century, Sade's third dialogue of *La Philosophie dans le boudoir* links homosexuals' desires to their physical make-up and to a congenital *caractère* which caused typically feminine traits: "Is it not clear that this is a class of men different from the other, but also created by nature . . . ?" Sade is very close to the forensic pathologists of the nineteenth century who would look for distinguishing stigmata of homosexuality (and all criminal types) on individuals' bodies. He is not very far, in his defense by natural cause, from the idea of a "third sex" and from the psychologists' creation of a category of genetic abnormality, which at the end of the nineteenth century would lead to the mutually exclusive categories of homo- and heterosexuality.

Translated by   *Michael Rey*
Robert A. Day & *Robert Welch*   Paris

NOTES

1. Paris, Bibliothèque de l'Arsenal, Archives de la Bastille, MSS 10.254 to 10.260.
2. Paris, Bibliothèque Nationale, MS Clairambault 985.
3. See Arlette Farge, *Vivre dans la rue à Paris au XVIIIe siècle* (Paris: Gallimard, 1979), and Daniel Roche, *Le Peuple de Paris* (Paris: Aubier, 1981).
4. MS 10.254, P. Deu, 31 Oct. 1723 and F. Solle, 15 July 1723. MS 10.255, abbé de Boisrenard, 10 Feb. 1724.
5. MS 10.254, T. Ranard, 23 Aug. 1723.
6. See Alan Bray, *Homosexuality in Renaissance England* (London: Gay Men's Press, 1982): Chap. 2, "The Social Setting."
7. MS 10.255, S. Guillard, 26 Apr. 1724.
8. MS 10.254, J. Fourty, 30 Aug. 1723 and C. Delamotte, 11 July 1723.
9. MS 10.254, L. Gouffier, 3 May 1723 and marquis de Bressy, 15 Apr. 1723.
10. Paris, Bib. Nat., MS Fond Français 10970.
11. See in particular, Nicole and Yves Castan, *Vivre Ensemble. Ordre et désordre en Languedoc (XVIIe et XVIIIe siècles)* (Paris: Gallimard, 1981).
12. MS 10.259, Veglay, 25 June 1748.
13. MS 10.258, P. Champ, 10 May 1736 and L. Chaumont, 1738; MS 10.259, Tranchant, Oct. 1748.
14. MS 10.254, L. Gobert, 21 Oct. 1723.
15. MS 10.254, F. Solle, 15 July 1723.
16. MS 10.258, Brunet, Bourbonnais, Dijon, and Courtois, 22 Sept. 1737.
17. See in particular Alexandre Mericskay, "Le Chatelet et la répresion de la crimilalité à Paris en 1750," Thèse dactylographiée, Paris IV—Sorbonne (1984).
18. MS 10.258, Leveillé, 26 May 1738.
19. MS 10.254, J. Berlet, 10 Apr. 1723.
20. P. Veyne, "La Famille et l'amour sous le Haut-Empire Romain," *Annales E.S.C.* 1 (1978): 35-63, and "L'Homosexualité à Rome," *L'Histoire* 30 (1981): 76-78, and B. Lapouge, "Les comportements sexuels déviants à Paris au XVIIe siècle," Mémoire de Maîtrise, dactylographié, Paris-Sorbonne.
21. MS 10.258, S. Fontaine, 1738; MS 10.259, J. Favé, Nov. 1748.

22. MS 10.257, P. Lemoine, 26 Oct. 1735; MS 10.256, C. Galard, 22 July 1725; MS 10.255, F. Gallimard, 3 Oct. 1724.

23. J. L. Flandrin, *Familles, Parenté, maison, sexualité dans l'ancienne société* (Paris: Hachette, 1976, and Ed. du Seuil, 1984), and "Amour et mariage an XVIIIe siècle," in *Le Sexe et l'Occident. Evolution des attitudes et des comportements* (Paris: Ed. du Seuil, 1981), pp. 83-96; Philippe Ariès, "L'amour dans le mariage," in *Sexualités Occidentales,* Communications, No. 35 (Paris: Ed. du Seuil, 1982), pp. 116-22.

24. MS 10.256, J. Damien, 3 Jan. 1725.

25. MS 10.255, F. N. Gromat, 11 June 1724.

26. MS 10.259, Charpentier, Nov. 1748.

27. Bib. Nat., "Extraits d'interrogatories faits par la police de Paris de gens vivants dans le désordre, et de mauvaises moeurs, renfermées au château de Bicêtre": no. 81, S. Langlois.

28. MS 10.259, Caron, 23 Jan. 1748.

29. MS 10.259, Pinson, Jan. 1748.

30. MS 10.257, J. Baron, 25 Oct. 1735.

31, MS 10.258, A. Guy, 12 Feb. 1737; MS 10.258, M. Lalonde, 7 June 1736; MS 10.259, Ferret, May 1748 and Feuillon, Apr. 1749, MS 10.260.

32. MS 10.259, Marandel, Feb. 1748 and J. B. Thomas, March 1748; MS 10.260, J. Boudin, Jan. 1749.

33. Paris, Archives Nationales, Y 13408. J. Prainguet, 11 and 20 Oct. 1781 and L. Dufresnoy, 1 Dec. 1781.

34. Bray, *Homosexuality*; Randolph Trumbach, "London's Sodomites: Homosexual Behavior and Western Culture in the 18th Century," *Journal of Social History* 11 (1977): 1-33. L. J. Boon, "Those Damned Sodomites: Public Images of Sodomy in the 18th Century Netherlands," in *Among Men, Among Women: Sociological and Historical Recognition of Homosexual Arrangements,* text for the international conference of this title, University of Amsterdam, 22-26 June 1983.

The Censor Censured:
Expurgating *Memoirs of a Woman of Pleasure*

My Lord Duke

    Your Grace ordered a prosecution against the Printer and pub-
lisher of the *Memoires of a Lady of Pleasure*. The same Bookseller, one
Griffiths (as I apprehend) has published within a few Days a Book
called *Memoires of Fanny Hill*, the Lewdest thing I ever saw; It is, I am
told, the same with the other, after leaving out some things, which
were thought most liable to the Law and to expose the Author and
publisher to punishment—But if there is not Law enough in the
Country to reach this vile Book after all the pretence to correct it, we
are in a deplorable condition.

    I beg of your Grace to give proper orders, to stop the progress of
this vile Book, which is an open insult upon Religion and good
manners, and a reproach to the Honour of the Government, and the
Law of the Country.[1]

    The writer of this splenetic letter (15 March 1750) is Thomas Sherlock,
Bishop of London, who in addressing the Duke of Newcastle, Secretary of
State, is urging him to suppress a newly published work, *Memoirs of Fanny
Hill*, an expurgated version of John Cleland's *Memoirs of a Woman of
Pleasure*. The unabridged edition, as Sherlock points out, had already
been prosecuted and suppressed. Less than four months earlier, on 24
November 1749, Cleland, the printer Thomas Parker, and the publisher
Ralph Griffiths had all appeared in court, charged with producing an
obscene book. They were found guilty; the novel was withdrawn from
circulation and has remained an illicit work in England to the present
day—although editions have been published since 1970 without government harassment.[2]

    Despite losing their case, Cleland, Parker, and Griffiths seem to have
escaped lightly. No record of any punishment survives; and in his obituary notice of Cleland, John Nichols even suggests that he was "rescued
from the like temptation" of writing further pornography by a government pension of "£100 a year, which he enjoyed to his death."[3] Like much
of Nichols' obituary, this charming and often repeated story is probably a
fabrication; according to Boswell's journal, Cleland complained of having
been offered but then denied a government pension.[4] It is, however,
remarkable that so shortly after their arrest, Cleland, Parker, and Griffiths were producing another edition of the *Memoirs*. Clearly they believed

that this time they would be safe from prosecution. Cleland, who was heavily in debt to Griffiths, had been commissioned to "strike out the offensive parts" of his work and "compile a Novel from it which might be inoffensive."[5] Prominently featured in the publisher's advertisement was the sententious epigraph to the new edition:

> If I have painted Vice in its gayest Colours, if I have deck'd it with Flowers, it has been solely in order to make the worthier, the solemner Sacrifice of it to VIRTUE.[6]

"VIRTUE," the term so closely associated with Richardson's *Pamela; or, Virtue Rewarded*, is placed in capitals, while "Vice" receives no such emphasis. The already notorious *Memoirs of a Woman of Pleasure* was now being promoted as an edifying, didactic novel.

Thomas Sherlock, however, was not appeased by such sophistry, and his outburst brought immediate results. On the same day that he wrote his letter, warrants were issued for the arrest of Cleland, Parker, and Griffiths;[7] the forces of repression seemed again to be in the ascendant. Pressing home his advantage, Sherlock published on the following day his *Letter to the Clergy and People of London and Westminster on Occasion of the Late Earthquakes*. The second of these earthquakes, fortunately for the Bishop's polemical purposes, had taken place a week earlier, on 8 March, the day on which *Memoirs of Fanny Hill* was published. In his letter, the Bishop, alluding to Cleland's novel, enquires rhetorically: "Have not the histories or romances of the vilest prostitutes been published?"[8] On the same day (16 March), Cleland, Parker, and Griffiths were taken into custody and all available copies of the abridgment were seized. On 20 March, Griffiths was called before Lovel Stanhope, Law Clerk in the Duke of Newcastle's office, to defend the work that he had published.

Unimpressed by Bishop Sherlock's fulminations, Griffiths was convinced that the expurgated *Fanny Hill* could not be found obscene. In his testimony he denied that "there is any harm in the said Book & that had the King's Messengers given him Notice that the said Book gave offence, he would have Cancelled the whole Edition."[9] In a review for his own *Monthly Review* of March 1750, published shortly after this statement, he declared that, unlike *Memoirs of a Woman of Pleasure*, "a very loose work" which he claimed falsely never to have seen, *Memoirs of Fanny Hill* contained nothing "more offensive to decency, or delicacy of sentiment and expression, than our novels and books of entertainment in general have."[10] Far from countenancing immorality, Cleland had striven "to exhibit truth and nature to the world, and to lay open those mysteries of iniquity that, in our opinion, need only to be exposed to view, in order to their being abhorred and shunned by those who might otherwise unwarily fall into them." Unlike "the more solemn declamations of a sermon"—an obvious hit at Bishop Sherlock—Cleland's fiction would at least find attentive readers, whom it would thus be able to reform. Griffiths' arguments were compelling. On at least two occasions in 1750, the Earl of Newcastle wrote to the Attorney General requesting that charges be brought against those responsible for the expurgated *Fanny Hill*,[11] but they seem to have escaped prosecution. As James Basker has recently shown, Griffiths continued to advertise the abridgment openly in catalogues of his books of 1752 and 1753;[12] he would hardly have done so, if it had been successfully suppressed.

Unlike *Memoirs of a Woman of Pleasure*, therefore, *Memoirs of Fanny Hill* has always been legally available in England—and yet it is scarcely known. In contrast to the original novel, which appeared in numerous pirated editions in English and in translation, the abridgment was not reprinted in the eighteenth century. Although *Memoirs of Fanny Hill* was used as the copy-text for an edition of 1841,[13] no Victorian critic gave the abridgment any consideration. In the twentieth century, the book disappeared from sight until the British Library acquired a copy in 1965—one of only two known to exist today.[14] After its reappearance was announced by David Foxon, *Memoirs of Fanny Hill* was discussed briefly by William Epstein in his biography of Cleland, by Peter Naumann and by Raymond Whitley in their doctoral dissertations, and by James Basker in a recent paper; but no one has yet compared the two versions of Cleland's novel.[15] The purpose of this essay is thus to examine the nature and extent of Cleland's revisions and to consider the status of his long neglected recension.

Memoirs of a Woman of Pleasure was first published in two volumes containing 482 pages; *Memoirs of Fanny Hill*, published in a single volume of 273 pages, is less than two-thirds the length of the original. The new title page neutralizes the salacious effect of that of *Woman of Pleasure* in several ways: by removing the phrase that identifies Fanny's profession; by inserting the epigraph about the triumph of virtue over vice; and by changing the pseudonymous publisher, "G. Fenton" (a cover for Fenton Griffiths), into a well known personage: Fenton's brother, Ralph Griffiths. Preceding the text of *Fanny Hill*, but not of *Woman of Pleasure*, is a table of contents, guiding readers towards a didactic interpretation of the text; the effect is similar to that of the table of contents added by Richardson to the 1742 edition of *Pamela*. Like Richardson, Cleland shows readers how to respond to his novel. Thus, on Fanny's arrival in London he notes "the Distress she immediately falls into there"; of her first encounter with Charles notes that "she falls deeply in Love"; and of Charles' deception of Fanny's first procuress, Mrs. Brown, notes that this is a "Laudable Imposition."[16] Mr. H.'s scheme to make Fanny his mistress constitutes a "base Advantage taken by him, over her, in her unhappy Circumstances"; Fanny's "Manners are corrupted" by those of her fellow-prostitutes; but finally, after her marriage to Charles at the end of the novel, she becomes "virtuous for Life." Homosexuality is described as "that unnatural Taste," and the homosexual whom Emily, disguised as a boy, unwittingly attracts at a masquerade is labelled a "S_____te." Such pejorative terminology, even masked, as here by a dash, is entirely avoided in the aptly entitled *Memoirs of a Woman of Pleasure*.

In both versions of the novel, Fanny's memoirs are cast in the form of letters to an anonymous correspondent, addressed as "Madam." In the original, there are only two such letters, each filling a volume; in the abridgment their number is increased to eleven. In both editions, Fanny begins her first letter in compliance with the wishes of "Madam"; but the first paragraph of *Fanny Hill* contains a significant insertion, in which Fanny expresses distaste for her assignment:

> Yet surely you cannot think the task you set me, a pleasant one. Tho', in truth, there is a pleasure in relating past follies, and past misfortunes, when once one is free from their effects. Without much regret then, I shall recall to view the false steps of my life, out of which I have at last emerg'd, to the enjoyment of more happiness than indeed I ought to have hop'd for.
>
> (pp. 1–2)

It is, however, striking that Cleland does not make use of the openings or closings of Fanny's subsequent letters to insert further didactic commentaries of this kind. The letters serve as chapter divisions for the reader's convenience, but there is little attempt at epistolary verisimilitude; most of the letters begin and end abruptly, without acknowledging the presence of their supposed internal reader, "Madam."

The new title page, added table of contents, and the revised epistolary format of the expurgated edition are readily apparent, but largely cosmetic, revisions. The essential difference between the two versions lies in the abridgment's massive deletion of sexual passages. At times the censored matter is simply passed over in silence; elsewhere, Fanny is given such phrases as "I shall here draw the curtain," "let me check my forward pencil," and "I leave it to your imagination" (pp. 50, 68, 243). Despite its moralistic pretensions, however, *Memoirs of Fanny Hill* was not intended to become merely a didactic tract; some of the lubricious material had to remain. In general, Cleland's system was to preserve matter leading up to each sexual scene, expunging description only when disrobing and foreplay get underway. Thus, in Fanny's first sexual encounter, her lesbian dalliance with Phoebe, the abridged version breaks off after the two are in bed together and Phoebe's hands "like a lambent fire ran over my whole body, and thaw'd all coldness as they went" (p. 24), but before the description of their bodies, their mutual stimulation, and their orgasms. In the case of the homosexual episode, Fanny interrupts her narrative at the point when the two young men begin to embrace and disrobe, adding the indignant exclamation: "And O! what a shocking scene ensued" (p. 232).[17]

Cleland's censorship, however, is not always so logical and anodyne. At times, the bowdlerized text pruriently draws attention to deleted material, in Sterneian fashion, through a row of asterisks—such as those that replace the words "I felt his hand on the lower part of my naked thighs," in the original (*FH*, p. 37; *MWP*, p. 18). Since the asterisks invite readers to greater flights of sexual fantasy than did the relatively innocuous deleted words, Cleland is slyly abusing his ostensible role as censor. Both here and elsewhere, a comparison of the two versions reveals cunning witticisms which have hitherto gone unappreciated. In the abridgment, for example, Harriet's statement that "it was out of the power of all my modesty to command my eye away from him, and seeing nothing so very dreadful in his appearance, I sensibly look'd away all my fears" (pp. 162–

63) seems innocuous enough. But the words "him" and "his" have re-placed "it" and "its" in the original, in which the pronouns refer to a phallus that Harriet cannot help admiring (p. 102). By a fine sleight of hand, Cleland has thus made Harriet's beloved, in the expurgated ver-sion, a synecdoche for his own penis. More mischievously, when Fanny describes one of her sexual encounters at Mrs. Cole's brothel, Cleland allows the expurgated text to suggest that she is being sodomized:

> Coming then into my chamber, and seeing me lie alone, with my face turn'd from the light towards the inside of the bed, he, without more ado, proceeded to a repetition of the last night's indulgence, and that in a way peculiar to a taste I was not till now acquainted with. (p. 183)

By omitting the sexually explicit details of the original, Cleland also omitted the observation that Fanny's lover has "ascertain[ed] the right opening" (*MWP*, p. 126); the reader of the abridgment is left in doubt.

Like other censors, Cleland fashioned arbitrary sets of rules for his expurgated text. One of his working guidelines was to retain descriptions of breasts, but to delete even casual mentions of thighs—as in the row of asterisks mentioned above. Thus, for example, a graphic account of Mrs. Brown's pendulous breasts remains uncut: "A more enormous pair did my eyes never behold, nor of a worse colour, flagging-soft, and most lovingly contiguous" (*FH*, p. 50); yet the footman's "new buck-skin breeches, that clipping close, shew'd the shape of a plump well made thigh" (*MWP*, p. 71) can be found only in the original. Elsewhere, "thighs" are modified to "legs": as when Fanny writes of keeping "my legs so lock'd, that it was not for a strength like his to force them open" (*FH*, pp. 199–200; *MWP*, p. 133).

Bishop Sherlock might reasonably contend that such mechanical modi-fications of the text were merely superficial tinkering. In some inserted passages, however, Cleland makes a more concerted effort to alter the focus of his novel. At times, Fanny is given moralizing commentaries that justify her apparently amoral actions, as when Charles first becomes her lover:

> Yet can I hardly allow myself to say that, as yet, I lost my virtue, tho' I lost, indeed, my virginity: for my love for this dear youth, was so sincere, so tender and intire, that if to be constant to one, is to be virtuous, I am sure I should ever have continu'd so, had my fortune shewn me fair play.
>
> (*FH*, p. 64)

The responsibility for Fanny's subsequent career as a prostitute is thus ascribed to ill fortune, rather than to her own inconstancy. Conversely, once she has become a prostitute Fanny is now more ready to condemn her own activities. Her self-reproach for having seduced Mr. H.'s footman is a characteristically didactic insertion:

> And I believe, and with remorse now think on it, that I was the first seducer of the innocence of this raw country youth, whose native modesty did, in truth, oblige me to go great lengths in impudence, before I could conquer it. (p. 124)

Some of these passages replace lengthy sexual scenes in the original. The abridgment omits entirely Fanny's first bacchanalia at Mrs. Cole's brothel, while adding a typically sententious remark by the reformed narrator:

> after being an eye-witness to, and personably concern'd in, such a profound plunge into the deepest and most undisguis'd excesses of sensuality, it is to be suppos'd but that I was sufficiently seasoned to any frolicks of this sort. (p. 180)

Similarly, instead of describing her painful dealings with the flagellant Barvile, Fanny less graphically states that she "went thro' the whole of a process, which was not more terrible in its beginning, than surprising in its conclusion" (*FH*, p. 220).

The style has necessarily been much impoverished. In *Memoirs of a Woman of Pleasure*, Cleland's delicately periphrastic prose created numerous metaphorical variations for the male and female sexual parts, and for orgasm; almost all of these have been removed, so that we hear no more of the "master member of the revels," the "oval reservoirs of the genial emulsion," the "soft laboratory of love," or the "extacy, that extended us fainting, breathless, entranced." Another rhetorical strategy—that of matching metaphors for the sexual act with the occupation of Fanny's partners—has also disappeared: no longer can she admire the nautical briskness of her sailor, who "seiz'd me as prize," "fell directly on board me," and "drown'd in a deluge all my raging conflagration of desire" (pp. 140–41). Much of the sly ribaldry that runs through the novel, beginning with Fanny's invocation of "Truth! stark naked truth" (p. 1), has also been removed in the interests of propriety. Fanny does not, in the abridgment, apologize "for this minute detail of things, that dwelt so strongly upon my memory after *so deep* an impression" (p. 84); such bawdy wordplay was too overt to be retained. In the original novel, Cleland enriched innocuous proverbs with sexual connotations, as in Mrs. Cole's description of the enmity between homosexuality and "the common cause of woman-kind, out of whose *mouths* this practice tended to take something more precious than bread" (p. 159); the passage is deleted in the abridgment.

Cleland's treatment of Fanny's reunion with Charles at the end of the novel exemplifies his expurgatory technique. Somewhat surprisingly, the abridgment retains Fanny's dry remark that "my woman had taken all imaginable care of *Charles*'s travelling companion" (*FH*, p. 265; *MWP*, p. 180); the double entendre here is sufficiently delicate to escape the red pencil. Fanny is still "laid in bed" in the abridgment, but the phrase "got between the sheets" is deleted (*FH*, p. 267; *MWP*, p. 182). An innocuous account of Fanny's sense of "renew'd happiness" replaces her much more tangible sense of Charles' "glowing body in naked touch with mine" (*FH*, p. 268; *MWP*, p. 182). Some of Cleland's most extravagantly metaphorical prose, in a lengthy description of lovemaking, is necessarily omitted, as in an extended comparison between the hydraulics of sexuality and those of a baby at suck:

> the sensitive mechanism of that part thirstily draws and drains the nipple of Love, with much such an instinctive eagerness, and attachment, as, to

compare great with less, kind nature engages infants at the breast, by the pleasure they find in the motion of their little mouths and cheeks, to extract the milky stream prepar'd for their nourishment. (p. 185)

Cleland's remarkable conversion of penis and semen here into "nipple of Love" and "milky stream" helps account for Boswell's terming the *Memoirs* "that extraordinary Book."[18] The abridgment, bereft of such stylistic pyrotechnics, is merely ordinary.

An important feature of the original novel is Cleland's analysis of his own stylistic techniques. The second volume begins with a three-paragraph discussion of tone and diction in erotic fiction, expressing the need to find a "mean temper'd with taste, between the revoltingness of gross, rank, and vulgar expressions, and the ridicule of mincing metaphors and affected circumlocutions" (p. 91). Fanny is a self-conscious narrator, acutely aware of the dangers of monotony in writing of sexuality, and knowing that such common terms as *"joys, ardours, transports, extasies"* will "flatten, and lose much of their due spirit and energy" through their inevitable repetition. Subsequently, she admits to having "too much affected the figurative style; though surely it can pass no where more allowably than in a subject which is so properly the province of poetry" (p. 171). These passages exemplify Cleland's attitude to the writing of erotic prose, and resemble his much later conversation with Boswell, recorded in Boswell's journal for 1779, in which Cleland claimed that he began writing *Memoirs of a Woman of Pleasure* while still in his early twenties, to show Charles Carmichael, his colleague at the East India Company, "that one could write so freely about a woman of the town without resorting to the coarseness of *L'Ecole des filles*, which has quite plain words."[19] Composing *Memoirs of a Woman of Pleasure* posed a stylistic challenge to Cleland; his success in confronting this challenge accounts for much of the novel's permanent value. Shorn of the sexual scenes, *Memoirs of Fanny Hill* inevitably loses much of the original's vitality. Cleland's meditations on questions of style are omitted, since there are few stylistic problems to solve: neither coarseness nor circumlocutions need be avoided when no sexual activity is to be depicted.

Cleland took the opportunity, in preparing *Memoirs of Fanny Hill*, to make hundreds of corrections and revisions unconnected with sexual propriety; in some respects, therefore, the abridgment is a more finished work than the original. Many of the numerous misprints were corrected, oddities of spelling and punctuation were removed, and relatively few new errors were introduced. In view of Cleland's popular reputation as a hasty Grub Street writer, the careful attention that he paid to stylistic accuracy in revising the *Memoirs* is surprising. Yet the same consideration for detail is later found in his painstaking rewriting of J. F. Dreux du Radier's *Dictionnaire d'Amour*, as *The Dictionary of Love* (1751), and in his heavily revised version of his own poem, *The Times! An Epistle to Flavian* (1759).[20] In *Memoirs of Fanny Hill*, however, the surface polish gained is small recompense for the stylistic accomplishment lost. Instructed by Griffiths to "strike out the offensive parts" of *Memoirs of a Woman of*

Pleasure and "compile a Novel from it which might be inoffensive,"[21] Cleland was largely faithful to his wearisome task. Fanny's sexual life is no longer the focus of the novel; instead, her non-sexual activities become central, while her sexual life is submerged in fragmented and truncated episodes. In expurgating his first novel, Cleland created a work akin to his subsequent, non-erotic fiction: *Memoirs of a Coxcomb* (1751), *The Surprises of Love* (1764), and *Woman of Honor* (1768). And like these later works, *Memoirs of Fanny Hill* lacks the one quality that has immortalized *Memoirs of a Woman of Pleasure*: its ability to render, in prose that is neither fulsome nor gross, the pleasures and frustrations of the flesh. Furthermore, the expurgated version has lost Fanny's ingenious parody of Pamela's writing-to-the-moment technique: "I see! I feel! the delicious velvet tip!—he enters might and main with—oh!—my pen drops from me here in the extasy now present to my faithful memory!" (p. 183). In the *Memoirs* this passage completes an elaborate network of allusions to both Richardson's *Pamela* and Fielding's *Shamela*:[22] the rigid application of censor's rules in the abridgment destroys many of these allusions and makes the surviving ones seem oddly sporadic and purposeless.

In the second part of *Memoirs of a Woman of Pleasure*, published in February 1749, Fanny declares her intention of devoting a third letter to her life with the "rational pleasurist," recounting "all the particulars of my acquaintance with this ever, to me, memorable friend" (p. 174). Cleland's arrest in November 1749 must have dissuaded him from writing such a sequel—though not, as we have seen, from producing the expurgated abridgment. Despite Bishop Sherlock's complaints, the Duke of Newcastle had succeeded in deflecting Cleland's energies from the one area in which he excelled. The author of the most celebrated erotic novel in English would never again compose erotic fiction, but dwindle into an undistinguished writer of miscellaneous novels, dramas, verse, journalism, and semi-learned works.

Had *Memoirs of Fanny Hill* been successfully prosecuted, there would have been, as Ralph Griffiths claimed in his review, a miscarriage of justice. That, instead, Griffiths' stock languished unsold testifies to the good sense of readers, who sought out illicit, pirated editions of the original text. Although Thomas Sherlock, in his diatribe against the abridgment, claimed to have read the work in question—unlike many other would-be censors—Griffiths rightly implies otherwise, in concluding his review of *Memoirs of Fanny Hill*:

> As to the step lately taken to suppress this book, we really are at a loss to account for it; yet, perhaps, all wonder on this head will cease, when we consider how liable great men are to be misinformed, how frequently obliged to see with other men's eyes, and hear with other people's ears.[23]

The implications of this remark extend further than Griffiths could have envisaged. For over two hundred years the shape of Cleland's literary career has been obscured by a series of erroneous statements passed down from one source to the next. It is remarkable that as recently as 1979, Roger Lonsdale could add seven works to Cleland's canon while, conversely, in 1981 Maurice Renfrew could confidently attribute to Cleland a novel, *Memoirs of Maria Brown*, that he almost certainly did not write.[24] The misinformation of which Griffiths complained continues to be disseminated. Although *Memoirs of a Woman of Pleasure* is both a popular bestseller and, increasingly, the subject of scholarly discourse, most of Cleland's subsequent writings, as well as *Memoirs of Fanny Hill*, are difficult to find, seldom read, and known primarily through inaccurate, second-hand accounts. The only effective censor, in this as in many other cases, has proved to be time and changing taste.

Peter Sabor
Queen's University, Kingston

NOTES

1. Cited in David Foxon, *Libertine Literature in England 1660-1745* (N.Y.: University Books, 1965), pp. 56-57.
2. See John Sutherland, *Offensive Literature: Decensorship in Britain 1960-1982* (London: Junction Books, 1982), p. 40.
3. *Gentleman's Magazine* 116 (1789):180.
4. See Boswell's journal for 25 Apr. 1778; *Boswell in Extremes*, ed. Charles McC. Weis and Frederick A. Pottle (N.Y.: McGraw Hill, 1970), p. 316.
5. Griffiths' statement to Lovel Stanhope, 15 March 1750; see Foxon, p. 57.
6. *General Advertiser*, 8 March 1750; cited in Foxon, p. 56.
7. Foxon, p. 57.
8. Cited in William Epstein, *John Cleland: Images of a Life* (N.Y.: Columbia Univ., 1974), p. 80.
9. Foxon, p. 57.
10. *Monthly Review* 2 (1750):432.
11. Letters of 12 Apr. and 27 Nov. 1750; see Foxon, p. 58.
12. "The Wages of Sin: *Fanny Hill* and the Later Career of John Cleland," unpublished paper delivered at the Northeastern American Society for Eighteenth-Century Studies Conference, Syracuse, (Oct. 1983).
13. See Foxon, "The Reappearance of Two Lost Black Sheep," *Book Collector* 14 (1965):76.
14. A second copy was recently acquired by the Houghton Library, Harvard Univ.
15. Foxon, "Reappearance"; Naumann, *Keyhold und Candle: John Clelands "Memoirs of a Woman of Pleasure" und die Enstehung des pornographischen Romans in England* (Heidelburg: Carl Winter, 1976), pp. 240-42; Whitley, "Rationalizing a Rogue: Themes and Techniques in the Novels of John Cleland," unpub. Ph.D. diss. (Dalhousie Univ., 1978) pp. 41-44; Basker.
16. *Memoirs of Fanny Hill* (London, 1750), pp. [i] - [iii]. Subsequent refs. to *Memoirs of Fanny Hill*, abbreviated to *FH*, are to this edn. Refs. to *Memoirs of a Woman of Pleasure*, abbreviated to *MWP.*, are to the World's Classics edn., Peter Sabor (Oxford: Oxford Univ. 1985), which is based on the first edn. (1749).
17. The widespread assumption that the homosexual passage is an interpolation stems from a note by Bohn in his edn. of Lowndes' *Bibliographer's Manual* (1864), stating that Cleland's "language was considerably altered for the worse by Drybutter, the bookseller, who was punished for it by being put in the pillory" (cited in Foxon, *Libertine*, p. 61). As Foxon points out, however, no record of any bookseller named Drybutter exists; and since the homosexual passage appears in the first edn. of *Memoris of a Woman of Pleasure*, Bohn's note is highly misleading.

however, no record of any bookseller named Drybutter exists; and since the homosexual passage appears in the first edn. of *Memoirs of a Woman of Pleasure*, Bohn's note is highly misleading.

18. Journal entry for 1 Jan. 1793, in *Private Papers of James Boswell from Malahide Castle*, ed. Geoffrey Scott and Frederick A. Pottle, 18 vols. (Mt. Vernon, N.Y.: priv. ptd., 1928-1934), 18:192.

19. Journal entry for 13 Apr. 1779, in *Boswell Laird of Auchinleck*, ed. Joseph W. Reed and Frederick A. Pottle (N.Y.: McGraw Hill, 1979), pp. 76-77.

20. In a seminal article, "New Attributions to John Cleland," *RES* n.s. 30 (1979):268-90, Roger Lonsdale discusses the *Dictionary of Love*, as well as the first, but not the rev., edn. of *The Times! An Epistle to Flavian*.

21. Foxon, *Libertine*, p. 57.

22. See the author's introduction to *MWP*, pp. xxii-xxvi.

23. Foxon, *Libertine*, p. 58.

24. Lonsdale, "New Attributions"; Renfrew, intro. to *The Memoirs of Maria Brown* (N.Y.: St. Martin's, 1981). Cleland's putative authorship of this novel is dismissed by Epstein "for various stylistic and chronological reasons," p. 233, n. 108.

Chthonic and Pelagic Metaphorization in Eighteenth-Century English Erotica

⁕ ⁕ ⁕

In Shakespeare's *Venus and Adonis* (1593), the goddess of love, while trying to seduce a coyly reluctant Adonis, compares her body to a deer park and develops the metaphor of her erotic topography with graphic precision:

> I'll be a park, and thou shalt be my deer.
> Feed where thou wilt, on mountain, or in dale;
> Graze on my lips, and if those hills be dry,
> Stray lower, where the pleasant fountains lie.
>
> Within this limit is relief enough,
> Sweet bottom-grass, and high delightful plain,
> Round rising hillocks, brakes obscure and rough,
> To shelter thee from tempest, and from rain. (11.229-38)

Beyond the popular Ovidian tradition, Shakespeare was availing himself of a stock of erotic imagery as ancient as the "Song of Songs," with its subtle blend of sacred and profane love in the description of the female body. Its metaphorical transmutation into a country described with (apparently) painstaking topographical accuracy is not particular to eighteenth-century erotica, but was first used—at least in book-length form—in *Erotopolis: The Present State of Betty-Land* (1684), attributed to Charles Cotton.[1] In France, La Mothe Le Vayer (1588-1672) published his *Hexaméron rustique* in 1670, in which the chapter devoted to the fourth day gives a most ingenious, if covertly bawdy, interpretation of Homer's description of the Naiads' cave in Book 13 of the *Odyssey*.[2] La Mothe Le Vayer's interpretation rests on a line-by-line and nearly word-by-word gloss of Homer's text. Thus, long before Our Father Freud and his dreary band of servile epigones, the French sceptic views the olive tree near the head of the harbor as what clearly amounts to a phallic symbol, while the bowls and jars of honey stored within the shadowy cave sacred to the nymphs cannot in fact mean anything but precious sperm in the uterus.[3] In pre-Lacanian fashion—but with much more deadpan humor—La Mothe Le Vayer analyses the *nymph/nymphae* semantic nexus, and sees the webs of purple dye woven by the nymphs as a symbolical representation of the hymen that bleeds when violently deflowered. He finishes his protopsychoanalytical parallel "entre la spelunque [cavern, from Lat. *spelunca*] enigmatique du Poëte, & la naturelle," by identifying the back-door of the cavern—presided over by Venus Postica—as the anus, an organ hardly fit to be named, although reserved as a way of penetration for the heathen gods only. In the light of so much recent heavy-handed Freudo-Marxist criticism, this lightly borne scholarly spoof makes delightful reading. But it also affords an apt illustration of the pelagic element in the metaphorization of the female body, in accordance with the central Odyssean trope of the amorous voyage, the sea being an archetypal symbol of life, immensity, and eternity. Finally, as will be shown in the study of a corpus of English erotica ranging over half a century—between the 1730s and the 1780s—the chthonian and the pelagic metaphors are closely linked by a botanical one, what might be called a "hortus sexualis," easily traceable in the frequent assimilation of male and female genital parts with plants.

Why did these anonymous or obscure authors of erotica resort to such tropes? Although it is impossible to furnish a fully satisfactory answer within the limited space of this essay, two tentative solutions may be briefly examined. First, the recourse to metaphorical parlance is a traditional approach to a taboo topic. Metaphorization, because of its distancing effect, acts as a convenient protection: it is a lexical and eidetic screen. The notorious four-letter words are studiously avoided, as in Cleland's *Memoirs of a Woman of Pleasure* (1748-49). Thus, the book (theoretically) did not offend chaste ears and eyes (although—as Peter Sabor points out in his essay in this volume—author, printer, and publisher were found guilty of publishing an obscene book). The "bewitching grove" or "Love's grotto," while meaning precisely the same thing, are euphemistic metaphors vastly less shocking than the use of what Grose in his *Dictionary of the Vulgar Tongue* listed as the "Monosyllable." This is the hypothesis formulated, for instance, by Roger Thompson.[4] A second theory might be termed "socio-cultural," or perhaps "sexo-cultural." My contention is that erotica, as part of eighteenth-century subculture, reflect—in a more or less distorted and fragmented way—the development of such sciences as topography, cartography, geography, obstetrics, and botany. It is needless to stress at great length that the eighteenth century was an age of maritime exploration. It is striking that, among others, the names of such travellers as Henry Maundrell (1655-1701)—whose *Journey from Aleppo to Jerusalem A.D. 1697*, published in 1703, reached its sixth edition by 1740—as well as those of three authors of well known geographical and/or cartographic compilations—Patrick Gordon (fl. 1700); Captain Greenville Collins (d. 1694); Thomas Salmon (1679-1767)—should appear in an impudent pseudo-bibliography of confessed plagiarisms in Thomas Stretser's *Merryland Displayed: Or, Plagiarism, Ignorance and Impudence Detected, Being Observations upon a pamphlet Intituled A New Description of Merryland* (1741). Patrick Gordon's popular *Geography Anatomized: Or, a Compleat Geographical Grammar* (London, 1693; 16th edn., 1740) combines elementary definitions of general geography with the didactic functions of a compendium and gazetteer of the various countries of Earth. It contains geographical problems, puzzles, and paradoxes. In describing the countries, it follows a set method and nearly invariable plan: Name; Air; Soil;

Commodities; Rarities; Archbishoprics (when applicable); Universities; Manners; Language; Government; Arms; Religion. This is a systematic approach that will be taken up and parodied by the authors of erotica, where the female body is transformed into a country—"terra incognita," if not always "intacta"—to be discovered and thoroughly explored. Likewise, Stretser quotes Collins' *Great Britain's Coasting Pilot*, published in 1693 and reprinted twenty times between 1723 and 1792.[5] This famous manual of coastal navigation by the hydrographer to Charles II betrays the same desire for encyclopaedic knowledge as Gordon's book. The lengthy title of the 1693 edition—still retained verbatim in the 1753 one—expresses perfectly this striving for topographical omniscience, akin to the sort of encyclopaedic vertigo that obtains throughout the eighteenth century:

> Describing All the Harbours, Rivers, Bays, Roads, Rocks, Sands, Buoys, Beacons, Sea-Marks, Depths of Water, Latitude, Bearings and Distances from Place to Place; the Setting and Flowing of Tides; with Directions for the knowing of any Place, and how to Harbour a Ship in the same with Safety.

Like Gordon's geography, Thomas Salmon's *Modern History; or the Present State of All Nations* (1736-38), containing cuts and maps by Herman Moll, was often reprinted during the century.

Finally, without attempting to give even a schematic outline of the complex historiography of such sciences as geology and botany, it is necessary to mention the works of John Woodward (1665-1728), a pioneer sometimes carried away by his theoretical speculations, such as the *Essay towards a Natural History of the Earth* (1695) and his catalogue, *An Attempt towards a Natural History of the Fossils of England* (1728-29). In the same realm of geology, the works of Leibnitz and Buffon on the continent should also be borne in mind. As for botany, John Ray (1627-1705), often referred to as the father of natural history in Great Britain, is still remembered for his system of classification set forth in his *Historia Generalis Plantarum* (1686-1704). But it was the Swede, Carl von Linné (1707-78), who laid the foundations of modern botanical classification in his *Systema Naturae* (1737). Such, very briefly, is the intertextuality of the erotic corpus to be examined here. This rapid sketch is all the more incomplete as it should take into account—which is impossible here—the progress of medical sciences, especially obstetrics. For example, at the end of his *Merryland Displayed* (1741), Thomas Stretser quotes two pioneers in those "Books from whence the *Author* of *Merryland* has borrowed Assistance." The French obstetrician François Mauriceau (1637-1709) published his *Aphorismes touchant la grossesse, l'accouchement, les maladies et autres dispositions des femmes* in 1694, a work which met with considerable success both in France and in England during the first half of the eighteenth century. Sir Richard Manningham (1690-1759) is likewise mentioned by Stretser, certainly one of the most celebrated accoucheurs of the period, who wisely avoided being taken in by the imposter, Mary Toft, the "rabbit breeder" in 1726, and who founded the first ward for parturient women in a parochial infirmary (St James's, Westminster) in 1739. His *Artis Obstetricariae Compendium* (1739) was published in English in 1744.

Probably toward the end of October 1740 was published *A New Description of Merryland. Containing, A Topographical, Geographical, AND Natural History of That Country*, written by one of Curll's hacks, Thomas Stretser, about whom nothing is known.[6] Although the publishing history of the *New Description* is beset with many uncertainties, due to the notorious Curll's deliberate confusion of dates and places of publication, which make the imprints less than reliable, it is an attested fact that *New Description* enjoyed a great success, reaching a tenth London edition in 1742. It was also translated into French about 1770 and condemned to be burnt by a Parisian tribunal in 1822,[7] a belated and prudish judicial overreaction to a by then well-established piece of not very naughty erotica. The work has been frequently reprinted, pirated, and imitated for the last two centuries or so.[8] Curll, an astute promoter of the books he produced as a bookseller and publisher, paid Stretser to write an apparently virulent counterblast to *New Description*, a fairly tame piece of bawdy badinage, yet aggressively subtitled, dated 20 October 1741, shortly after the seventh edition of the *New Description*.[9] Obviously nobody knew better than Stretser the many faults and plagiarisms of his own *New Description*, which he gloats over zestfully in *Merryland Displayed*—an unusual but not unknown case of an author acting as a Zoilus to his own work in order to stimulate waning interest in it and thus boost sales.

The parodic elements and structure of *New Description*, admitted to by Stretser in *Merryland Displayed*, derive directly from the geographical manuals briefly referred to above. It is easy to detect Gordon's and Salmon's systematic approach throughout the twelve chapters of *New Description* that deal with the following points: name; situation; air, soil, rivers, canals; extent, divisions, and principal places of note; ancient and modern inhabitants; products and commodities; curiosities; government; religion; language; tenures; coastal survey, with "Directions for strangers steering safe into Merryland." But beneath the thin pretence of topographical description, the chthonic metaphor is omnipresent. Its effect is twofold: it both reifies and eroticizes the female body, apprehended as a passive object, but also dynamized by the sexual pulsions of "Merryland." This makes for a Brobdingnagian macrocosm, swarming with potential activities, animated by such natural forces as winds, waters, tides and currents, peopled with a particular flora and fauna. The reified body abandons itself to the theoretically neutral explorer, in spite of his ominously (and doubly so) phallic name, Roger Pheuquewell (p. [i]). In his Preface (pp. ix-xv), the author keeps up the pretence of being a true explorer, refusing all fabulous relations. Out to tell the truth, and nothing but the truth, he virtuously deplores the neglect of a wonderful land by such modern geographers as Moll, Gordon, and Salmon.

Stretser invents toponyms borrowed directly from anatomical nomenclature, with a few letters (usually vowels) omitted here and there to render them both unrecognizable and innocuous enough. Thus, the geographical situation of Merryland:

in a *low* part of the Continent, bounded on the upper Side, or to the Northward, by the little Mountain called MNSVNRS [Mons Veneris], on the East and West by COXASIN [Coxa Sinistra] and COXADEXT [Coxa Dextra], and on the South or lower-Part it lies open to the TERRA FIRMA." (p. 3)

But still more interesting is the pervasiveness of the phallic principle of penetration, even when tentatively disguised by the use of scientific or technical lexemes. In order to determine the longitude and latitude of that country—which is none other than the female genitalia—the explorer has tried to assess them "with a *proper Instrument, of a large Radius,* and in perfect good Order" (p. 4). But, some years later, they turn out to have changed, because his "instrument," often used, may have been inaccurate, and also because a surprising increase of longitude and latitude takes place in Merryland whenever there is "a *fruitful season* in that Country" (p. 5). Several methods for reducing the latitude—i.e., restoring the vagina to supposedly virginal straitness by the use of astringents[10]—have failed. The same obsessive concern with phallic penetration is to be traced in all the chapters of this geographical anatomy, which is also an anatomical geography of the female parts. The author makes fun of those who prefer the podex to Merryland, "the *Italian* Geographers are pretty much inclined that Way; some of the *Dutch* have likewise come into it, and of late years a few in *Great-Britain* have appeared not altogether averse to it" (p. 7). This is the usual type of attack against the loose mores of the continentals, the French and the Italians taking pride of place in that effeminate homosexual fifth column, which was thought at the time to sap British virility. The premium set by religious, medical, legal, and popular opinion on physical virginity in females reappears under the slight metaphorical disguise of aratory lexis:

The Parts which have never been broken up, nor had Spade or Plough in them, are most esteemed; and so fond are People of having the first tilling of a fresh Spot, that I have known some Hundreds of Pounds given to obtain that Pleasure." (pp. 10–11)

Erotic poliorcetics quite predictably follows as a metaphorical means of describing precisely the female genitals. In such a context of male/macho-dominated erotic subliterature the phallic onslaught on the female fortress can only be successful:

two Forts called LBA [labia], between which every one must necessarily pass, that goes up the Country, there being no other Road. The Fortifications are not very strong, tho' they have *Curtains, Hornworks,* and *Ramparts;* they have indeed sometimes defended the Pass a pretty while, but were seldom or never known to hold out long against a close and rigorous Attack." (p. 15)

Poor innocent Uncle Toby, who in *Tristram Shandy* hardly ever suspects that the vocabulary of poliorcetics may be put to less chaste uses than the straightforward description of the siege of Namur! Pubic hair, not surprisingly, becomes a spacious forest that "seems to have been preserved for the Pleasure of Variety, and Diversion of Hunting," a description admittedly lifted from a volume of Chamberlayne's *Present State of England* (*New Description*, p. 17). The cynegetic allusion heralds in the peripatetic metaphor when Stretser alludes to the obstetrical works of Mauriceau, "who was a great Traveller in that Country, and surveyed it with tolerable Exactness" (p. 18).

To buttress this erotic metaphorization of the female body Stretser resorts throughout *New Description* to ubiquitous and insidious double entendre, from the lightest innuendo to the heaviest and bawdiest pun or quibble. With his customary brazenness he readily admits the implicit lewdness of all his pseudo-topographical descriptions. In *Merryland Displayed* he confesses, while seeming to attack *New Description*, that chapter six of the earlier work ("Of the Product and Commodities, such as Fish, Fowls, Beasts, Plants, etc.") consists "in general of low Puns, Quibbles, and Conumdrums, and even those are not of our Author's Invention, but many of them are much older than himself" (p. 40). It is quite true: demotic, or more distinguished, bawdry relies on lexical polysemy and the unbridgeable gap between word and world, which so much haunts Locke's *Essay concerning Human Understanding*, and which enables Sterne to let off his verbal pyrotechnics in *Tristram Shandy*. When Stretser mentions that in the great canal of Merryland "*Cod* indeed are often found about the lower end of the great Canal, and *Crabs* in Plenty on its Banks" (*New Description*, p. 23), this is little more than a schoolboy's feeble smutty joke; but when he casually mentions that rabbits have also occasionally been bred in Merryland (p. 24), this implies a more sophisticated devious reference to Mary Toft's attempted hoax of 1726 in Godalming. Minerals are also to be found in Merryland: not only gold and silver—an allusion to prostitution and the buying of more or less skilfully "repaired" hymens—but also blue or Roman vitriol "which is of great Use to eat away proud Flesh" (p. 24), a medical quibble on the sexually charged set phrase "proud flesh," and an allusion to the therapeutic use of vitriol in removing chancres. No contemporary would have missed the jokes about those

> *precious Stones*, here being a Kind very much esteemed, tho' very common, to be met with on the Surface; so fond are they of them, that a Man would be looked upon with Contempt in MERRYLAND, if he had not at least two of them, which they always carry about them in a Purse; they contribute very much to the Fruitfulness of the Soil. (p. 25)

More subtle, perhaps are the red and white flowers, which refer to the menses and *fluor albus*, i.e., leucorrhea (p. 26). Also allusively, Stretser informs his readers that no manufactures are to be found in Merryland, "except for *Pins* and *Needles* . . . made in great Plenty in some of the most trading Provinces, and . . . famous for their *exquisite Sharpness*" (p. 26)—a medical jest on the stinging and burning pains caused by gonorrhea during micturition.

Thus though the reified female body should be diseroticized by the constant recourse to the topographical metaphor, this does not occur.

First because of the structural function of double entendre throughout *New Description* and, second, because of the agonistic tensions within eighteenth-century society, which was far more repressive than its traditional, but inaccurate, label of libertinism leads too many historians and critics to believe.[11] Eroticism is notoriously difficult to define, but it should at least be clear that in the eighteenth century it fulfills a didactic and an oneiric function.[12] Such erotica may be viewed as the clumsy, often objectionable, predecessors of our current sex manuals; they are rather naive attempts at outlining a primitive sexology, envisaged exclusively from a masculine angle (naturally enough in a male-dominated society). Any form of eroticism, even the crudest one, is a pulsating and exacerbated celebration of the forces of life against those of death, an especially haunting omnipresence in the eighteenth century, before efficient remedies could curb infant mortality, the ravages of fevers, septicaemia, and rampant venereal infection. But even this festive celebration of life is not devoid of the ontological *Angst* surrounding the sexual act and its ejaculatory acme of erotic bliss.[13] *New Description*, like all erotic literature, is marked by the diffuse myth of what might be called the "precious sperm." To copulate means *spending* a precious balm of life, a quintessential liquor originating, some thought, from the brain, others from the marrow, or from the "better blood" after ingested food had been duly "concocted." The first inhabitants of Merryland—Adam and his offspring after the Fall—were given to change and variety, behaving like extravagant rakes "as they *spend all they can,* and glory who *spends most*" (p. 19). Sperm also appears as "an excellent Cosmetic" and "undoubtedly a great Sweetener" (p. 25) much in demand to cure sharp humours and green sickness in lovelorn maidens, which harks back to one of the most deeply rooted myths of Occidental sexology, the therapeutic value of semen, the sexual act being always more or less explicitly considered as the affirmation of a potentially violent domination of women by males. This twofold thematic myth—the preciousness of sperm and man's phallic domination—has been traced and analysed by Michel Foucault in texts of classic Greek authors and has been named "le schéma éjaculatoire"[14] and "le principe de la . . . soustraction précieuse,"[15] whereby the feeling of weakness and diffuse post-coital melancholy is accounted for.

P. J. Kearney contends that "these extended sexual metaphors did not find a great deal of favor elsewhere in Europe; some translations appeared in France, but in general they appear to have been a peculiarly English fancy" (*History*, p. 57). As "the last of these horticultural and geographical tours of the human anatomy," he quotes a naughty parody of Sterne's *A Sentimental Journey* entitled *La Souriciere. The Mousetrap. A Facetious and Sentimental Excursion through Part of Austrian Flanders and France* (London, 1794), by a "Timothy Touchit."[16] He fails to make the point, however, that throughout the eighteenth century recourse to such metaphors in erotica was widespread and quasi automatic. In *Harris's List of Covent Garden Ladies for the Year 1788* (London, 1788), a popular guide to the meretricious talents in Town, Miss Lister's anatomy is thus temptingly described:

the *neighbouring hills* below full ripe for manual pressure, firm, and elastic, and heave at every touch. The *Elysian font*, in the centre of a *black bewitching grove*, supported by two pyramids white as alabaster, very delicate, and soft as turtle's down. (pp. 16–17)

The focus on the female pudenda, with systematic recourse to Greek and Latin mythology, is best instanced in *The Secret History of Pandora's Box* (London, 1742), where the anonymous author, with the help of glib references to Homer, Virgil, and other classical poets, demonstrates that the *partes propriae quae foeminis* are fit objects of adoration. Had they been made dieties, that would have brought about the extinction of polytheism; but he also hints that these parts may well have been the original Pandora's box "and that this box was neither more nor less than an allegory of the characteristical nature of woman" (p. 51). "Pandora's box" was but one of many coy periphrases, mostly mythological, as is evidenced by the lavish use of them in *A New Atlantis* (London, 1758), where within half a dozen pages or so (pp. 36–43) the female parts are variously referred to as "the magic circle," "Cupid's grotto," "the procreative ring," "Cytherea's cell," "Venus's *camera obscura*," "the sanctuary of love," and "the blissful altar."

Likewise, a frequent rhetorical epiphenomenon of the nuclear chthonic metaphor is the use of a bellicose lexis to describe the inevitable "amorous Combat," especially that of poliorcetics, Captain Shandy's hobbyhorsical love. In *The History of the Human Heart* (London, 1749), Camillo vanguishes the fair Charlotta:

He pushed boldly forward, laid her gently back on the Couch, removed the Outworks, and Sword in Hand charged the Breach. The Engagement was warm on both Sides for some Moments, each strove for Victory with equal Vigour, till their Ammunition on both Sides being spent, the Swain first made a decent Retreat, and left the Field to recruit his Forces, in order to renew the Charge. (pp. 89–90)

These erotic encounters of Mars and Venus will remain, down to our times, well established clichés graphically underlining what Michel Foucault calls "la pénétration comme jeu 'stratégique' de domination-soumission et comme jeu 'économique' de dépense-bénéfice."[17] Even on such occasions as a wedding night, more dedicated to the cult of Venus than Mars, poets could use surprisingly bellicose accents:

To arms! to arms! now Cupid sounds,
Now is the time for grateful wounds.
Here VENUS waves the nimble spear—
VENUS is warlike-goddess here.[18]

The pelagic and botanical metaphors are practically inseparable from the chthonic in mid-eighteenth-century erotica, as though those unknown authors felt an unconscious nostalgia for a return to such archaic elements as earth, sea, and vegetal life. If the title page is to be trusted— which is dubious in view of the heavily parodic quality of the imprint, "London for J. *Conybeare* in *Smock-Ally* near *Petticoat-Lane* in *Spittlefields*"—

A Voyage to Lethe, by Samuel Cock, was published in 1741. It was "Dedicated to the Right Worshipful Adam Cock, Esq.; of *Black Mary's Hole*, Coney-Skin Merchant." Between *cock* and *coney* the erotic space of *A Voyage to Lethe* is firmly circumscribed. *Cock* reappears with predictable regularity in the names of the fancy subscribers, such as "Rev. Mr. Slowcock, for himself and Parishioners, to bind up with the Octavo Edition of *Pamela*, 3000 ditto"—which shows that the anonymous author of the *Voyage* was aware of literary novelties. Then follow Mr. Smallcock (50 copies), Mr. Badcock (25), Mr. Nocock (12) and Miss Shuttlecock (50). The onomastic punning on *cock* continues throughout the whole pamphlet and soon gets wearisome, with its obsessive focusing on genital parts and sexual activities. The author's father is "Sampson Cock of Coney-Hatch," and his mother comes from a Laycock family residing at Cunnington in Huntingdonshire. The male genital parts are described in the same topographic manner as the female in *New Description*. Here is a description of the author's manor of (inevitably) Allcock:

> most singularly curious for its Shape, and situate withal in a very pleasant and fertile Part of the Country, being a long Neck of Land, shaded by a Grove of Trees, and supported by a couple of Hills, impregnated according to the Virtuosi, with a white sort of Metal, which being liquify'd is deem'd an excellent Restorative. Its Figure towards the End is in the Form of a large Nut; and there is an Aqueduct thro' it, that terminates in a *jette d'Eau* [sic], as often as it is properly supply'd with Water. (*Voyage*, p. 8)

The "ejaculatory pattern" analysed by Foucault is easily detected here again.

It is only with the nautical metaphorization of the female body as a ship—*The Charming Sally*, commanded by the ubiquitous Captain Samuel Cock—that the pelagic metaphor, pursued throughout the *Voyage*, appears. The rhetorical assimilation of woman with a ship, usually a "leaky vessel," belongs to popular erotic subculture, as witness the countless, more or less humorous, jokes purporting to explain why "ship" is of the feminine gender. The following is one of the less objectionable: "when a woman or a ship are on the rocks, they both send out signals of distress." *The Charming Sally* must be fitted with her main-mast before sailing, a phallic manoeuvre described with the graphic precision of a seasoned mariner and a wealth of double entendre (which Smollett exploited more tactfully, but no less effectively, in the polysemic parlance of his sea-characters, Pipes, Hatchway, and Trunnion in *Peregrine Pickle*, and Captain Crowe in *Launcelot Greaves*). Here is the description of the operation:

> The Main-Mast being a Long-side, we strove to heave it in, but found much Difficulty; indeed I thought once I should never have got it righted in her, being somewhat of the largest; but by greasing and working it to and fro, the third Day it went tolerably plumb into the Socket. I work'd Night and Day upon the rest of her Rigging." (p. 13)

Then Captain Cock with his *Charming Sally* sails off to various allegorical and erotic climes, such as "Buttock-Land" and its "charming Circumference" (p. 28). There he pays visits to antithetical temples, dedicated to the goddess Dildona, and, on the opposite shore, another one dedicated to an idol, Paederarstia [sic]. Dildona is worshipped by women of all ranks and ages, making shameless use of the dildo, and fittingly called "Sterilians," while the adorers of Paederarstia, the "Sodomanians," turn out to be

> a very infamous People, of a mean sallow Complexion, and with an odious Squeak in their Voices. . . . The Idol, or rather Monster, is in a most unseemly Attitude, representing a young Boy, crouching down, with his Head pendent, and his Posteriors projecting to his Votaries. (p. 36)

Among his votaries: Alexander, Caesar, Pompey, and various kings and princes.

Here two remarks should be made. First, the *Voyage* affords yet another example of the moralizing teleology inherent in the implicit discourse of eighteenth-century erotica, apparently an unlikely place for didacticism, yet one where almost invariably homosexuality and masturbation are virtuously condemned. Even erotica may conceal a repressive discourse beneath their apparent sexual permissiveness. Not before Sade and his *Les 120 Journées de Sodome*, where instructions how to masturbate are given, was the taboo on solitary pleasure openly transgressed.[19] In the *Voyage* the idol Mastupro (p. 37), therefore, is described with obvious dislike and great contempt. With similar moral thrust, *The Charming Sally* sails on to Cape Venterino, makes Point Cornuto, then "Agonia, the most noted Island on the Coast of Lethe" (p. 73), where Captain Cock bids an eternal farewell to his ship, returns to England, and marries a rich widow, declaring himself "determine'd to make no more voyages to *Lethe*."

In the final chapter of *New Description* Stretser also has recourse to the pelagic metaphor to define man's possible erotic routes to the sexual conquest of woman. It is noteworthy that the fusion of the chthonic and pelagic metaphors was graphically achieved in a set of plates entitled *A Compleat Set of Charts of the Coasts of Merryland* (1745), of which, unfortunately, no copy is known to survive.[20] According to Stretser, to steer safely into Merryland a man may take either the "upper Course"—via "LPS" [lips], along the shore to "BBY [bubby] mountains," then proceed only if there is no storm, or else let the squall blow over and "lie-by"—or "the lower Course," up "*the Straits of Tibia,* with the Coxadext bearing close on the Larboard-Bow, and so run-a-head, directly as the Current carries you, into the Harbour; and indeed when the Trade-Winds set in, this Course cannot fail" (p. 44). In either of these courses the "Forestaff" should always be kept at hand and in good order. Such erotic navigation is greatly facilitated by Aretino's "charts" (p. 46). Sexual interdicts make themselves obstrusively felt even in such erotica as this: catamenial and anal intercourse is best avoided. The menses are compared to spring tides running out of harbor, while anal intercourse is referred to as "go[ing] about the *Windward-Passage*" (p. 46). The final sailing and docking instructions keep up the nautical metaphor with a great (protective) display of apparent technicalities:

> After you are fairly entered the Mouth of the Harbour, go up as far as you can, and come to an Anchor, *veering* out as much Cable as possible; the more you *veer*, the better you will ride. The chief thing is to beware of anchoring in *foulground*; for here is some much gruffer than others, and a great deal so very bad, that it will soon spoil the best of Cables; the *sandy* or *grey Ground* are not good to anchor in, the *brown* is best, in my Opinion: But as People cannot always have their Choice, they must be contented with such as they can get. (p. 47)

On these goodly words of maritime sexology *New Description* comes to a didactic close, but not before the author has coyly remarked that in voyages to Merryland, it is generally easier to sail into harbor at night than in daylight, another minor taboo still current in our so (mis)called *New Description* called "permissive society."

A mythological link could be found between classical antiquity and those mid-eighteenth-century erotica making extensive use of the horticultural metaphor: Priapus was also the god of gardens, as Fielding slyly reminds his readers when describing Joseph Andrews' bird-scaring activities at the outset of his menial career. A more direct and contemporaneous reason is the publication in 1730 of *Catalogus Plantarum*, by the famous Scotish gardener, Philip Miller (1691-1771), soon followed by extremely popular works repeatedly reprinted throughout the century: *The Gardener's Dictionary* (1731) and *The Gardener's Kalendar* (1732). It is probable that it was the publication of Miller's *Catalogus* that prompted the production of two erotico-horticultural skits, both published in 1732 in London: *The Natural History of the Arbor Vitae, or Tree of Life* and *The Natural History of the Frutex Vulvaria, or Flowering Shrub*, the latter by an onomastically evocative Philogynes Clitorides. Both pamphlets are often attributed to Thomas Stretser.[21] The botanical metaphor is used throughout *Frutex Vulvaria* with as much thoroughness as the topographical one in *New Description*, the "vulvaria" being defined as the female Arbor Vitae. The whole range of puns, quibbles, double entendres, sexual allusions, and innuendos is likewise to be found in the opening description:

> The *Frutex Vulvaria* is a flat low Shrub, which always grows in a moist Valley, at the Foot of a little Hill, which is constantly water'd by a Spring, whose Water is impregnated with very saline Particles, which nevertheless agree wonderfully well with this Shrub; it is guarded round about with *Fibrillae*, or *Capillary Tendrils*, of the same Nature, and Use, with those at the Root of the *Arbor Vitae*. (p. 6)

The author fully exploits the polysemic potentialities of such words as *hot-houses*—which, not unexpectedly, are made to mean brothels "in and about the *Hundreds of Drury*; not a few about St James's and *Westminster*; that celebrated Female *Botanist* Mother *Needham* in her Time kept a very famous one" (p. 14)—and amply uses mythology and Latin periphrases to designate the female genitalia, e.g. *Arma Veneris, Fons Vitae, Incus Vitae, Natura, Frutex Scientiae Boni et Mali, Concha Veneris, Annulus Regum* (because there kings set their "precious Stones") (p. 21). It is noteworthy that, for once, the ubiquitous myth of the "precious sperm" gives way to that of the "all-healing vulva." The "vulvaria" works miracle cures for melancholy, choler, stone, gravel, and tumors; it makes misers generous and cowards bold, transforms oafs into wits, clodpates into machiavels, and coxcombs into the greatest politicians.

In *New Description* Stretser also exploits the horticultural metaphor. The penis is likened to a plant resembling red coral, yielding "a *whitish viscid Juice*, which when taken inwardly, has a bad Effect on some people, causing a large Tumor in the Umbilical Regions, which is not got rid of again without great Pain"; the "hortus sexualis" in Merryland is well stocked with bawdily polysemic plants, such as rue (in great plenty), carrots (much used), some true-love and sweet-marjoram, "and the Plant called *Maiden-hair*; but the last is very scarce" (p. 25). Stretser also mentions a submarine plant "of the *Sponge-kind*," used "not only as a *Cleanser*, but also as an Antidote against the bad Effects of the Juice above mentioned" (p. 26)—a clear reference to the contraceptive use of small sponges inserted in the vagina.

In a mildly erotic and, at times, rather amusing spoof of pseudo-philosophical and scientific treatises, *The Man-plant: Or, a Scheme for Increasing and Improving the British Breed* (London, 1752), Vincent Miller, M.E., and self-styled "Professor of Philosophy," similarly exploits fully horticultural metaphor. He describes no less than the transplant of a fertilized human ovum not into another uterus, but into a bladder filled with a nutritious liquid prepared by the author from food extracts. The whole is planted in baskets of earth in a hot-house, duly watered, and covered by a bell-glass. The experiment proves successful, and the author is soon pestered with many offers of laying fertilized eggs (pp. 18-19) from "nominal Maids, Wives of Absentees, and wise Widows" (p. 33). Miller displays some knowledge of both botany and medicine, but the botanical metaphor is not kept up throughout, especially after the birth of the hale "man-plant" in the hot-house; yet, *The Man-plant* is an interesting avatar of the horticultural metaphorization of the body and a comic anticipation of embryo-transplants.

The most complete assimilation of the penis with a phallic plant is made by John Wilkes in his infamous *An Essay on Woman* (1763), "by Pego Borewell, Esq.; with Notes By Rogerus Cunaeus, Vigerus Mutoniatus."[22] Pego appears as a robust plant that "will shoot forth most amazingly, quite on a sudden, especially in a *Hot-bed*, and as suddenly shrink back," while the clitoris is described as "a bastard Plant . . . though seldom large; I mean in this country; for at Lesbos it was the formidable Rival of Pego" (p. 215). Sexual intercourse becomes a hunting scene, a cynegetic metaphor fusing the chthonic and the vegetal:

> Together let us beat this ample Field,
> Try what the Open, what the Covert yield.
> The lateut [latent] Tracts, the pleasing Depths explore,
> And my Prick clapp'd where thousands were before. (p. 217)

The "Arbor Vitae" metaphorization of the phallus, probably because of its biblical origins, haunts the erotic unconscious during the century. As late as 1789 in the anthology, *The Pleasures, that Please on Reflection*, "The Geranium," a poem "Ascribed to Various Writers, Mr. Whalley, Mr. Ers—e, etc.," is reprinted (pp. 35-38):

> Then straight before the wondering maid,
> The Tree of Life I gently laid;
> Observe, sweet Sue, his drooping head,
> How pale—how languid—and how dead.
> Yet let the sun of thy bright eyes
> Shine but a moment, it shall rise.
> Let but the dew of thy soft hand
> Refresh the stem, it straight shall stand.
> Already see it swells, it grows,
> Its head is redder than the rose.
> Its shrivell'd fruit of dusky hue,
> Now glows a present, fit for Sue.
> The balm of life each artery fills,
> And in o'erflowing drops distills. (pp, 36-37)

This last quotation may not belong to the most refined strain of ethereal love-poetry, but it affords an apt illustration of several recurrent sexual myths, still persisting today to a certain extent. Mid-eighteenth-century erotica are not only phallocratic but phallocentered. The "tree of life" is clearly an object of amazement for the bemused maid. The hackneyed use of the solar metaphor in amorous verse ("the sun of thy bright eyes") all the same finds some justification for once, as the phallic plant—unlike its vegetal counterparts drooping in the sun—receives fresh vigor from the cosmic heat of Eros. Likewise, "the dew of thy soft hand" may not be the most successful metaphor, yet its aqueous referent suggests strongly the association of woman with the primal life-giving element, water.

In other words, mid-century erotica belonging to a more or less recondite subculture—as opposed to such a work as Cleland's *Memoirs of a Woman of Pleasure* that was published, sold, and reviewed quite openly— are perhaps less interesting *per se* than for their sexo-cultural discourse, or counter-discourse, which reflects all the contradictions, difficulties, and major problems of an age torn between an ancient tradition of fierce individualism within the community and the formidable forces at work in the mercantilist, pre-capitalist socio-economy of the time. There is little doubt that the often horrified rejection of both onanism and homosexuality may partly be ascribed to the mercantilist dictum that no energy should be *spent* in vain. But, conversely, erotica were also often presented by their authors as helpful and conducive to procreation, in virile reaction against the dangerous effeminacy of the "mollies" and the masturbators.

Finally, what perhaps remains most striking about those erotica is the compulsive need for sexual confession. As Diderot's *Bijoux indiscrets* (1748) illustrates so well, never was sex more discursive, not to say talkative, than in the eighteenth century, when the erotic rituals of sexual confession first became fixed, progressively building up what Michel

Foucault rightly calls "une grande archive des plaisirs du sexe."[23] In that perennial quest for sexual knowledge, still pursued today, eighteenth-century erotica display an instinctive, if not instinctual, recourse, via metaphorization, to the primeval sources of life: earth, sea, and plants.

Paul-Gabriel Boucé
Université de Paris III—Sorbonne Nouvelle

NOTES

1. See Roger Thompson, *Unfit for Modest Ears* (London: Macmillan, 1979), pp. 190-93.
2. See the trans. by A. T. Murray, Loeb Classical Library (London: William Heinemann, 1966), 2: 9-11, 11. 96-112.
3. François La Mothe Le Vayer, *Hexaméron rustique* (Cologne: P. Brenussen, 1671), pp. 96-103. On p. 98, sperm is referred to as "ce miel métaphorique de l'antre des Nymphes."
4. Thompson, p. 190.
5. See Coolie Verner, *Captain Collins' Coasting Pilot* (London: Durrant House, 1969).
6. On the complex bibliographical history of the pamphlet, apart from the BL *Catalogue* and NUC, see: R. Straus, *The Unspeakable Curll* (London: Chapman and Hall, 1927), pp. 308-14; Patrick J. Kearney, *The Private Case* (London: Jay Landesman, 1981), pp. 319-20. The edn. used here is the 2nd., Bath (in fact, London), pub. Nov. 1740, but dated 1741. See also Kearney, *History of Erotic Literature* (London: Macmillan, 1982), pp. 55-57.
7. See Pascal Pia, *Les Livres de l'Enfer* (Paris: Coulet & Faure, 1978), 1:299.
8. See Kearney, *Private Case* p. 320.
9. The edn. cited bears a probably false Bath imprint. Like *NDM*, *MD*, Sold for 1s.6d.
10. On the myths of virginity, and the various ways of repairing a damaged one, see my essay "Some Sexual Beliefs and Myths in Eighteenth-Century Britian" in P.-G. Boucé, ed., *Sexuality in Eighteenth-Century Britain* (Manchester: Manchester Univ., 1982), pp. 28-46, passim.
11. For an analysis of sexual tensions and repression in 18th-c. Europe, see Jacques Solé, *L'Amour en Occident a' l'époque moderne (1976; Bruxelles: Editions Complexe, 1984), pp. 253-60. Solé's Marxist approach is at times reductive, and his grid of interpretation turns into a bed of Procrustes.
12. See P.J. Kearney's working definition in his *History* p. 7: "Erotica, for the purpose of this book, is seen as a matter of intent in that the authors and publishers had it in mind to provide the reader of their wares with sexual stimulation of one sort or another." This pragmatic outlook is too narrow and incomplete.
13. See P.-G. Boucé, "Aspects of Sexual Tolerance and Intolerance in XVIIIth-Century England," *The British Journal for Eighteenth-Century Studies* 3 (1980): 173-91 and Peter Wagner, "The Veil of Medicine and Morality: Some Pornographic Aspects of the *Onania*," ibid. 6 (1983): 179-84.
14. Michel Foucault, *L'Usage des plaisirs* (Paris: Gallimard, 1984), p. 146.
15. Foucault, p. 148. See also pp. 146-50 ("La Dépense") and 150-56 ("La Mort et l'immortalité").
16. *La Souriciere* is but a poor imitation of *A Sentimental Journey*, and does not in fact qualify as an extended horticultural or anatomical metaphor. It is just a slightly titillating tale of peripatetic philandering on the Continent.
17. Foucault, *Le Souci de soi* (Paris: Gallimard, 1984), p. 44.
18. "The Bridal Night," "Translated from the KISSES OF SECUNDUS, by a Gentleman of *Trinity-College*, Dublin," in *The Pleasures, that Please on Reflection* (London, 1789), p. 49.
19. See note 13.
20. See Kearney, *History*, p. 57.

216

21. Thompson, p. 194, thinks such an attribution groundless. Both pamphlets were rep. 1741; *Arbor Vitae* was rep. in Curll's *The Merryland Miscellany* (1742 & 1745), and in 1749. Of the same eroticohorticultural type, see also *Teague-Root Display'd* (1746) by "Paddy Strong-Cock," mentioned by Kearney, *History*, p. 57, and the verse satire, *The Fruit Shop*, 2 vols. (London, 1765), mentioned by Ivan Bloch, *A History of English Sexual Morals* (London: Francis Aldor, 1936), pp. 548-49.

22. *The Infamous Essay on Woman*, ed. Adrian Hamilton (London: Deutsch, 1972) reproduces Wilkes' erotica.

23. *La Volonté de savoir* (Paris: Gallimard, 1976), p. 85.

Modes of Discourse and
the Language of Sexual Reference
in Eighteenth-Century French Fiction

The French eighteenth century holds particular interest for a study of systems of sexual reference. It is not fortuitous that *libertinage* was a key term for the culture, used to denote both sexual and intellectual license, and it seems in retrospect almost inevitable that as the century moved into its final eruptive phase an author such as Sade should have insisted upon the necessary alliance between the two. Heir to the tyrannical *bienséances* of the recently triumphant polite society (*le monde*), yet philosophically dedicated to epicureanism, governed by an authoritarian complex of political institutions yet driven by a "modern" ethos of freedom and individualism, the culture exhibits nearly everywhere the same isomorphism: a visible, official orthodoxy overlaying, but not quite hiding from view, the scandal of a heterodoxy attempting always to emerge. Whatever stability the culture possessed, in fact, was assured neither by the power of the orthodoxy nor by the strength of its cultural antagonist, but rather by the evolving symbiotic relationship between the two. The tension between these opposing forces gives the age its peculiar historical identity. Significantly Rousseau, the cultural outsider who denounced the tension itself and refused to be part of it, found himself denounced in turn and cast out by the representatives of both sides, officialdom and *philosophie*.[1] Sade, proposing a different but equally radical dissolution of the tension through the definitive triumph of libertinage, was to meet with the same fate.

Within the world of words that played so preeminent a role, the structural tension manifested itself as an encounter between two kinds of discourse. The inherited discourse of orthodoxy, purified to the extreme by the assiduous linguistic and literary trustees of neo-classicism throughout most of the seventeenth century, reigned with a supremacy whose sway was such as to constrain Voltaire: when moving from institutional and ideological concerns to matters of language and style in his *Lettres philosophiques* (1733), he exchanged his revolutionary red bonnet for the most conventional of plumed hats. The extreme self-assurance he displays everywhere in his writings concerning *le bon usage* reflects perfectly the belief of his time that the French language and its modes of expression had reached their apogee.

The counterforce to proper expression makes itself felt in the gradual emergence of improper expression, still only partially documented.[2] The drama of the encounter between the two types of discourse finds its most telling realization in *Le Neveu de Rameau* (1762), in which Diderot weaves into the debate between the two dialogists an extended *agon* between Right Discourse and Wrong Discourse. Less energetically, many other eighteenth-century writings reveal the same effort of "illegitimate" discourse to proclaim its own legitimacy in the face of "legitimate" discourse.[3]

The situation described above gave rise to a form of tacit legitimacy afforded to sexual reference in discourse, whereby intellectually curious adherents to a naturist philosophy and an ideology of freedom could speak of sexual matters, but always and only in coded language. Daniel Mornet discerned the emergence, during the Regency, of a *bon ton* style that allowed people to "parler de choses basses avec élégance et de distractions grossières avec distinction." The austere Rousseau provides, in borrowed voice, a memorable example of this witty preteritive style when he quotes an aristocratic lady's designation of licentious novels as those books that are "incommodes en ce qu'on ne peut les lire que d'une main" (*Oeuvres*, 1:40).

While not officially formulated, the rules governing sexual reference were clearly understood. Montesquieu, for example, carefully emended the 1721 text of the *Lettres persanes* in later editions to eliminate the term *membre viril*, felt to be referentially too direct.[5] Lenglet Dufresnoy, in 1734, speaks of an obscure piece of realist fiction from 1701 (*Les Amours libres dex deux frères* [Cologne]) as "un ouvrage [qui n'est pas] fort délicatement écrit."[6] Recognizing the linguistic hypersensitivity of his time, Lenglet adds with wry irony: "Si nous sçavons vivre, nous sçavons encore mieux parler: notre discours est ce qu'il y a de plus réel dans nos moeurs" (p. 56). Later in the century, Voisenon proudly remarks in the introduction to *Le Sultan Misapouf* (1746): "J'ai évité tous les mots qui pourraient blesser les oreilles modestes; tout est voilé; mais la gaze est si légère, que les plus faibles vues ne perdront rien du tableau."[17] And in his *Rêve de D'Alembert* (1769) Diderot picks up the image of the veil that must be cast over the language of sexual reference when he has Mlle de Lespinasse warn Dr. Bordeu, as he is about to launch into a discourse on sexuality: "De la gaze, docteur, un peu de gaze."[8]

The image of a filmy material that hides and at the same time reveals the shapes behind it is drawn not from the theatre but from the world of feminine fashion, where the erotic bodily curves artfully appeared behind the veil of modesty required by orthodox morality.[9] Much alluded to in fiction, where the male is depicted silently appraising the carefully but ineffectually obscured female contours (the "beautés cachées" of rococo parlance), the gauze is the visual analogue of the linguistic and stylistic code used for the veiling of sexual reference. It remains for us to analyze this code, and to discuss the emergence, at two different moments in the eighteenth century, of a discourse whose deliberate discarding of the veil will both create the ultimate scandal and, paradoxically, threaten an end to scandal by proposing the triumph of radical modernism over the inherited orthodoxy. First, however, it is necessary to glance briefly at the interaction between the society's rules concerning sexual language and the mimetic bias of narrative fiction.

The social rules governing sexual discourse were, predictably, situational. From what skimpy evidence we have (drawn largely from anecdotes) it seems that, in male society and in informal situations, use of the relatively restricted number of lexical items regarded as scandalous *per se* was not uncommon. Chamfort, for example, reports that Duclos, a well-regarded gentleman and a scholar of considerable reputation,

> avait l'habitude de prononcer sans cesse, en pleine Académie, des B . . . [bougre], des F . . . [foutre]; l'abbé du Renel, qui à cause de sa longue figure était appelé un grand serpent sans venin, lui dit: "Monsieur, sachez qu'on ne doit prononcer dans l'Académie que des mots qui se trouvent dans le dictionnaire."[10]

The anecdote is valuable, for it indicates both a fairly widespread and easygoing use of taboo words among the "gens de lettres" and a stricture upon their use in situations reserved for formal, even if oral, discourse. The academician's comical reference to the dictionary points directly to the authority of a closed corpus of official, orthodox language from which unveiled sexual terms are proscribed.

An equally valuable passage from Diderot's *Jacques le Fataliste* (1771) reinforces the message of Chamfort's anecdote, and at the same time reveals the discomfort of the mimetic writer forbidden to use the full lexicon of his society's language in his writings, which fall by definition into the domain of official discourse. At the end of the lengthy episode in which the crafty Père Hudson manages to turn the tables on a young monk who has tried to expose the father-superior's sexual misconduct, the latter says to his defeated nemesis: "Mon cher Richard, vous vous foutez de moi, et vous avez raison." Even though its denotation here is not specifically sexual, *foutre* is the most powerfully scandalous item in the century's lexicon; and Diderot (in his persona as "Author") feels compelled to apologize to the "Reader," arguing that occasionally use of the "mot honnête" ruins the effect. Then, as if to underscore the distinction between the written and oral proprieties, he cites a conversation between Piron and the Abbé Vatri, the details of which he refuses to divulge to the "Reader," saying only: "Allez la demander à l'éditeur de ses ouvrages, qui n'a pas osé l'écrire; mais qui ne se fera pas tirer l'oreille pour vous le dire."[11] Though unwilling to commit the obscenity to paper, Diderot encourages the process of oral transmission.[12]

If, as the foregoing suggests, the rules governing sexual reference varied from oral to written discourse, of what use might novels be for a study of sexual language in society? First of all, the novel's special status among literary genres as the one consecrated deliberately and self-consciously to supposedly unmediated representation of the empirical world provides a limited guarantee of equivalence between the language we read and the language actually used. The novelists' awareness of the special license awarded them by this empirical principle is neatly expressed by Andréa de Nerciat in his *Les Aphrodites, ou fragments thalipriapiques pour servir à l'histoire du plaisir* (1793). Whereas the narrator has used the metonymic *boute-joie* to refer to the penis, one of the characters—one earthy Madame Durut—uses the hard-core term *vit*. This linguistic shocker occasions a footnote by the author:

> On s'engage avec le lecteur à lui épargner dans ce récit toute expression incongrue, mais on ne peut lui promettre de faire parler un acteur autrement que le comporte soit son éducation, soit le délire dans lequel une situation violente peut le jeter. Madame Durut, par example, n'est pas femme à user de périphrases, et dans un emportement de colère ou de joie, elle lâche fort bien un *foutre*, un *bougre*, ou nomme quelque chose d'indécent par son vilain nom.[13]

The epithet, "vilain nom," is delivered not entirely in bad faith; for Nerciat, pornographer though he is in this work, must uphold the decency of his professional role as a *writer*. Nonetheless, as a *novelist* he must bow to the rule of empirical mimeticism. The defensive footnote results from a tension between the neo-classical linguistic heritage and the modern generic aesthetic.

An intermediate stage in the movement away from authorial decorum is marked by the appearance in 1783 of the Comte de Mirabeau's purportedly autobiographical novel *Ma Conversion* (rep. 1784 as *Le Libertin de qualité*), written in prison three years earlier. Mirabeau launches his work (dedicated to "Monsieur Satan") with a fireworks display of taboo sexual language; and we may surmise that this gesture of liberation is on his mind when he refers to his novel, in a letter to Sophie Monnier written during the composition of the work (5 March 1780), as "absolument neuf" (p. 243). The first-person narrator here is, in a sense, the author, at least insofar as the work is autobiographically based, and to that extent it is the *author* who is taking responsibility for the language. Nonetheless, *Ma Conversion* is unlike a true autobiography (of which Rousseau's would, of course, already have provided an outstanding recent example, even for those who had not had direct knowledge of it) in that the author does not name himself as such—i.e., the "autobiographical pact" is not established. Hence, the narrator's voice emanates from a space between the authorial and the fictional. Bachaumont's reproof of Mirabeau for having "levé le voile sur ces scènes intérieures qu'il faut laisser couvertes des ombres épaisses où elles se passent" (p. 231) would presumably have been far stronger had the author presented a formally authentic autobiography in the same linguistic vein.

Only near the close of the century, with Sade's *Philosophie dans le boudoir* (1795) and *Nouvelle Justine* (1797), will the decisive break occur. In the first version of the latter (1787-88), there is not the slightest example of linguistic impropriety. In those few instances where the unfortunate heroine is obliged to recount material of a sexual nature, her stylistic attenuations are so indirect and convoluted as to be comical. Indeed, one suspects that Sade was parodying the typical rococo licentious style of the

1780s.[15] In the second version (1791), the language still conforms to the rules of propriety (with an occasional "garce" or "catin" hurled at the heroine by her tormentors), but Sade is clearly moving in the direction of greater referential explicitness. In the final version, however, a fundamental shift in narrative perspective occurs: from first to third person. No longer restricted by the problem of verisimilitude posed by the choice of a virtuous female character, Sade storms the linguistic Bastille, liberating the forbidden words in a flood of obscenity. Henri Coulet interprets this outpouring of taboo language as a sadistic aggression against the reader.[16] While no doubt accurate, his psychological analysis calls for an ideological supplement. The tacit or (as in the case of Nerciat) avowed agreement between author as "man" and readers as "men" to observe certain rules of linguistic propriety flows from the neo-classical assumption of an order in society generated and sustained by rules and restrictions. While sadistic in its effect, Sade's use of taboo language in the *Nouvelle Justine* acts as an ideological battering ram against an entire culture and the rule of order whence it is conceived.

Sade is, however, the patron saint (perhaps self-appointed) of hopeless causes. The inefficacity of his authorial gesture can be measured by the immediate literary reaction it produced, Restif de la Bretonne's *Anti-Justine* (1798). The mutual antipathy between Sade and Restif was profound, and the latter seized upon the *Nouvelle Justine's* scandalous appearance in order to outdo his enemy in scandal. The chapter entitled "Du fouteur à la de Sades" reads, in fact, very much like a parody of the Marquis. But Restif sanctimoniously presents his pornographic work as an antidote to the *Nouvelle Justine:* it will provide jaded couples with the stimulation necessary for renewed procreative activity, and will thus further Nature's aims.[17] Already Sade's radical ideological message has vanished into thin air, as Restif shepherds the forbidden vocabulary back into the domain of nature and social harmony.

Although, as we have seen, the novel managed to assert its right to complete linguistic freedom in sexual reference, few indeed were those who availed themselves of their license. In addition to the few who did so during the final twenty years of the century, we will see an equally small number during the 1740s "go the limit." By far the most common form taken by sexual reference throughout the century was preterition, the various strategies of which we will merely designate in passing: anagram, logogriph, metaphor, metonym, the use of foreign terms (usually Italian), and whatever other rhetorical devices the writer may have delighted in using. The eighteenth-century context of literary education and practice constituted a particularly felicitous background for writers involved in what one might rightly call the "sexual reference game." Paid to provide society its "distractions les plus grossières" under a veil of politeness, they had at their disposal all the writerly tools for carrying out their task. The tropes themselves range all the way from the petrified "preuves d'amour" of the legion of uninspired novelists to the functionally brilliant "raison suffisante" of Voltaire's invention. A fuller taxonomy of sexual preterition will be presented elsewhere.

What remains to be discussed is, rather, the emergence of unveiled, uncoded sexual language in a relatively small number of works of fiction and at two distinct moments in the eighteenth century. I have not found any uncoded language in narrative fiction before the appearance in 1741 (1740?) of Gervaise de Latouche's *Le Portier des Chartreux*. In this pornographic classic published with considerable frequency during the century under the alternate titles of *Histoire de Dom B____* or *Mémoires de Saturnin*,[18] the code of preterition is deliberately and calculatedly discarded, in the name of truth and freedom. Early in the novel, a libertine nun explains to a young postulant the "true" meaning of the expression "être amoureux." She reduces the attenuation to its purely physical basis:

> Quand on dit. Monsieur . . . est amoureux de Madame . . . c'est la même chose que si l'on disoit, Monsieur . . . a vu Madame . . . sa vûe a excité des desirs dans son coeur, il brûle d'envie de lui mettre son Vit dans le Con. Voilà véritablement ce que cela veut dire: mais comme la bienséance ne veut pas qu'on dise ces choses-là, on est convenu de dire, Monsieur . . . est amoureux.   (p.54)

The publication of *Le Portier des Chartreux* opened the floodgates of sexually oriented fiction, usually built around a highly voyeuristic conceit, and the succeeding decade saw the appearance of Crébillon *fils' Le Sopha*, *Le Canapé couleur de feu* (probably by Fougeret de Monbron),[19] Caylus' *Nocrion*, Bret's *Le Bidet*, Fougeret de Monbron's *Margot la ravaudeuse*, Diderot's *Les Bijoux indiscrets*, and the Marquis D'Argens' *Thérèse philosophe*. Curiously, however, very few of the licentious underground novels of the decade display the daring of the *Portier des Chartreux* in the use of unveiled sexual language. The female narrator of *Margot* includes a small number of quotations in which other characters cross the linguistic barrier. The narrator of *Thérèse* never uses the taboo lexicon, but full license is granted to secondary narrators, especially to Mme Bois-Laurier, whose narrative is far more frankly libertine than that of Thérèse.[20] This novel, considered by contemporaries as one of the most scandalous works of an epoch that relished its scandal, shares with the *Portier des Chartreux* a significantly strong component of overt naturist ideology in combination with the eighteenth-century pretense to documentary realism. The convergence between the two (which one finds to a lesser degree in *Margot*) seems to determine the crossing of the linguistic Rubicon, as was already suggested in our discussion of Sade's *Nouvelle Justine*.

The power of the internalized resistance to the use of frankly sexual language in writing may be deduced from the preface to Meusnier de Guerlon's *Histoire galante de la tourière des Carmélites, ouvrage fait pour servir de pendant au Portier des Chartreux* (1743, according to Barbier, who is probably right, considering the habit of capitalizing very quickly on a recent popular success). The author writes:

> L'ouvrage est écrit purement et plus soutenu [sic] que Dom B. quoiqu'aussi libertin que ce dernier livre, puisque c'est proprement l'histoire d'un mauvais lieu, il n'y a pas un seul mot obscène ou grossier. . . . C'est une petite

débauche d'esprit qu'il [l'auteur] a faite pour son propre amusement, et pour essayer, à ce qu'il m'a dit, jusqu'où l'on pouvoit porter la license, sans user de termes licencieux: ce qui est faire, à mon avis, la censure de tous nos Sotisiers modernes.[21]

The female narrator, in her foreword, boasts of having respected her reader's eyes and ears: "c'est tout ce qu'on demande aujourd'hui, et pourvu que les objets soient voilés, la qaze n'est jamais trop fine, même au gré de notre sexe" (p.7). So quick and decisive a return to the veiling strategy after the linguistic unveilings of the *Portier* point to something more than merely a tyrannical cultural superego. A hidden pleasure accompanies the flirtation with the forbidden object, a pleasure directly identified by the narrator of Gaillard de la Bataille's delightful *Frétillon*, almost exactly contemporaneous with the *Portier*. The (once again female) narrator alludes to the conversation she had with an abbé who was undertaking to seduce her, in company: "Nos discours renfermoient un sens fort éveillé; mais nos expressions étoient limées, et malgré le ménagement des termes, la Compagnie ne perdoit rien du fond de la matière; *ce qui la rejouissoit beaucoup*" (emphasis mine).[22]

The image of the gauze that can never be too thin and the references to the pleasure derived by the company from the veiling of the nonetheless clearly perceived sexual discourse suggest a form of shared or public voyeurism, a social counterpart to the voyeuristic component of so much of the fiction and art of the period. This clearly has something to do with the underlying motives of the Enlightenment: to penetrate, to know, and to rejoice in the sharing of the heretofore inaccessible (or even forbidden) knowledge. Once again it seems highly significant that Rousseau and Sade, both critics of the linguistic veiling game, should have been, in different ways, the most profound and radical critics of the Enlightenment.

After the publication of *Thérèse philosophe*, the direct sexual language almost completely disappears from the novel,[23] to resurface in 1783 with the appearance of Mirabeau's *Ma Conversion*. French fiction had not, between 1748 and 1783 become overly modest, far from it, but the pornography of a writer like Nougaret is purveyed behind the fashionable rococo veils; and, as we have seen, in 1771 Diderot flirted, but only flirted, with the kind of linguistic frankness he no doubt envied the authors of the *Portier* and *Thérèse*, whose naturist ideology he of course shared. Mirabeau's novel marks a sudden and dramatic return to the earlier directness of reference, and the way is now open to the classic pornographic fiction of the final twenty years of the century: Sade's underground novels, Nerciat's *Les Aphrodites*, and Restif's *Anti-Justine*.

We can only speculate on the reasons for the appearance of linguistically scandalous fiction at two separate moments in the century. In the case of the earlier manifestation, it is possible to adduce at least three contributing factors. First, the novel had been moving throughout the century (certainly since Challe's *Les Illustres Françoises*, 1713) toward greater realism, which would ultimately include unvarnished linguistic realism. The language of the coachman and the milliner, in Part II of Marivaux's *La Vie de Marianne*, had shocked a sector of the neo-classical reading public in 1734, but certainly not on the grounds of inverisimilitude; and the author defended himself by invoking his responsibility to the *truth*.[24] *La Vie de Marianne* was not, however, a clandestine novel, and the violation of linguistic propriety is therefore relatively mild. The second factor was the novel's movement underground, as a result of the secret "prohibition of novels" established by the government as early as 1737.[25] With the disappearance of this immensely popular genre into the socio-literary darkness, public and official control was lost, at least until after publication, at which point an awesome amount of time and energy was spent attempting to apply sanctions. The movement underground, by breaking institutional orthodoxy's hold on the novel, allowed a complete liberation of expression. It is not surprising that the *Portier des Chartreux* should have appeared at the threshhold of this new period of clandestinity.

The third factor is less specifiable in hard empirical terms, but is to my mind as important as the two preceding. The 1740s in France, and particularly in Paris, bear a special stamp of daring. The first wave of Enlightenment writers such as Challe, Montesquieu, Marivaux, and especially Voltaire had, in a sense, "softened up" the society and had accustomed the public to think in new and modern ways. The reader of 1733 implied by Voltaire's strategies of presentation in the *Lettres philosophiques* is that of a curious, literate person who has not yet thought his way very far into the great political and ideological issues of the day, but who is ready to be transformed through instruction. By the 1740s, this reader has become an Enlightenment sympathizer, and the public can't get enough of the new and radical ideas. The situation will not last far beyond the decade, for the supposed "excesses" of the free-thinkers will produce a growing backlash, and from the affair of the Abbé de Prades (1752) until at least the mid-1760s French history chronicles an ever-increasing abatement in the kind of heady freedom that had characterized the 1740s. Writers took to heart the persecutions visited upon many of their fellows, and Diderot's own notorious prudence was no doubt motivated in good part by his brief imprisonment in 1749. (Significantly, one of the misdeeds charged to him was the publication of a pornographic novel.)

The decade saw, then, an adventitious convergence of literary, social, and political factors that, taken together, help to explain the enormous increase in sexual reference in fiction and, in some cases, its total linguistic freedom.

When we turn to the later resurgence of linguistic scandal, the causes are more difficult to assign, and it would be tempting merely to invoke a pre-Revolutionary Zeitgeist as the vague but all-powerful cause. It seems significant, however, that Mirabeau, Sade, and Restif were all strongly oriented toward the newly triumphant naturist philosophy and were enemies of the existing order (or at least dreamers of a new order). All three were of the same character, as well: energetic, self-willed, and self-centered, romantic demons and *enfants terribles* before their time. While

Nerciat does not present exactly the same ideological or personal profile, he was a faithful *homme à la mode*, and as such was willing to straggle after the pornographic leaders. *Les Aphrodites* draws its authorization from the tradition: the epigraph is taken from Piron's "Ode à Priape" and in the novel itself Mme Durut provides a jaded Countess with a copy of Mirabeau's *Ma Conversion* for the purpose of sexual reawakening. It is also perhaps not coincidental that *Les Aphrodites* is filled with allusions to the social upheavals caused by the Revolution.

❖

As suggested earlier, the question of discourse was a burning question and should occupy a prominent place in our attempts to understand the period. The importance of erotic discourse in particular is determined by the special role of the erotic within the Enlightenment, as is underscored by Aram Vartanian in his "Erotisme et philosophie chez Diderot":

> on constate qu'une forte dose d'érotisme, se manifestant dans un champ assez restreint, a agi d'une façon créatrice à l'intérieur du mouvement des lumières, et que cette étrange et unique synthèse de deux tendances si dissemblables reste un des caractères les plus marquants, et peut-être le moins compris, de la culture intellectuelle de l'époque.[37]

If the two tendencies, eroticism and enlightenment, are indeed so dissimilar, it is because the rather self-congratulatory public image that the official Enlightenment presented to the world was one of reason and order, while the erotic always threatens irrationality and disorder. Laclos devastates the Enlightenment's self-image in the ironic "Avertissement to one of the most subversive of eighteenth-century writings:

> En effet, plusieurs des personnages qu'il [l'auteur] met en scène ont de si mauvaises mœurs, qu'il est impossible de supposer qu'ils aient vécu dans notre siècle; dans ce siècle de philosophie, où les lumières répandues de toutes parts, ont rendu, comme chacun sait, tous les hommes si honnêtes et toutes les femmes si modestes et si reservées. (*Liaisons dangereuses*, p 5)

Clearly, this master-analyst well understands that the official self-portrait needs completion and rectification by means of a "forte dose d'érotisme," which he intends to provide in its most corrosive form. It is richly significant that, in a brilliant perception of the aristocracy's ultimate collusion in the destruction of "their" order, he has Valmont teach Cécile, in the sexual propaedeutics he administers, the "mots techniques" (i.e., the taboo terminology) in gleeful anticipation of the havoc this will create on her wedding night. "Rien n'est plus plaisant que l'ingénuité avec laquelle elle se sert déjà du peu qu'elle sait de cette langue! elle n'imagine pas qu'on puisse parler autrement" (p.264). Valmont's linguistic program parallels the intention to subvert, permanently, the family line of his rival Gercourt by sending Cécile into his connubial arms already carrying his, Valmont's, offspring. The sacred order of the *ancien régime* collapses into sinister bedroom farce.

The special function of erotic scandal within the "strange synthesis," then, is to subvert. Most obviously, it creates a fundamental disrespect for order in a world where sexual repression, a legacy of the Counter Reformation, and absolute respect for social decorum, imposed and handed down by the world of Louis XIV, acted constantly both as tokens and as guarantors of order. With its intrinsic power greatly magnified by the very insistence with which it was officially decried and repressed, the erotic is invested with the capacity to carry out the more radical part of the culture's program, the part that its ultimately rather respectable sister the Enlightenment cannot permit herself to be involved in. Rather than a torch raised high, the eighteenth-century erotic might be visualized as a dark lantern (much used at the time) casting a beam of light into hidden corners; and it is not accidental that the most powerful writers and artists of the time should have used this dark lantern: Voltaire, Diderot, Montesquieu, Rousseau (whose sexual revelations in the *Confessions* created enormous scandal), Laclos, Restif, Sade, Watteau, Fragonard, to name only the most conspicuous.

The discourse of eroticism functioned as a metonym for the erotic in the context of the preceding argument, and its scandal was equal to that of erotic acts. It may be, indeed, that the scandal of discourse was greater than the scandal of acts, for two reasons. First, discourse is by its very nature *public*, no matter how carefully one may attempt to privatize its use. Erotic acts—including fantasies, which are acts of a sort—can and often do remain completely private. The history of the century is instead one of persistent unsuccess in maintaining the privacy of discourse. The discourse of the age inevitably feeds the obsessive curiosity the public had concerning who wrote what, who said what, what was really said, and (especially) how it got out. It would almost seem that clandestinity existed for the sake of its scandalous emergence.

The second reason for the superior scandal of discourse can be found in Lenglet's wry comment: "notre discours est ce qu'il y a de plus réel dans nos moeurs." His sarcasm is more than a figure of speech, and within an order that hypostasized discourse it is only natural that discourse would serve as the ultimate weapon of destruction, at least prior to the installation of that orally isomorphic machine with incisors of steel. It is not surprising, then, that scandalous sexual language should have reached its fever pitch in the 1790s, nor for that matter, that this language should by then already have been living on borrowed time, soon to be silenced by the triumph of the new social and political discourse of the Revolution itself, and by the return to sexual repression that was to accompany the Revolution's own reinstatement of order—a new order that surely could not have come into existence without the earlier sapping from below of the old order's foundations by the liberation of sexual discourse. In this light, we may see the frank refusal, by a handful of daring writers, to play the compromise game of indirect sexual reference as the critical ingredient that transformed a harmless powder into a powerful explosive. At the ending was the Word.

Robert J. Ellrich
University of Washington

NOTES

1. Rousseau's own words in *Emile* on the question of sexual reference are pertinent: "La Langue française est, dit-on, la plus chaste des Langues; je la crois, moi, la plus obscène; car il me semble que la chasteté d'une langue ne consiste pas à éviter avec soin les tours deshonétes, mais à ne les pas avoir. En effet, pour les éviter, il faut qu'on y pense; et il n'y a point de langue où il soit plus difficile de parler purement en tout sens que la françoise. Le lecteur, toujours plus habile à trouver des sens obscénes que l'auteur à les écarter, se scandalise et s'affaroûche de tout. . . ." *Oeuvres complètes* (Paris: Gallimard, 1969), 4: 649.

2. Historical discussions of French language and style have, understandably, been largely oriented towards the creation and maintenance of a standard or orthodox discourse whose values reflect the official culture. Alexis François devotes space to "le néologisme" and the "genre ordurier" that appears during the Revolution, but presents his material as momentary, trivial veerings away from the "true" language (F. Brunot, *Histoire de la langue française* [Paris: Colin, 1968], 6: 1053–1274; 10: 167–237). Jean-Pierre Seguin, in his *La Langue française au 18e siècle* (Paris: Bordas, 1972), follows in general A. François (see section on "Le baslanguage" during the Revolution, pp. 250–52).

3. A few studies have been devoted to the pressure exerted by the "other" discourse. The best-documented instance is no doubt that of the "new style" of the 1730s, for which see Frédéric Deloffre's *Une Préciosité nouvelle: Marivaux et le marivaudage* (Paris: Belles Lettres, 1955). The documentation, readily available for the preceding, is not always of easy access or interpretation for one pursuing the question of the "other" discourse.

4. *La Pensée française au 18e siècle* (Paris: Armand Colin, 1930), p. 19.

5. Brunot, 6: 1205.

6. *De l'Usage des romans* (Geneva: Slatkine, 1970), p. 137.

7. *Contes et poésies fugitives* (Paris: Garnier, n.d.), p. 40. Alexis François incorrectly places this statement in the introduction to a 1767 collection of Voisenon's tales. The correct dating—1746—is important, for in the same liminary text the author refers to the current vogue of "contes peu modestes, où l'on ne se donne pas souvent la peine de mettre une gaze légère aux discours les plus libres" (p. 3).

8. *Oeuvres philosophiques* (Paris: Garnier, 1956), p. 374.

9. In *Liaisons dangereuses* (Letter X), Mme de Merteuil boasts of a boudoir dress of her invention: "il ne laisse rien voir, et pourtant fait tout deviner" (Paris: Gallimard, 1951), p. 30.

10. *Caractères et anecdotes* (Paris: Garnier Flammarion, 1956), p. 374.

11. *Oeuvres romanesques* (Paris: Garnier, 1959), p. 682.

12. Much of the linguistic obscenity of the age appears to have been preserved through faithful oral transmission, ultimately finding its way into print with the advent of the Revolution. For a pertinent analysis of the ways in which underground literature of noble and royal obscenity (which in the ephemeral *chansons* and pamphlets appears earlier than in other printed sources) helped pave the way for the Revolution, see Robert Darnton's *The Literary Underground of the Old Regime*, (Cambridge: Harvard Univ., 1982), pp. 199–208.

13. "Lampsaque" (1793; rep. 1909), p. 16.

14. (Alençon: 1929), "notice bibliographique" by |Louis Perceau|.

15. In Nerciat's *Félicia, ou mes fredaines* (1776) the narrator, a former woman of pleasure, recounts a scene involving cunnilingus, standard intercourse, and an attempted homosexual anal rape (presented in some detail) without once using an improper term (Paris: L'Or du Temps, 1969), pp. 200–02.

16. "La Vie intérieure dans Justine," p. 94, in *Le Marquis de Sade*. Centre d'Etudes et de Recherches sur le Dix-huitième Siècle (Paris: Colin, 1968). See pp. 89–94 for a penetrating analysis of the evolution from the first to the third version. In "La Langue de Sade," in *Eroticism in French Literature*, French Literature Series, vol. 10 (Columbia: Univ. of South Carolina, 1983), pp. 103–13, Beatrice Fink has argued via a lexical, stylistic, and linguistic analysis that the real subversion in Sade is directed at the classical edifice of language and that this is done by combining the "style galant" and obscenity. Also, see Philippe Roger's *Sade: la Philosophie dans le pressoir* (Paris: Grasset, 1976).

17. *L'Anti-Justine, ou Les Délices de l'amour*. Nouvelle édition sans suppressions conforme à celle originale de 1798 (Amsterdam: n.d.), 2: 4.

18. Pascal Pia, in his "Histoire d'un livre traqué: *Le Portier des Chartreux*" (rep. as an appendix to the Paris, L'Or du Temps, 1969, edn. of the novel), opts for the sole authorship of Gervaise, to whom the novel is usually attributed, while including evidence for a collaboration with Gervaise's young colleague Billard. An attentive stylistic reading of the work strongly suggests, however, different authorship of the two parts into which it is divided. See pp. XVII–XX.

19. On the authorship of this work (of which a scholarly edn. is needed), see Kay Landolt (Gee), "*Le Canapé*: une erreur bibliographique rectifiée," in *Revue d'Histoire Littéraire de la France* 78 (1978): 790–92.

20. *Thérèse philosophe, ou mémoires pour servir à l'histoire du P. Dirrag et de Mademoiselle Eradice* (La Haye, 186–); based on orig. edn. (La Haye, 1748). The Bois-Laurier interpolation appears on pp. 118–48.

21. (N.p.: 1774), p. 3. Bibliothèque Nationale, Enfer 1261.

22. *Histoire de la vie et des moeurs de Mlle Cronel dite Frétillon, écrite par elle-même. Actrice de la Comédie de Rouen* (La Haye, 1739–40). Quotation from the La Haye, 1742, edn., p. 68.

23. A few clandestine novels include a sparse representation of taboo words, but with little of the ideological energy or stylistic verve of the works of the 1740s. The anon. *Vénus en rut, ou Vie d'une célèbre libertine* (Interlaken, 1771), e.g., while daring in subject matter includes only three such instances (pp. 14 and 40). Mostly, the works that appeared between 1748 and 1783 use elaborate, self-consciously witty forms of indirection.

24. (Paris: Garnier, 1957), pp. 55–56. See chaps. 4, 6, and 7 of Georges May's *Dilemme du roman au 18e siècle* (New Haven: Yale Univ., 1963).

25. May (chap. 3) gives a full account of this obscure but important episode in the political context of the 18th-c. novel. Nerciat's *Félicia* provides endless examples.

26. *Cahiers de l'Association Internationale des Etudes Françaises* 13 (June 1961): 372.

The *Mélange de poésies diverses* (1781) and the Diffusion of Manuscript Pornography in Eighteenth-Century France

With the rise of the middle class in eighteenth-century France and a general increase in the literacy level of all classes (a phenomenon by no means confined to France), more people began to read, and more books were printed to satisfy the demand. Since the increase in the reading public was not paralleled by as marked an increase in higher or advanced education, the kinds of books that proliferated dramatically were especially to be found among practical works (devotional, educational, culinary, and the like) and leisure literature: novels, plays, and poetry. Silas Jones' bibliography covering the first half of the century lists only 26 new works of French prose fiction for the years 1700-1701 (excluding translations), whereas in contrast Martin, Mylne, and Frautschi list 113 new works and 38 new translations for 1800 alone, with the total number of reeditions reaching 114 (85 originals and 29 translations).[1]

In brief, as the century wound its way to a bloody conclusion, more people were reading an expanding body of works which were, generally, becoming more and more moralistic and sombre. The evidence put forth by Martin, Mylne, and Frautschi in their elegant tables on fiction is also true of other genres, and it reflects a general change, or development, in attitudes and values which was especially evident in France. For example, the public enjoyed Richardson's *Clarissa* and especially the French adaptations which tended to tone down or even eliminate scenes of rape and violence. When Edward Kimber's *Maria: the Genuine Memoirs of a Young Lady of Rank and Fortune* (1764) was translated into French (1765), its often harsh realism was edulcorated.[2] French was a far more universal language than English, but judicious censoring was certainly a factor that led to the French version's being more popular than Kimber's English. In short, the French had developed, on the surface anyway, a fairly stringent notion of propriety, embodied in a series of unformalized strictures which we could term the "bienséances" of fiction. To Eric Trudgill's remark that "flagrant vice [became] a sign of inferior taste" I would add, "among certain classes." And pornography suffered the same fate as "flagrant vice."[3]

Now all this does not mean that pornographic fiction containing explicit licentious detail had ceased to be composed and/or republished. For example, after Cleland's *Memoirs of A Woman of Pleasure* (1748-49) was rendered into French by Lambert (expurgated in 1751 and somewhat reworked in 1770; see Martin, Mylne, and Frautschi 51.17 and 70.41), it went through quite a few editions. Furthermore, passion and lust were certainly present in non-pornographic works, not only in the bible, but in such widely read books as Rousseau's *La Nouvelle Héloïse* (1761); and works which in the 1730s and '40s had been banned in France by the authorities were, a few decades later, upon occasion receiving tacit or official government approval. Publishers were allowed openly to print and sell works by Prévost and Crébillon *fils*. Voltaire posed a special problem: the censors forbade the printing or distribution of his complete works in France; but on more than one occasion, permission was granted to allow individuals to retrieve their copies of, for example, the Kehl *Oeuvres complètes* (1784-89), in spite of the ban.[4]

During the period ca. 1735-89, however, the obscene was hunted with as much vigor and rigor as before: editions seized, printers and distributors often thrown in jail (or worse), and books inevitably burned by the public executioner or condemned to the "pilon" (shredder, as it were). In the second half of the 1780s, a further change occurred. By this time, nearly all levels of French society enjoyed some degree of literacy; and in the printed word the lower classes, especially the urban ones, had acquired a powerful weapon which could be used on the political front, often in a satirical and obscene way. From 1789 on, many pamphlets, richly pornographic, were directed against members of the royal family— pamphlets in which one of the kinder epithets hurled against the queen, for example, was that of "the Austrian whore"—and the revolutionary period set off an explosion of salacious books, including Sade's.

All of this is important in understanding the circulation of clandestine literature in general, more specifically obscene literature, and especially that in manuscript form. When pornographic works were printed in a given locale, they faced the difficulty of distribution not only in the town where they were produced, but also outside town walls—for police spies were everywhere. The government attempted to keep strict control on the movement of every book. That it failed is easily understood when we realise that individual books and private libraries were subject to the same constraints as trade material. If a traveler arrived on the ferry in Calais with a novel or devotional work in hand to help while away the time, that book was supposed to be carried to the local guild office of the booktrade (the "chambre syndicale") to be inspected by the police. If a gentleman of quality wished to move from Versailles to Paris and not abandon his library, he had to obtain a special authorization from the government to permit such a translocation. Otherwise his books would have to be gone through, one by one, by a police inspector; and unless his holdings were strictly conservative, he stood every chance of losing many of them.[5] It must often have been difficult for a police inspector to ascertain whether he was dealing with a banned work, unless like Rousseau's *Emile* (1762) or Raynal's *Histoire philosophique . . . des deux Indes* (1770) it were at the center of one of the more famous scandals. Although supplied with lists, printed decrees, registers, and the like, these could not have been complete; so even by dint of thumbing through a book, an over-worked, harrassed functionary could hardly have seized controversial nuances or harmful satirical overtones, assuming there were any. But although pornography shared the same problems as controversial works dealing with politics and religion, it was particularly vulnerable because it could be easily recognized by anyone who could read.

Thus the obscene, though extant in printed form, was especially circulated in manuscript. Here again, however, problems arose for the would-be pornophile: manuscripts were also, again in principle, subject to restrictive controls. A public postal system had been established in France in the sixteenth century and continued to develop over the years, being consolidated during the revolutionary period. But letter writing was the domain of the privileged few: letters were not infrequently opened and were thus subject to a form of censorship which could be circumnavigated only by the well-to-do who could afford their own couriers, or who had the connections to send missives via a third, influential, party who would not be subject to inspection.

Another form of manuscript literature was the hand-written newspaper, the "nouvelles à la main" which grew out of, on one hand, the rise of periodical literature and the increase of letter writing in general—the kind of letter writing that addressed itself particularly to the news and gossip of the day. The "nouvelles" became so popular that the government tried to control them via a series of official directives, culminating in the total prohibition of the genre by royal decree on 18 May 1745.[6] The lieutenant-general of police, Marville, rendered judgments against several of those dealing in such clandestine manuscript literature (official government document F.F. 22092, No. 26, 23 September 1747; signed "Menard"). In spite of official condemnation, however, by the early 1750s a hybrid genre had come into use: manuscript news sheets, with printed or stamped headings. *Le Courrier de Paris*, in its manuscript prospectus, boldly titled itself an "ouvrage polémique" and stated its goals: "We intend to unveil the mysteries of the future and to illuminate the secret anecdotes of Paris and Mount Parnassus. Will we succeed? Reader, be you the judge."[7]

In such a way did manuscript and semi-manuscript literature reveal the licentiousness of social life, for it often focused on the more scandalous peccadilli and sins of contemporaries. Sometimes these revelations were even published fairly soon after their composition or even as they were being composed (e.g., Louis Petit de Bachaumont's *Mémoires secrets* (1780-89) and François Métra's *Correspondance secrète* (1787-90). Then, too, salacious gossip and libertine news, intermingled with slander, was not infrequently composed for immediate publication, often abroad. Such is the case of many of Théveneau de Morande's salacious books which cashed in on the scandals of the day: *Le Gazetier cuirassé* (1771), *La Gazette noire* (1784), *Mélanges confus sur des matières fort claires* (1771), etc. (Many of these were printed in England, despite the imprints.)

More privately, manuscripts were diffused in sheets and in either book or pamphlet form. In book form, aside from common-place literature dealing with recipes, medicine, and the like, these were largely related to religion, politics, and the libertine; and they were usually created by or for specific appreciative individuals. In the case of religious works, the owner might have wanted to possess an elegant, personalized copy of some devotional tract, for example the carefully conceived and elegantly executed *Psautier (1773), beautifully bound for some pious "âme sensible."[8] The same aesthetic motive might have applied to a political work, but it would have been coupled with the difficulty, even impossibility, of obtaining a printed copy of the book, even assuming it had been published.[9] Sometimes, too, a printed work was, or at least had become, rarer than contemporary manuscript copies, as Ann Thomson has pointed out in her introduction to Le Matérialisme du 18ᵉ siècle.[10]

Clandestine literature that circulated in manuscript sheets and pamphlets was common. For example, the patriarch of Ferney, like other wealthy people who lived far from the capital, had agents in Paris who sent him tidbits of slander and satire that were making the rounds. Such a tidbit was the satirical *Parody of a Scene from Corneille's "Cinna," which cost Marmontel a stay in the Bastille.[11]

An interesting example of a pamphlet that circulated in manuscript is the Rules and Regulations Governing the Royal Academy of Music [*Statuts pour l'Académie royale de musique] by Nicholas Thomas Barthe (1734-85).[12] The Statuts were later published (22 October 1791) in the Mercure de France (pp. 121-30). An editorial note states that the Statuts had circulated in 1767, which can be verified by reference to various contemporary sources. Furthermore, and somewhat rare for 1791, the editor explains that as a sop to public opinion and because some of those concerned were still living, he left out one particularly wounding stanza; but the truth of the matter is that far more was deleted, names appear in the printed version by initials alone, and there are many important variants. All of this, of course, was not unique to France; for in other countries, especially those with repressive forms of government, circulation of particularly satirical manuscript verse was on the rise.[13]

Leaving aside satire, slander, and gossip, let us examine the more specialized domain of the libertine. In France, a fairly common form of manuscript literature containing naughty verse was that of the chansonnier, or song-book. The manuscripts contain bawdy tavern songs, an occasional popular song from an opera or operetta, and romances in some of which off-color licence evolves to the obscene. These collections of ribald poems indicate what the educated middle and lower classes were collecting, reading, and singing in the period before the Revolution. An example is the *Receuil de chansons appartenant à Jean Baptiste Delmaire, the titlepage of which gives a real place and date: "à Valenciennes le 11 Novembre 1783." Another is the *Receuil de chansons. Dedié et presenté à Mlle. . . . ("A Cythère." 1787). A presentation copy, the latter is far more elaborate and elegant than Delmaire's book.[14]

A far less conventional collection is the *Mélange de poésies diverses, par différents auteurs. The titlepage bears "A Paris. 1780," with the indication "f.p. fecit." The latter might refer to the scribe, who possibly was the owner. The *Mélange* contains an unusually wide variety of pornography: over fifty pieces in verse, a prose *Proclamation Establishing the Salary and Prerogatives of Ladies of Pleasure*, and five plays.[15]

The principle scribe took considerable pain with his labor and copied from various printed sources and probably manuscripts. In at least one case, that of Alexis Piron's "Ode à Priape," the variants from the known printed sources are significant enough to suppose that he had at his disposal a copy of the work (in printed or manuscript form) that must have been unique—or nearly so for I have found no trace of the original—and it is possible the scribe might have introduced some changes of his own. (Indeed, some of the shorter poems might be either of his own composition or transcribed from oral tradition, in the vein of the *chansonniers*.)

One example will serve to show how different the text in the *Mélange* is from that in **Lettre philosophique, par Mr. de V**** (1747)[16] or the modern edition of Piron's *Oeuvres*:

> Que l'or, que l'honneur vous chatoüille,
> Sots avares, vains conquerans,
> Vivent les plaisirs de la coüille,
> Et foutre des biens & des rangs (*Lettre*, stanza 5, ll. 1-5).

> O vous qu'un vain honneur chatoüille
> Empereurs, Rois, Princes et grands
> Vive le plaisir de la Couille
> foutre des biens honneurs et rangs (*Mélange*, stanza 9, ll. 1-5).

Though five strophes longer, and though its strophes are in different order, the text in Dufay's modern edition[17] is similar to that printed in 1747. These brief citations amply indicate the originality of the version in the *Mélange*. And that holds true for many other pieces in the manuscript, which demonstrates the importance of this manuscript collection in establishing not only the authorial texts but the texts as known during the period.

Aside from this and other important poems, of which some of the more interesting are Piron's *Le Chapitre général des Cordeliers* and Charles Borde's *Parapilla*,[18] this manuscript is unusual for containing five full-length plays, among the most pornographic published in the eighteenth century: *The New Messalina*; *The Countess of Olonne*; *The Pleasures of the Cloister*; *Vasta, Queen of Bordelia*; and *The Art of Fucking, or Paris in Heat*.[19] Several of the plays bring to mind John Wilmot, earl of Rochester's equally explicit *Sodom, or the Quintessence of Debauchery, Written for the Royall Company of Whoremasters*. Indeed, *The Countess of Olonne* was often attributed to Roger de Rabutin, comte de Bussy (1618-93). If there be any truth in that, it would have been composed around the time that *Sodom* was making the rounds. Rochester and Bussy-Rabutin were both bon-vivants and the reader is reminded that the former spent some time in France.[20]

In the case of *The Art of Fucking*, the *Mélange de poésies diverses* is of special importance, for the text of the play was obviously copied from the first edition, no copy of which has come down to us. To my knowledge, the last time a copy of the first edition was recorded (in the Soleinne sale catalog) it was apparently destroyed. In fact, the only other known copy of *The Art of Fucking* (in printed form and a later edition), is in the Arsenal Library in Paris, and is as yet uncataloged. Thus the transcription of the *Mélange*'s titlepage currently constitutes the most exact bibliographical record of one of the lesser known but more interesting plays by one of the most popular writers of the period, Baculard d'Arnaud.[21]

Suffice it here to remark that, like Rochester's *Sodom*, d'Arnaud's little rhapsody was actually staged (in Mistress La Croix's palace of pleasure, just as indicated on the titlepage). The performers who took part in the New Year's celebration were the whores of La Croix's brothel, aided by her clients and even the King's own! The madam exhorts:

> Fuck, fuck, don't ever give up!
> To the thrusts of hard pricks, let your cunts reply!
> Use every secret of the powerful Art of Fucking.
> Let the deep holes of our pussies be filled;
> Fuck, fuck, don't ever give up!
> Let happiness and good fortune glide into all cunts.

Elements of farce are sprinkled throughout this musical comedy-ballet, and the general impression is one of gaity alternating with serious fornication. Since there could not have been room for any spectators, *The Art of Fucking* might be considered a total, audience-participation experience. The last scene of the play is one of climactic, frenzied action. The dramatis personae by now include: the madam, three strumpets, a mixed chorus, six whores and their six stout fuckers, no less than thirty-six additional prostitutes with a corresponding number of musqueteers and their entourages, more pimps and procuresses. "Etc.," gasps the author at this point. But no theatre of the absurd or of total freedom, this: the musqueteers surge up from the back of the stage and, with their thirty-six whores, carefully and in cadence execute the various postures described by Aretino, while the original six prostitutes slip into their first positions. (Note that Aretino's *Thirty-Six Positions* is an item conveniently included in the *Mélange*.)

A strumpet being greased for fornication, sings langorously, parodying the love poetry of the times:

> Ah! que mon coeur
> Goûte le bonheur;
> Un feu divin m'enflamme.
> Je meurs . . . je sens . . .
> Quel trouble dans mon âme
> Quel ravissement. . . .
> Mes sens, pleins d'une douce ivresse
> Une vive ardeur
> Succède à ma langueur.
> L'amour me presse;
> Dans ses transports. [French modernized]

Finally the stage directions explain that all characters fuck away. This ends in a communal orgasm, which creates a cascade of sperm, forming the most beautiful theatrical climax in the world. The actors wind down with a couple more songs, and the play finishes with a melancholy morality: "We've done enough today with cock and cunt: Having told the gods to fuck off, let's beware of the clap."

The author was rewarded with a sojourn in the Bastille, as was everyone else connected with the performance or the publication of the play. As for poor Madame de La Croix, her fate is unknown—America, perhaps?

Another play of considerable interest in the *Mélange* is *The New Messalina*, a self-proclaimed tragedy in one act, and in classic French verse: heroic alexandrines disposed in rhyming couplets.[22] The characters of *The New Messalina* are:

> Messalina, daughter of Testiculus [Couillanus]
> Testiculus [Couillanus], father to Messalina, King of Venus-Mound
> Cuntita [Conine], Messalina's confidante
> Cockus [Vitus], in love with Messalina
> Umbilicus [Nombrillis], Pricket [Pines], Cuntitius [Matricius], Guards

"The action takes place in Fucklandia in the city of Venus-Mound situated on the banks of the Brothela, in the palace of Testiculus." Since this play is more or less readily available, having been inserted into several eighteenth-century compendia, it seems best to limit discussion largely to the events surrounding the publication of a couple of early editions and to its possible authorship.

Nearly all bibliographers give 1773 as the date of the first edition, presumably because the earliest known copy up to now has been that in the Enfer of the Bibliothèque Nationale. The only bibliography to allude to an earlier date is Barbier's, but 1752 is mentioned without commentary. Subsequent bibliographers and students of the theatre, with no proof of the existence of a 1752 edition, have chosen to ignore Barbier's oblique reference.[23] I can now offer proof that 1752 is the date of the first separate edition of the play. In the Department of Manuscripts of the Bibliothèque Nationale is a fat folio titled *Affairs of the Booktrade: Slanderous Libels and Other Prohibited Books, 1742-1754*. In it is the work which interests us here. Because of its rarity, uniqueness even, it merits a careful description:

> La nouvelle / Messaline, / tragedie. / En un acte. / Par Pyron, dit Prépucius. / [composite ornament: triangle formed by different sorts of fan-shaped flowers, with a sort of andiron in the center] / A Ancone, / Chez Clitoris, Libraire, rue du Sperme, vis-à-vis / la Fontaine de la Semence. / à la Verge d'Or. / M. DCC. LII."[24]

What happened is that Broncard, an apprentice printer, was caught manufacturing (or possibly distributing) this obscene play, apparently before he had a chance to sell any copies. The police kept one copy, doubtless to help them in their prosecution of Broncard, and nearly all other copies must have been destroyed, for so far as I know none have

236

come down to us. I write "nearly all," for there is a possibility that the 1773 edition, itself extremely rare, was copied from the printed text rather than a manuscript. In any case, the 1773 edition is so poorly printed that I strongly suspect it emanates from a private or clandestine press.

In a letter from Nicolas René Berryer to M. Baisle, governor of the Bastille, dated 21 December 1752, we learn that Broncard was to be incarcerated in the most dreaded of Louis' castles. Berryer also informs his correspondent that the latter would soon be receiving the necessary papers.[25] On the same day, Rochebrune, a sort of sargeant in the police force, was told that he was to accompany Joseph d'Hémery, the police lieutenant in charge of booktrade affairs, in his pursuit of Broncard.[26] Then there is a mysterious note, unsigned and undated, but probably written by d'Hémery himself, informing his correspondent that, of the men to be apprehended that day, Broncard was to be the first.[27] Was Broncard ever escorted to Bastille? If so, did he ever leave it? Since there is no mention of him in Funck-Brentano's monumental study concerned with prisoners of the Bastille,[28] I suspect that Broncard was done away with or that he managed to escape before being arrested.

Now, who was the author of *The New Messalina*? Brenner, in his standard bibliography of French plays, lists the full title of the 1773 edition (presumably after the Enfer copy, being the earliest edition known to him), and puts the play under Piron's name (No.7071). However, that entry bears an asterisk, indicating that Brenner is not sure about the attribution.[29] Barbier attributes *The New Messalina* to Charles François Racot de Grandval, mentioning that the 1752 and 1773 editions appeared under the pseudonym of "Pyron, dit Prépucius." Gay mentions that all editions of *The New Messalina* are very rare, although it was included in, for example, the various editions of *Le Théâtre gaillard* and in the *Théâtre de société* (Gay, III.390; no reference is given to the 1744 *Mélange de pièces curieuses*). The Soleinne catalog includes a copy of the 1773 edition (No.3848), with a truncated transcription of the titlepage, but no information is given about a possible author. In No.3883, an edition (no date, no place) is listed as being by Grandval the Younger. (The only separate editions of the play I know of are 1752, 1773 and the no place, no date one listed in Soleinne.) Pascal Pia, in his catalog of the Enfer, states that the play is not by Piron, but by Grandval the Younger, giving no reasons. He doubtless bases himself on Barbier or is just repeating Apollinaire.[30] Pia also lists an eighteenth-century manuscript copy of *The New Messalina* in the Enfer (Enfer 910), as does Apollinaire (No.910; Apollinaire follows the shelf-list), remarking that the scribe wrote "Par deux amateurs." Strangely, in light of his commentary on the previous item, Pia suggests that it is possible that the person who penned the attribution might have been better informed than we are concerning the origins of this "tragedy." Where does the truth lie? The only thing I can affirm is that my manuscript states unequivocally that the play is by Piron. However, Grandval the Younger did write plays akin to the one which interests us here, and Piron was not renowned in his own time for obscene dramas. It is quite possible that Barbier attributes *The New Messalina* to Grandval instead of Piron for those reasons alone. If so—and I know of no other reasons—the question of the authorship of the play has not yet been answered. Until more information comes to light, it is wisest to state that *The New Messalina* has been attributed both to Grandval the Younger and to Piron.

Whoever he was, the author enjoyed considerable literary talent. The play is well written, and the author was obviously imbued with the spirit and precepts of French classical drama. There are not a few verses comprising clever parodies of some famous classic French plays. For one example alone, Messalina's soliloquy, pronounced after Pricket's cock turns out to be considerably more flacid than desired by the princess, is a cleverly turned pastiche of Don Diègue's "tirade" in Corneille's *Le Cid* (I,iv). Indeed, the ironic humor of the situation is further underscored when the reader realises that Corneille's Don Diègue is quite precisely lamenting his impotence—weakness due to old age with no sexual implications—for he is unable to avenge the insults hurled at him by his rival in the King of Castille's favors (Don Gomès de Gormas). Messalina directs her rage against her would-be lover's sexual impotence:

> Ô rage, ô désespoir ô Vénus ennemie:
> Etais-je reservée à cette ignominie?
> N'ai-je donc encensé ton temple et tes autels
> Que pour être l'objet du faible des mortels? [modernized]

Etc., rather at length with some strong obscenities thrown in, but in a very clever way.

Unfortunately, space restrictions prevent a full discussion of individual items in the *Mélange*, among which are short poems of a couple of lines, rhyming puzzles (the answer to one is "le con"), an acrostic (the first letters of each line form "LE VIT," "vit" corresponding to modern French "bite," or cock), and a very naughty sonnet. There is also a mock-heroic epic in six cantos (Borde's *Parapilla*), which first appeared in the printed version in five. Literary pornography not infrequently takes the form of parodies or pastiches of famous works, which lends a certain amount of intellectual picquancy and humor to what might otherwise be a somewhat lackluster piece of smut. Such is the case of *L'Art de bien aimer et de le prouver* which any student of French literature would immediately recognize by diction and rhythm as being a take-off of Boileau's *Art poétique*:

> C'est en vain qu'à Cythère un débile fouteur
> Pense de l'art de foutre atteindre la hauteur.
> S'il ne sent point du con l'influence secrète. [modernized]

Besides containing the plays, the *Mélange* is unusual for its two prose pieces. The first is the *Déclaration qui fixe les droits et honoraires attachés aux fonctions des filles de joie*, in which the reader is presented with a philosophically conceived document establishing a utopian system for the management of prostitution in Paris. The distribution of favors by the capital's whores is discussed and defined in some detail. The four noblemen involved in the composition of this piece are: Francis Frig-Mound, Marquess of Thick-Prick (François Branle-Mott, marquis de Grosse-Pine);

James Cockerect, Count of Beau-Balls (Jacques Lebandeur, comte de Belles-Couilles); Anthony Squarecock, Baron of Hot-Ass (Antoine de Vit Quarré, baron de Cul-Chaud); Charles Spermachester, Knight and Lord of Clitoris, Vaginitis and other places (Charles Spermancourt, chevalier-seigneur de Clitoris, Vaginis et autres lieux). The second prose piece, *Les Trente-six postures de l'Arretin*, graphically and imaginatively describes, in considerable detail, thirty-six ways to make love.

So many pornographic books were seized and destroyed in the eighteenth and nineteenth centuries that it is a wonder any survived. In his rather tongue-in-cheek introduction to the obscene section ("Pièces libres") of the Soleinne catalog, Paul Lacroix, some hundred and fifty years ago, remarked upon this phenomenon, noting that such works were becoming daily rarer and rarer (III.323). He further implied that all works listed in that section were to be destroyed, an implication reinforced by a contemporary manuscript note in the Burt Franklin reprint. And well might they have been, although I cannot imagine that Lacroix would have been the one to light the match! This adds further interest to the manuscript volume of obscene literature under consideration. Had it ever been included in a public auction in the last century, or in most of this one, as part of a group of books (for the owner would not have been foolish enough to send it up on its own), it might well have vanished forever. Satirical pieces never really became an endangered species, especially if they surfaced some time after the events or person satirized could have taken offence. The same is not true for pornography, of course, because such works attack the frustrated libido, a phenomenon which over and over again causes the Hydra of prejudice and repression to raise its ugly head.

As far as pornography and particularly the second half of the eighteenth century is concerned, we might well reassess our conceptions of that period and come to a better and fuller understanding of it were more information available about such clandestine literature. So much remains to be done. For example, although Raunié took the trouble to wade through a great many eighteenth-century satirical manuscripts some hundred years ago, publishing selections in a ten-volume work (the *Recueil Clairambault-Maurepas* mentioned above), he omitted, as is usually the case, material which would fall into the category of the obscene. Not everything can be published of course, but the pornographic underground is particularly absent from nearly all anthologies; and there is no bibliography adequately dealing with the topic. Aside from explanations concerning genres and studies of individual works and authors, our conception of the eighteenth century would be further enhanced were we to have available a bibliography which would include the obscene in manuscript form, with incipits to facilitate future identification. With advances in technology, it would be feasible to establish a data base for the diffusion of such information, one that would grow over many years of research. In a way, this essay might be considered a small step in that direction.

In the past, students of French have largely had to rely on catalogs of manuscripts compiled in the nineteenth century. These are woefully inadequate, not to mention that access to various private cases remains difficult. We have come a long way from the time when the Goncourt brothers, writing on Piron, did not dare mention the famous "Ode à Priape."[31] Or when Capon and Yve-Plessis, in their book devoted to clandestine theatres of the eighteenth century and their plays found themselves obliged to discuss only in a very general way *La Comtesse d'Olonne* (pp. 28-29). But we've still a long way to go.

Robert L. Dawson
University of Texas

NOTES

I would like to thank the University Research Institute of The University of Texas at Austin for support without which this article could not have been written. My warm thanks are also due to the National Endowment for the Humanities for a grant which in part made this study possible.

Nota bene: a certain amount of the 18th-c. material used for this study, both books and mss, is unique. Rare and unique items in my possession are marked with an asterisk.

1. Silas Paul Jones, *A List of French Prose Fiction from 1700 to 1750* (N.Y.: H. W. Wilson, 1939) and Angus Martin, Vivienne G. Mylne, Richard Frautschi, *Bibliographie du genre romanesque français: 1751-1800* (London: Mansell; Paris: France Expansion, 1977). The scope of Martin, Mylne, and Frautschi exceeds that of Jones, for they have included translations, adaptations, short fiction in collections variously published, and even some marginal works. To complement the bibliographies of prose fiction dealing with the 17th and 18th cs., see my *Additions to the Bibliographies of French Prose Fiction: 1618-1806* (Oxford: Voltaire Foundation, in press).

2. See Dawson, *Additions*, No. 154.

3. Eric Trudgill, *Madonnas and Magdalens: The Origins and Development of Victorian Sexual Attitudes* (N.Y.: Holmes and Meier, 1975), p. 160. Trudgill and others see a turning point occurring somewhere around 1800. The post-revolutionary period might be viewed as reaffirming certain trends and values which began to develop before 1789. Then, too, a reaction set in against the brutality of the Terror. For England, see David Loth's *The Erotic in Literature: A Historical Survey of Pornography as Delightful as It Is Indiscreet* (N.Y.: Julian Messner, 1961), esp. chap. 7, "The Pornography of the Victorians."

4. In Voltaire's case, however, the paranoia of officialdom was directed largely (though not exclusively) at the socio-political implications of his controversial works rather than at libertine descriptions found in many of his novels, histories, and poems. When the Abbé Logerot proposed to edit the works of Voltaire, presumably highly expurgated, an edn. intended for the education of the young and for none less than the Dauphin, his good intentions were for naught. The official answer was decisive: "impossible" ("Cela ne se peut"; work session of 2 Sept. 1785, *Registre de la librairie, 1785*, BN MS F.F.21866, f.149ro).

The Kehl edn., largely because of its popularity, became the focus of special attention by the authorities, egged on by the archbishop of Paris. On 3 June 1785, the king's council met and subsequently issued an official decree banning the first thirty vols. (BN, MS F.F.21866, f.148ro). Cases of volumes were seized around Paris and elsewhere, but occasional exceptions were granted to influential persons. An elite had a fairly ready access to the Kehl edn. See, e.g., Giles Barber, "The Financial History of the Kehl Voltaire," *The Age of the Enlightenment: Studies Presented to Theodore Besterman*, ed. W. H. Barber, et al., (Edinburgh; London: Oliver and Boyd, 1967), pp. 152-70.

5. Such was the case with Regnier de Miromini, "Bailly honoraire de Versailles," who wanted to move to Paris. On 5 March 1785, he asked that his library be permitted to move with him, without undergoing an inspection at the Paris booktrade guild office. Five days later the chief of police, Jean Charles Le Noir, was kind enough to accede to the request (BN, MS F.F.21866, f.169ro).

6. See BN, MS F.F.22092, No. 17. This *Arrêt de la cour du parlement . . . extrait des registres du parlement* is a decree rare enough not even to be referred to in the *Recueil général des anciennes lois françaises depuis l'an 420 jusqu'à la révolution de 1789*, ed. Athanase Jean Léger Jourdan, François André Isambert, Decrusy, et al., (Paris: Belin-Le-Prieur, Verdière, 1822-33). It is also unknown to scholars today. E.g., François Weil cites a contemporary statement which refers to this prohibition, without being aware of the decree or its scope: "Les Gazettes manuscrites avant 1750," in Pierre Retat, ed., *Le Journalisme d'Ancien régime, questions et propositions: table ronde CNRS 12-13 juin 1981* (Lyon: Presses universitaires de Lyon, 1982), p. 95. Much research remains to be done concerning this aspect of the diffusion of clandestine ms literature, as the various articles in *Le Journalisme d'Ancien régime* amply show.

7. Arsenal Library (Paris), MS 7082, f.33. The issues present in the Arsenal ms extend from 10 Jan. 1753 to 5 July 1753. Many of the "letters" or issues bear a stamped heading, "Le courrier de Paris." This venture appeared weekly and contains tidbits of largely political and literary news. François Jérôme Bousquet de Colomiers was thrown into the Bastille 8 Nov. 1752 for having composed "nouvelles à la main." When we realise that his subscribers included the "président" Riquet, the archbishop of Narbonne, and the English and Dutch ambassadors, we can today appreciate the importance of the genre, and the police's concern, or paranoia, depending on which way you look at it! (See Bibliothèque nationale, MS F.F.14058, N.A.F.1891.) According to Frantz Funck-Brentano, *Les Lettres de cachet à Paris: étude suivie d'une liste des prisonniers de la Bastille, 1659-1789* (Paris: Imprimerie nationale, 1903), No. 4210, there is also further information to be had in the British Library, MS Egerton 1667.

8. This ms has an engraved titlepage (by Martinet), with a ms title in red and black ink within a central cartouche: *Psautier distribué pour tous les jours de la semaine, Traduit selon le texte Hébreu, avec des Titres et des Notes, pour en faciliter l'intelligence.* 539 quarto pp.

9. Here is an example of a ms book dealing with controversial political issues: *Nouvelle dissertation sur les moeurs, les droits, la dignité et l'origine de la noblesse française . . . présentée par un grand du royaume à messieurs les ducs et pairs* (1728). 59 quarto pp.

10. Olivier Bloch, ed., *Le Matérialisme du XVIIIe siècle et la littérature clandestine: actes de la table ronde des 6 et 7 juin 1980 organisée à la Sorbonne,* Bibliothèque d'histoire de la philosophie (Paris: J. Vrin, 1982). The reader who might be interested in pursuing this avenue of inquiry must of course consult Ira Wade's *The Clandestine Organization and Diffusion of Philosophic Ideas in France from 1700 to 1750* (1938; rep. N.Y.: Octagon, 1967).

11. My copy of this satire (which was actually composed by Bay de Cury[s]) contains corrections and additions in a different hand. This ms comes from a large group of Voltaire's papers that was sold in the late 1950s. Another copy belonged to Mme Du Deffand. After her death it passed into Walpole's collections and is now in the W. S. Lewis Walpole Collection of Yale University at Farmington, Conn. I am grateful to W. S. Lewis for so kindly answering my queries several years before his death. For the story of this affair, see Jean François Marmontel, *Mémoires,* ed. John Renwick (Clermont-Ferrand: G. de Bussac, 1972), 1:175-83 and notes. For a somewhat different version, see Charles Collé, *Journal et mémoires,* ed. Honoré Bonhomme (Paris: Firmin Didot, 1868), 2:201-06. The only ms copy of the *Parody* known to Renwick is the Du Deffand Walpole one.

12. This ms is supposed to be a holograph, but I have not yet been able to verify that. For the composition and circulation of particularly satirical poetry in France, see Emile Raunié, ed., *Recueil Clairambault-Maurepas: Chansonnier historique du 18e siècle publié avec introduction, commentaire, notes et index* (Paris: A. Quantin, 1879-84).

13. E.g., I have a contemporary ms version of Manuel Freyre da Silva's *Papeles jocosos*

con su poco de Moralidad satirica, q^e con titulo de papeles del Doende [Duende] se expancionan en esta Corte de Madrid en los ānos de 1735 y 1736. The author had to flee Spain, whereupon he disappeared. (The only other known ms copy of this mordant satire directed against the Spanish court is in the National Library, Madrid).

14. Discreetly located on the recto of the penultimate end-paper, there is inscribed in faded pencil "A Valerie Durie" (or "Duriez"). Many of the songs in both *chansonniers* deal with girls being seduced by their confessors, ardent shepherds making love to their ecstatic shepherdesses, ladies of quality screwed by their lackeys, etc. A few are humorously scatalogical. Here is an example, strophe 1 of No. 136: "Eloge de la Merde" ["In Praise of Shit"], "Air [To the tune of]: Aussitôt que la lumière" (from the 1787, "Cythère," collection):

> Vous qui connaissés la merde
> et en faites tous les jours
> craignés vous qu'elle ne se perde
> du mal arrettes le cours.
> Savés vous que la plus fine
> Celle que l'on aime tant
> dans les meilleures cuisines
> a pris son commencement.

15. The full title of the prose *Proclamation* is: *Déclaration qui fixe les droits et honoraires attachés aux fonctions des filles de joie de la ville, faubourg et banlieu de Paris, et prescrit le maintien, l'ordre et la [?] qui doivent s'observer dans les bordels soit publics soit particuliers.* (Donné au serail le 28 mars 1781). The *Mélange de poésies diverses* is on paper containing no figurative watermarks that might have enabled me to ascertain its provenance. Most of the text was written by a single scribe; various other 18th-c. hands finished it.

16. *Lettre philosophique, par Mr. de V***, avec plusieurs pièces galantes et nouvelles de différens auteurs* (A Paris, aux dépens de la compagnie, 1747) is of special significance to this essay, for it contains several pieces included in the *Mélange*. Another collection, which I have not been able to consult, apparently containing a few items included in the *Mélange* is the *Mélange de pièces curieuses . . .* (Londres, 1744) for which see Jules Gay, *Bibliographie des ouvrages relatifs à l'amour, aux femmes,* 6th edn., ed. J. Lemonnyer (Paris, 1894-1900), 3:97.

17. *Oeuvres complètes illustrées,* ed. Pierre Dufay (Paris: Francis Guillot, 1928-31), 10 vols. Dufay included works by Voltaire and others in his edition, sometimes without bothering to mention so. This doubtless stems from his having used various 18th-c. editions of Piron's selected and collected works which also bore no indication of being collected works (poems usually) *largely* by Piron.

18. *Parapilla* was first pub. in 5 cantos in Lyon, 1776 ("Florence" on the t.p.). The *Mélange* version is in 6. When was the sixth canto added? Dominique Grandmont, in an art. devoted to *Parapilla,* gives an outline of five cantos; a sixth is not even mentioned (*Dictionnaire des oeuvres érotiques: domaine français,* ed. Gilbert Minazolli, with Pascal Pia and Robert Carlier (Paris: Mercure de France, 1971), pp. 377-78. It is a verse adaptation of Marino's *Novella dell'angelo Gabriello* which appeared in *Il Libro del perche et la pastorella del cavalier Marino colla Novella dell'angelo Gabriello,* 16th c., rep. in Paris ca. 1757 according to J.-M. Quérard, *Les Supercheries littéraires dévoilées, seconde édition,* ed. Gustave Brunet and Pierre Jannet (Paris: Paul Daffis, 1869-70), 1:560-63. See also Gay, 1:561-63 who points out that it is possible that *Parapilla* is not by Borde after all. Like other obscene works rep. in the 19th c., it was again condemned to be destroyed (on 12 May 1865; Gay, 3:630–31), placed on various lists of prohibited works, and so on. Gay himself sentenced to a four-month prison term (the Poulet-Malassis case). See esp. Fernand Drujon, *Catalogue des ouvrages, écrits et dessins de toute nature poursuivis, supprimés ou condemnés depuis le 21 octobre 1814 jusqu'au 31 juillet 1877 . . .* (Paris, 1879; rep. Bruxelles: Culture et civilisation, 1968), pp. 297-99.

19. Some details concerning three of the plays, the other two being discussed in the text:

I. *La Comtesse d'Olonne, tragédie*—has been attributed to Grandval the Elder, and was apparently first pub. 1738. See Guillaume Apollinaire, with F. Fleuret, L. Perceau, *L'Enfer de la Bibliothèque nationale: bibliographie méthodique et critique de tous les ouvrages composant cette célèbre collection avec une préface, un index des titres et une table des auteurs, nouvelle edition* (1919; rep. Geneva: Slatkine, 1970); Clarence D. Brenner, *A Bibliographical List of Plays in the French Language: 1700-1789* (Berkeley, 1947) rep. . . .*With a New Forward and an Index* by Michael A.

Keller and Neal Zaslaw (N.Y.: AMS, 1979); Pascal Pia, *Les Livres de l'Enfer: bibliographie critique des ouvrages érotiques dans leurs différentes éditions du 16ᵉ siècle à nos jours* (Paris: C. Coulet and A. Faure, 1978). The attribution to Bussy-Rabutin seems false, and if bibliographers have occasionally associated his name with the play, that is probably because Bussy-Rabutin devoted a sizeable section to Mme d'Olonne in his *Histoire amoureuse des Gaules*. Gaston Capon and Robert Yve-Plessis, in *Les Théâtres clandestins* (Paris: Plessis, 1905), while agreeing that the play has been attributed to Bussy-Rabutin and to Grandval, see no reason to attribute it to the latter and leave it under the former's name (pp. 27-28). This play is not to be confused with the much earlier *Comédie galante*. See too Fernand Drujon, *Les Livres à clef: étude de bibliographie critique et analytique pour servir à l'histoire littéraire* (Paris: Edouard Rouveyre, 1888), 1:211–13.

II. *Les Plaisirs du cloître, comédie en trois actes et en vers*—apparently first pub. 1773. Ms t.p. claims that it is by a "M.D.L.C.A.P." See Quérard, Soleinne, and Gay. The latter remarks that it was once again condemned in the 19th c. (12 May 1865), 3:765, and also, justifiably, underscores the obscene nature of the "comedy" without however alluding to the pornographic Lesbian scenes. (The play's main sexual theme deals with homosexuality, male and female.) See too Drujon, *Ouvrages condamnés*, p. 321 (the Poulet-Malassis case). A brief but discreet outline of the play is included in Capon and Yve-Plessis (pp. 43-44).

III. *Vasta*—ms t.p. reads: "Vasta. / Reine de Bordellis / Tragedie / En trois actes Et en vers / Par / Mʳ. Piron." This play has been somewhat hesitantly attributed to Piron by various bibliographers. Brenner seems to feel certain that it is by him (No. 9964). Barbier (4:915e) is unsure (Antoine Alexandre Barbier, up-dated by Olivier A. Barbier, Paul Billard, et al., *Dictionnaire des ouvrages anonymes*, 3rd edn., 4 vols. [Paris: Fechoz and Letouzey, 1882]; fifth vol. supp. by Gustave Brunet [1889]). I do not know where the truth lies. The first edn. I know of is 1773. My manuscript indicates "Piron" with no question implied. Capon and Yve-Plessis, without entirely accepting the attribution to Piron, do point out that the latter wrote the "Ode à Priape" and that he would have had the talents required to compose such a well structured "tragedy."

20. The relationship of Rochester to France and vice-versa, the authenticity of *Sodom*, and all the questions such problems raise are far too complex to be but mentioned here. Suffice it to say that Rochester might have been aware of a certain *Comédie galante* which antedates *Sodom* by quite a few years and that *Sodom* was in any case rendered into the French. See Paul Lacroix, *Bibliothèque dramatique de Monsieur [Martineau] de Soleinne, catalogue rédigé par P. L. Jacob, bibliophile* [i.e., Paul Lacroix], 6 vols. (Paris, 1843-45; rep. N.Y.: Burt Franklin, n.d.), 3: nos. 3835-36. Gay apparently had access to Soleinne's mss, for he cites from one of them (Gay, 3:1121). These ms pieces were dated 1682 and 1744, respectively. There is a ms copy of a French *Sodom* in the Arsenal Library, Paris. Brenner also refers to Rochester, but puts the play with the anonyms (Brenner No. 2480; Arsenal MS 9449). I am attempting to sort this out in a study titled "*Sodom* in France." *Sodom* was apparently pub. in 1684, and like the first edn. of d'Arnaud's *Art of Fucking*, all copies seem to have disappeared.

21. The unique printed copy of *The Art of Fucking* follows an edn. of a work attributed to the Comte de Caylus by Barbier and to Charles François Racot de Grandval by Brenner: *Le Bordel, ou le Jean-Foutre puni*, [*The Brothel, or Johnny Fuckalot Meets His Reward*] (1747). For events surrounding the performance and publication of the *Art of Fucking*, see my "Baculard d'Arnaud, Life and Prose Fiction,", *Studies on Voltaire and the Eighteenth Century*, 141-42 (1976), 1:55-60. For further bibliographical details, see 2:659-60. The t.p. in the *Mélange* reads as follows:

L'art de foutre ou Paris / foutant. / Sur la musique du Prologue de L'Europe / galante, qui commence ainsi; frappez, frappez / ne vous lassez jamais &c. / Ballet. / Representé aux Porcherons dans le Bordel / de Mademoiselle Delacroix fameuse / Maquerelle, le Premier de Janvier 1741. et / remis au meme Théâtre, presque tous les / jours de fête de la dt. [la dite] année. / à Paris / Chez Dom Bougre jmprimeur de tous / "les fouteurs et de tous les cocus du / "Royaume a L'Enseigne du Vit / a la grenadiere. / Avec Privilege de tous les Seigneurs de la Cour.

22. T.p. in the *Mélange*: "La Nouvelle / Messaline / Tragedie / En Quatorze Scênes / Et en vers. / Par Mʳ· Piron". Capon and Yve-Plessis give a very brief synopsis, not having dared to do more, and attribute the play to Grandval *fils*.

23. The *Dictionnaire des anonymes* went through several edns. but is far from complete and, though an excellent reference work, contains quite a few errors, which helps to explain why so many have chosen to ignore 1752 as the date of the first separate pub. of *The New Messalina*. All bibliographers concerned with *La Nouvelle Messalina* seem to be unaware that it apparently first saw the light as a one-act *comedy* by "Prépucius" in that collection of heteroclite works, the *Mélange de pièces curieuses*. I am assuming that it is the same play as the one under discussion here, for I have been unable to consult that rare book.

24. MS F.F.22092, No. 69, f.204-12. These sheets comprise a printed book; a ms note reads "Broncard 13. X^bre. 1752."

25. Bibliothèque Nationale MS F.F.22092, No. 68.

26. Bibliothèque Nationale MS F.F.22092, No. 70.

27. Bibliothèque Nationale MS F.F.22092, No. 71, f.214ro.

28. Funck-Brentano went through many more sources than just the Bastille archives preserved in the Arsenal Library, today a department of the BN. The reason that this affair has remained unknown is that not only is there no mention of it in Funck-Brentano, but it is also not cited in the index to Ernest Coyecque, *Inventaire de la collection Anisson sur l'histoire de l'imprimerie et la librairie principalement à Paris: Bibliothèque Nationale, F.F.22061-22193* (1900; rep. N.Y.: Burt Franklin, n.d.). Any user of Coyecque should be aware that though in his introduction Coyecque states that the index contains the names of *all* people and places, with the exception of those encountered on just about every page, this is not true. A researcher interested in a particular person, place, or incident must read through the entire two vols.

29. Unfortunately, nowhere does Brenner explain the meaning of such asterisks. Not long before his death he was kind enough to explain his use of them to me.

30. See Apollinaire No. 721 for more info. Albeit useful, Pia's bibliography is descriptive rather than historic and little research was done to update previous bibliographies.

31. Edmond and Jules de Goncourt, *Portraits intimes du dix-huitième siècle*, ed. with a postface by Jean Ajalbert, 2 vols. (Paris: Flammarion, [1940]?), 2:235 81. Moreover, in an art. devoted to an "Introduzione al teatro di Alexis Piron," *Convivium: revista bimestrale di letteratura, filologia e storia* 35 (1967): 385-429, Antonio Frescaroli makes no mention at all of Piron as the possible author of erotic or obscene plays, and indeed only mentions in passing the saucy aspect of his career, with a ref. to the "Ode à Priape" hidden in n. 133, p. 429.

Obscene Literature in Eighteenth-Century Italy: an Historical and Bibliographical Note

Conscius ecce duos accepit lectus amantes:
Ad thalami clausas, Musa, resiste fores!
[Behold, a guilty bed received two lovers:
Stop at the chamber's closed doors, O Muse!]
Ovid, *Ars amandi*, II, 703-04

In the eighteenth century, foreigner travelers like Montesquieu found Italy a magnificent but dusty museum. Yet in the general conception of European men of letters, especially in the second half of the century, the peninsula also became the exotic stage for aberrant passions. "Aberrance"—the word evokes that *déraison* which had enjoyed its moment of glory in the courts of the Renaissance, and which was dear not only to Stendhal, but to Gothic novelists, to Elizabethan dramatists, to Shakespeare, and to Meissner, Tieck, and Schlegel.

The Marquis de Sade was in Italy from 1775 to 1776, and described it as a marvelous country ("le plus beaux pays de l'univers"), but one inhabited by the most decadent race ("habité par l'espèce la plus abrutie").[1] This latter fact so delighted him that he chose the area between Turin and Naples as the site for the journey of debauchery which constitutes more than half of Juliette's interminable adventures. Casanova's *Mémoires*, although scarcely a reliable source, corroborate the Marquis' observations. And it was precisely the historical reality of this darker world which fueled the imagination of Stendhal in his *Chroniques italiennes*. His tales of Accoramboni and the Borgias, of Pier Luigi sodomizing the bishop of Fano, and of Francesco Cenci raping his own daughter are all well-documented historical facts.

The person most responsible for establishing this inane legend—which survives even in our century, thanks to vacationing writers from northern Europe—was Mme de Stael. In her *Corinna ou de l'Italie* and *De la littérature considerée dans ses rapports avec les institutions sociales*, we find a fundamental notion (already present in Rousseau's *Essai sur l'origine des langues*): while northern climes foster meditation and melancholy, the fertile sentiments which favor the works of a genius, warm climates draw people together in society, fomenting their passions and licentious behavior. This theory provided a sort of answer to the questions raised, both then and now, by the "peculiarity" of Italian culture during the eighteenth century, which we are inclined to call "European." Perhaps it would be better to speak of missing elements, rather than peculiarity. For not only did eighteenth-century Italy not share in the flowering of the novel which took place in other European countries, she seems never to have produced literature which assumed the task of developing a "realistic" discourse concerning love and sexual passion.

For Mme de Stael, the reason is simple: Italians don't write about passion because they experience it all too strongly in their daily lives. It is the reverse of Ovid's saying: *Lasciva est nobis pagina, vita proba est* ("My writings are lewd, but my life moral"). Hence, we seem to find a difference between the Enlightenment European and the ageless Italian, or (citing Stendhal for an apt contrast) between Julien Sorel and Fabrizio del Dongo—between the calculating Frenchman and the impulsive Italian.

No one has yet attempted to exhume the poor remains of the unorthodox literature of eighteenth-century Italy in order to see whether any group of texts existed which might be classified in the category which we may tentatively call "erotic realism." Yet such an undertaking of literary archeology is surely called for, if only because it is during the first half of the eighteenth century, in England and especially in France, that the erotic novel emerges as a forerunner of the realism of the middle-class novel.

If it were true that we could view the image of readers mirrored in contemporary publishing practices and in the guidelines used to found public and private libraries, we would be led to believe that the passion expressed in eighteenth-century Italian literature is merely that of a late and pallid Petrarchism. Unfortunately, this view has been codified by literary historians, who usually pay little attention to underground and unorthodox sources, and its persistence has been insured by an almost complete lack of the necessary studies and research.[2]

In the limited space available, I do not propose to offer the reader a learned and comprehensive census, but rather to provide him with an initial overview (necessarily rather generic) of bawdy literature as represented by the authors and works most significant for their success or circulation.

The scope of the present study is limited to sexual obscenity. I avoid the term "pornography" because I believe it has ambiguous and misleading connotations. And concerning the vexed question of the boundary between "erotic" and "lewd," I prefer to reject any notions based either on the haphazard and meaningless categories of literary history, or on criteria of moral responsibility such as the author's intention (physiological or aphrodisiac effects, for example). I consider only rhetorical and stylistic distinctions as heuristically valid. Simply stated, we recognize eroticism when the author euphemistically replaces terms describing sexual activities or the sex organs either by non-expression (suppression or omission) or by using expressions which tone down his meaning. Eroticism consists in leaving something unsaid, more or less explicitly, so that the reader's active participation is required. By contrast, obscenity consists either in avoiding euphemistic replacement, or in employing it in such a way as to emphasize even more the term replaced. Hence, an obscene text requires no act of interpretation.

Eroticism is a game which avoids acknowledgment by exploiting the semantic indirectness of figures of speech, but it is also an explicit acknowledgment. The use of metaphor tends to capture the reader's attention precisely because its meaning seems clichéd or faded. As I noted, this is perhaps the only distinction which is heuristically useful, for by it the two "spurious" categories are rendered independent of changes in historical periods and cultures.

It has been said that the eighteenth century was the age of the discovery of sexual pleasure. Now, the ideological foundations for the *roman libertin* which flourished in France between 1740 and 1760 were laid by the pleasure which rococo taste dramatized in pastoral and mythological settings. And the key features of this taste were miniaturizing and metonymy, as Patrick Brady has observed in his recent definitive study concerning various aspects of rococo literary culture.[3]

In terms of an esthetic of sentiment, the first of these concepts suggests that the narcissistic and hedonistic psychology of the rococo miniaturized passion, so that *l'amour passion* was no longer acceptable. As for the second, the "horizontal" contiguity of metonymy supplanted metaphor's "vertical" relationship between things, which had characterized earlier styles. Objects became personalized, and substitutes, such as Belinda's lock, were preferred to reality. Reality was replaced by fetishes.

Gallantry was precisely the miniaturizing of sexual passion and its reduction to metonymy. It is evident that gallantry exorcized *l'amour passion* and reduced it to a harmless game of society. Less evident but more important is the fact that the banishment of passion by *l'amour goût* constituted a decisive step toward liberating the senses. The era of the rococo, which situated paradise in the here-and-now, coincided with the spread of empiricism and the development of sensationalism.

At the beginning of the eighteenth century, the literary world was invaded and overwhelmed by Nature in the form of its principal fetish, Woman: hence the dominance of first-person narratives assigned to her by French novelists. In short, after the misogynism of the seventeenth century, passion was reinstated in the miniaturized dimensions given her by rococo hedonism. Whereas rococo eroticism, by regarding nature as human, unreasonably refused to consider sex a problem, soon the libertine novel reversed this position and made sex an emblem of all problems. This was the next step in the process of regarding man as natural, a process which culminated in the *Liaisons dangereuses,* in which *volupté* and *débauche* can no longer be distinguished, and in which beauty becomes simply the appearance most inviting to sexual satisfaction.

If every other form of liberty came to be subsumed under sexual liberty, it was the result of this first non-pathological approach to sexuality, which the rococo aesthetic of sentiment had made possible. This aesthetic, properly considered, made no attempt to shut man up in a shell, but rather made him assume the dimensions of the universe as conceived by Locke or Newton.

But what about Italy? Rather than in the erotic writers of Arcadia, such as Savioli and Rolli, the new aesthetic may be found in the conception of Francesco Algarotti's short work, *Il Congresso di Citera* (Naples, 1745), which was inspired by Montesquieu's *Temple de Gnide* (Amsterdam, 1724). Yet in the entire panorama of "official" eighteenth-century Italian literature, only one author seems to have kept pace with European culture by assimilating the "sweet system" of the new hedonism. In his *Arte di piacere alle donne,* published posthumously in 1769, Tommaso Crudeli (1703-1745) asserts decisively that "We obey and follow nature when we approach a woman who charms us."[4]

Crudeli, a crypto-libertine arrested in 1739 on charges of being a Freemason, was undoubtedly the only free-thinker among the Arcadians. Echoes of sensationalism are not heard until the second half of the century, when in his brief *Filosofia per Giulietta,* Aurelio De Giorgi Bertòla (1753-1798) praises Ninon de Lenclos and the *Temple de Gnide,* and also launches into a defense of carnal pleasure. "We are born for pleasures, and without exception all our actions have them for their purpose," his philosopher instructs Giulietta: "See that you assign a great part of your system to that pleasant error which love bids us commit and which love itself justifies" ("Siam nati per i piaceri: ad essi mirano indistintamente tutte le nostre azioni . . . quel grato errore, che l'amore fa commettere, e che l'amore istesso giustifica, quegli formi una gran porzione del vostro sistema").[5] But the times had already changed, and the drawing-room epicureanism of De Giorgi Bertòla probably seemed short-winded and surprised no one.

While it was the rococo which discovered the fertile and subversive partnership of love and the human body—which was to create a "geometrical" view of amatory passion—we should note that in eighteenth-century Italy this passion seems to have enjoyed only probationary freedom. Thus in the figurative arts, where Boucher portrays women of vivid sexuality such as Madame Pompadour and Victoire O'Murphy, the portraits of women by Rosalba Carriera and other Italian artists before 1750 seem even today severe ornaments of a culture more reminiscent of a seventeenth-century *Wunderkammer* than of a lively *salon.*[6]

Before attempting to explain why Italian culture did not share in this development, it is necessary to explore beyond the official horizons of literary history.

❖

Of the ten laws of the Arcadian Republic of Letters, only two actually speak of letters, and one of these absolutely prohibits "evil, infamous, obscene, superstitious, or impious poems" (*Mala carmina et famosa, obscaena, superstitiosa impiave*). In fact, Italian men of letters had to defend their image from the Bernesque poets, whose very number made them a national calamity. In 1766, Saverio Bettinelli lamented: "Look at Italy—

how for three centuries full she has been full of such buffoons!" ("Or mirate l'Italia com'e, da tre secoli in qua, piena di tai buffoni!).[7] Francesco Berni himself, convinced that literature no longer had the power to edify, had established a kind of poetry which was attentive to form but devoid of content. Initially both satirical and bawdy, the Bernesque style became exclusively bawdy, and scatological topics became a principal constituent and source of humor.

Rather than among popular and dialect writers, Bernesque poets are to be found in higher society, in educated circles, and among full-time courtiers. One of the last was Carlo Innocenzo Frugoni (1692-1768), a facile versifier at the court of the dukes of Parma, where his works were printed with the ducal coat of arms.[8] The vast and extremely vulgar Bernesque portion of his works shows that farting and defecation occasioned great amusement in courtly drawing rooms. But significantly, with only one exception, excretory functions were never replaced by obscenity of an erotic nature.[9] Gasparo Gozzi (1713-1786) goes further; in his burlesque verses, written before 1760, there are allusions to physical arousal.[10] But these are isolated cases. Doubtless the audience took pleasure in the elegance with which the poet managed to avoid being too explicit. Gozzi, for instance, avoided making clear that, in describing the "flower of women" he meant the female genitals.

Elsewhere, as in the *Poesie bernesche* of the abbot Giuseppe Cherubini (b. 1738), the poet limits himself to a hint—"I burn to find myself stretched out in her bed" ("Bramo vedermi steso nel suo letto"). Or, like poets since Berni himself, he employs vocabulary not countenanced by the Accademia della Crusca: "An arse is an arse, not a martin or a basket; once even the nuns in the convent called it an arse, which was a decent name" ("Il culo è culo, e non martino o cesto; / E allora fin le monache in convento, / Culo lo chiamavano, ch'era un nome onesto").[11] By this point, the poet had already blushed, the public was laughing, and they went no further.

The comical basis of Bernesque style and burlesque poets generally relies on the unchanging and unperishing topics of tradition. Narrating defecations, conjugal mishaps, and the contagion of the "French malady," writers felt secure in the presence of a most ancient tradition. In the burlesque mode, we possess a veritable *summa* in the interminable satirocomic poem on marital misadventures, *La Corneide* by Giovanni De Gamerra (1743-1803), a compendium in 71 cantos of famous cuckolds from every age and country.[12]

De Gamerra apologized for the nearly 70,000 verses of his *Corneide*. Cherubini regretted writing his Bernesque verses. And Gaspare Gozzi refrained from publishing his poems. Similar repentance may be found in Gresset's *Perroquet,* a work which enjoyed great success in translation during the entire century. In the work, a parrot learns foul language from boatmen and repeats them in a convent, but repents in the end. Burlesque defecatory language consists in dropping conventions for a while, precisely where they are most accepted and enforced, in order to shock nuns and make polite society laugh.

One of the theses of Karl Rosenkranz's *Aesthetik des Hässlichen* is that ugliness and obscenity become comic when they recall and reinforce an ideal opposed to them.[13] Sexual obscenity in all burlesque literature is merely a caricature, because it actually stengthens a belief in what it seems to reject, namely, the ideals of chastity and purity. We laugh because in the end we know that man's true essence is incorporeal. Yet, if this form of obscenity has no value as ideology, there are a number of authors, interesting for different reasons, who go far beyond *mauvaise plaisanterie*.

In the first part of the eighteenth century, lyric poetry drew inspiration from this popular taste; and as years passed, even Arcadia seemed to become less modest and timid. Gallantry never resorts to euphemism, since it always stops on the threshold of "the bounds one may not utter" ("quel confine che dir non lice").[14] In Niccolò Forteguerri's burlesque poem *Ricciardetto* (1738), an innkeeper tells how a priest resorted to Boccaccian stratagems to enjoy the favors of a young bride. But at the tale's finest moment, "the keeper's speech was cut short, so many voices were heard in the street" (XXX, 101: "dell'oste il favellar fu rotto, / tanti s'udivan voci per la via"). Thanks to the providential clamor, we find an *obscaenus interruptus,* and appearances are saved, even if we knew perfectly well what was going to happen, since these were the customary events repeated *ad nauseam* in novellas of the fifteenth and sixteenth centuries.

Let us briefly consider some authors for whom crossing the bounds of propriety was not so much a *divertissement* as a conscious program. They may be subdivided into two groups. The first group employs non-rhetorical revelation, i.e., a direct obscenity with a quantitative recording of obscene *topoi*. The second employs an ambiguous use of rhetoric of obscenity which emphasizes the qualitative aspect.

In the first group, the place of honor belongs to the Venetian Giorgio Alvise Baffo (1694-1768), who was the greatest priapic poet of all time, as Apollinaire was the first to recognize. Now, there are a number of Venetian dialect writers, generally scurrilous, whose works survive in manuscript.[15] But they are not in a class with Baffo, since for them obscenity was only one of many possible topics. Baffo has left us more than 700 short poems which feature a patent rhetoric of "anti-euphemism" that may perhaps be comparable only to that in Aretino's *Sonetti*. His obscenity lies not so much in the situation as in the obsessive repetition of certain vocabulary: one noun in three is an obscenity like *potta* ("pussy") or *cazzo* ("prick").[16] "I'll say 'cunt' to a cunt and 'prick' to a prick," Baffo declares as his poetic manifesto: "Dirò mona alla mona e cazzo al cazzo." "I'm best at following my true nature," he explains: "El mio forte xe de star sul *natural*." And: "When I must call a prick 'that thing,' I shall sing poorly" ("Quando che al cazzo go da dir cotal / Canterò sempre mal").[17]

Baffo's poetic output occupies a special place in the history of the obscene literature through the ages. The reason lies not in his pandering to carnality. After all, we are dealing with oral banquet literature, and his poems were written for declaiming. Rather, the reason lies in his unrestrained expression of sexual Pantagruelism and in his obsessive and boundless allusions to genitalia, which seem like a pagan rite of the Mediterranean. In his poetry, Baffo writes, he speaks "only of fair, pleasant, and good things, most delightful things, that is, of mouths, tits, arses, pricks, and cunt" ("sol de cose belle, allegre e bone, / Cose deliciosissime cioé / De boche, tette, culi, cazzi e mone").[18] He so closely adheres to his manifesto that the female genitalia ("mona") become the *leitmotiv* in poetry which is otherwise characterized by a lack of dramatic episodes, by bestial physicality, and by an almost compulsory repetition of filthy refrains. Indeed, it was this unreflecting and "sunny" physicality which won Baffo great popularity, even outside Italy. Dialect poets rarely enjoy such international popularity, but perhaps we should recall that, until the fall of its republic in 1797, Venice lived in the imagination of many Europeans as a great lagoon which harbored every vice.

While the Venetian whore or "donnazza," which Baffo made his muse, enjoyed great success, Goethe and Foscolo did not hesitate to express their admiration for another writer, Domenico Luigi Batacchi (1748-1802). Foscolo called him "cheerful and original" ("gaio," "originale"), and said his language was not barbarous ("non barbaro nella lingua").[19] Such qualities would seem rare in a writer whose only aim was to amuse his readers with a pinwheel of episodes revolving around men's lust for what he calls that "oval sweetest orifice" ("bislungo amabile orifizio").

The comicality of his *Novelle* is in fact consistently effective. Their emblematic lesson is that chastity is a mere dream, since "fucking is a necessity, and Nature gave man his dangler for that purpose" ("il fottere è un bisogno, e la Natura / Fe' quel ciondolo all'uomo a questo effetto").[20] Besides his novellas, he also wrote *Il Zibaldone* [*The Miscellany*], a poem in twelve cantos which relates how the country priest Don Barletta contracts the French malady from his maid, and how after various episodes he is punished by heaven. Near the end, a grotesque God tells St. Peter: "I won't cut his off, thanks to your intercessions, but still I'll fine him his erections." ("Non glie lo taglio di vostra intercessione, / Ma però gli confisco l'erezione").[21] Don Barletta is driven to suicide. While Batacchi's creativity seems lower-class in his *Novelle* and *Zibaldone*, his *La Rete di Vulcano* [*Vulcan's Net*] shows that he was a man of refinement.[22] Indeed, Batacchi also translated Richardson's *Clarissa*, and was suspected of Jacobinism.

Batacchi's obscenity is overt. When the heroine appears in his *Zibaldone*, the men present feel a swelling in their breeches ("gonfiar nella brachetta") and Don Barletta has a stiff cock ("ritto l'uccello").[23] Batacchi doesn't mince words or attempt to moralize, but exploits the comic scene for all it is worth. In his preface to the *Zibaldone*, he writes: "Let no one expect to find sentimental poetry here; nay, here is graphic imagination, and everything that will provide a few moments of comfort, good humor, and gaiety" ("Non credasi dunque di trovare qui poesie di sentimento, non, ma una fastasia pittrice, e tutto cio' che puo' procurare qualche momento di sollievo, di buon umore e di allegria"). It is the merit of Batacchi's poetry that his folk-like farce is sustained by a certain level of taste, and by a learned tradition which includes the ever-present Boccaccio, from Masuccio Salernitano, La Fontaine, oriental tales, and Lesage. In fact, his novella *La mala notte* [*The Night of Ill*] imitates an episode from *Liaisons dangereuses*.

One of the main ingredients of obscenity in Baffo and Batacchi is its Pantagruelian aspect. Yet if we analyse their works qualitatively, we find that gross comicality is replaced by slyness. And if we compare Baffo and Batacchi to the other numerous Italian authors of obscene tales, we find the same difference of quality as that between Boiardo and Marino. When Boiardo describes the lovemaking of Fiordelisa and Brandimarte, he is explicit but decent: "Six times they repeated their dance before their desire was spent" (I, xix, 63: "Sei volte ritornarno a quel danzare/ Prima che il lor desio ben fosse spento"). By contrast, Marino's taste for ambiguity permits his fisherman to spend four octaves describing a domestic eel with two hangers ("due pendenti") which he is saving for Lilla *(Adone, IX, 48-51)*. Even though he says that it soon raises its head if anyone touches it—"se la tocca alcun, tosto si drizza"—the reader can still read the passage without blushing, at least in theory.

With writers like Marino, we leave the middle-class readership of Baffo and Batacchi for a more refined public with higher social implications. It was precisely this courtly public which determined the success of the novellas by Giambattista Casti (1724-1803). An abbot and courtier, Casti gained fame by his *Novelle galanti* [*Gallant Tales*], which he wrote in *ottava rima* beginning in the 1760s. These tales may strike the modern reader as insipid by comparison with those of Batacchi, for they constantly play on an ambiguous alternation between obscenity and feigned prudery. But Casti's false delicacy merely serves to disguise his use of the traditional obscene commonplaces employed by Boccaccio, Firenzuola, Voltaire, Grecourt, and Diderot (Casti's *Berretto magico* [*The Magic Cap*] reworks Diderot's *Bijoux indiscrets*). And his persistent and insincere moralizing interrupts the flow of the narrative.

To be sure, there are some bold defenses of sexual pleasure: "It is ridiculous and bizarre to think that love can feed on metaphysical nourishment for very long" ("Ridicolo è il pensiero e stravagante, / Che amor di metafisico alimento / Pascere si possa a lungo andar").[24] But there is only one passage in which Casti describes the sex organs in non-euphemistic terms, and there he employs the *linqua franca* of medicine. Indeed, what his contemporaries most valued in the tales of the "obscene abbot" was his evident ability to say anything by using, not the language of the stables, but decent vocabulary, and by avoiding any trace of explicit description.[25] "I can only say that I don't know if she was a virgin that evening, but I know she was no virgin by morning" ("Dirò sol, ch'io non so, se fu la sera / Vergin, so che il mattin vergin non era").[26]

Casti's tales did not survive the society which they had amused. Today we see in them only the taste of a mediocre talent who succeeded in rendering inoffensive any reference to the libertine need for satisfying the "innocent instincts of nature" ("innocenti / Instinti di natura").[27] Yet Casti nearly gave rise to a school of licentious novella writers. For example, in his six *Novelle galanti* in *ottava rima* (Paris, 1802), Giuseppe

Fuerroni[28] attempted—with horrendous results—to imitate the "gallant little tales that noble Casti told with skill" ("Galanti novellette, / Che il gentil Casti vi seppe narrare"). And Gaetano Fornasini (1738-1808) likewise produced ten tales in verse in his *Giornata campestre* [*Day in the Country*] (Brescia, 1807), which reveal Casti's influence but are much closer to the Bernesque style.[29] Success nearly equal to Casti's was enjoyed by Filippo Pananti (1766-1837), author of epigrams and short tales in verse based on the comical plights of cuckolded husbands, betrayed women, and so on. Worthy of note are Pananti's two short poems devoted to the subject of female genitalia, "La Civetta" ["The Owl"] and "Il Paretaio" ["The Fowling Net"].[30]

Let us complete this bibliographical survey with a quick look at some anthologies patterned after the *musées secrets* which circulated in the eighteenth century. These were miscellaneous collections of the best of Italian obscene literature. One example is the *Scelta di prose e poesie italiane* [*Selection of Italian Prose and Poetry*] (London, 1765), which contained brief anonymous poems, nearly all from the eighteenth century, including a translation of Piron's *Ode à Priape* attributed to the Venetian Francesco Gritti, and the collection of anti-clerical letters, *Il Gazzettino* by Girolamo Gigli.[31] Another is *Gli Scherzi geniali, ovvero Raccolta erotica degli più famosi autori* [*Ingenious Jests, or Erotic Collection from the most famous Authors*] (Cythera, c. 1780).

Undoubtedly the most famous collection is the *Libro del perché* [*Book of Wherefore*], of which I have identified six eighteenth-century editions, but none of which contains publication data. Most of the collection consists of three long compositions in verse, purportedly "derived from the great Aristotle's *Book of Wherefore*. The subjects treated include an epic war between male and female genital organs *(cazzi* and *potte)*, the complaints of women before Jupiter that the human penis is smaller than that of animals, and so on. To these tales, various editions occasionally add short novellas and other compositions, such as Niccolò Franco's *La puttana errante* [*The Wandering Whore*] or the ever-present translation of Piron's "Ode à Priape." Many of these are works of an earlier era, however, and there are in fact seventeenth-century editions of the *Libro*.[32]

✳

Italy was the cradle of libertine ideology, and of that school of thought which was to use literary obscenity to justify the naturalistic freedom of man. In the sixteenth century, Giacomo Zabarella, an Aristotelian thinker in Padua, argued in his *De Anima* that the sexual act was necessary for maintaining the balance between man's body and soul. And seventeenth-century Italy produced *livres de chevet* on ethical naturalism, such as Ferrante Pallavicino's *La retorica delle puttane* [*Rhetoric for Whores*] (1643), or Antonio Rocco's *L'Alcibiade fanciullo a scola* [*Alcibiades as Schoolboy*], a defense of sodomy published in 1662 but written at least fifty years before Rochester's *Sodomy*.

This particular kind of naturalism was adopted by d'Argens, Mirabeau, and the *esprits forts* of the French eighteenth century. Yet the general picture which I have just drawn indicates that Italy was not on the same level, in either quantity or quality, with France and the other European nations. The Italian libertine tradition of the seventeenth century disappeared, only to reappear in Enlightenment France, while no trace remained in Italy itself. A representative case is that of Ferrante Pallavicino, perhaps the only true libertine of seventeenth-century Italy. After his death in 1644, he was completely forgotten in Italy, while in France he survives in a tradition that leads from Guemadeuc to Lesage, and even to the Ferrante Palla of Stendhal's *Chartreuse de Parme*. We must also remember that between the nineteenth and early twentieth century it was French bibliographers who appreciated and published certain texts from the Italian tradition of obscenity.

Beginning with the eighteenth century, the Italian obscene tradition lived in Parisian exile. Thus, the most common edition of Aretino found in Italy is the *Recueil des pièces choisies* printed in France (Anconne, 1725). And Brunet, Bonneau, and Apollinaire were the first to publish critical editions of the authors discussed above.[33] Unfortunately, we still must refer to their studies even today, since in Italy much of the terrain of eighteenth-century obscenity remains unexplored.

This gap in literary history was largely the result of the censures of the Savoyard critics during the nineteenth-century Risorgimento and of the idealistic critics in the twentieth century; for they paid little attention to underground sources which contributed nothing to the evidence (which had to be positive at all costs) that Italian literature had developed independently with a dignity equal to that of other nations. The requisite historical researches, moreover, were hindered by the fact that publishing activity until the Unification remained scattered in countless small states with different laws and customs. Indeed, our knowledge of eighteenth-century publishing is still in an early stage of development, and must concentrate on single regions under the same jurisdiction. Consequently, it is difficult to achieve a unified and complete picture of the situation.

Italian literature suffered a blow in the sixteenth century which was felt until the end of the eighteenth century, namely, the consolidation of the Roman Church's ideological control which the Council of Trent had made possible. While fervent religious reformers beyond the Alps believed strongly in conversion by the printed word, orthodox authorities in Italy feared the press as one of the main instruments which might spread the contagion of heresy. Sarpi relates a remarkable utterance made by a major prelate at the Council in 1562: "We have no need of books. There are far too many in the world, especially after the press was invented; and it is better to prohibit a thousand books, even if faultless, than to permit one which deserves to be prohibited." In the view of the Council, books were tantamount to hand weapons.[34] While in England Milton was expounding his extraordinary defense of freedom of the press in his *Areopagitica,* in Italy the monstrous baroque novel represented the. last blow struck by publishers who would be forced, if they were to survive, to accept the supervision of institutions created to protect orthodoxy.

Everywhere the effects of the *Index librorum prohibitorum* were paralyzing. We have no reason to discount the testimony of Gaspare Gozzi, Superintendent of the Press in Venice in 1765, who writes that between the sixteenth and seventeenth centuries the *Index* struck such a blow to publishers that "in a few months the printing presses were reduced from 125 to 40, for lack of material to print."[35]

My remarks are not meant to imply that ecclesiastical censorship hindered the composition of obscene texts. But we should note that the continuous conflict between Italian culture and the powerful institutions which sought to exorcize all dissent and heterodoxy had disastrous consequences in the long run. After the Jesuits had failed in the seventeenth century to establish a cultural hegemony over the entire peninsula, a similar attempt was made at the beginning of the eighteenth century by Arcadia, a mock "Republic" which reproduced the extremism of the counter-reformation Church in seeking to subordinate the entire national culture to one model with Roman ties.

If we view the history of Italy from the eighteenth century to the present in such a light, we may discover a continuous series of totalitarian and all-encompassing world views which link the Counter Reformation, the Risorgimento, and Fascism. *Extra ecclesiam nulla salus*: "Outside the Church there is no salvation." Inevitably, such world views must exclude and exorcize all minor and unorthodox practices, including those literary. At the same time, the extreme political fragmentation and the divergence of practical interests of the Italians hindered their anxiety, artificially imposed from above, to embrace a supranational orthodoxy. Thus, in terms of literature, Petrarchism, the Accademia della Crusca, and Arcadia all constitute a *souvenir des Antiques*, insofar as they attempt to turn back ideologically to recover a lost identity which could have provided a foundation for this cultural totalitarianism.

But let us return to the eighteenth century. The effects of censorship should not be overestimated, in part because ecclesiastical censorship gradually relaxed as the century progressed, and yielded to political censorship as jurisdictional ideas came to dominate the various regimes. Yet as laymen replaced the Dominicans, they took the same precautions to prevent "impious" doctrines from entering Italy—those of Locke and Newton early in the century, and those of Helvetius and d'Holbach later. It is clear that Italy was only superficially touched by the philosophical revolution which ultimately defined a mechanics of sensations. Hence, while in France one spoke of a *Venus physique*, the Italian Venus continued to be the Venus Urania of Plato's *Symposium*. One almost has the impression of witnessing a sort of national self-censorship and ideological torpor.

At any rate, we cannot fail to reckon with the two great spheres of cultural influence, namely, the traditional Jesuit and Aristotelian culture with its cloistered perspective, and what we call the popular sphere, even though it is difficult to divide Italy into social strata. "Popular" here connotes a sphere which we may infer from a sort of marketing survey *ante litteram*: witness the mass-produced novels of Chiari and Piazza, Italy's Bibliothèque Bleue, as it were. In fact, the absence of a refined middle class, together with the slow emergence of new social strata, greatly delayed the diffusion of those foreign ideologies which proclaimed the emancipation of man and the discovery of his natural being.

✣

The abbot Anton Maria Donadoni, a zealous officer of the Venetian Customs from 1769 to 1795, has left us two very important documents—a register of the books confiscated at the Customs and submitted to the magistrates of the Republic as suspect, and a list of books considered dangerous.[36]

Prior to examining these documents, it is important to recall that the Venetian Republic was not typical of the governments of eighteenth-century Italy. For example, it was the only state in which the *Encyclopédie* freely circulated. Yet while anyone caught possessing it in Rome was excommunicated, the Venetian government managed both to maintain good relations with Rome, by observing certain rules of the *Index*, and to safeguard the profession of the booksellers, whose profits often derived in large part from the sale of prohibited titles. The magistrates often looked the other way, less concerned with overseeing ideology than with preventing pirate editions which might harm the Venetian printers. Consequently, Donadoni's records, which deal more with marketed books than with private collections, should be examined with some reservation. Still, if we carefully consider them with obscene literature in mind, they make an interesting contribution to our study.[37]

We know with certainty that 20% of the "foreign" books (books from outside the Republic of Venice) came from France. Thus, Voltaire was perhaps not correct in complaining that Hannibal and Brennus crossed the Alps with less difficulty than books in his day.[38] Rather, there existed a profound and real exchange between Venice and French culture.

Donadoni's *Registro* covers 26 years and 486 titles. Of these only 37 were seized as obscene, and all of them (except for De Gamerra's *Corneide*, Baffo's *Poesie*, and Casti's *Novelle*) were of French origin. Donadoni's other document, a *Catalogo* which was sent to the Riformatori dello Studio di Padova as a memorandum to the censors, contains a section of obscene books ("Libri osceni"). Of the 45 titles listed there, the following are Italian: Antonio Rocco's *Alciabiade fanciullo a scola*, Aretino's *Ragionamenti* and *Sonetti*, Baffo's *Poesie*, Alessandro Piccolomini's *Della bella creanza delle donne* [*On the Fine Manners of Women*] (a work containing no obscenity), *La cortigiana di Smirne* [*The Courtesan of Smyrna*] (a work about which I have no information), *Il libro del perché*, Masuccio Salernitano's *Novellino*, *La matrona di Efeso* (probably the tale from Petronius), three works by Ferrante Pallavicino, Niccolò Franco's *La puttana errante*, Gregorio Leti's *Il puttanismo romano* [*Roman Prostitution*], Luigi Tansillo's *Il Vendemmiatore* [*The Harvester*], and an obscure work called *Rosalia*.[39] There are few Italian authors, then, and only Baffo belongs certainly to the eighteenth century.

From Donadoni's two documents, we learn that the most widely diffused works of obscenity were d'Argens' *Thérèse philosophe*, Dulaurens' *Imirce ou la fille de la nature*, Chorier's *Aloysiae Sigeae* (in Latin, but also in French as *Académie des dames*), and Cleland's *Memoirs of a Woman of Pleasure* in French (*La fille de joye*) and Italian (*La meretrice*). We also find the complete works of Crebillon, Diderot's *Bijoux indiscrets,* and so on. There is no need to continue the list: it would simply repeat the titles of the Bibliothèque Nationale's Enfer or the British Museum's Private Case. Apparently, the limited public of free-thinking readers turned to the foreign market.

While these documents speak for themselves, there is one thing to be noted. If we read carefully the dates of the various entries, we have the impression that the influx of obscene texts gradually increases as we approach the end of the century. It may be true that late in the eighteenth century there were still occurrences like that of a young woman who was called before the Inquisitor in Piacenza to defend herself against charges of having praised the *Encyclopédie* in a drawing-room conversation. But toward the end of the period covered by Donadoni's documents, we observe a marked secularization in book publishing and in the public's interests.

New elements entered Italy late, following in the wake of Napoleon's troops, and only in the nineteenth century did moralistic surveillance gradually disappear. An important indication of this may be seen in the appearance of the editions of Italian obscene writings in the decades which close the eighteenth and open the nineteenth century. The new century is heralded by a collection of tales called *Il Convito Borgesiano in cui si raccontano dieci piacevolissime novelle. Opera di Messer Grappolone* [*The Borghese Banquet, Containing Ten Delightful Tales, by Mr. Grappolone*] (London [actually Milan], 1800). The author of this Borghese banquet—so named because it is set in the Villa Borghese in Rome—was Tommaso Grapputo, an obscure Venetian lawyer. The tales merit our consideration, for some of them are decidedly unusual. Besides their physiological details and the pervasive anti-clerical tone (the protagonists are nearly all priests who have difficulty in observing their vows of chastity), we find here the first appearance of explicit pathological behavior, of sexual excess used as a narrative element.

True, there had been some strange cases before. Boiardo had included an episode of necrophilia in his *Orlando Innamorato* (I, viii, 46); and in Tommaso Stigliani's poem *Mondo nuovo* (1628), a nymphomaniac named Gebra seduces her twelve-year-old brother and then couples with an ape. But Grapputo adds particular touches. He undertakes a serious account of indecent delights ("disonesti diletti"), and makes no concessions to the comical terminology which we have surveyed above. I cite a few examples. In the fourth tale, a rejected suitor kills his beloved and then takes his pleasure of her. In the seventh tale, a mother conceives a bestial passion ("bestial furore") for her fourteen-year-old son. Pretending to be the maid, she sleeps with him for two months, and secretly bears his child, a daugher whom he later meets and marries, unaware of their incest. The mother dies of grief.

Before this work, I doubt whether a woman in Italian literature had ever so completely abandoned herself to abnormal passion. In the very country where the cult of the Virgin Mary had always limited obscenity to misogynistic comedy, such obscenity was meant to exorcise man's dread of woman's power of seduction—a power revalued by the notion of *amour goût*. In Grapputo's seventh tale, the protagonist "in shame kept this bestial passion and boundless lust locked in her heart, whereby she fed it the more and made it more powerful" ("Questo bestial furore, questa sfrenata libidine . . . tenevala per vergogna ben chiusa nel petto, e con ciò le dava maggiore alimento and rendevala più potente").[40] This passion is no longer on probation; at the end of the tales a young woman sings, "And you, fair Venus, mother of all delights, chase far from the fresh young maid the dark and gloomy figures of blushes and modesty and chastity" ("E tu Venere bella / D'ogni diletto madre, / Caccia lunge da fresca giovincella / Le immagini fosche, ed adre? Di rossor / Di pudor di Castitade").[41]

The very presence of religious characters is no longer comic by itself, and most of the tales have a tragic end. The main characters either commit suicide or enter a convent, and Grapputo implies that there is little difference. In place of Don Barletta and the cheerful friars of Batacchi and Casti, we find the unhappy people whom Bayle had subtly mocked in his learned notes to the *Dictionnaire*.[42]

✣

We have seen two fundamental typologies of obscenity: the bestial and farcical priapism of Baffo and Batacchi, whose folk-like metaphors of "riding" and "trading" distinguish them from the false refinement of allusive obscenity in Casti and in the novella tradition with its classic and refined precedents. We may now add a third: ideological obscenity, that is, sexual realism subordinated as a weapon in the conflict of ideas, whether in the service of anti-clericalism, of evangelical or heretical claims, or of simple naturalism. Thus, in the obscenity of the first two groups, a reference to a woman's *potta* provoked laughter behind which there lurked misogynism and fear of the woman as devil. For Grapputo, in turn, as for libertine French novelists, the claim for a natural approach to sexual pleasures betokens something more profound: woman has at last ceased to be Pandora, and has become Demeter. But with this new image we are already on the threshold of the nineteenth century.

It is not trivial to assert that confessional intolerance hindered the emergence of a secular tradition in Italy. The bawdy literature of eighteenth-century Italy is misogynistic or scatological because realistic descriptions of sex are always an end in themselves, and never a means of spreading a polemical idea or world view.

On the one hand, we find the erudite obscenity of the *Ex gemmis* and the *Monumens de la vie privée des Douze Césars*, with their engravings taken from ancient gems and coins, or of the *Erotopaegnion*.[43] These texts intended for a refined public which read Latin (an Italian translation of *Aloysiae Sigeae* appeared only in 1799) and which chose to assign certain topics to a classical and timeless world. On the other hand, we find the obscenity of

258

the authors we have examined in this study—Baffo, Batacchi, Casti—an obscenity imprisoned in a world of religion and thus condemned to tend toward scatology and buffoonery.

The actors in these bawdy farces in the Italian style resemble Vaucanson's *authomates*, incapable of reflecting on the causes of their instincts and physiological acts. We realize that obscene literature becomes literarily concrete and interesting only when the performers of such sexual workouts succeed in becoming *philosophes* like d'Argens' Thérèse, or as boring as Sade's characters. Yet Italian obscene literature never posed any real danger for those institutions whose ideological power commanded such obedience that, early in the century, Prince Pamphili hammered the genitals off the statues in his villa and replaced them with copper ivy.

Translated by   *Armando Marchi*
James Coke & David Marsh   Parma

NOTES

1. D.A.F. de Sade, *Voyage d'Italie*, in *Oeuvres complètes* (Paris: Éditions Tête de Feuilles, 1973), 16:439.

2. Today we have two anthologies of Italian obscene literature: *Erotismo e pornografia nella letteratura italiana*, ed. P. Lorenzoni (Milano: Il formichiere, 1976) and *L'altra faccia della poesia italiana*, ed. R. Reim and A. Veneziani (Milano: Savelli, 1982). However, they are hasty commercial publications, which is apparent in the sloppiness of their texts, especially in Lorenzoni's anthology.

3. P. Brady, *Rococo Style versus Enlightenment Novel* (Genève: Slatkine, 1984).

4. T. Crudeli, *Rime e Prose* (Parigi: 1805), p. 151.

5. A. De Giorgi Bertòla, *Amori, ossia Rime e Prose* (London: 1801), pp. 78, 80.

6. Although figurative arts extend beyond the scope of this work, I would note some oil paintings of Alessandro Magnasco (1667–1749) of Genoa which represent hetero- and homosexual couplings among nuns and friars: they should be remembered together with the erotic art that the court of France commissioned from Boucher.

7. S. Bettinelli, *Lettere virgiliane e lettere inglesi* (Torino: 1977), p. 155.

8. C. I. Frugoni, *Opere poetiche* (Parma: 1779), Vol. 3, and see the coprolitic sonnets: 59 *Contro il Galateo di Monsignor della Casa* ("Against Monsignor della Casa's Code of Politeness"), 60 *Lode del cacare* ("Praise of defecating") and 61 *Per un magnifico stronzo* ("To a magnificent turd"), pp. 159–64.

9. We are dealing with the sonnet *E chi questo agitò spergiuro letto?* ("Who did shake this perjured bed?"), that in fact was not included in Frugoni's poetical works but can be found in the *Poesie* by Giorgio Baffo (Milano: A. Mondadori, 1974), pp. 263–65 together with two translations in Venetian dialect (see further on).

10. When the protagonist of *Il fiore delle donne* sees his beloved, his *Amore* promptly *sì gonfia* (swells up) and "becomes so big and stiff, and rises so immoderately that it tears apart the belt of his trousers": Venice, Biblioteca Marcianna, MSS C1.IX, no. 332, Vol. 3, p. 49.

11. G. Cherubini, *Poesie bernesche* (Venice: 1767) pp. 122, 98.

12. G. De Gamerra, *La Corneide poema eroi-comico* ([Livorno]: 1781).

13. K. Rosenkranz, *Aesthetik des Hässlichen* (Königsberg: Gebrüder Bornträger, 1853). An anthology of the most renowned Italian scatological literature is the *Raccolta di poesie toscane; la Culeide del sig. Abate Pasquini; e di diversi autori; il Canto sopra le corregge; le lodi spora il*

Cacatojo; la Girandola dei cervelli. Lettere diverse e poesie del sig. Girolamo Gigli (London: 1786). For Italian and previous foreign writers, see the *Bibliotheca Scatologica ou catalogue raisonné des livres traitant des vertus faits et gestes de très noble et très ingenieux Messire Luc. . . .* (Scatepolis, 5850; i.e., Paris, 1849).

14. De Giorgi Bertòla, *Amori*, p. 38.

15. I am referring to Antonio Ottoboni (1646–1720), Marcantonio Zorzi (1703–87), Angelo Maria Barbaro (1726–79), and Pietro Buratti (1772–1832). For an anthology of their poems, see *Il fiore della lirica veneziana*, ed. M. Dazzi (Venice: N. Pozza, 1956). Another remarkable vernacular writer is the Sicilian Domenico Tempio (1750–1821), who aside from his "official" production wrote obscene verses: see *Canti erotici* (Catania: 1974).

16. There is now a philologically accurate edn. of Aretino's "lustful sonnets" with the original engravings by Giulio Romano and Marcantonio Raimondi: *I modi*, ed. L. Lawner (Milano: 1984).

17. Baffo, *Poesie*, pp. 176, 175. The 1st edn. of his works was (Cosmopoli, i.e. Venice: 1789).

18. Baffo, *Poesie*, p. 19.

19. In spite of his licentiousness, Foscolo wrote of himself: "you could say that he, like Ariosto, would rather delight than corrupt his readers; he is as free and easy as Berni and as naive as La Fontaine. Perhaps he had their same genius" (*Opere* [Napoli: F. Rossi, 1970], 5:449).

20. D. L. Batacchi, *Raccolta di novelle* (London: Anno VI; i.e., Bologna: 1792), p. 283. These tales were trans. into French as *Nouvelles galantes* (Paris: 1805). The *Index librorum prohibitorum* of 1819 prohibited them, which demonstrates their renown.

21. Batacchi, *Il Zibaldone* (London: 1805; i.e. Bologna: 1792), p. 331.

22. Batacchi, *La Rete di Vulcano* (Sienna: 1799; i.e. Milano: 1812).

23. Batacchi, *Zilbaldone*, pp. 6, 2. As happens in the purest tradition of obscene literature, the characters are all built around comic gestures and attributes such as genital size and sperm production.

24. G. B. Casti, *Raccolta di poesie, o sieno novelle galanti* (Parigi: 1804), 1:227.

25. Or, as Parini defined him in 1780: "an ugly, old and stinking priest, entirely disfigured by the French disease, and called chaste after the name of his family for the freaks of fortune" (*Opere* [Milano: U. Mursia, 1967], p. 435).

26. Casti, *Raccolta*, 3:142.

27. Casti, *Raccolta*, 1:163.

28. I have no biographical data about him.

29. It still remains in ms.—a portion from six tales published under the date: Yverdun (i.e., Forli) 1839—the production of Luigi Cerretti (1738–1808), who, as local biographers say, wrote nearly thirty obscene tales and an "extremely licentious" poem in six cantos entitled *La Frusta di Pietro il Grande* ("The Whip of Peter the Great") under the pseudonym Nebulone Fragosi di Vallombrona. By Guiseppe Rillosi (1768–1822), lawyer from Bergamo, there are some *Novelle* (Italia: 1797) and a few compositions spread in several collectaneous volumes.

30. The *Paretaio* is an instrument to capture birds with nets (in Italian "bird" also indicates the penis). The works by Pananti are collected in *Epigrammi e novellette galanti. Poemetti* (Catania: Libraria Tirelli, 1927).

31. The *Gazzettino*, by Girolamo Gigli (1660–1722) had been published between 1712 and 1714: it is a burlesque anticlerical epistolary.

32. We can find most compositions of the *Libro del perché* in the *Novellette ed epigrammi del celebre Pananti con la Civetta poemetto del medesimo ed altre rare, e galanti poesie d'amore composte da diversi insigni autori*, Calè Anno XI (i.e., 1803). The tradition of these collections continued into the nineteenth century: for example, *L'Erotiade, fiori galanti* (n.p., n.d. [ca. 1840]) or the *Tempietto di Venere* (London, n.d. [ca. 1850]), which collected some works of such eighteenth-century authors as Casti, Rillosi, Pananti, Batacchi, and Forteguerri.

33. Gustave Brunet trans. the *Alcibiade fanciullo a scola* into French; Alcide Bonneau published Baffo's and Casti's tales; and Guillaume Apollinaire dedicated one of the two vols. of *L'Oeuvre libertine des conteurs italiens* (Paris: Bibliothèque des curieux, 1910) to Casti, Baffo, and Batacchi.

34. P. Sarpi, *Istoria del Concilio tridentino* (Torino: G. Einaudi, 1974), 2:757, 261

260

35. G. Gozzi, *Scritti* (Firenze: F. Le Monnier, 1849), 2:421.

36. *Registro de' Libri Fermati nelle Dogane dal Revisore Deputato D. Antonio Maria Donadoni e dal sue successore Don Giacomo Morelli* ("Register of the Books Seized at the Customs by the Revisor Deputed Don Antonio Maria Donadoni, and by his successor Don Giacomo Morelli"): Venice, Biblioteca Querini-Stampalia, MSS C1.IV, Cod.506. *Catalogo de libri contro la Religiene, e contro i Principi* ("Catalogue of the books against Religion and Princes"): Venice, Archivio di State, Riformatori delle Studio di Padova, Filza 372.

37. For an overall evaluation of these documents, see the studies by M. Berengo, *La società veneziana alla fine del Settecento* (Firenze: 1956), pp. 134–36; A. Machet, "Censure et librairie en Italie au XVIIIe siècle," *Revue desétudes sud-est européennes* 10 (1972): 459–90; F. Piva, *Cultura francese e censura a Venezia nel secondo Settecento. Ricerche storico-bibliegrafiche*, Memorie dell'Instituto Veneto di Scienze, Lettere ed Arti, vol. 36 (1973), and "Censura e libri proibiti a Venezia: il Registro Donadoni–Morelli (1769–1795)," *Aevum* 5–6 (1974): 546–69.

38. Voltaire, letter to Francesco Algarotti (Dec. 1759), *Correspondance* in *Oeuvres* (Lyon: 1792), 8:529. And so writes Voltaire in a letter to Father Bettinelli (Mar. 1761) about Italian customs' censorship: "you will judge it proper that I do not go to a country where at the gates of towns they seize the books a poor traveller has in his suitcase. I am absolutely not eager to ask a Dominican's permission to speak, to think, and to read; and I shall simply confess to you that I hate this vile Italian slavery" (9:31–32).

39. For the attributions of titles that are mostly anonymous in the documents, I refer to: G. Melzi, *Dizionario di opere anonime e pseudonime di scrittori italiani o come che sia aventi relazioni all'Italia* (Milan: 1848–59); P. Pia, *Les livres de l'Enfer, du XVI siècle a nos jours*, (Paris: C. Coulet & A. Faure 1978); P. Kearney, *The Private Case. An annotated Bibliography* (London: J. Landesman, 1981).

40. T. Grapputo, *Il Convito Borgesiano* (London; i.e. Milano, 1800) pp. 103–04.

41. Grapputo, *Convito Borgesiano*, p. 155.

42. I am referring to scarcely known passages by Bayle, such as the learned comment affirming that he who has sexual couplings with a nun dies with an erect penis (*virga tendente*), or the quarrel about the truthfulness of the apparition of San Domenico spearing the thighs of a possessed nun with some kind of love unguent (*unguentum amoris*). See *Dictionnaire* (Rotterdam: 1702), p. 2049 n.*a*, and p. 2057 n.*b*.

43. *Erotopaegnion, sive Priapea veterum et recentiorum* (Lutetiae Paris: 1798). We are dealing with a mostly complete anthology of Latin hymns to Priapus by Italian and foreign authors of all ages.